THE CHARTISTS

Popular Politics in the Industrial Revolution

DOROTHY THOMPSON

Pantheon Books, New York

Library of Congress Cataloging in Publication Data

Thompson, Dorothy, 1923-
The Chartists.

Bibliography: p.
Includes index.
1. Chartism. 2. Labor and laboring classes—Great Britain—Political activity—History—19th century. 3. Labor and laboring classes—Great Britain—History—19th century. I. Title.
HD8396.T44 1984 322'.2'0941 83-21984
ISBN 0-394-51140-9
0-394-72474-7 (pbk.)

Manufactured in the United States of America

First American Edition

Contents

FOR MARTY AND DAVID MONTGOMERY

Preface

FOR the ten years from 1838 to 1848 the authorities in Britain were faced with a popular movement which came nearer to being a mass rebellion than any other movement in modern times. Working people in all parts of the island – in Scotland and Wales as well as in England – demonstrated in favour of a political programme, formed organisations to promote it and in many ways set up a whole alternative culture and life-style in the process. A mass of published material was produced, newspapers, pamphlets, broadsides, placards and books were circulated, sermons were preached, plays and pageants performed, hymns and songs were written and sung. Traditional forms were adopted alongside new forms of organisation and demonstration.

The programme around which all this activity took place was deceptively simple and straightforward. The programme which gave the Chartist movement its name, the People's Charter, published in May 1838, called for universal male adult suffrage, protected by the ballot, the abolition of property qualifications for Members of Parliament, the payment of Members, equal electoral districts and annual parliaments. These six points were to give all citizens access to the political processes of the country, and through them the outstanding grievances of all sections were to be solved. (One or other of these points, however, was sometimes omitted, which accounts for occasional references to 'the five points'. O'Connor, for example, was ambivalent about the ballot and others did not favour numerically equal electoral districts.) The purpose of this book is partly to show why so many people believed that political change could bring about an improvement in their situation, and partly to show the scale of the movement which grew up around this conviction. Every tactic was considered to bring the achievement of the programme about, from rational argument with those in power to the taking up of arms against them. In the end, the authorities remained unshaken, although the movement was of far greater proportions than the movements which overthrew governments in many other European countries in 1848. The particular circumstances in Britain produced both a wider-spreading popular movement and a more secure structure of authority than existed in the main countries of continental Europe.

Preface

Historians continue to be fascinated with Chartism. Interpretations range from the view that the world's first potential proletarian revolution was allowed to founder through lack of theoretical clarity and through inept and opportunist leadership, to the view that the leadership encouraged its followers to believe in the possibility of a national political remedy for what were essentially minor and very local growing pains of an industrial society. Much of the argument ranges around the question of the nature of classes in modern society – the extent to which there was a working class in Britain in these years whose national interest was greater than the conflicts of interest between trades, localities and strata. Since the Chartist movement was the movement above all on which Marx and Engels based their analysis of class consciousness, the Chartists have inevitably been tested by some historians in the light of this analysis. The arguments are raging all around us.

In a short account of a large and widespread movement, I have not attempted to enter all these discussions. I have tried to supply some empirical data, to make clearer the patterns of behaviour which were evident in the movement, and to show the extent of participation by the different sections of the working population of Britain. If the consciousness of these workers did not always conform to what the theoreticians consider should have been correct for their stage of industrialisation, it may help to stand back a bit from theoretical preconceptions, and see what the people actually were demanding, what they were defending, and why they took certain forms of action. Women, labourers, Irish workers, artisans, alehouse keepers and itinerant dissenting clergymen took part in the Chartist movement as well as factory workers, miners and keelmen. These people shared a common sense of class, based on the feeling of exclusion from the political system, and of exploitation by the new merchant and industrial powers which were growing up in the country. This unity of outlook can be amply demonstrated, and can clearly be seen to have faded with the end of the Chartist movement. The reasons for its growth and decline may be those suggested by the theoreticians of economically-defined class, or they may have been a more complex interaction of factors which include such things as the size of the towns and villages in which people lived and the strength of occupational and local traditions as well as the level of wages. Certainly the kind of control which the Chartists sought over their work, over the education of their children and over the way in which they spent their leisure has not yet been achieved by their more prosperous descendants, who may well have achieved a higher standard of living at the expense of the sort of independence which the Chartists sought in such reactionary schemes as the Land Plan or the early redemption societies.

Much has to be left out in such a short treatment, and perhaps one thing I have omitted is a sense of balance. This is an account of the movement written in general sympathy with it. Other cases could be made, and I am well aware that some points of view hostile to those of the Chartists have been foreshortened or omitted. Our library shelves, however, are loaded with the self-expression of the middle and upper classes of the nineteenth century, and I hope that readers will compensate for the necessary omissions in this book by going back to the many works which discuss the same questions from different viewpoints, from the diaries of Greville and Broughton to the writings of the 'Condition of England' novelists.

Acknowledgements

THIS book has been many years in preparation, and very many institutions and individuals have helped with advice and resources. Quotation from material in the Public Record Office is by permission of the controller of HM Stationery Office. I am also grateful for the help given by the staff of many libraries, including the British Library of Political and Economic Sciences, Goldsmiths Library, the Bishopsgate Institute, the Reading Room, Manuscript Room and Newspaper Library of the British Library, the Special Collections Library of Columbia University, Weslyan University Library, the International Institute of Social History Amsterdam, the Marx-Engels Institute in Moscow, Birmingham Public Library, Bradford Public Library, Halifax Public Library, Manchester Central Reference Library, the John Rylands Library Manchester, the Working Class Movement Library Manchester, the New York Public Library, and the University Libraries of Birmingham, Leeds and Warwick.

The bibliography on which this book is based has already escaped into a separate volume. If I were to mention all the people who have helped me with material, ideas and encouragement an even larger volume would be required, out of all proportion to the book itself. I have been extremely fortunate in my students, colleagues and friends and feel that it would be invidious to mention only a few but pretentious to try and list them all. Working in the field of social history in the last twenty years has been rewarding in every way, and I can only hope that this book will make some contribution to the many discussions going on in the field. Parts of it have been presented at seminars and talks in Britain, Europe and the United States, and have benefited from the criticism and comments of many colleagues. I am only too well aware that many of the questions raised have not been answered, and that many of my suggestions will be very critically questioned.

To engage in research and writing as well as teaching and bringing up a family inevitably puts strains on all three activities. Without my husband and children this book would have been written twenty years ago, but it would have been a very different book, as they have all contributed to it and to the ideas contained in it. In particular my husband, Edward Thompson, has made an enormous contribution, not only by discussion and argument and generous help with research, but also by taking on family responsibilities which have enabled me to get time and space for my own work. Finally I want to thank the number of friends and helpers who have made this and other books possible by not only coping with much of the housework which would otherwise have taken up the time needed for research, but by also taking on a great deal of responsibility for the smooth running of the domestic side of the Thompson academic factory. In particular my thanks go to Joan Murray of Halifax, Myrna Squib of Leamington and Bridget Davis of Broadheath in Worcestershire.

Introduction

One problem in writing about Chartism is that of definition. Chartism might perhaps be called the political facet of the total experience of the working people of Britain in the second quarter of the nineteenth century. But if we call it that, it is clear that it cannot be studied apart from that experience. And since we are now talking about the experience of the great majority of the population of the nation, and since that experience was profoundly affected by the attitudes and actions of those in authority, and since the behaviour and the understanding of society and the economy which was held by the upper classes in society was affected by the actions and beliefs, as they saw and interpreted them, of the lower orders, we are coming near to saying that the study of Chartism is the study of British society in these years – society in its entirety, and in its thought and beliefs as well as in its actions.

In effect, this is how Chartism has to be seen. For a short period, thousands of working people considered that their problems could be solved by a change in the political organisation of the country. They believed this passionately. Hundreds of them went to prison for demonstrating their belief and for demanding political change. Many hundreds more gave up time, money and the chance of advancement in their jobs. The political question dominated all others. The story of the Chartist movement is the story of how this came to be so, and why the conviction was finally abandoned. But while they held it, people saw the Charter as a liberating force which would affect all their lives, and not simply admit them in a formal way to full citizenship of the country.

An all-embracing narrative history of Chartism could only be written in a multi-volume form. Already a number of district studies have produced full-length doctoral and masters theses,[1] and book-length biographies have been written of a number of the leaders.[2] 1848 alone has been treated in one study almost at book-length, and further work on that year in Britain is in the process of being written.[3] Attempts to get into the wider experience of the industrial areas in which Chartism flourished are fewer – there is still a tendency to precede Chartist studies with a social and economic run-down of the district which is somehow separate from the main experience, although these regional introductions may often be of value in themselves. To coordinate this work into a new interpretation of the Chartist movement, fully illustrated with documentation from all the regions, would demand a series of studies, probably divided chronologically. The present volume is an attempt to look at Chartism globally at least in some of its aspects, and to suggest some possible re-interpretations for consideration by those making future detailed studies. It cannot attempt the total narrative account which we still lack.

Very few people today are without some fairly clear idea of what the Chartist movement was about. The dates, the names of some of the leaders and some at least of the issues with which the movement was concerned have become clichés of nineteenth-century history. The search for controversies around which to build A-level courses or college entrance exams has led to the emphasising of the moral force/physical force conflict within Chartism – often seen as a decisive conflict and disagreement which weakened the movement – and to the emphasis on other divisive issues – London against the provinces, disagreement on the possibility of a compromise and an alliance with progressive allies among the middle classes, failure of leading Chartists to work together, and the conflict between 'backward-looking' aspects of the movement (the Land Plan, for example) and 'modernising' aspects such as the search for socialist solutions, the acceptance of the factory and its discipline – which pressaged the modern labour movement. Some or all of these issues have been seen as explanations for the failure of Chartism – for a failure it is universally agreed to have been. Historians have been ready enough to point out the reasons for its failure, most of them agreeing to a great extent with Hovell's verdict on the first petition: 'The Petition was dead, slain by the violence of its own supporters, the tactlessness of its chief advocates, the inertia of conservatism, and its own inner contradictions.'[4] They have been less prepared to suggest what they understood by the vision of Chartist success. As Asa Briggs has emphasised in considering the often-repeated suggestion that the failure was due to shortcomings on the part of the movement's most powerful leader, Feargus O'Connor,

> In fact it is very difficult to see how, given the nature of English society and government in the Chartist period, the Chartists could have succeeded in the way that O'Connor's critics claim that they might have done. The cards were too heavily stacked against them. Both Chartism and O'Connor in my view were doomed to failure. . .[5]

For most writers about the movement, however, the assumption of the possibility of success for the petitions has been an essential part of the narrative. Tactical failure by the active leadership and theoretical failure by the analysts of the political scene and the formulators of programmes have been criticised in the light of such an assumed possibility.

To Whiggish historians, watching the inevitable unfolding of British democratic institutions, the Chartists were premature. By trying to bring within the pale of the constitution the uneducated, the Irish, the women of the lower orders, they were anticipating a degree of participation in the processes of representative government which would only be possible after a further three-quarters of a century of education and instruction. Had the policies of the LWMA (London Working Men's Association) in its earliest days been followed, this argument implies, the better sections of the lower classes – the educated and rational – might have been admitted to the franchise well before 1867. Only the behaviour of the undisciplined mob, under the influence of unscrupulous demagogues, frightened those men of goodwill among the powerful who would otherwise have followed the course of history by promoting the gradual admission to participation of those who had shown themselves to be worthy of it. This view had its exponents during the Chartist years, as we shall see, and it underlies the view of Chartism which sees the failure of Lovett's attempts at leadership as the chief reason for the movement's lack of success. Mark Hovell certainly held it, and among contemporaries it was expounded by men with some sympathy for aspects of the Chartist movement, such as Henry Solly, as well as by those who used it to condemn the whole movement.

Another framework is suggested by the view of history which sees it as developing towards a classless socialist society. In some versions of this explanation, industrial capitalism, with all its brutality and exploitation, is seen as having been a 'necessary' stage through which British society had to pass before the resources could be developed which could form the basis of the new, non-exploitative society. Working-class agitation could therefore only be seen as helping forward the historical process if it involved the acceptance of industrialisation, of large productive and marketing units, large factories, large-scale agriculture and large towns. An anti-capitalist ideology was needed, but one which accepted these inevitable developments and which looked forward to a society without private property, to be attained through the expropriation of the capitalists by the working class. Those aspects of the Chartist movement which were based on the defence of 'artisan values' – the independence of the craftsman, his control over his personal environment, the defence of craft standards – or on the desire felt by many factory workers to leave the industrial districts and join communities of rural or semi-rural producers, are seen as backward-looking, peasant-inspired, and are often blamed on the Irish origins of Feargus O'Connor. In this socialist teleology, many of the most highly-charged and powerful impulses behind the protests of the common people are seen as manifestations of 'false consciousness'. The failure of the movement lay in the inability of its leaders to transform the energy of protest into a genuinely revolutionary consciousness which would have made possible the transfer of class power and the overthrow of the capitalist system. This was the philosophy behind much of the writing about Chartism in the 1930s.

Both these sets of assumptions see Chartism as a political movement, aimed primarily at changing the political forms in Britain. Both also imply a political and an economic teleology. The Chartists were wrong in parts of their programme and activity not only because they tried to resist the inevitable development of political institutions, but perhaps even more because they were setting themselves against inevitable economic developments. For the liberal historians the dogma of the free market and the need for the progressive freeing of trade required no justification. Hovell, for example, considered the arguments of those Chartists who mistrusted the conception of a total removal of government interest or control over manufacture and trade as being too feeble to require any refutation. For many Marxists and other economic historians, the protest movements of the early nineteenth century contained large elements of purely destructive ideas, were aiming simply to put back the clock of economic advance and hinder the transformation of society and the economy, a transformation which would in the end bring nothing but good to all classes of society. They dismiss, therefore, protests against the unrestricted introduction of machinery, and attempts like those of Fielden and Maxwell in the House of Commons[6] to temper the wind of economic change, to slow down some of the transformations in the interests of the producers. In the end, in this view, such protest was going against a determined pattern of economic development, and must therefore have been either futile or actively reactionary.

To the people in the manufacturing districts of Britain in the earlier nineteenth century, however, the truths of political economy were not self-evident. Experience of industrialisation in other parts of the world since has shown that there is not a single unique road along which industrialising nations must travel. If we are to listen sympathetically to the voice of Chartism, we should perhaps set aside some preconceptions about historical absolutes and listen to the contemporary debate without being too fixated on our *ex post facto* knowledge of its outcome. It was not only the starving weavers and irrational cloth finishers who urged the case against unrestricted freedom in the development of the quickest and cheapest methods of production, irrespective of short-term human cost. A look at some of the defeated arguments, as well as a look at the areas in which some success was achieved, may teach us more about the sort of people who made up the society of the time than a simple dismissal of the losers as blind and ignorant. The partial victories of the Chartists as well as their failures and defeats help to explain the particular nature of the institutions which developed in Britain in the later years of the nineteenth century.

The publication of the People's Charter was only one of the events which dates the beginning of the Chartist movement. The years 1837 and 1838 contained a number of events of significance for the beginning of a movement different, in scale if not in its immediate programme, from anything which had occurred before in history. That the world's first labour movement should take place in Britain is not surprising – no other country had such a clearly defined labouring sector of its population, a sector defined by its absolute reliance on wage labour. The great Reform Act of 1832 had defined more clearly than at any time before or since in British history, and more clearly than had been done in any other country, a qualification for the inclusion in the political institutions of the country based entirely on the possession of property and the possession of a regular income. The line drawn for the exercise of the franchise was precisely made to include all members of the middle and upper classes and to exclude all wage-labourers. Voters had to be men, but no other qualification, whether of race, religion or educational achievement, was considered apart from property. A movement to extend the franchise was bound to divide the country on class lines.

Britain, with the exception of the agricultural areas which were almost untouched by the mass activities of the Chartist movement, was a nation of growing urban manufacturing districts – districts made up of clusters of communities in which one or two industries were carried on. Many of these districts had grown up during the century preceding Chartism, and had grown up comparatively independent of many forms of traditional authority. They had developed their own traditions for regulating their trades and the behaviour of their inhabitants, and had incorporated these into their own notions of customary standards. The Chartist movement gained its greatest strength in manufacturing districts in which the actual communities were small enough to sustain a unity of purpose, in which communication was quick and easy, and in which the traditional authority of church and state was weak. Such communities could be centres of factory production, mining, or hand trades. It was the size and nature of the community together with the comparative homogeneity of the industrial experience within it which gave strength to the movement, rather than the actual nature of the productive process on which its members were engaged.

Britain was an area of comparatively high literacy levels among the working population. Chartism was preceded by a number of movements of varying size and influence in which printed journals, pamphlets and broadsides played an important part. It was itself organised and made into a national movement by the growth of a national working-class press: indeed it perhaps makes more sense to date Chartism from the foundation of the *Northern Star* in November 1837 than from the publication of the Charter six months later. Protestantism, dissent and the vulgar traditions of broadsides and ballads had in the past contributed to a leaven of literacy in the population, to which the more recent dissemination of radical journals in the main urban centres had added a political dimension and a further incentive to master the basic skills of literacy.

The British labouring population was prepared by its living and working conditions, its recent history in a series of struggles to preserve customary institutions and practices, its ready access to printed material and to the oratory of the platform and the pulpit, to produce a national labour movement at the end of the 1830s. The ruling classes, at the time, appeared particularly vulnerable to demands for concession. A new reign was beginning, one which represented a change in generations, which seemed to be a move away from the corruption and cynicism of the monarchy thus far in the century. Republicanism was to play a small part in the rhetoric of Chartism for this reason. The Reform Bill of 1832 which had admitted the urban middle classes to the parliamentary franchise had itself been achieved amidst a resounding rhetoric of the ending of corruption, monopoly and patronage. The Whig leaders who had ridden to power on the tide of reform were open to the charge of reneging on their principles if they declared too firmly their opposition to any further reform. Lord John Russell's 'finality' speech in reply to Wakley's motion for franchise extension on the occasion of the Queen's speech to her first Parliament in 1837 enforced the sense of betrayal and heightened the atmosphere of class conflict. The British landed and commercial interests may have been the most solidly entrenched in Europe in 1838, but to the populace they appeared not as an *ancien régime* encrusted with traditional power and privilege, but as a ruling class which owed its legitimacy to a recent Act of Parliament, and which might be persuaded or frightened into using the same machinery to extend parliamentary rights to the rest of the nation. Disillusion with the actions of the reformed Parliament was combined with a certain optimism as to the possibilities of further peaceful reform if enough pressure could be brought.

For Chartism was not essentially a desperate or hopeless movement. It contained elements of fear and desperation, but also, always, a basic belief in the possibility of success, which imposed on it a discipline and a rationality in which it differed from earlier popular movements. It produced within itself older forms of demonstration and protest, but these were almost always controlled by a sense of longer-term purpose than the older and more traditional forms of riot or conspiracy. In many ways the years between 1836 and 1856 saw considerable changes in forms of political and industrial organisation in Britain. The changes which took place in organisations of the working people were among the most important of these. Chartism contained for a time elements of old and new forms, and was able to combine a national leadership with the participation of working men and women at all levels in the communities in which they lived. 'Modern' argument, printed matter and bureaucratic organisation combined for a time with 'traditional' demonstration, crowd action and intransigent resistance. The combination produced one of the most impressive movements in modern history.

PART ONE:

1838–1841

CHAPTER ONE

The Politics of the Reformed Parliament

Of the population of Britain in the 1830s, only a very small fraction took any active part in national politics. The electorate in England and Wales was around 653,000 from a population of just over 13 million, and in Ireland 90,000 from 7·8 million. The Reform Act of 1832 had enlarged the electorate by about 50 per cent above the figure in 1830, mainly by the inclusion in the borough franchise of the £10 householder. Excluded from the vote were all women, all people under the age of twenty-one and the majority of men in the country. Even among the enfranchised, a majority never used their votes independently, for the system of open polling, by which the name and vote of every individual was publicly recorded, meant that every kind of pressure could be put on the voters, and that most people therefore used their vote instrumentally – tenants to gratify landlords, tradesmen to ingratiate themselves with rich customers, the comparatively weak to win the favour and influence of the powerful. Serious choice, and the exercise of influence over the make-up of the House of Commons, remained the privilege of a very small number of people. Why then did such a strong and sustained movement arise at the end of the thirties for an extension of the franchise and the exercise of political rights by the whole population?

The answer lies partly in a changing perception of politics. High politics had traditionally had no real place in it for the non-elector. The old-fashioned carnival which had accompanied contested elections in the eighteenth century, where rival crowds and brass bands paraded in support of the landlord or patron's candidate, was rapidly going out of fashion. The politics of the crowds who had demonstrated in favour of Queen Caroline in 1820, and even more the threatening crowds which had controlled Bristol and burnt parts of Derby and Nottingham during the reform agitation, had banished for ever the image of the jolly drunken crowd of loyal supporters at election celebrations. In the 1830s the good, self-respecting workman did not mix in politics. The word 'politician' applied to a working man by his fellows or by his superiors invariably meant that he was interested in radical politics. Benjamin

Wilson was first introduced to Chartism by his aunt, 'a famous politician, a Chartist and a great admirer of Feargus O'Connor'.[1] When HM Inspector of Prisons interviewed the men in prison for Chartist activities in 1840, he spoke approvingly of the decision some had made to 'give up politics'.[2] It did not occur to him that former Chartists should become Whigs or Tories. Politics in any form was not the business of the working man. Loyal support for church and government of whatever political complexion was all that was required of the non-electors.

The reform agitation had introduced a new dimension into politics, with the crowds demonstrating for a principle rather than for particular candidates. To some conservative members of the higher orders this had been the most worrying thing about the whole reform episode – the assumption of an interest in political matters by the hitherto non-political crowd. The political radicalism which grew up in the manufacturing districts and in the cities of Britain in the 1830s was totally independent of either of the two established parties, the Whigs and the Tories. It was a turning towards political solutions for a variety of activities and problems which had hitherto been dealt with at a local and largely non-political level. Chartism was the channelling into a series of demands for political rights of a large number of grievances and experiences of oppression felt by the common people in the early decades of the nineteenth century.

The issues which drew people into the Chartist movement after 1838 had nearly all been present during the reform agitation of 1830-2. In the debates and excitement of those years there had been a general optimism and a sense that, could the corruption and inefficiency at the top of society be reformed, no problem would be insoluble. Throughout the country there were working-class radicals who had become part of the movement for reform in the years immediately after the wars, or at the time of Peterloo, or who had taken part in the agitation in support of Queen Caroline at the time of George IV's coronation, or who had bought and sold the infidel publications of Richard Carlile or the illegal unstamped journals of Carpenter and Hetherington, or had read Cobbett's *Political Register*, or joined the crowds listening to Henry Hunt and his provincial followers demanding the reform of Parliament. These men and women had been nourished on a variety of radical journals, had joined Hampden clubs to agitate for parliamentary reform in the years immediately after the wars, or Zetetic societies to explore free thought and challenge the intellectual dominion in the 1820s. They had turned out to protest against the massacre at Peterloo, half expecting that their funeral processions would be met with the same kind of attack as had killed the victims they were mourning. In many districts the radicals formed merely an active minority, perhaps grouped around a bookseller or coffeehouse keeper who stocked radical journals, or the shop of a radical shoemaker or tailor whose workplace provided a meeting point for kindred spirits. In other places, like some of the cotton towns of Lancashire or the woollen districts of the West Riding, whole villages and townships supported the reforming cause. Here the agitation of 1830 aroused unbounded hope and enthusiasm.

When Sydney Smith said that every unmarried woman in England thought that the Reform Bill would get her a husband, he was, as so often, putting a flippant finger on a serious point. Nearly everyone who supported reform expected it to produce a government which would deal rationally with the country's problems and find acceptable solutions to them. They believed that nearly every problem had a political solution. Some of the more sophisticated among the working-class radicals saw that the extension of the franchise to the middle classes was not going to help the working class, and said so. They stood out from the beginning for universal suffrage, and many of them went on to become founders of the Chartist movement a few years later. Peter Bussey of Bradford, Matthew Fletcher of Bury, John Knight of Oldham, Thomas Sidaway of Gloucester, and many others up and down the country defended 'the Bill, the whole Bill etc.' but declared that at best it could only be a first instalment of political rights for the whole people. But the majority of people in all classes who shouted for reform in 1832 maintained great hopes of the reformed Parliament.

There were many issues at the beginning of the 1830s for a reformed legislature to tackle. For working people in the manufacturing districts, life had in very many ways become much tougher since the end of the wars. The main trades had been flooded with new entrants, and old controls in the form of apprenticeship regulation were breaking down. The power of trade societies and unions to control entry to trades, agreed price lists, and methods of fixing rates and prices had been challenged, in almost all cases successfully. Most major industries throughout the country had seen strikes or lock-outs during the 1820s – episodes like the strike of Bradford woolcombers in 1825 which had lasted for twenty-three weeks, the strike of carpet weavers in Kidderminster in 1828 which lasted three months, those of the London shoemakers in 1818 and 1824, the Lancashire cotton spinners in 1824 and 1828, the shipwrights in 1824, powerloom weavers in 1826 and the handloom weavers in the same year, had all taken place in defence of existing wages in the face of threatened cuts. All had failed, in spite of considerable support from fellow tradesmen and unionists throughout the country. Although trade unions had nominally been made legal in 1824, the repeal of the Statute of Artificers in 1814 had withdrawn the last remnant of legal protection for apprenticeship, and the main unions had been unable to enforce their own regulations by industrial action. Many hoped for government intervention to restore trade standards and to protect the wage-bargaining machinery of the craftsmen.

Closely associated with the need to defend working conditions was the vexed question of poor relief. Although the agitation against the 1834 Poor Law Amendment Act was later to invoke the pre-1834 law to an extent favourably, there was at the time of the Reform Bill general agreement that the structure of relief needed overhauling. As O'Brien declared in the course of an attack on the new law,

> . . . talk of 'abuses of the old Poor Law system'! Who denies these abuses? Who denies that that system was full of glaring abuses? Who denies that that system was full of glaring defects which called loudly for amendment?[3]

The demoralisation of the agricultural districts, the restriction on mobility imposed by the settlement laws, the wastage and corruption existing among the administrators of parish funds in many districts, and the humiliation involved in applying to the parish for relief were all grievances felt strongly in many parts of the country. Middle-class ratepayers were not alone in looking to Parliament for a reform of the system. Associated with this was the need for a wider reform of parochial and municipal government. Many of the radicals who went on to found the Chartist movement had already cut their teeth on the politics of the select vestry or the conflict over freemen's rights. Coventry and Newport, for example, had experienced battles over freemen's rights, and the radicals of the London borough of Finsbury had taken the lead in vestry politics.

A fourth issue which affected people in their working lives was the question of factory reforms. In the cotton industry in particular an increasing volume of production was being carried on in factory premises, where half the workforce was children and a further substantial section women. The complexity of the problems which arose from this, and from the increasing tendency towards the concentration of other work into factories, was considerable. Most of the operatives in Lancashire and the West Riding were in favour of legal intervention to limit the working hours in factories, whether this was to protect children from excessive exploitation or to decrease the competition between child and adult labour by putting 'artificial' restrictions on the work of children, or simply to decrease the working hours of all factory operatives. The case for legal intervention was supported by a few radical manufacturers in Lancashire, among them the reformer and Chartist sympathiser, John Fielden. The radicals of Lancashire may have been encouraged by the election to the reformed Parliament of more than one convinced factory reformer. Across the Pennines, however, there was less cause for optimism. The leader of the factory reform movement in Parliament, Michael Saddler, lost his seat in the first post-Reform-Bill election, to be replaced by a member of one of the most notorious mill-owning families, Marshalls the flax-spinners. The disillusion which the factory reformers of Yorkshire had already experienced with middle-class radicalism left them with a less optimistic view of the possible results of reform. It has sometimes been suggested that they were 'Tory Radicals', but this is hardly a useful ticket, except for the eccentric figure of Richard Oastler himself. When the Yorkshire reformers put forward a parliamentary candidate in Oastler's own stamping-ground, Huddersfield, in the first reformed election, it was a universal suffrage candidate, like that of every other working-class radical constituency in the country, and like the rest he fared ill at the poll.

A Ten Hours Bill was already in preparation before the dissolution of the last unreformed Parliament, the work of Michael Saddler. The new administration was confidently expected by many to continue on the basis of the report of the Saddler Committee, and to produce a Bill limiting the working hours of children to ten. Factory reform was expected, as was the long-overdue repeal of the punitive taxes on newspapers and journals which had been imposed by the Government in the aftermath of Peterloo to limit the circulation of cheap radical publications.

Apart from the question of the extension of the suffrage, the main political question which agitated radicals at the time of the Reform Bill was the question of Ireland. A third of the population of the British Isles was Irish by 1841, a large section of the workforce in England and Scotland was well as in Ireland itself. The Act of Union of 1801 had brought Ireland under the government of Westminster, but government had been sustained by a series of Coercion Acts which in effect put large parts of the country under martial law. Draconian powers were given to the authorities, particularly in districts in which agrarian terrorism was carried out. Catholic emancipation in 1829 had brought the possibility of a more representative delegation of MPs from Ireland to Parliament, and radical opinion hoped for – if not the immediate repeal of the union – at least an end to coercion and the rationalisation of relations with Ireland. The decay of the Irish textile industry after the final abandonment of protection in the 1820s had had the effect both of impoverishing the country and of driving many of the workers to England, where some of them were already part of the radical movements in London, Lancashire, South Wales, Yorkshire, Glasgow and other districts. Apart from the resident Irish, migrant labourers regularly came to England to work, often seasonally for harvest work, sometimes seeming to threaten English workers by the low wages they would accept, and sometimes appearing as examples of the depths to which an oppressed and exploited population could sink. In British radical politics, Ireland stood for several things. On the grounds of natural justice and human rights, Ireland had the right to her own government. Most radicals believed that universal suffrage would produce a repeal of the Act of Union. On the same grounds, coercion was unjust and tyrannical. But not only this, for most radicals considered that measures which were used to hold down the Irish might well be used in the 'disturbed districts' of the rest of Britain. In the same way, the low level of Irish wages could be used to force down the level in Great Britain – Cobbett described the process in *Legacy to Labourers*: '. . . the farmer, pressed by the tax-gatherer, pressed by the parson, pressed by the landlord, a jail-door opening to his eyes would, with tears in those eyes, screw the labourer down in a short time to *Irish wages*'.[4] Irish coercion, like Irish poverty, was a threat to the working class of England, Scotland and Wales. In addition, each of these three countries contained a large Irish constituency who could be relied on to keep the problems of Ireland before their fellow-radicals.

But basically the reason for optimism on the part of those non-electors who joined in the enthusiasm for the Reform Bill was the belief that it heralded a new age of enlightenment. The £10 household voting qualification was to be the beginning of a gradual widening of the franchise which would come with other benefits in the years following the reform of Parliament.

The reform agitation itself had produced a great political awakening among all classes. Political unions, whether jointly organised by middle- and working-class reformers or separately by the two distinct interests, had organised meetings and demonstrations, enrolled members, and provided quasi-respectable platforms for many people who until their foundation had been outside politics altogether. A combination of mass pressure and threats of violence as well as reasonable argument and constitutional petition had apparently achieved the impossible. Faced with popular pressure, a corrupt Parliament, based on patronage and interest, had voluntarily extended its privileges to a section of the hitherto unenfranchised. The lessons seemed clear. The unenfranchised *could* make themselves heard. The demonstrations which had shaken the country had brought about a peaceful revolution, turned out an entrenched and reactionary ministry and established the power of popular opinion. Bronterre O'Brien in the *Poor Man's Guardian* decried the Bill, but pointed up the lesson of its achievement.

> Firm, peaceable, and intelligent determination to resist an odious faction has been crowned with success, and the united people of this country have scared from their prey the basest and most odious reptiles the earth has ever beheld, and filled them with dread, without so much as one drop of blood being spilled – or even a single instance of the peace and good order of society being disturbed. Let us not forget this lesson. Let us continue to bear it in mind, for we still have our battle to gain. 'The Bill' . . . will benefit none but the proud and arrogant 'shopocracy'. My friends, you know what use they make of their power. Will adding to the power they already possess to oppress you benefit you? You are not ignorant enough to think so. We have then our battle still to gain.[5]

Disillusion with the results of reform set in almost as soon as the Act was passed. Universal suffrage candidates with massive support at the hustings were defeated at the polls almost without exception. A few ultra-radicals were returned – William Cobbett and John Fielden at Oldham, and Thomas Attwood at Birmingham supported universal suffrage. But Henry Hunt lost his seat at Preston where the new franchise was narrower than the old, as Michael Saddler lost his to the new middle-class electorate of Leeds. The new £10 householder franchise had drawn the line between the classes more sharply than ever.

The new House of Commons contained, apart from Fielden and Cobbett, supporters of factory reform in the persons of Charles Hindley, Joseph Brotherton and Lord Ashley; the latter took over the leadership of the parliamentary movement from Saddler, and continued to work for the Ten Hours Bill. Daniel O'Connell, at the head of a group of Irish Members, supported many radical demands; he and his sons continued to vote for universal suffrage motions as long as they remained in the House, although they never initiated such motions, and they were, of course, expected to be the strongest proponents of the repeal of the union. William Sharman Crawford, among the Irish Members, was an ultra-radical and supporter of what was to become the Chartist programme, and Feargus O'Connor was himself the Member for Cork until 1835. Thomas Slingsby Duncombe, elected for the radical borough of Finsbury, where the electorate included many long-standing radicals and future Chartists, was probably the most radical Member of the House, as well as having the reputation of being the best-dressed. He consistently presented the radical and Chartist case in Parliament, and investigated a range of problems on behalf of the working-class radicals from the treatment of Chartist prisoners to cases of the ill-treatment of paupers in workhouses. He spoke on Chartist platforms, chaired meetings of trade unionists, and he and his fellow-Member for Finsbury after 1835, Thomas Wakley, founder and editor of the *Lancet*, were the only two Members of Parliament to take membership cards in the National Charter Association. Cobbett died in 1835, and O'Connor was unseated in the same year. Attwood withdrew in 1839. During most of the years of Chartist activity, only Duncombe, Fielden and Wakley could be said to support the major part of the Chartist programme. Up to forty Members would usually vote in support of the extension of the suffrage, while others, not in most cases the same people, would vote for the suspension of the Poor Law regulations. In the main, however, the membership of the reformed House of Commons differed little from that of the unreformed, except for a greater sensitivity to the interests of the new electorate.

Almost the first act of the new Government was to pass a Coercion Act for Ireland which surpassed in the restrictions it imposed on political action of all kinds even the Coercion Acts of earlier administrations. The thirties saw the beginning of a 'tithe war' in Ireland, and the Whig Government associated the agrarian terrorism of this movement with the repeal agitation led by Daniel O'Connell. They therefore forbade not only acts of terrorism but many kinds of ordinary constitutional political action. The Act has been called 'perhaps the most repressive Irish measure ever proposed by an English Government',[6] and was described by a contemporary Tory as 'a compound of the Proclamation Act, the Insurrection Act, the Gagging Bill, the Suspension of the Habeas Corpus Act and Martial Law'.[7] Its provisions shocked radicals of all kinds; they were accustomed to the widespread presence of the military in Ireland, although many hoped for a review of the Irish question in the aftermath of reform. What was new and shocking in the 1833 Act was the inclusion of powers for the suppression of ordinary political activity. The Lord Lieutenant was empowered to 'suppress any meeting deemed by him to be dangerous to public safety'. Meetings so suppressed were to be unlawful, and anyone present at them was to be guilty of a misdemeanour. The Lord Lieutenant was also empowered to proclaim any county to be 'disturbed', and in such districts no meetings 'to petition parliament etc.' could be held without ten days' notice and the permission of the Lord Lieutenant; any person found outside their house after sunset 'in suspicious circumstances' could be deemed guilty of a misdemeanour; courts martial were to take the place of civil courts, and only in them could any action taken by the authorities be questioned.[8]

The reaction to the Irish Coercion Act of 1833 is a most essential ingredient in the development of Chartism. It helps to account for the strongly defensive attitude which was present in the early years of the movement. The Whigs had, as almost their first action in government, fired a salvo at popular radical political action, and had been supported in doing so by the overwhelming majority of the new House of Commons. The radicals of Nottingham were voicing widespread fears when they declared that the Government's Irish policy was 'a subject of vital importance to the people of Ireland, and scarcely less so to the constitutional liberty of every subject in the British Dominions'. A large meeting forwarded a resolution to the House of Commons, declaring: 'Should your petitioners witness these acts of injustice done to Ireland, the most fearful apprehensions will be excited in their minds, that the same odious tyranny will be perpetrated towards themselves.'[9] Nottingham had, after all, been among the 'disturbed districts' mentioned in the Six Acts, and might well become one again. The determined opposition put up in Parliament to the Bill by Daniel O'Connell also helps to explain the enormous respect with which he was viewed by working-class radicals, and therefore the shock of his apostasy – first in entering in 1835 into the Lichfield House compact (see below, p.26) with the very Whigs whom he had so forcibly denounced for their base and bloody brutality at the time of the Coercion Bill, and then, perhaps even more, for his denunciation of trade unions, particularly of the Dublin trades, who had been among his most ardent supporters in opposition to the Act and in support of repeal. Dan was not the only parliamentary radical to go back on aspects of radical policy, nor was he the only one among them who accepted the main doctrines of *laissez-faire* philosophy. His eloquence and tenacity in support of popular political rights in Ireland, however, and his widespread extra-parliamentary activity in the protests against the

Coercion Act, led the radicals to expect far more of him, and therefore to be more bitter at his apparent desertion.[10]

The first anti-Government demonstrations after the Reform Bill were called to protest against the Irish Coercion Act. They were massively supported in traditional radical areas. At Birmingham the meeting at Newhall Hill in May, addressed by O'Connell and Thomas Attwood – a tough and consistent opponent in Parliament of the Government's Irish policy – was held to protest against that policy. It was certainly one of the largest meetings ever held in the district.[11] In Manchester an open-air meeting on Camp Field which rivalled the reform meetings in attendance was addressed by cotton spinners' leader John Doherty; a petition launched at the meeting against the Act was later presented to Parliament by William Cobbett with 14,000 names attached.[12] The issue of Irish coercion was at the head of the grievances which radical speakers emphasised in the years immediately preceding the publication of the Charter.[13]

If the Government's response to the Irish situation provoked a shocked response in those who had high hopes of the reformed administration, more such shocks were soon to follow.

An improvement in trade in 1833 turned the attention of many of the leaders of the trades towards union organisation, and in particular towards general unionism, as the protection against the kind of defeat which particular trades had experienced in the 1820s. The early thirties saw widespread attempts to build trade unions, both national or metropolitan alliances of particular trades, and the more ambitious attempt to build general unions to include skilled, unskilled, even female and juvenile labour.[14] The lock-out of Derby silk-weavers in 1833-4 became the kind of *cause celèbre* amongst unionists that some of the great strikes of the 1820s had been, and the collection of supporting funds accompanied the move for protective general union organisation. Any idea that the authorities in the post-Reform-Bill era would be more sympathetic to trades organisations was, however, short-lived. The employers' response to the strikes and to the organisation of national unions was predictably the use of the 'document' – the forcing of all employees to sign an undertaking not to belong to a trade union. In March 1834 the conviction of six Dorchester labourers for forming a branch of a trade union and administering oaths in the process seemed to bring the endorsement of the law and the Government into the battle clearly on the side of the employers. The Dorchester case again provoked an immediate response from radicals and unionists all over the country. Meetings and processions of protest were organised in

Leeds, Manchester, Birmingham, Newcastle, Oldham, Nottingham, London, and all the main manufacturing centres, at which thousands of men and women from the districts around joined in demonstrating and petitioning against the conviction and sentences. The motives for union organisation may well have been 'economic' or 'industrial'. The response to the sentences was certainly 'political'. The London demonstration and many provincial organisations sent delegations and petitions on behalf of the men to the Home Secretary, making the point repeatedly that the laws were heavily biased against the unrepresented. George Loveless, leader of the Dorchester labourers, threw into the crowd which watched him being led away from court a poem which began:

God is our guide! from field, from wave,
From plough, from anvil and from loom;
We come, our country's rights to save,
And speak a tyrant faction's doom:
We raise the watchword, liberty,
We will, we will, we will be free!!![15]

Already, two years after the passing of the Reform Bill, the Whig Government had become a 'tyrant faction'.

The collapse and crushing of the general union movement, highlighted by the Dorchester case, turned radical attention back to the suffrage and to political reform in general. All over the British Isles, men who had taken part in union actions were among the first Chartists. In the crucial year of 1837, when the movement really began to take on a national character, another trade-union case was one of its most important precipitants. In that year the cotton-spinners were on strike in Glasgow – along with members of other skilled trades – against wage reductions. In the course of the strike, a blackleg spinner was shot, and as he died he claimed that his shooting was due to his having continued work during the strike. The leaders of the strike were arrested, and finally the president, secretary, treasurer and assistant secretary, together with another member of the union, were charged on twelve counts, including murder and conspiracy to murder. After a lengthy trial they were found not guilty on the most serious charges – indeed no evidence of any kind to connect them with the actual crime was produced – but guilty of being leading members of an association engaged in illegal activities. All five were sentenced to seven years' transportation in January 1838.[16] The arrests and trial took place in an atmosphere of mounting tension throughout Britain. Every aspect was reported in detail in the *Northern Star* and the *Northern Liberator*, as well as in the *New Liberator*, a journal edited by Dr John Taylor and partly financed by the spinners' union. In all these journals the cotton spinners' case was linked with the radical political programme, indeed the prosecution of the spinners' committee was seen by many of the ultra-radicals as part of a planned attack on the whole working-class movement. Lawrence Pitkethly of Huddersfield wrote to his friend Joseph Broyan of Sutton-in-Ashfield:

Have you had a meeting respecting the Glasgow Cotton Spinners Committee. I hope you have this *is* a case peculiarly interesting to all working men if they submit to this they deserve their wages still lower than they have required the Glasgow men to go viz. one half. This case is far worse than the Dorchester labourers, be up, & have a large meeting & talk as with cloven tongues we are in continual Agitation here.[17]

Pitkethly was untiring in his work for the cotton spinners, raising money, organising meetings and petitions. He was himself the organiser in the background, while O'Connor, Beaumont and Taylor wrote and spoke in public in the spinners' defence. Trade unions throughout the kingdom supported the campaign, which emphasised the unity between the trades and political radicalism. A broadsheet printed in Newcastle in 1838 put the spinners' experience into rhyme.

Ye working men of Britain come listen awhile,
Concerning the cotton spinners who lately stood their trial
Transported for seven years far, far awa'
Because they were united men in Caledonia.

Success to our friends in Ireland, who boldly stood our cause,
In spite of O'Connell and his support of whiggish laws,
Away with his politics, they are not worth a straw
He's no friend to the poor of Ireland or Caledonia.

Success to O'Connor who did nobly plead our cause,
Likewise to Mr Beaumont, who abhors oppressive laws,
But after all their efforts, justice and law,
We are banished from our country, sweet Caledonia.

Whigs and Tories are united, we see it very plain,
To crush the poor labourer, it is their daily aim,
The proverb now is verified, and that you can all knaw,
In the case of those poor spinners in Caledonia.[18]

The sentence of the spinners' leaders was passed only a few months after the return to England of the first of the six Dorchester labourers, pardoned, in 1836, after a long campaign on their behalf. Radicals of course made connections between the two cases. The female radicals of Elland issued an address to the returned men, congratulating them and urging them to join the campaign for remission of sentence on the spinners.[19] Bronterre O'Brien urged that the Dorchester men should tour the country in support of the spinners' case.[20] The meeting of the London trades to support the spinners, called as soon as the sentences were passed, was chaired by Robert Hartwell, who had been the secretary of the Dorchester committee in its earliest days and who now became a member of the supporting committee for the spinners.[21] As the rhyme indicated, the case also brought to a head the differences between Daniel O'Connell and the working-class radicals. For the latter the difference between 'political' and 'industrial' issues was never as sharp as modern historians have suggested, nor was it seen in the same way as the political economists saw it. The Glasgow spinners had been prosecuted by the Sheriff of Lanarkshire, Archibald Alison, to whom trade unions were a 'moral pestilence', and who described Glasgow during the strikes as being in a state of 'insurrectionary fever'. Alison, a High Tory, had no doubt about the political nature of his prosecution. He considered that the door to anarchy had been opened by the Reform Bill and by the spread of liberal principles, and saw his duty as the re-imposition of authority, including the authority of the employers to determine the conditions on which they employed their hands.[22] The harsh sentences imposed for offences which were amongst the least serious of those with which the men were charged again reinforced the political nature of the prosecution. The whole experience of the decade for those who were concerned with union organisation and with wages was calculated to underline the close connection between the status of men as workmen and their status as citizens. When O'Connell chose the spinners' case as his opportunity to attack trade unions, and demanded a parliamentary enquiry into their character and organisation, he seemed to have changed sides completely. Another aspect of politics highlighted by the case was the often-repeated belief, 'proverb', as the ballad calls it, that there was nothing to choose between Whigs and Tories as far as their attitude to the working classes was concerned. 'Whigs and Tories are united, we see it very plain.' In Glasgow the unity was underlined when the Tory sheriff brought the case before the Whig judge, Lord Cockburn. If Alison's case was exaggerated, Cockburn's sentence was a draconian response.

The years between the Dorchester and Glasgow cases had seen other actions by the Government calculated to complete the disillusion with the Reform Bill and to heighten the tension felt in the manufacturing districts. Foremost of these, and the one which has received the most attention from historians, was the passing of the 1834 Poor Law Amendment Act. Before that occurred, however, it should be noted that the ten hours campaign had also received a serious set-back. Historians of factory reform have rightly seen Althorpe's Act of 1833 as a landmark, since it established at least in principle a neutral inspectorate to monitor the implementation of its provisions, and so laid the basis for effective reform later in the century. In the context of the short-time movement of the 1830s, however, the Bill was a serious defeat. All energy had gone into the demand for a ten-hour day for children and young people, with the barely-disguised aim among the organisers of the movement of establishing ten hours as the norm for all ages. The Royal Commission which had been set up by the first reformed administration, at the instigation of the Lancashire factory masters, had no illusions about the matter. Their report, published in the spring of 1833, and couched in the language of political economy, attributed the activity of the ten hours movement to trade-union 'agitators' and rejected clearly and specifically the idea of any interference in the hours of work of adults or adolescents. The authors of the report recognised that children were not free agents, and should therefore receive some legal protection: 'the period of childhood, properly so-called', however, ceased at the age of thirteen, and after that 'the same labour which was fatiguing and exhausting at an earlier period is in general comparatively easy'. They therefore proposed that children under nine years of age should not be employed at all in factories, and that between that age and their thirteenth birthdays their working hours should be limited to eight a day, with no night work. In addition children should receive two hours a day of schooling. Adolescents between thirteen and eighteen years of age were to be limited to a twelve-hour day, again with no night work. All textile factories except silk mills were covered by the Act, and its provisions were to be introduced gradually over the following years.

Response to the Act and to the report was predictable. Factory reformers and working-class radicals saw the reformed Parliament declaring its attachment to the doctrines of *laissez-faire* political economy. The attack on trade unions, the specific rejection of any legal interference with the hours of work or the wages of adult workers were in line with the economic doctrines of the employers. The figure of eight hours allowed for young children's work meant that employers could operate a relay system, using two shifts of child workers for each adult shift, a procedure which could actually lengthen the adult working day. On such a system, spinners who employed their own piecers could find themselves paying more for child assistants, introducing more children into the factories and therefore potentially into the trade, and themselves having to work longer hours. The 1833 Act was undoubtedly a defeat for the short-time movement, and in so far as that movement had concentrated on trying to effect reform in one area only by pressure on existing parliamentary institutions, it again turned radicals towards more generalised political demands. Richard Oastler, the powerful and charismatic leader of the Yorkshire factory movement, was never a believer in universal suffrage as the answer to the problems of the working class. Although working constantly with people to whom the suffrage seemed the most important possible reform, he maintained: 'My opinion on "Universal Suffrage" is, that if it were the law of the land next week, it would in a short time produce "universal confusion" and would inevitably lead to "despotism".'[23] He did, however, on occasion preach forms of direct action, wrote for the unstamped press, and in both his factory and anti-Poor-Law campaigns, orchestrated popular crowd action which bordered the frontiers of legality. Reacting in rage to the 1833 Act, he made very broad hints about the possibility of direct industrial action – the limitation of the working day by the workers themselves refusing to do more than ten hours a day – and even of direct sabotage.[24] In the following years, his contribution, like that of the Rev. Joseph Rayner Stephens, to the mounting feeling, was to encourage the idea of direct action rather than to encourage the growth of popular constitutionalism. But it is important always to remember that both these elements were present in Chartism. Both elements were also present in the factory movement, many of whose leaders were, like Fielden and Doherty, ardent supporters of universal suffrage. All the movements which originated among the non-electors had continually to consider all forms of action as well as pressure on Parliament. As the decade proceeded and the bad effects of Althorpe's Act were observed, other forms of action were proposed. The Society for the Promotion of National Regeneration, founded in Lancashire, proposed direct industrial action in support of a legal eight-hour day. William Benbow's pamphlet proposing a month's 'National Holiday' to enforce universal suffrage was again published and discussed. These forms of activity were to be considered again by the Chartists.

In 1836, when the last phase of Althorpe's Act was to be brought into operation, and the hours of twelve-year-olds brought within its restriction, the free-trade lobby made an attempt to prevent it. Poulett Thompson, President of the Board of Trade, proposed an amendment to restrict the application of the Act to children under twelve years old, proposing that children of twelve be allowed, like their seniors, 'to decide for themselves; and if they think proper [to] work twelve hours a day'. The debate on the amendment is one of the most interesting of the decade, with the free traders arguing against control of working hours but in favour of the repeal of the Corn Laws, and the defenders of the Act marshalling their arguments from statistical evidence to scriptural injunction. The 1833 Act had not pleased anybody – petitions against it were presented from operatives, spinners and overlookers, as well as from manufacturers. Nevertheless the attack on it was universally seen as an attack on the principle of legislative interference, and the majority of operatives feared that a victory for the amendment would be the prelude to the total repeal of the Act. In the event the amendment was accepted by the House of Commons, but with a majority so slim, two only, that the Government treated it as a rejection, and proceeded with the implementation of the last phase.

For the radicals, who by 1836 were becoming organised nationally into clubs and unions, the experience and the debate emphasised again the importance of parliamentary decisions for the daily life of the operatives. It also marked a further deterioration in the standing among radicals of Daniel O'Connell. It has too often been suggested that a personal quarrel between him and Feargus O'Connor lay at the root of the attacks upon him by Chartist and radical groups, and that this personal factor also accounts for the attacks made by the *Northern Star* on the London Working Men's Association, of which O'Connell was an honorary member, in 1837 and 1838. This was certainly not the case. O'Connor's quarrel with O'Connell was founded on real political differences. Of course, personalities soon came into it, but essentially O'Connor's attitude to O'Connell was shared by all the radicals who became Chartists, including eventually Lovett and his associates.

The full story of O'Connell's sacrifice of the independence of the Irish party is a long one, and has been described in detail elsewhere.[25] Essentially, however, by the so-called Lichfield House compact of 1835, O'Connell pledged the support of his party to the Whigs, in return for certain concessions in their Irish policy. These concessions were not seen by Irish radicals as being of great significance – the main ones being the appropriation of part of the money collected as tithes in Ireland for rather vaguely defined 'religious and moral instruction of all classes of the community' in Ireland, and the reform of the Irish municipalities. The long-drawn-out struggle for these measures in both Houses of Parliament kept O'Connell and his party tied in entirely with the Whigs for the second half of the decade. Although O'Connell and his sons voted consistently in favour of any universal suffrage motions that were introduced into the House, and for the motions on the presentation of the Chartist petitions that the petitioners be heard, on an increasing number of other issues they voted with the mainstream Whigs and against the radicals. The Poulett Thompson amendment was an example of this. Of the Government majority of two, one was Daniel O'Connell, and undoubtedly the majority was achieved by the adhesion of his followers. O'Connell had been a passionate supporter of the original Act, and had supported the ten-hour day for everyone under eighteen. But by 1836 he had changed his mind. Feargus O'Connor reminded him:

> You pledged yourself – you were the Chancellor of the infant children – eighteen years at least, was the age for such labour as you consigned your babes to – you proposed the resolution at the Crown and Anchor – and what did you do? Why give your vote, the very casting vote, against unprotected innocence![26]

O'Connell had voted with the ultra-radicals on a number of occasions during the passage through the Commons of the 1834 Poor Law Amendment Act. Although he had decided that the sentence on the Dorchester labourers was legal, he had spoken out against its severity, and he and his sons had voted in favour of Wakley's motion for the remission of the punishment. But after 1835 his attitude hardened. During the discussions of the Irish Poor Law, towards which his attitude was ambivalent, he was often found defending the English system. His liberal attitude to the Dorchester labourers contrasted strongly with his hostile reaction to the Glasgow case, in which he took the lead in condemning both the cotton spinners and trade unionism generally, and his change of front on the factory question looked like straightforward apostasy. By the time the Chartist movement had begun, O'Connell had reverted to his position as an orthodox Benthamite in philosophy, and was committed by his political tactics to all-out support for the Whigs. His achievement as the single-handed victor in the struggle for Catholic emancipation, his stirring oratory against the Whigs in the days of the Irish Coercion Act of 1833, his support for universal suffrage and the repeal of the union between Ireland and England were remembered with bitterness by radicals throughout the British Isles. Amongst the Irish in Ireland he remained the overwhelmingly popular leader he had always been, at least until the very last year of his life. Among the Irish in England the position was less clear-cut, but he certainly created a split in the loyalties of the Irish, retaining by and large the support of the priests and their flocks, particularly among the recent immigrants in the large cities, but creating divided loyalties among the generality of first and second generation Irish men and women in the manufacturing districts. He was not among the supporters of Wakley's Amendment to the Address from the Throne in 1837.

The Irish Coercion Act, the emasculation of the Factory Act, the attacks on trade unions, all contributed to the disillusion felt by working-class radicals with the Reform Act and the administrations which followed it. The interests of the manufacturers and shopkeepers which had seemed to many in 1832 to be allied to those of the working people, now seemed to be being advanced in every area in which they conflicted with working-class interests. The Municipal Reform Act of 1835 established a system of government in the municipalities which mirrored that at Westminster. A ratepaying franchise was set in most places high enough to exclude those who were already excluded from the parliamentary franchise, and the powers which the new authorities were permitted to assume included the establishment of modern police forces, modelled on the unpopular metropolitan force which had already flexed its muscles on post-reform radicals in London in the Calthorpe Street affair in 1833.[27] Proposals were afoot for the extension of policing to areas outside the boroughs, and in 1836 a commission was set up to enquire into the establishment of rural police forces. The questionnaire sent out by the Commissioners asked particularly about 'riots and tumults' in the parishes, and their 'supposed objects'. The report, when it was issued in 1839, was clearly as much concerned with putting down industrial unrest as with the suppression of more traditionally defined crime. The rationalisation of local government may be seen in retrospect as a neutral process, an essential part of 'modernisation'. To many of those involved it implied attacks on their customary expectations – attacks at work on the regulations of their trade and the societies they had created to protect their standards and traditions, and attacks outside work on their leisure activities and on their family life.[28]

Of all the controversial acts of the reformed administrators during the 1830s, the two which aroused the most sustained reaction in the country, and which led directly into the Chartist movement, were the 1834 Poor Law Amendment Act, and the Government's treatment of the whole question of the duty on newspapers, leading to the 1836 Newspaper Act.

The working-class radicals were never in any doubt about their opposition to the new Poor Law. Bronterre O'Brien, in the *Poor Man's Guardian*, attacked the first reformed Parliament, which 'instead of RE-forming, has DE-formed, and instead of extending our rights and liberties . . . has invaded the one and considerably abridged the other. It began with a Coercion Bill for Ireland – it ended with a Starvation Law for England'.[29] The unstamped *Political Penny Magazine* was started specifically to campaign for the Act's repeal, declaring: 'The Cotton Lords of Manchester, the Iron Lords of Birmingham, the Sugar Lords of Liverpool, and the Monied Lords of the whole Kingdom, want to have the power placed in their hands to enable them to still grind and subdue the poor through their accursed machinery and commercial wealth . . .'[30]

In the House of Commons support for the Bill divided the philosophical radicals from the few radical Members who retained a popular following outside the House. It became the litmus test for distinguishing the radicalism of the middle class from that of the working class. Inside Parliament and out, John Fielden opposed the Act. 'I tell you [he said on its introduction] that the introduction of this new law into my constituency will meet with resistance, and I do not mind telling you frankly that if such resistance takes place, I would lead it. . .'[31] William Cobbett devoted the last year of his life to opposing the 'poor man's robbery bill', and the presence among the opponents of the Bill of eccentrics from both major parties, as well as the overwhelming support it gained locally and nationally from the majority of the Whig and Tory authorities, helped to accentuate the alienation of popular protest from either of the two parties' programmes.

What was at issue in the opposition to the Act was at first the apparent philosophy and intention behind it. Malthusian ideas of 'surplus population' were widespread, and were clearly seen to be embodied in the provisions of the Act which stressed the need for stopping any kind of outdoor relief based on family size, and which provided for the separation of families taken into the workhouse for relief. It was also widely believed that the Act aimed to reduce the possibility of survival without working, so that people would be forced to work at any wage rather than starve. The two themes – the defence of the working-class family and the defence of wages – brought together in political action against the Act whole communities of men and women. Samuel Kydd, a young shoemaker in the 1830s, later wrote:

The passing of the New Poor Law Amendment Act did more to sour the hearts of the labouring population, than did the privations consequent on all the actual poverty of the land. Rightly, or wrongly, may be a subject of discussion, but the fact is undeniable, that the labourers of England believed that the new poor law was a law to punish poverty; and the effects of that belief were, to sap the loyalty of the working men, to make them dislike the country of their birth, to brood over their wrongs, to cherish feelings of revenge, and to hate the rich of the land.[32]

The operation of the Act was resisted in nearly all parts of the country. In agricultural areas resistance was isolated and sporadic, though none the less bitter for that. In areas where the radical journals were read, however, populations were encouraged to resist in every possible way the application of the provisions of the act to their districts. Kydd spoke of the opposition of 'working men' to the Poor Law, but it was above all the resistance to it that brought the women of the manufacturing districts into political activity. The considerable presence of women in the early years of the Chartist movement can partly be accounted for by their passionate opposition to the new Poor Law, and the philosophy which lay behind it.

The new law was introduced into the northern manufacturing districts in 1837. This was the year of the foundation of the *Northern Star* and the *Northern Liberator*, the year of the arrest of the Glasgow cotton spinners, the year of the Crown and Anchor meeting in London at which the proposal for a new petition to Parliament for Reform was agreed. Although the name of *Chartist* is not used until after the publication of the People's Charter in May 1838, it is really from 1837 that the movement may be said to have begun nationally. So far from the northern anti-Poor-Law movement fading into the Chartist movement, it should rather be seen as an episode in the continuous radical activity which marks the first phase of Chartism. It is significant of Mark Hovell's view of politics that he found the two movements not only separate but contradictory.

The Poor Law divided the working-class radicals from the Philosophical Radicals more sharply than any other issue. It is confusing that the term 'radical' has to be used in the first half of the century for two groups which were in many ways so disparate. The parliamentary group known as the Philosophical Radicals had little in common with the extra-parliamentary radicals, or indeed with parliamentary radicals like Cobbett or Fielden, except a willingness to accept change. The fact that some of them believed in universal male suffrage, and that some signed the original People's Charter, adds further to the confusion, since before the publication of the Charter the Chartists were in fierce public confrontation with some of these signatories. The issue of the Poor Law was the test. John Arthur Roebuck, a signatory of the Charter, spoke approvingly in the House of Commons on the aims of the new law.

He advocated it not on the ground that it had decreased the expense of maintaining the poor – that was, indeed, a great point; but he must beg to remind the House that there were two classes of poor, the industrious poor, and the poor that were not so. Now he believed that the interests of the industrious poor were deeply involved in the bill, and it was as a friend to those interests that he should continue to vote for the measure.

John Bell, of the *London Mercury*, countered the argument vigorously.

I deny the existence of any *class* of idlers, out of the ranks of the aristocracy, and of the middle orders. There is no class of idle poor . . . yet Mr. Roebuck, in his place as a law-maker, talks of dividing the producers of all wealth into the idle and the industrious – as if the one class, the class of idlers among the poor, counterbalanced in numbers and importance the class which toils . . . In talking after this fashion, Mr. Roebuck proves his expertness in repeating by rote the false assumptions of a frigid and shallow system of philosophy. . . The fault of the poor is not, I contend in opposition to Roebuck and Hume and all that set of complacent retailers of Malthusianism – the fault of the poor is not that they work too little, but that they work too much. . .[33]

Cobbett and others had argued that the right of the poor to relief in time of need was a constitutional right which could be traced back to the period of the dissolution of the monasteries, when the charitable functions of the holy orders were assumed by the state. But the Chartists increasingly set aside this kind of argument in favour of a bolder and more political case. Bronterre O'Brien articulated this in the early months of 1837.

. . . I hate long discussions and disquisitions upon the rights and privileges of the oppressed. I hate such arguments as go to prove that hawks should not prey upon doves; wolves on lambs; or the idlers of society upon the productive classes; I hate all appeals to the morality of monsters. . .

We have had enough of moral and learned strictures upon abstract rights and duties, which have left the respective parties *in statu quo* – the one plundering, the other being plundered. . .

My motto is '*Qui capet ille habet*'. 'What you *take* you may have'. I will not attempt to deal with the abstract question of right, but will proceed to show that it is POWER, solid, substantial POWER, that the millions must obtain *and retain*, if they would enjoy the produce of their own labour and the privileges of freemen.

The old Poor Law, the famous 43rd Elizabeth, had, he maintained, been wrung from the rulers of the day by the threat posed by 'valiant beggars' who were prepared to help themselves 'when charity did not make them welcome'.

This famous Act, with slight local variations, has been the law of the land since the time of its enactment; the Reformed Parliament of our ruling classes undertook to repeal it, and again drive the necessitous to the alternatives of plunder or starvation. Our sturdy ancestors, as has been seen, were not long in deciding. They had not, to be sure, been trained in the '*Useful Knowledge*' school – their inborn sense of justice had not been frittered away by the interested jargon of the economists and anti-population reasoners; they had not learned 'that there was no place for them at nature's board'; they therefore gave nature credit for inviting them, and *took their places* at her board accordingly. . .[34]

Such arguments were not confined to the north, but were to be found in radical journals throughout the country. Only the London Working Men's Association, which has ironically often been credited with originating the Chartist movement, held back from criticism of the new law in return for promise of support for an extension of the suffrage from some of the parliamentary radicals. It was this combination which made up the original signatories of the Charter, but by the time that document was actually published the tenuous alliance of O'Connell, Roebuck and others with the radicals of the working-class movement had been broken.

The vigour of the anti-Poor-Law movement in the north owed much to the already existing organisations of the short-time movement. The network of committees took on the new agitation, and the growing number of radical associations associated all these issues with the demand for further parliamentary reform.

In 1836, 1837 and 1838 leaders of the radical movement were making provincial tours. Feargus O'Connor was first in the field, touring the country and speaking at dinners and meetings arranged for him by radicals in the main provincial centres. The missionaries from the London Working Men's Association followed, and in 1837 and 1838 Hetherington, Cleave and Vincent toured Britain, setting up Working Men's Associations or speaking at meetings arranged by existing radical associations. However much some of the London leaders had been affected by the approval given to the 1834 Act by the philosophical radicals, and by their advisors, Dr Black and Francis Place, once away from the metropolitan atmosphere the missionaries were as fervent in their opposition to the Act as Feargus or as their provincial hosts.

The arrival of Feargus O'Connor at a radical meeting was often the occasion for the fracture of alliances between radicals of the middle and working classes which had survived the first few years of the reformed administration. In Halifax in 1836 he was invited to a dinner held to honour the two anti-Tory candidates, the Whig Charles Wood and the radical Edward Prothero. When the Whigs, in some alarm, withdrew the invitation, the radicals went ahead with a separate function. This, however, turned out in the end to be far too radical for Prothero, and made clear the impossibility of continuing the anti-Tory alliance. As guest of honour, Feargus stressed the importance of breaking with the Whigs. 'Are we so blind as we have taken ourselves from the fangs of one party, to present ourselves to another?' He attacked the new Poor Law strongly, and the Irish Coercion Bill, spoke in favour of the Ten Hours Bill and called for universal suffrage. In his speech he specifically addressed the non-electors, reminding them that they paid the nation's military bills through their taxes, but that the army would be used against them to protect those taxes.[35] This tour, on which O'Connor visited Nottingham, Newcastle, Kilmarnock, Cumnock, Leith, Edinburgh, Glasgow, Dundee, Dunfermline, Paisley, Halifax, Bradford, Hull, Barnsley and Huddersfield, was of great importance. He held meetings, was welcomed with processions and attended dinners in the various towns. In some places, as in Newcastle, these events were organised by the old Reform Bill alliance; in others the alliance was already fractured by the winter of 1836. Feargus rallied the supporters of universal suffrage, and at the same time made contacts who were to be of great value when he came to found the *Star* in 1837. At a dinner in Halifax in May 1838, held to celebrate the first half-year of the *Northern Star*, shareholders who sat down to the meal included Robert Wilkinson, Thomas Cliffe, Henry Rawson, William Thornton and Thomas Tetley, all of whom were among the group of radicals who had supported Prothero, and of whom Tetley at least had been on the committee which had arranged the 1836 dinner. By 1838 all were leading Halifax Chartists and *Star* shareholders.[36] The dinner took place at the Labour and Health Inn in Southgate, which had been the main distribution point for unstamped journals in the district[37] and was the meeting-place for the Chartists in the early years of the movement. Radical groups had been formed in and around Halifax during the thirties, and well before the publication of the Charter a public meeting adopted five of the six points (the missing one being the payment of members); this meeting was chaired by another member of the 1836 radical dinner committee, William Thorburn, and speakers included many of the same group, with the addition of two of the leaders of the handloom weavers in the district, Benjamin Rushton and John Crossland, both of whom were soon to become leading Halifax and West Riding Chartists, and Abram Hanson, radical shoemaker from nearby Elland. The platform represented the traditions of political radicalism, the agitation for the suffrage and for the freedom of the press, the trades (both Rushton and Crossland had given evidence to the handloom weavers' commission) and the anti-Poor-Law movement. Benjamin Rushton and William Thornton were also popular lay preachers, and brought their abilities in this field into the Chartist movement. Robert Sutcliffe, another handloom weaver, made the first speech, particularly attacking the Irish Coercion Act. 'While Daniel O'Connell was stating that the radicals of England had no sympathy for Ireland, he would assure him that they felt as keenly for their Irish brethren as for their own suffering.' The motion for the adoption of the petition was moved by John Crossland and passed by acclamation by the crowd of between three and four thousand who stood in the snow to hear him. The ingredients of Chartism were already all present, the main points of the Charter, accepted without question, the unity of social and political grievances on the same platform, the hostility to the 'betrayal' by the Whig reformers – Thomas Cliffe recalled that Edward Baines had 'called on the people to come forward in their thousands and hundreds of thousands in order to carry the Whigs into office', but had then proclaimed against the anti-Poor-Law meetings – and the particular resentment shown by all speakers against Irish coercion and the new Poor Law. Benjamin Rushton proposed the motion for the repeal of the new Poor Law, declaring that 'He had now been a common labourer thirty-three years, and after having toiled fifty or sixty years he had the consolation of knowing that he might retire into a bastille and finish his existence upon fifteen pence halfpenny a week.'[38]

Among the women, the Poor Law was a question of the greatest concern. The bastardy clauses of the 1834 Act shifted the responsibility for children born out of wedlock to the mother alone, unless she was able to prove in a court of law the paternity of the child. These clauses were bitterly resented. But it was above all the attack on the family and on the control by the parents of their homes and children that was most hated. This was the nerve in his audience that responded passionately to the emotive rhetoric of Joseph Rayner Stephens, the former Methodist clergyman who was, by 1838, leading his own independent congregation in Ashton-under-Lyne, in a chapel built there for him by his supporters.

For Stephens, the 1834 Poor Law was part of a deliberate policy of the factory owners to force down wages and to use the cheap labour of women and children instead of men's labour. His apocalyptic rhetoric was enormously popular throughout the manufacturing districts.

> I will fight to the death sooner than that law shall be brought into operation on me or on others with my consent or through my silence. . . Perish trade and manufacture – perish arts, literature and science – perish palace, throne and altar – if they can only stand upon the dissolution of the marriage tie – the annihilation of every domestic affection, and the violent and most brutal oppression ever yet practised upon the poor of any country in the world.[39]

Some of this tone appears in many of the manifestos of the female radical associations. From Newcastle-upon-Tyne early in 1839, the Female Political Union declared that 'the solace of our homes, the endearments of our children and the sympathies of our kindred are denied us – and even in the grave our ashes are laid with disrespect'.[40]

When the miners' leader, Thomas Hepburn, spoke to the women of Newcastle in March 1839, he made the defence of the family the main theme of his talk.[41] By the 1834 Act, politics had intervened to attack the most intimate areas of the family, and the women reacted at least as strongly as the men. The challenge to the politics of the reformed administrations was moral as well as political. John Fielden was cheered when he said, simply:

> If Parliament was composed of working men, they would not have suspended the laws and constitution of the country and have passed a coercion Bill for Ireland. If Parliament was composed of poor men, they would not have passed the new Poor Law Amendment Act, but would first have secured to the working class fair remunerative wages. . .[42]

Increasingly, during the second half of the decade, the men and women of the manufacturing districts were taking up again the question of parliamentary reform, but this time in opposition to their former allies in the agitation. As Bronterre O'Brien wrote soon after the passing of the 1834 Act:

> In one respect the New Poor Law has done good. It has helped to open the people's eyes as to who are the real enemies of the working classes. Previously to the passing of the Reform Bill, the middle orders were supposed to have some community of feeling with the labourers. That delusion has passed away.

It barely survived the Irish Coercion Bill. It vanished completely with the enactment of the Starvation Law.[43]

By the beginning of 1838 the same tone was being nationally spread through the columns of the *Northern Star*, which from the beginning linked the new law with a series of other grievances.

The London journals are in error when they suppose that, in the North, all agitation is directed against the new Poor Law Amendment Act. No, but *it* is the basis of a new Constitution, and therefore do we work the battering ram of discontent against it. Its provisions are to give effect to the new system of the political economists . . . and therefore do we denounce it. The auxiliaries to this infernal law are the Factory scheme, the Rural Police and the complete destruction of Trades Associations, which was the last remnant of power in the hands of the working classes, and by which supply and demand could be wholesomely regulated.[44]

CHAPTER TWO

The Chartist Press

CHARTISM came about because the people in the different manufacturing districts found themselves agreed on the need for a movement to protect their existing institutions and achievements, to resist the attacks being mounted on them by the newly-enfranchised employing class, and to press forward for more freedoms and a more equitable system of taxation, employment and citizenship than the society of the 1830s offered them. Other beliefs and other programmes were added to the central political demands of the Charter, and there were regional and occupational differences of emphasis. What was new and powerful about the movement, however, was its national character and the speed with which ideas and proposals for action were disseminated. This speed and this national dimension were achieved largely through the press.

The Chartist press was one of the foundations on which the movement was built, and one of the bridges with earlier movements. Of all the immediate precursors of Chartism, the 'war of the unstamped' was among the most significant and influential.[1] Not only were many of the leading journalists and platform orators veterans of the unstamped, but very many of the leading provincial radicals had first come to feel themselves part of a national movement through the part they had played in selling and distributing the papers. From the time of the Six Acts onwards, the Government's attempt to price newspapers out of the working people's reach by the imposition of a heavy stamp duty on each issue had been challenged by a number of radical journalists and publishers. Their main tactic was simply to publish and sell cheap periodicals without the necessary stamp, and to accept the inevitable punishment of fines or imprisonment.

The best and most influential of the unstamped journals was the London-based *Poor Man's Guardian* (1831-5). Its publisher, Henry Hetherington, a leader of the campaign, was a signatory of the People's Charter, and remained a radical and a Chartist until his death from cholera in 1849. The *Guardian*'s editor for most of its life was Bronterre O'Brien, at his best the ablest of all the radical journalists of this period. His main positive contribution to Chartism was made in its early years, when he ran *Bronterre's National Reformer* for the first quarter of 1837, edited the *Operative* from November 1838 to June 1839, and contributed regular columns to the early editions of the *Northern Star*. John Cleave, after Hetherington the most important of the metropolitan unstamped publishers, became the London agent for the *Northern Star* and published, among a great deal of other radical literature, the *English Chartist Circular* from 1841 to 1843. William Carpenter, whose *Political Letters* in 1830 had been one of the first unstamped journals to earn its publisher a prison sentence, was editor of the *Charter* in 1839 and 1840, and the *Southern Star* in the first half of 1840. John Bell, editor of the *London Mercury* in 1837 and later associated with the Newcastle *Northern Liberator* in 1839 and 1840, had been associated as editor and publisher with the unstamped *New Political Register*, as well as having edited the radical, stamped, *True Sun*. William Benbow, a veteran of the National Union of the Working Classes in 1831 and 1832, and of almost all the radical agitations since the wars, had edited the *Tribune of the People* in 1832 and the *Agitator and Political Anatomist* in 1833, and continued to publish journals and pamphlets, including several editions of his *Grand National Holiday*; he was early in the Chartist movement, and was imprisoned for sedition in 1840. The inspector of prisons who interviewed him in 1841 noted:

> The name and character of this prisoner is familiar to all acquainted with agitation. The associate of Carlisle [*sic*] Hetherington and others, he is now 56 years of age and time seems to have abated nothing of his warmth in the cause of republicanism.[2]

J. B. Lorymer, who had edited several of the republican unstamped journals, was a founder member of the East London Democratic Association, and contributed to its journal the *London Democrat*. Richard Lee, printer and editor of the *Man* in 1834, was London correspondent of the *Northern Star* from 1839 to 1841 and the printer of the *English Chartist Circular*. In Yorkshire, Joshua Hobson, editor and publisher of the unstamped *Voice of the West Riding* (1833-5) and three times prosecuted, became the publisher and for a time the editor of the *Northern Star*, while his associate William Rider, who edited the *Voice* while Hobson was in prison, became a founder and leading member of the Leeds Working Men's Association and a delegate to the first Convention.

Continuity between the two movements can be seen in the persons of agents and distributors of the papers, as well as of journalists and publisher. Of the hundreds who sold the unstamped papers and served terms of imprisonment for doing so, many turned up as agents for the

Chartist journals, and many more whose names have not survived may be assumed to have been among the earliest Chartists. The governor of Coldbath Fields prison, who had had charge of many of the vendors in the early thirties, recalled:

> Many of them were really good-tempered, and even facetious declaimers on popular rights, whose erratic ideas and mental dreaminess were of a very unusual stamp, and quite explained the visionary nature of their political creed. They delighted to call themselves 'working men', although they were unlike the general mass of working men. . . . A judicious alteration in the act regarding newspaper stamps deprived me of all my 'martyrs' and I have not the slightest notion how those men thereafter developed their political tendencies, but I surmise they swelled the cry for the 'People's Charter'.[3]

Best-known of the former vendors in later years was G. J. Harney, who had been imprisoned while still in his teens and went on to become editor of the *Northern Star* and one of the national leaders of Chartism throughout its existence. But other less well-known figures throughout the country bridge the gap between the two campaigns, people like Alice Mann in Leeds, Joshua Hobson of Ashton-under-Lyne, and Abel Heywood of Manchester, who had the Manchester agency for the *Northern Star* and acted for a time as Feargus O'Connor's business manager. In the West Riding James Ibbotson of Bradford, Titus Brooke of Dewsbury and Christopher Tinker of Huddersfield, all former prisoners of the Government, appeared as early agents for the *Star*. In Barnsley Joseph Lingard and his wife, who had been vendors of the unstamped journals, were agents for the Chartist papers, whilst four of the six agents listed as handling the *Star* in Birmingham in 1838 had been prosecuted for selling unstamped papers, including James Guest, who had first introduced the metropolitan journals to Birmingham when he began to sell *Carpenter's Political Letters* there in 1830.[4]

Among the immediate ancestors of the London Working Men's Association was the Association of Working Men to Procure a Cheap and Honest Press, formed early in 1836 with the help and encouragement of the American Dr Black, for the purpose of raising money and support for the imprisoned unstamped publishers. There was considerable overlap between this body and the LWMA formed later in the year. John Gast, the shipwright's leader, was a member of both, as were Robert Hartwell, Richard Moore and William Lovett.[5] Both in and out of Parliament, Feargus O'Connor was a prominent speaker on behalf of the unstamped, and of press freedom in general. He had been the chief supporter of the radical editors of the *True Sun*, imprisoned in 1834 under the law of libel for recommending the non-payment of house and window tax in the campaign for a property tax, had spoken in their defence at public meetings, and presented in the House of Commons the petition against their imprisonment. The Marylebone Radical Association which he helped to found in 1835 had the freedom of the press as one of its founding aims, and the Univeral Suffrage Club which he started in association with Augustus Hardin Beaumont also included the fight against the stamp duty as one of its prime objects.[6]

The unstamped campaign was therefore part of the early political experience of a very large number of Chartism's first leaders. Taking part in it had taught them certain important practical lessons. They had learnt how to write, publish and disseminate a tough, immediate radical propaganda, how to finance and organise a movement of resistance to authority, how to organise support for members and their families who were prosecuted and imprisoned. The campaign also brought home political convictions which were to form part of the consciousness of the Chartist years. After the Reform Bill, working-class radicals expressed feelings of betrayal towards those reformers among the middle classes who had used the rhetoric of liberty and equality, but who accepted the finality of the 1832 settlement. There were middle-class radicals in Parliament and outside, however, who continued to advocate an extension of the suffrage, and to accept a degree of cooperation on the question with working-class radicals. Some of these men were strongly opposed to the newspaper taxes, and mounted a campaign of petitions and meetings in support of their abolition. But as the campaign developed, a strong division emerged between this middle-class campaign and the law-breaking campaign of the unstamped. Even Cobbett, writing in friendship to Joshua Hobson in gaol, warned him of the folly of deliberately breaking the law and urged him not to do so again.[7] The parliamentary lobby against the taxes, and the educational and political-economic speakers outside the House, found the actions and the language of the radical unstamped sheets an embarrassment. On occasion they found it necessary to make public criticisms, and to dissociate themselves from such unwanted allies.[8] When the Newspaper Bill was brought in in 1836, and proposed to reduce the stamp duty to 1d, instead of to abolish it altogether, Thomas Wakley could find only one supporter for his motion for complete abolition. To the working-class and ultra-radical reformers this was betrayal on the lines of 1832. As the *Northern Star* later put it, the reduction 'made the rich man's paper cheaper, and the poor man's paper dearer'. An address issued by the Association of Working Men to Produce a Cheap and Honest Press declared:

> The stamp duty is to be reduced to a point which will permit newspapers to circulate freely among the middle classes, as if the press were actually free; while so much of the stamp duty is to be retained, and such an inquisitorial law is to be enacted in addition to all those now in force, as shall utterly prohibit the circulation of newspapers among the working classes.[9]

The radicals drew three conclusions from the experience – firstly the need to gain access to the law-making process, secondly the essentially property-defined nature of the social attitudes of the existing legislature, and thirdly the folly of relying on the support of allies and sympathisers among the higher classes. The Newspaper Act was another of the issues over which the radicals quarrelled with Daniel O'Connell. In the earlier days of the campaign he had supported the complete repeal of the taxes, but in the event he supported the limited repeal of the 1836 Act. John Bell wrote:

> The productive classes of England have once more been betrayed by their leaders. Had Mr. O'Connell chosen, he could have forced the Whigs to repeal the whole of the taxes on political intelligence. It has suited Mr. O'Connell, however, to desert this mighty cause. His price is the Irish Corporations Bill. . .[10]

The 1836 Act, besides reducing the duty from 4d to 1d per copy (pre-paid) on all newspapers, greatly increased the penalties for producing or possessing unstamped newspapers. In the two years before the Act, the unstamped publishers had become bolder, and had replaced the original small format of their journals by a full newspaper-sized broadsheet, and by an approach to the presentation of news which was more like that of a conventional stamped newspaper. In 1834 a judgement in court had declared that the *Poor Man's Guardian*, which had occasioned so many prosecutions and punishments, was not in fact a newspaper within the meaning of the Act. This decision, and the passing of the 1836 Act, left publishers with the alternatives of going back to small-sized cheap journals, carrying comment only, or of converting the large unstamped papers into legal newspapers, selling at a higher price. Hetherington decided to make his *Twopenny Dispatch* into a stamped journal, and in September 1836 it appeared as *The London Dispatch and People's Political and Social Reformer*, priced 3½d. Its publisher was apologetic about his submission, but justified it on the grounds of the new harsher penalties: 'Against a power like this, personal courage is useless . . . unless . . . some means can be devised either to print newspapers without types and presses, or render the premises . . . inaccessible to *armed force*, no unstamped paper can be attempted with success.'[11] Bronterre O'Brien used the other method. In January 1837 he produced a small paper, *Bronterre's National Reformer, In Government, Law, Property, Religion and Morals*. It consisted of four thin sheets, and sold for 1d, but contained no news. 'A hard case it is to be sure, for it is hard to write politics without glancing at the '*goings on*' around us, but the fault is of the liberal Whigs, not mine.'[12] The *Dispatch* needed to sell, Hetherington considered, 16,000 copies a week to pay its way. Bronterre need perhaps have sold far fewer, but his sale of 4,000 copies was not sufficient to sustain the journal, and it closed before the end of March.[13] The *Dispatch* was more successful, and lasted for three years; however, it never circulated outside London to any great extent, nor was it ever in any sense the journal of the Chartist movement. It was Radical in tone, supported universal suffrage and social and political equality, but was, like the LWMA itself, somehow too cautious and pompous in tone to become the journal of a movement as varied and popular as the early Chartist movement.

Before the foundation of the *Northern Star* in November 1837, Daniel Whittle Harvey's *True Sun* in London, and George Condy's *Manchester and Salford Advertiser* in the provinces were the newspapers most widely supported by radical working men. Few individual working people bought them, but in the alehouses and coffee-shops a selection of the most popular journals was available, and among serious-minded people the practice of joining together to subscribe to a weekly paper was clearly established well before the Chartist period, when it became very widespread. John Snowden recalled going as a young boy in the early thirties to the house of a 'good old radical' to read the *Leeds Mercury*, which cost 7½d a copy.[14] But like all the established journals, even the most liberal, the *Mercury* in the years after the reform agitation took an approach on certain critical issues which alienated its working-class readers. For a time the Yorkshire radicals moved their loyalties to the Tory *Leeds Intelligencer*, whose support for the factory movement under Richard Oastler was an important factor in the Tory–radical alliance which preceded Chartism in parts of the West Riding. The founding of the *Leeds Times*, under the more radical-liberal editorship of Robert Nicoll in 1837, was welcomed by the working-class radicals initially, until their loyalties were transferred to the *Star* later in the same year.

The *Manchester and Salford Advertiser* was unique among the commercial journals of the North of England in having as its editor a radical who not only supported the main planks of the working-class radical programme, but consistently urged the creation of independent working-class political organisations. George Condy, who shared with Thomas Ainge Devyr the unusual component of Irish Methodism in his ancestry, was an ultra-radical, factory reformer, strong opponent of the 1834 Poor Law, an advocate of universal suffrage and a founder-member of the Society for the Promotion of National Regeneration.

The *Advertiser* was the only stamped journal outside London to report the radical activity of the year 1834, and to record the widespread protests at the sentences on the Dorchester labourers. Its circulation was mainly in the radical strongholds of Lancashire, although its style made few concessions to a popular readership. The fact that its circulation dropped after the *Northern Star* started, and even more sharply after the end of 1839 when, after having initially welcomed Chartism without reserve, Condy declared it to have been betrayed by 'the pike and musket violence of the extremists', and offered the support of his journal to the Anti-Corn-Law League, suggests that it had been sustained between 1833 and 1837 by at least a section of those who were to find the paper they really wanted in the *Northern Star*.

The unstamped journals had been in the main individual voices in the tradition of Cobbett. Among the Chartist journals this tradition was also maintained, and a series of mostly unstamped, usually locally-produced journals appeared. *Udgorn Cymru* (*The Trumpet of Wales*) was published in Merthyr Tydfil from the blacksmith's forge of David John, Unitarian minister and organiser of a Chartist school and Sunday school.[15] In Glasgow the *Chartist Circular* carried throughout its three years of life the measured, self-educating tone of its editor William Thomson. Its English near-contemporary, *The English Chartist Circular and Temperance Record for England and Wales*, edited by James Harris, had, in spite of a somewhat similar tone, a very different personality. It was made up far more of fairly long articles and disquisitions by reflecting Chartists from a variety of localities which varied from the verbosely uninformative addresses of poor John Watkins (whose own *London Chartist Monthly Magazine* appeared briefly in 1843)[16] to the interesting and sensitive biography of William Ellis which Thomas Cooper submitted in the aftermath of the Staffordshire riots. As the forties proceeded, more and more of these small, personal unstamped journals appeared. Peter Murray McDouall produced *McDouall's Chartist and Republican Journal* from Manchester in 1841, in whose columns he discussed political questions in a general manner, but in the context of current events. Thomas Cooper ran a whole series of small journals, starting with the *Midland Counties Illuminator* in 1841 which, for all the restriction of actual news, gives a good idea in its editorial and correspondence columns of the breadth of Chartist activities in the Leicester area in that year. The *Extinguisher* and the *Chartist Rushlight* appeared in 1841, *The Commonwealthsman or Chartist Advocate* in 1842.

It is clear that Cooper saw his work of organising and teaching his Chartist followers in the two years of his activity in Leicester as necessitating the use of regular printed material. In his letters some of the problems of the unstamped as against the stamped journals can be seen.[17] The stamp, as well as being a tax, was also the legal definition of a newspaper, and carried the privilege of free post. The *Northern Star*, for which Cooper was the local agent, was sent post-free, was despatched in large quantities and was invoiced by an efficient central office. The small unstamped papers which retailed at ½d or 1d a copy got no concessions from the post or railway, and could rarely have been worth the effort of handling them in terms of the profit they produced. Nevertheless, if they could be made to cover the cost of production, these small sheets enabled particular positions within the movement to be articulated, and the views or grievances of particular members to be aired. After his release from prison, Cooper found for a time that book-length work, lecturing and some occasional journalism in London filled his time. By 1849, however, he was again helping to edit a small journal, the *Plain Speaker*, which was followed in 1850 by *Cooper's Journal or Unfettered Thinker and Plain Speaker for Truth, Freedom and Progress*.

The last phase of Chartism saw a great proliferation of these small, personal journals. Harney edited the *Democratic Review* in 1849 and 1850, and the *Red Republican*, which started in June of the latter year, changing its name to the less controversial *Friend of the People* after a few months. Ernest Jones and Feargus O'Connor jointly edited the small monthly *Labourer* in 1847 and 1848, which closed with Jones's imprisonment. When he came out of gaol he started his weekly *Notes to the People*, which contains some of his best writing in prose and verse. In the introduction to the first volume, issued after six months, he complained that the paper had lost him money. Newsagents had refused to handle it or to display his bills. Where the bills had been displayed, the police, or on some occasions hostile radicals, had torn them down. But above all he complained that he had alienated his potential supporters.

> The readers of the 'Notes' may be expected to consist of political democrats, social democrats, trades' unionists and co-operators. A correspondent tells me,

I have set to work just as though I intended systematically to destroy the circulation. Firstly, I estrange a large portion of the political reformers, by exposing and assailing demagoguism and pointing to the paramount importance of social measures. . . Secondly, by endeavouring to show that social reforms are unattainable to any great or permanent extent without previously securing political power, I am told that I alienate a second class of readers – those who look down with contempt on political agitation and think that the discussing of philosophical problems will batter down stone walls. Thirdly another body of readers are said to be driven away by my attempt to expose the injurious tendency the present cooperative movement has been assuming. . . . Fourthly a further section of readers are supposed to be estranged by the articles that seek to show the futility of any mere trades' union regenerating the social happiness and power of the working-classes.[18]

Nothing could illustrate more clearly the difference between the paper that is the voice of an individual and the paper that is the voice of a movement than this catalogue. By the early fifties the old Chartist journalists, including Jones, who did try, with his *People's Paper* from 1852 to 1858, to publish a national broadly-based weekly, had divided into small groups, publishing journals based on their own particular viewpoints, which had little sense of speaking for or to a movement. The tradition of popular radical journalism had been inherited by ex-Chartists like G. W. M. Reynolds and Edward Lloyd, for whom it was a commercial project. *Reynolds's Political Instructor*, issued weekly during the winter of 1849-50, while its editor was still very much committed to Chartism, survived for a further century as the radical weekly *Reynolds' News*.

As long as the newspaper stamp and advertisement duties existed, there was a place for the small non-newspaper, a vehicle for political opinions and controversy which could be produced well below the cost of a newspaper. Harney, who produced more than one such journal in the early 1850s, noted in the last volume of the *Northern Tribune*, which ended with the abolition of the stamp duty in 1855: 'The abolition of the 1d stamp on newspapers . . . will cause a revolution in journalistic literature, and in all periodical publications partaking of a political character. Indeed, for political periodicals there will be no place; they must become newspapers or nothing.'[19]

Small, unstamped journals and a mass of pamphlets and broadsides formed the basis of much of the political education and discussion in the Chartist movement. But the most important by far of all Chartist publications was the *Northern Star*. Most historians have suggested that O'Connor's leadership of Chartism derived from his ownership and control of the *Star*. Alone among Chartist journals it made a profit. It was taken in every part of Britain. Every kind of organisation, from the collection of funds to the organisation of rallies and lecture tours, was recorded in the *Star*, political issues of all kinds were thrashed out in its columns. News of the movement was printed in it, national and international news was printed and explained. The owner of such a vital part of the whole movement must have had an enormous advantage over any potential rivals for its leadership.

But this judgement, like so many, is an over-simplification. The *Star* was indeed a powerful force, but there was no intrinsic reason why it should have had a monopoly of Chartist support. At the time of its foundation several possible rivals were either in the field or soon to be launched. The *London Dispatch* might have exercised hegemony on behalf of the 'moderate' radicals in the movement, the *Manchester and Salford Advertiser* was already supporting the issues of trade union defence, hostility to the new Poor Law, support for the Canadian rebels and the demand for universal suffrage, which may have been said to have constituted the main issues on which radicals were exercised in the summer of 1837. The *Birmingham Journal* was under ultra-radical editorship, and was strongly in support of all the main radical demands; indeed it has often been considered as a Chartist newspaper in the early months of the movement. Had the majority of potential customers wanted a different kind of radical journal, a more moderate one, and one less committed to the particular views of Feargus O'Connor, there were such papers on offer. And since it is usually suggested that O'Connor started the paper with little or no contribution from his own pocket, it could also be said that any one else who wished to do so could have started a paper in opposition, or as an alternative to the *Star*. Other later attempts were made, notably the *Operative* and the *Southern Star*, both of which, incidentally, were welcomed and encouraged by O'Connor, but neither ever became financially viable.

The fact is that, so far from being used to impose his leadership on the movement, the *Northern Star* owed its success to the fact that it was Feargus O'Connor's paper. The immediate response and phenomenal early success of the paper showed that Feargus and his collaborators had judged the mood of provincial radicals correctly, in the timing, location and tone of the new paper. The continued and increasing success throughout 1838 and 1839 showed that O'Connor's method of running the paper satisfied a large readership.

Anyone who has read the *Star* knows that it is very far from being the kind of one-man paper that was traditional among radical journals. The paper had an editor who was a determined and opinionated radical, the Rev. William Hill, a Swedenborgian pastor from Hull who had formerly been a linen handloom weaver in Barnsley. Editorial control rested with Hill, and later with the other editors, Joshua Hobson from 1843 to 1845, and G. J. Harney from 1845 to 1850. O'Connor's role was as a major contributor – most weeks he wrote a front-page *Letter*, he occasionally wrote other columns, and he always ensured that his speeches were reported in full. But for the rest – the greater part of the paper – he allowed his editors and other staff considerable freedom. The *Northern Star* was run in accordance with O'Connor's idea of what a radical newspaper should be – and this was much more like a radical *Times* than like a reincarnation of Cobbett's *Political Register*. The paper succeeded because it was considered by its readers to be the paper of the Chartist movement, not simply the voice of Feargus O'Connor. This was a strength not only of the paper, but of the whole Chartist movement, and it was to a large degree O'Connor's contribution.

Chartism differed from earlier radical movements in scale more than in its programme. Its significance lay in its ability to hold together over a period of years a variety of impulses within a single programme, and to cover the whole of the British Isles in its appeal and its organisation. Corresponding societies were still illegal in Britain, and in any case the corresponding and organising abilities and experience among the varied groups which made up the movement would never have been sufficient to have created a unified movement capable of mounting a sustained programme in the way that the Chartist movement did. The essential organising power was the *Star*, and the qualities which made it so were the abilities of its editorial directors and the overall policy of its owner.

The *Star* welcomed and reported all radical initiatives. Outright hostility was usually reserved for the Government and its supporters, the exponents of anti-radical policies or programmes, or occasionally for what were seen as divisive moves within the radical forces. It was this latter approach which has been held to show that the journal supported one faction only of the movement. Writers like Hovell used the term 'O'Connorite' as if it had been one faction among many contending for the loyalty of the ordinary supporters of the Charter, and suggested that the *Star* was used unfairly to assert the control of that group. But apart from the fact that the journals put out in direct opposition to what could be called 'O'Connorite' but should more properly be called 'mainstream' Chartism all failed to gain support and readership among the Chartists, a reading of the *Star* must dispel this picture. An enormous range of radical activity is reported. Socialism,

Owenism, cooperation, Christian radicalism of many kinds, trade-union activity, all appear regularly. Correspondence about the correct path for Chartists to take, criticism of the leadership – including on many occasions that of O'Connor himself – wrangles, accusations of bad faith or outright dishonesty, as well as thousands of reports of meetings, lectures, demonstrations and organisational matters of all kinds fill its columns. Most historians of the movement have abstracted their most telling criticisms of O'Connor from the columns of the *Star* itself, and certainly the information from which the biographies, political and personal, of the other leaders and activists of the movement are constructed derives almost entirely from the paper. It is a record of a movement which is remarkable for the fullness and variety it presents – compared with earlier and with subsequent radical journals.

The strength and novelty of the *Star* lay in several things. Feargus was unquestionably the owner of the paper. He paid off the original shareholders as soon as he was able, and retained in his own hands the control and disposition of the profits. This was, of course, no new thing for radical publishers. Hetherington, Watson, Cleave, Carlile, all lived from their publishing ventures. Most of the earlier radicals had invested their profits in further publishing, often subsidising less popular or successful items with the profits from successful ones. O'Connor made a new departure in using the profits from the paper to subsidise the movement rather than further radical publishing. He appointed agents in the main provincial centres whose task was to report for the paper and to act as full-time organisers for the Chartist movement. Harney was paid £2 a week to do this in Sheffield in the early forties, George White in Birmingham, Edmund Stallwood in London, and a number of others at various times. In addition the profits from the sale of the paper enabled radical booksellers to rely on a regular income, and to themselves form a nucleus for the spreading of radical ideas and the sale of less profitable literature. Subventions from the *Star* profits went to help defray defence costs for Chartists on trial – including the very heavy costs of the Welsh trials – and to support the families of imprisoned Chartists. In 1848-50 payment from O'Connor relieved the London Chartists from the degrading punishment of oakum-picking. All these uses of the money helped, of course, to reinforce the power and prestige of the *Star*'s owner, and the patronage which he exercised within the movement. It also enabled a movement, which consisted in the main of people who would have been hard put to it to supply any kind of regular income, for ten years or more to sustain a reasonably stable leadership, and to offer at least some protection and care for those who suffered persecution and hardship for their part in it. The success of the *Northern Star* would have been impossible without the Chartist movement, but it is equally impossible to imagine Chartism without the *Star*.

The *Northern Star*, like the *London Dispatch*, felt it necessary to apologise to its readers in its first issue for its concession to the law in the form of payment of stamp duty. Clearly Feargus, just as much as Hetherington, expected his readers to come from among those who had supported the unstamped: 'Reader – Behold that little red spot, in the corner of my newspaper. That is the Stamp; the Whig *beauty* spot; your *plague* spot.' The issue of the remaining 1d duty was not forgotten, although it did not become a major part of the Chartist platform again until the end of the forties, when Harney joined in the lobbying which eventually led to its abolition in 1855. But once the *Star* got under way, it was able to make full use of the postal concessions, and soon took the lead in circulation among all the provincial weekly newspapers.

1837 was a good year to start a newspaper. New techniques of production were beginning, and the *Star* was able to gain the advantage over many of its rivals by the very fact that no provincial printer at the time had the resources to print a full-sized journal of the kind O'Connor proposed. Once the idea of the paper had been accepted by the northern radicals, the energy and enthusiasm which were O'Connor's chief characteristics would brook no obstacle. Machinery and type were bought in London and elsewhere, money was raised, some personally by O'Connor from the sale of property, more from loans and the sale of shares among radicals of some means – men like Lawrence Pitkethly and Peter Bussey helped to raise money in their localities, and Joseph Rayner Stephens sent £20 from Ashton. In November 1837 the first issue of three thousand was printed, and by the end of the year the paper was making a profit.[20]

The first editor was William Hill, a man who has left little impression of his personality for historians of Chartism to assess. Comments from contemporaries suggest a rather unsympathetic man, tough and ungenerous in many ways, as his replies to correspondents in the *Star* suggest, particularly some of his replies to aspiring poets. One writer describes him as humourless and verbose, and suggested that when a sharp and lively piece appeared in the editorial columns, it was generally assumed that it had been written by his wife. Yet under his editorship the *Star* was an excellent paper. The editorials are clear, well argued and hard-hitting, and there can be no doubt that in its most successful years the paper owed an enormous amount to Hill's guidance. There were other contributors who helped maintain the paper's standards. O'Brien brought a genuine journalistic talent to the work, and also the associations of the heroic age of the unstamped. Oastler wrote to Stephens urging him to 'tell O'Brien to put the *Poor Man's Guardian*'s *soul* in the *Star*',[21] and in his regular letters in the early issues of the paper much of Bronterre's best writing can be found. Oastler too wrote long letters in the early issues of the paper, and the 'sermons' and other political speeches of Stephens were regularly reported.

The centre for the publication of the *Star* was the Leeds office of Joshua Hobson. Here the paper was set up, and the many pages of reports from Chartist leaders and correspondents throughout the country were sent. The tone was sharp, combative and provincial. The initial response came above all from the provincial centres. London was, as the delegates to the first Convention were to discover, out of step with the provinces in its political awareness. Writing from London in April 1838, O'Brien made the comment: 'Gentlemen – While you are rousing the sections in the north, we, in London, have fallen into a sort of Endymion's sleep, as though the combined juices of Mandrake, poppy and hemlock were our only potations. . .'[22] The provinces were ready for the *Star*, however, and it soon became the most widely-read journal of its time in Britain. It is difficult to make a numerical assessment of its readership. The practice of buying an individual copy of a newspaper hardly existed among the working people. Papers were read in coffee-shops, alehouses, reading-rooms. The correspondence of Thomas Cooper, when he was acting as agent for the *Star* and other papers, gives some indication of the way in which journals circulated. Single copies would be ordered, as when a correspondent ordered one copy of the *Star* and one of the *Nonconformist* 'for a newly-opened reading-room', but there is no way of computing how many readers would see each copy. George Robinson of Hinckley wrote:

> A party of friends met at my house last night and subscribed for the Star so be so kind as to send it without fail on Saturday. . . We think of meeting on a Sunday morning at some central spot between us and the villages and reading the Star and conversing together when weather is fair, otherwise at my house.[23]

This kind of joint subscription was very common, and most Chartist autobiographies and memoirs include an account of regular meetings to read the paper on Saturday afternoon or Sunday morning.

> As a schoolboy my Saturday forenoons were occupied in walking from Newton Heath to Abel Heywood's in Manchester and bringing back a copy of the

Northern Star and a penny number of a tale about William Tell. In the afternoons I read aloud much of these for the edification of others, and I doubt not derived some good myself

one writer recalled more than half a century later.[24] Thomas Wood of Bingley recalled his early attempts at self-education in the West Riding weaving community:

When near my sixteenth year I began to join in some fashion at a newspaper. A man lent me his newspaper when it was a week old for a penny, I giving him the paper back when I had had it a week. The paper was the *Northern Star*, edited by Fergus O'Connor a name at that time familiar as a household word throughout Yorkshire and Lancashire.[25]

Ben Brierly of Failsworth recalled that the *Star* was 'the only newspaper that appeared to circulate anywhere in that part of Lancashire.'[21] As a boy he read it weekly to his father and five others who subscribed to it jointly. From Dublin Peter Brophy took four hundred copies a week in 1842, and declared:

The principles of the Charter are by means of the *Star* finding their way into the extremest towns in Ireland, and with all the opposition which our Association has met with and is likely to meet with from those that are interested in keeping up the delusion, we still progress. . .[27]

Clearly the paper's readership was much in excess of its circulation. Samuel Fielden recalled that in Todmorden in Lancashire in his father's time the people lined the street to await the arrival of the *Star* each week.[28] Such a weekly event must have developed its own significance, and the ritual of the arrival of the paper have been followed by the public reading and discussion of its contents. The 1,330 copies ordered weekly in Ashton-under-Lyne in February 1839 must have circulated among perhaps thousands of factory workers and provided the basis for many hundreds of readings and discussions.[29] In Rochdale, it was remembered that the *Star* had 'an enormous circulation, so much so that at last the mail coach was unable to carry them and a special conveyance drawn by four horses had to be employed to transport from town to town the heavy loads of this newspaper through Rochdale to Manchester'.[30]

It is possible from the returns of the newspaper stamps to get a rather more accurate idea of the number of copies that were printed of the *Star* than was possible for unstamped journals. Annual returns are given, and by averaging these it is possible to get some picture of the figures. In 1839, the year of the greatest numbers, the average weekly imprint was

36,000. The *Star* itself quoted 42,000 as the average for the period April to June of that year, so that the figure given by some contemporaries of 60,000 a week might just have been possible for one or two peak periods of excitement and interest. Such enormous numbers of newspapers caused distribution problems at all levels. Mail coaches to some provincial area were not accustomed to carrying large numbers of newspapers, and the postal authorities had to hire extra carts or wagons.[31] The small premises occupied by radical booksellers were often uncomfortably crowded. But the distribution system seems to have worked well. Sales never again reached the heights of those of 1839, but a very large printing continued to be distributed for another ten years.[32]

When it reached the agents, the paper was eagerly collected by coffee-house and beer-house keepers and local subscribers. Saturday evenings, Sundays and Mondays were the days on which it was read aloud to waiting groups by people like Gabriel Redfearn, blanket weaver of Littletown in the Spen valley, who would 'take up a position on the Bridge wall and read the paper to the loungers for hours at a stretch', in the summer, or in the winter read to a more select group around his fire.[33] The *letters* of Feargus, reports of speeches by all the leading figures, and probably the main leading articles could be communicated in this way. Feargus's letters were clearly intended to be read aloud, and to this extent the Cobbett tradition of direct communication with the readership was kept alive. The famous address which they often carried – to the fustian jackets, unshorn chins and blistered hands – was an oratorical device to extend the range of the printed word, and to limit any divisive effect which the use of print might have between the literate members of the community and the rest. The giving away of engravings of Chartist leaders and the use of blocks and cartoons in the paper had something of the same intention.

Nevertheless, each issue of the paper did contain matter that required closer attention. Donations and contributions to the National Rent collected to support Convention delegates in the early days, figures of returns of signatures to the national petitions, the names of committee members of the National Charter Association after its formation in 1840, the numbers of cards issued to branches, acknowledgement of the receipt of money for cards, and a host of important organisational details were published every week. The itineraries of travelling lecturers, location of large demonstrations, announcements of new publications, results of elections to the National Executive, all these required closer attention by the leaders and organisers in the localities.

There were also parliamentary reports, foreign reports and other news items which required reading closely rather than mass declamation. The regular reports from the localities, of meetings, lectures, delegate meetings and discussions provided a record of the movement, and a chance for localities to see themselves in print and as part of a great number of similar groups. The paper appealed at some level to most of the active people in the movement. Its literary contents – and it published poems and reviews in every number – tended to appeal to the more serious readers, although there was an occasional comic or satirical poem and even more occasionally one in the form of a broadside ballad. As the forties continued, the quality of the staff employed on the paper became very high. Harney joined it in 1843, G. A. Fleming in 1844. In 1846 Ernest Jones became literary editor, by which time Harney had taken over the editorship. In 1844 it moved to London and changed its title to the *Northern Star and National Trades Journal*, and included, even more than hitherto, information and news about trade-union activity throughout the country. To some extent these later developments illustrate a process which was taking place in other aspects of the movement after 1842, the development of the structured and organised aspects of Chartism, and the pull away from the more popular, less self-conscious elements which had formed an important part of the movement and of the *Star*'s public in the early days. A sense that the journal was losing the attention of its provincial readership lay behind O'Connor's censure of Harney for his too great concentration on socialist news, home and foreign, in the late forties. He wrote to Harney, denying that he had advocated the exclusion of foreign news as such.

> . . . You . . . knew that in my directions about foreign news that I did not include either American, nor yet French, nor Irish, or Italian when of interest, but that I did refer to the fraternal news and conventions of nations. I had before given Mr. Jones and you instructions to court a good understanding with the French and American Democracy, and we have had less of American and French news than from any other quarter. . .[34]

In his own letter at this time, he urged his 'dear Friends' to

> . . . wean your minds from the consideration of foreign questions further than the effect they may have on ministerial action. Keep your minds steadily and steadfastly fixed upon 'Home sweet Home' . . . do not, I beg you, allow any question of the form of government to be mixed up in our defined principle of representation. Get the Charter, and your united will is omnipotent; no matter whether the Pope, the Devil, or the Pretender is on the throne.

To the last, he objected to the concentration on sectarian interests, and tried to keep the paper on a level to interest the widest possible spectrum of radical working-class readership.

O'Connor always hoped that Chartism would support a daily paper. From August 1842 to February 1843 his ambition was realised, and he edited the London *Evening Star* as a Chartist daily. The paper, however, did not prosper, and lost several thousand pounds before it finally went out of business. No other attempt to found a daily was made, although O'Connor never totally abandoned the hope of doing so.

There were, as has been noted, a number of other Chartist journals in the movement's early years. None of these achieved the stability of the *Star*. Indeed, Francis Place, who kept a very close watch on the radical press, said that none of the Chartist papers with the exception of the *Northern Star* paid its expenses 'even at the time of the greatest excitement'.[36] Whether or not he was right about the *Northern Liberator* may be doubted. This was the longest-lived and liveliest of the other English Chartist newspapers. Founded originally by Augustus Hardin Beaumont, O'Connor's former colleague, it was bought in early 1838 by a local radical, Robert Blakey, a one-time mayor of Morpeth. Beaumont continued to edit it until his death in February 1838, when the direction was taken over by a talented team which included Thomas Ainge Devyr. Although a stamped journal, the *Liberator* did not make a bid for a national readership. It relied heavily on the *Star* for items about news from outside the north-east, and made use of the *Star* office in Leeds for any business transactions outside Newcastle. Its advertisement proclaimed:

> The Political Creed of the *Northern Liberator* may be thus abridged –
>
> FREEDOM OF THE PRESS
> UNIVERSAL SUFFRAGE.
>
> The *Northern Liberator* will urge the principles thus avowed by all the means that reason and truth can supply, the only moral arms which are worthy of the people and its advocates.[37]

Nevertheless, Devyr and his colleagues were at the centre of the arming and conspiracy in Newcastle in the winter of 1839-40, and nothing in the paper's tone distinguishes it from that of the *Star*.[38] Its circulation in 1838 was said to be 4,000 copies a week, which probably increased in 1839. In 1840 it combined with the *Champion*, and continued as *Northern Liberator and Champion* until it closed finally in December of that year.

North of the border also several journals seem to have held their own in the early years of the movement. *The True Scotsman* edited by John Fraser was often coupled with the *Northern Star* as a place in which Chartist information should be recorded. Its editor was strongly opposed to violence and a supporter of temperance, but neither of these attitudes precluded an extremely militant tone on occasion. It continued to be published from the end of 1838 until the summer of 1843. The *Scottish Patriot*, published in Glasgow and edited by Robert Malcom, had a shorter life, lasting from mid-1839 until late 1841. It was the organ of the Glasgow trade unions as well as of the Chartist movement. In Dundee, the *Dundee Chronicle* was edited by R. J. Richardson in 1841 and John La Mont in 1842, and carried radical material including poetry. As in England, there were a number of smaller, short-lived journals putting over the views of sections of the movement in Scotland. In Wales, apart from *Udgorn Cymru* and its English-language companion the *Advocate and Merthyr Free Press*, Henry Vincent's *Western Vindicator*, published in Bath in 1839 and 1840, circulated widely and carried some articles in the Welsh language. After his release from prison, Vincent re-started the paper as the *National Vindicator and Liberator of the West and Wales*, editing it jointly with Robert Kemp Philp. In neither incarnation does the paper seem to have had a very large issue, but there is no doubt that in its early years it circulated widely in Wales and the West Country, where its editor was one of the most popular leaders. In London both the London Working Men's Association and the London Democratic Association had their papers – the *Charter* for the former, which ran from January 1839 to March 1840, and the *London Democrat*, journal of the LDA, edited by J. C. Coombe and G. J. Harney. In 1842 the supporters of the New Move put out the *National Association Gazette* edited by John Humffreys Parry, which ran for six months, but like the Association itself appeared to gain little popular support.

The thousands of copies of the *Star*, taken with the many smaller or shorter-lived journals, amounted to an enormous number of pages of print. If the great mass of pamphlet literature is added to this, it becomes clear that Chartism was in many places a movement of literate people. How far the printed word was a unifying force and how far it was a divisive one is a difficult question. Quite clearly the press provided a sense of national unity which the platform could not provide. It reached districts regularly which would have been inaccessible to speakers or organisers. But it also allowed oppositional views to be circulated – some of O'Brien's later publications, for example, like the *National Reformer* published in the Isle of Man between 1844 and 1847, were largely concerned with carrying on personal vendettas against other leaders. Pamphlets like those which John Watkins issued attacking O'Connor, or the series of hostile publications aimed at Ernest Jones in the later years of the movement, leave a strong sense of bitter and strident disagreement – a quality which many of the rank and file members found distasteful. When Ernest Jones started the *People's Paper* in 1852, Benjamin Wilson recorded:

> I wrote Mr Jones a letter asking him to keep personal quarrels out of the paper as they did no good. I received the following reply. . . . 'You may rest assured that as one of the objects of the paper is to lift the movement out of the grovelling depths of personal contention and ambition, so not one syllable of personality shall intrude itself into its columns.'[39]

The promise was not kept – indeed the fifties were to be the period of the most bitter quarrelling and recrimination among the old Chartists.

CHAPTER THREE

'We, Your Petitioners'

THE unstamped press and the agitation against the Poor Law Amendment Act, together with resistance to the persecution of trade unions, created between them a disturbed and anxious population in the manufacturing districts. The response, in the form of radical political leadership, came from a number of directions. The formation in London of the London Working Men's Association has in general been given more prominence as a precipitant of the Chartist movement than it deserves. Of far greater significance were the foundation of the *Northern Star*, and the revival of the Birmingham Political Union with its proposal not only for a national petition but – more significant in terms of political action – the calling of a general convention. The main contribution made to the radical programme by the actual publication of the People's Charter was an elaborate exposition of the methods for the implementation of a system of universal male suffrage. The proposals embodied in the six points had already been widely canvassed in London by an earlier petition launched in 1837, and in the provinces by the Birmingham petition launched in the same year. The name of the Charter defined the working-class radical movement, and distinguished it from the middle-class radicals. The proposal for a national petition was, however, regarded with scepticism in many provincial centres. So far from being a new idea, the petitioning of Parliament was the oldest form of peaceful political action available to the non-electors, and when the radical leaders decided to advocate support for the Charter, one of their first tasks was to overcome the reluctance of many of their provincial followers.

In order to re-furbish the traditional instrument of the petition, the radicals' leaders were already proposing variations well before the Charter. In February 1837, O'Brien discussed the question in relation to the 1834 Poor Law and the opposition to it.

> But how are you to proceed? There are but two courses – Insurrection and Petition. . . . Insurrection is out of the question. . . . Petition then is the only course. – But what sort of petitions? In my opinion petitions for the mere repeal of the new Act would be useless. – They would be disregarded and thrown contemptuously under the table, as all petitions from the oppressed classes are. . .

. . . I would recommend that instead of petitioning for a mere repeal of the Act, we should petition –

THAT THE POOR OF ENGLAND SHALL BE HEARD BY COUNCIL AT THE BAR OF THE HOUSE OF COMMONS AGAINST THE LATE TYRANNICAL AND INHUMAN ENACTMENT MISCALLED THE POOR LAW AMENDMENT ACT.

A petition of this sort, accompanied to the House by 200,000 people and headed by all the popular leaders of good repute throughout the country, would be worth ten thousand of the ordinary kind. Mr. Feargus O'Connor, who first suggested the idea to me, would make a capital counsel on the occasion. . .[1]

This new kind of petition, backed by the physical presence of the leaders and petitioners, and coordinated throughout the country, was what was new about Chartist petitions. But in many districts there was considerable reluctance to be overcome. At the great meeting in June 1838 at Newcastle, all the speakers said they had agreed to petition no more, but were responding to Birmingham's lead for just *once* more.[2] Writing from the Convention in February 1839, O'Connor urged: 'Sign the petition. It is the last – the very last.'[3] The subject recurred. In March 1840 James Rawson of Halifax told a Manchester delegate conference that 'his constituents were opposed to petition any more. He did not see any reason why they should petition a house constituted as the House of Commons was constituted at present. . .'[4]

The original People's Charter was a very moderate document. Whether or not its authors were, as many provincial radicals believed, acting under instructions to divert popular anger and popular activity from the anti-Poor-Law and other radical movements in the provinces, the very moderation of the tone of the Charter induced a cautious, even suspicious response. The *Northern Star* was not alone in restraining its enthusiasm in the early days, as a glance at the radical press will show. The 'working men' signatories were, with the exception of Henry Vincent, middle-aged men, employers of labour and living in the metropolis. Although all of them had good radical pasts, they had not been associated with all the issues which were agitating younger radicals in the provinces. The six signatories who were Members of Parliament were by no means the most radical of MPs, and they were not, in fact, to remain very long in association with the Chartists. The Charter was presented to Parliament by radical members – Thomas Attwood and John Fielden in 1839, Thomas Slingsby Duncombe in 1842 and Feargus O'Connor himself in 1848 – none of whom had signed the 1838 Charter. What was more, in the interval between the first initiative of drawing up the Charter and its actual publication in May 1838, Daniel O'Connell had made his attack on trade unions, and there had been public discussion in radical journals of the allegation that he had stated that he had signed the Charter with the deliberate intention of using the LWMA to divert potentially dangerous political energies into safer channels.[5] It was widely known that Francis Place had made a condition of his help in drafting the Charter an understanding that the radicals were to avoid any attacks on the new Poor Law, or any advocacy of socialism on their platforms.[6] Historians who see the final coming together of the Charter and mainstream provincial radicalism as bandwagoning by the latter have relied far too heavily on the far from disinterested evidence of Place. In fact, the *Northern Star* was neither the only, not even the most vociferous, critic of the London Working Men's Association. The *Northern Liberator* attacked the Charter signatories as Malthusians. Matthew Fletcher, the radical surgeon of Bury in Lancashire – who had established himself as a leading radical in the town by his opposition to the new Poor Law, his support for the factory movement, his opposition to the establishment of rural police forces and his protests against the importation of metropolitan police into the borough later recalled:

> When honest and humane men of every political opinion which has regard for the ancient principles of the constitution, and for the ordinary rights of humanity, were banded in determined opposition to it [the Poor Law]; when the mandates of the Commissioners were defied and their pretended authority set at naught; some of these people set to work to devise means of drawing off the attention of the 'masses' and depriving the anti-poor-law agitators of their support. . .[7]

Oastler too thought the national petition had been floated to quieten the turbulent provinces and divert the people from direct action to the future chimera of the suffrage.[8] Even *The Times* suspected a lack of spontaneity, a deliberate attempt to channel the turbulence into controllable directions.

> It is very strongly suspected that the Whig Ministers were the actual founders of this Chartist agitation, and that many of the individuals now forming the National Convention were originally employed by them and paid out of the public purse (secret service of course) to agitate for the Charter. Wise and wary politicians, who know something of the party, even the people's friend, Mr. Oastler, is of this opinion. They knew very well that the respectable portion of the community would be with them against granting any such preposterous claims, but it was an excellent trick to divert the people's attention from unanimously demanding the repeal of the New Poor Law Bill. . .[9]

In spite of these doubts, however, the Charter definitely filled a need. Provincial radicalism required a focus, and the collection of signatures and even more the preparations for the Convention – the election of delegates, the raising of the national rent and the circulation and discussion of the journals and pamphlets associated with the movement – fused the various local agitations into a campaign of national dimensions. The hundreds of thousands of people who turned out to the mass meetings held to launch the Charter and to elect delegates to the Convention show the extent to which the timing was right. As John Bates recalled,

> There were [radical] associations all over the country, but there was a great lack of cohesion. One wanted the ballot, another manhood suffrage and so on. . . The radicals were without unity of aim and method, and there was but little hope of accomplishing anything. When, however, the People's Charter was drawn up . . . clearly defining the urgent demands of the working classes, we felt we had a real bond of union; and so transformed our Radical Associations into local Chartist centres. . .[10]

Nevertheless, the actual collection of signatures to the petition does not seem to have been a major preoccupation of the new groups. By no means all the areas which had radical associations in 1838 returned large numbers of signatures to the first petition, and throughout the years of Chartist activity, there is no clear correlation between signature collection and other indices of Chartist strength – membership of National Charter Association localities, collection of national rent, organisation of mass meetings, support for the national Land Company or sales of the *Northern Star*. It is also noticeable that none of the recollections of ex-Chartists mentions the collection of signatures as a remembered form of activity. Meetings, lectures, tea parties and the regularly-shared reading of radical newspapers, above all the *Star*, are what the Chartists remembered.

When the Charter was published, in May 1838, it was adopted by an already-existing network of organisations. Working Men's Associations, Radical Associations, branches of the Great Northern Union, Democratic Associations, Political Unions, all these were waiting for the national leadership offered by the *Star* and the Charter. Associations of one kind or another are recorded in 609 places in 1839. Some of these were small associations centred on a larger district, some were considerable units in their own right. Some had existed since the Reform Bill period without interruption, most had been formed or re-formed since 1836. The summer of 1838, when mass meetings to elect delegates to the Convention were held throughout the country, saw the formation of many more. Little documentary evidence has survived of any of these organisations, except reports in the local press or the national radical press. In some cases there is evidence of continuity of organisation throughout the Chartist years, in others the earliest bodies seem to have died out without re-forming. Some places where there is no record of an organisation in 1838-9 set up branches of the National Charter Association after 1840. Local studies will certainly reveal more organisations, since those areas which have already been studied in detail have in many cases produced evidence of radical and Chartist organisations which were not reported even in the *Star*. The important point, however, is that the Charter did not create the organisations which carried it to such vast numbers of people in the twelve months after its first publication. It was taken up by organisations already in existence, propounded by speakers already practised in their craft in the factory, anti-Poor-Law and earlier radical movements, and above all popularised by the *Northern Star*, the *Northern Liberator*, and in the early days the *Manchester and Salford Advertiser*, all journals whose existence owed nothing to the London Working Men's Association or the signatories of the original People's Charter.

The response to the political initiatives of London, Leeds and Birmingham came above all from the villages and townships of the manufacturing districts of Britain. The places at which meetings were organised to welcome Feargus O'Connor on his tours, to hear Henry Vincent speak for the London Working Men's Association, where individuals and agents placed the first orders for the *Northern Star*, and where the radicals began to organise the collection of signatures to the 'Birmingham Petition' even before the publication of the Charter, were to be found in the main provincial centres of manufacturing industry. The tone of the Chartist movement and the nature of the organisation which sustained it were formed by the communities which were to be its heartland for the decade and a half after 1838.

Chartism has to be understood as a movement which took most of its character from these industrial communities. Their experiences in the half-century preceding the movement as well as in the years immediately preceding the publication of the Charter dictated much of the nature of the movement and the forms which it took.

Manchester, Birmingham, Sheffield, Leeds, Glasgow and some others among the major cities of England and Scotland had important manufacturing districts within their boundaries; Manchester and Liverpool had recently undergone and were still to some extent going through considerable expansion of their docks and transport systems. London, Bristol and some of the older ports and cities had felt the impact of the expansion in trade and the changes in technology very much less than the northern towns, and were less affected in their political structures by the Bills of 1832 and 1835. All these places had Chartist movements of a respectable size, all of them saw some conflicts between the city authorities and the populace during the Chartist period. But the districts in which the Chartists were for a time in control, and where traditional authority was most threatened, were in the textile towns of the West Riding – Bradford, Halifax, Dewsbury – of Lancashire and Cheshire – Bolton, Oldham, Ashton, Stockport, Staleybridge – of Nottinghamshire and Leicestershire, the mining and ironworking districts of South Wales and north-eastern England, and in places like Barnsley or Dundee in which a community of locality, of one or two major industries, and of shared leisure and recreational activities made for speed of communication, common concerns in work and in political action and the kind of mutual knowledge and trust which was essential for the maintenance of organisations which were always on the very frontiers of legality.

The study of the history of industrialisation in Europe has been the preoccupation of historians for many generations. The macro-history of the subject is well-known, but the micro-history of the communities in which the changes took place is only beginning to be studied.

The men and women of the industrial communities took up the agitation for the Charter with enthusiasm. The whole of 1838 saw the country flooded with meetings, pamphlets, lecture and speaking tours, all aimed towards the collection of signatures, and the election of a General Convention which was to meet early the following year. Conventions in the past had a history of governmental opposition and repression, and in its early months at least, the Chartist movement grew with the strong sense that it was challenging authority by its methods as well as by its programme. The central issue, and the issue which was to dominate the Convention when it finally met, was what would happen if – or rather when – Parliament rejected the Chartist petition. The 'physical force – moral force' debate was rehearsed many times during 1838, and in the years that followed.

The story of the Chartist Convention has been written several times. Some things, however, should be recalled in connection with it. In the first place, the Chartists did not have a model on which to base the conduct of their campaign. Earlier radical conventions had not proceeded to action, unless their number was taken to include the

French Revolutionary assembly. Perhaps George Julian Harney and even Bronterre O'Brien did see the gathering at the British Coffee House as potentially the Provisional Government of Britain, but most delegates set their sights lower. For some the function of the Convention was simply to see through Parliament the petition – it had no mandate to provide any further leadership to the country after that. For this view there was the precedent of the various petitions presented by trade societies and particular industries, when representatives of the organising committees would usually come to London to be available to the MP who was acting for them, to advise and if necessary to pressurise their political allies. Most views lays between the two extremes. The collection of the 'national rent' – the name for the money with which the expenses of Convention delegates were paid – a name which shows the influence of the Catholic Emancipation campaign on Chartism, had been a major part of the activity of every Chartist locality in the year before the Convention met. The delegates were the most trusted of local radical leaders. Clearly most Chartists looked to them for leadership beyond the purely organisational aspects of the movement. There is no doubt that most delegates accepted the role of extra-parliamentary representatives, indeed some added MC after their name in imitation of the title of Members of (the other) Parliament.

Like the petition, the idea of a Convention was not the discovery of the radicals of 1838. British parliamentary reform had been organised around the idea of an alternative Parliament since the middle of the eighteenth century.[11] Every previous attempt to assemble such a gathering had, however, ended in disaster. Peterloo had been the fourth in a series of meetings to elect alternative representatives – 'legislatorial attorneys' – to present the case of the unrepresented to Parliament.[12] The Calthorpe Street clash had been the determined attempt by the Metropolitan police to break up a large meeting assembled in Cold Bath Fields by the National Union of the Working Classes to plan a projected national convention. The renewal of the idea by the radicals in 1837 signalled another attempt to challenge the legitimacy of the existing franchise by electing an anti-Parliament by universal suffrage to challenge the unrepresentative nature of the House of Commons. The idea was closely associated with the other radical tactic of the 'National Holiday', and had been recently re-stated in the pamphlet by Benbow, whose full title was *Grand National Holiday and Congress of the Productive Classes*.

Not only were the Chartists divided about the exact function of the

Convention, they were also well aware that they were on very uncertain grounds legally. A central meeting of mandated delegates would certainly have been illegal under the Seditious Meetings legislation. The same regulations limited the number of representatives to under fifty. However, by calling the meeting the General Convention of the Industrious Classes, carefully avoiding the expression 'National Convention', by having the delegates chosen by acclamation at public meetings and by limiting the number of delegates to forty-nine, the Chartist leaders hoped to keep within the law. During the whole of its session, however, the Convention was always under threat. The West Riding Chartists elected three delegates to replace their original three in the expectation that all the members were likely to be arrested at any time.

The Convention met at the British Coffee House, Cockburn Street, on 4 February 1839. Delegates had been elected at mass meetings throughout the previous summer and autumn. The delegates represented at the beginning the contradictions which had been present in the movement since the publication of the Charter. Francis Place said that of the 53 delegates who presented themselves at the opening, 29 were middle-class and only 24 were working men.[13] Matthew Fletcher, one of the delegates, later recalled:

> It was a very different affair to the subsequent gatherings of Mr. Feargus O'Connor's tramping lecturers. . . . There were barristers, clergymen, merchants, as well as members of my own profession, and literary men, and a considerable proportion of honest and intelligent working men.[14]

Visitors commented on the sober and respectable nature of the gathering. Place included men like Hetherington and Lovett in his category of middle-class delegates, but he was probably right in doing so. The delegates from Westminster, who included all six of the 'working men' signatories of the Charter, were pretty solid tradesmen by this time. Many other districts had elected similar people – men with long histories of reforming and radical activity, like Matthew Fletcher himself, who were well enough known in their districts to win the votes of the crowds, and who also had sufficient independence of status, and sometimes of means, to be able to take time off from their normal work to attend. For a working man delegate there were many problems. Even if the local radicals were able to raise the money to make up lost wages, there was no guarantee that a job would still be waiting when the Convention was over. James Woodhouse, framework knitter, who replaced the Rev. Dr Wade as Nottingham's delegate, was unable to find a frame when he returned.[15] George Loveless, returned Dorchester labourer, attended for only four days, and wrote in April that he was unable to return.

> My reason and my only reason is the following – I find it utterly impossible under present circumstances to leave home. If I did I must hire a man to supply my place which at present I cannot afford to do.
>
> My best Respects to the Convention wishing them all prosperity.[16]

A detailed analysis of the delegates has been made by Thomas Kemnitz, and good accounts of the Convention can now be found in several published sources.[17] Its proceedings may perhaps be summarised therefore rather briefly.

The first question was the establishment of the exact function of the Convention. The discussion here divided the delegates into three groups. The first, whose spokesman was J. P. Cobbett, wanted to restrict the activity of the meetings simply to the supervision of the presentation of the petition. Whatever the outcome, the Convention's function must end there. Cobbett proposed a resolution to this effect, and when it was defeated became the first of the middle-class delegates to resign. Those delegates who remained, including to begin with the group of members of the Birmingham Political Union, agreed that their purpose did include the working out of a policy for the movement in the event of the petition's rejection. What caused the remaining resignations was a strong difference of view about the kind of leadership that they should be giving. Nearly every historian has picked up from the debates in the Convention the fundamental divergence between 'physical force' and 'moral force' proposals. Tactics were certainly argued about in these terms, and when the Birmingham delegation withdrew from the gathering on 28 March it was specifically in protest against the violent talk of many of the delegates. But the Birmingham delegates were by March something of an anachronism in any case. They were not individual members of the middle class who happened to have radical views, but the representatives of a city and a class which was for the moment in opposition to the Whigs, but which was in no way in sympathy with the radicalism of even its own city's artisan and working class. Like the Anti-Corn-Law League a little later, the Birmingham men were toying with the 'brickbat argument', hoping to bring pressure on the Government to alter its financial policy by supporting a popular movement. They had no intention of forming part of a country-wide movement under artisan or working-class leadership. They certainly believed that their financial proposals would solve many of the country's economic ills, and therefore provide a better way of life for the working people. They had a record, under the leadership of Thomas Attwood, of active agitation since the days of the Orders in Council, for the freeing of trade and the liberalisation of finance. They were, however, in a quite different tradition of radicalism from that which was already emerging as the distinctively Chartist tradition.

The 'new blood', in Feargus O'Connor's phrase, that came in to replace the delegates who resigned came increasingly from among the younger radicals who had become known in their localities since 1836. Those of the older generation who remained, men like John Frost, Matthew Fletcher, Peter Bussey, Lawrence Pitkethly, James Taylor of Rochdale, and Henry Hetherington, represented a different kind of lower-middle-class radicalism, something more akin to Jacobinism rather than to that of the Birmingham men and those who had resigned with or soon after them. The 'Jacobins' were committed to a policy of confrontation with the Government, and had in some cases already been involved in direct action against the new Poor Law. Although they were mostly by occupation men of a certain amount of independence, they were also, in 1838-9, on the wing of the movement which anticipated armed conflict, and indeed John Frost, draper, former mayor of Newport, until recently Justice of the Peace in that town, was to be the leader of the most significant attempt at armed rising before the end of the year. In retrospect many of these men – including the leaders of the Welsh rising – viewed their own behaviour with something like amazement. Matthew Fletcher recalled:

> . . . an excellent friend of mine, an Unitarian minister[18] suggested that we had better go home while we had yet a character. But there was a duty to perform. . . . We determined to remain. It was well we did so – some bloodshed was probably prevented. . . . Some people said I had 'played my cards well' not to get transported. They were right, for it required something more than good intentions and ordinary discretion, to save ourselves and others from such a fate.[19]

Others, however, like Harney and Thomas Ainge Devyr, recalled the atmosphere in 1839 as being so tense that everyone expected some recourse to arms to be imminent. The manufacturing districts were in a very different mood from that of the metropolis, as Henry Vincent had noticed in his tour the previous year.

> One feeling prevails in every town – or rather I should say *two* feelings – the first a general and almost universal radical opinion – resolved to aid *one more attempt* to obtain by peaceful means a full recognition of the universal rights of

the people – and *second* an apparent fixed resolution to appeal to *arms* should this last moral effort fail. . .[20]

Harney remembered many years later:

One marked feature of the proceedings had been the concensus of opinion that force would have to be resorted to to obtain justice and the acknowledgement of right. This opinion has been placed to the account of certain names, at the head of which stands Feargus O'Connor; but I venture to affirm that if any reader of these remarks has the opportunity to turn to the Newcastle papers of the time, he will find in their reports that it was not only Dr Taylor and others in unison with his views who referred to the probable employment of force, but also those who, at least later, acquired a character for moderation, who held the same view and expressed themselves in like terms. . . . The opinion was general. It was, so to speak, 'in the air'.[21]

This was the background to the physical force moral force debate. The question was much more one of tactics than one of fundamental principle. All delegates expected that the petition would be rejected. All expected that the rejection would be followed by punitive or provocative action by the Government. The question was, how far could resistance be organised in such a way as to use the only real advantage the Chartists had, the advantage of numbers? One way in which this advantage could be used was to back the threat of force. Even those leaders who had no intention of actually promoting an armed conflict employed a rhetoric of force, pointing to the power which the supporters and signatories represented in terms of at least hypothetical force. It was a game of bluff whose chief exponent was Feargus O'Connor, but which was played at one time or another by almost every leader. Like all games of bluff, it contained the insoluble problem of what to do when the bluff is called. The 'purely moral' use of numbers was an argument which few used, although it was part of the armoury of Daniel O'Connell, who had scored a notable triumph by the use of it in 1829. But as many speakers pointed out, even the middle-class supporters of the 1832 Reform Bill had appealed to the possibility of forcible resistance if the Government had tried to put down the reform movement, and had played the 'numbers game' up to the threshold of violence and occasionally over it in 1831-2.

The appeal to arms, contained in the manifesto issued by the Convention after the rejection of the petition, was only one of a series of proposed 'ulterior measures' to be followed. Others of them, including the calling of a month's 'national holiday' and the holding of massive simultaneous meetings throughout the country, also contained implicit possibilities of violent confrontation. Although some of its supporters considered the withdrawal of labour to be a peaceful tactic, most people realised that a general strike might very soon produce armed conflict, which could also eventuate from attempts by the authorities to suppress the great demonstrations. The slogan of the Newcastle Chartists – 'If they Peterloo us, we'll Moscow them' – reflected the constant fear that the authorities would act to break up the demonstrations, and provoke the anger of the population in response.

Once the Birmingham delegates had followed the Cobbettites out of the Convention, differences between the remaining members were more shifting. It was possible to hold together the various views. This was the responsibility of the two men who have sometimes been presented as representing opposite poles of Chartist beliefs. O'Connor was the best-known and most respected member of the Convention. He was known to all the delegates, and was the most certain crowd-drawer at the meetings which took place outside. During the sittings he did not present himself as the leader of a faction; on the contrary, his role seems to have been the reconciling of differences and the maintenance of unity. Lovett, as secretary of the Convention, also took pains to speak in the name of as many delegates as possible. The LWMA contingent were the nearest thing to a faction in the gathering, but Lovett seems to have felt a responsibility beyond that to his fellow delegates from Westminster. Looking back later in life, he dissociated himself from some of the proposals in the *Manifesto* which he signed in the name of the Convention: 'I believe I did an act of folly in being a party to *some of its provisions*; but I sacrificed much in the Convention for the sake of union, and for the love and hope I had in the cause. . .'[22] He was secretary to the sub-committee of Frost, O'Connor, Bussey, Pitkethly and Mills which had drawn up the document.

The *Manifesto* was the most specific outcome of the first Convention. The lethargy of the London Chartists, and the delay which the need to collect more signatures imposed on the presentation of the petition, led delegates to consider moving the location of the Convention. This discussion, together with the drawing up of the manifesto, led to the articulation of views on the function of the meeting of delegates which were much more in line with the idea of the Convention as an anti-Parliament, claiming for the non-electors some of the functions of the Parliament of the electors. O'Connor urged that they should leave London, where 'they dare not say that the Convention was the fountain of all law and justice – he dared them to say that in London, but let them go down to Birmingham, and they would be obliged at once to declare that they alone were the fountain of all law, order and justice'.[23] On 13 May the Convention moved to Birmingham, to meet on the days of that week, before adjourning until 1 July to enable members to attend the simultaneous meetings during the week of the Whit holiday, and generally to report on the activities of the Convention and discuss its manifesto before the date of the presentation to Parliament on 12 July.

The presentation of the petition by Attwood and Fielden coincided with the Bull Ring riots in Birmingham. The Convention had reconvened after its break, and was meeting in the city when the Birmingham authorities brought in a posse of London policemen to break up the regular gatherings of Chartists which had become customary in the Bull Ring in the evenings. The resulting riot led to much destruction of property, and to the calling in of troops. It was a strange action for the Birmingham authorities to have taken against meetings which were neither riotous nor threatening, and it is not surprising that Chartist leaders interpreted it as the long-anticipated attack on the Convention. A placard attacking the behaviour of the Birmingham authorities was posted in the city, signed by Lovett, the secretary, and John Collins, chairman of the Convention on the day of its issue.[24] Both signatories, together with Harney and Taylor, were arrested for sedition. Parliament contemptuously rejected the Charter by 235 votes to 46, and the question of ulterior measures became the prime one for the Chartists.

The meetings of the Convention between 13 July and the end of the month discussed the crucial question of what action should be proposed now that the petition had been rejected, and the *Manifesto* accepted in the localities. Of all the suggested 'ulterior measures', by far the most provocative was the proposal for a 'sacred month', a month's general strike throughout the country.[25] By the time these discussions took place, authorities throughout Britain had begun to take action against the Chartists. Vincent had been arrested in May; in Newcastle police and troops had broken up meetings, there had been serious riots in Birmingham and in Llanidloes, as well as lesser clashes like the incident at Bury in which a boy was injured by police fire, and considerable crowd action took place.[26] O'Connor was under arrest for seditious libel, for some of the reporting in the *Northern Star* of speeches asserting the right – or the intention – of the populace to resist by arms if their meetings were attacked. Clearly the movement was now at the frontiers of legality. Apart from the Convention, the press and the huge meetings addressed by prominent speakers, Chartists in all districts were beginning to engage in regular activity which took on an increasingly menacing aspect – menacing both in the increasing use of quasi-military formations and in the constant display of very large numbers. During the summer the tactic of going to church was pursued in many districts. The Chartists walked to church on Sunday. Their venue was always the parish church, and they invariably entered and took seats in the main body of the church, often in pews for which they had paid no rent. To the church authorities their very presence, peaceful enough as it usually was, represented a threatening attitude of no small dimension. Some clergy preached them sermons full of condemnation and warning. Francis Close told the Cheltenham women Chartists on their visit to his church:

> Take for instance this insane proceeding of endeavouring to possess themselves of our churches. . . . However peaceably it may be carried into execution, the nature of the transaction remains the same, it is a display of physical strength, it is *intimidation* and nothing else![27]

The Chartists were moving into many different areas of public life, making demands on the organisations of local and national government which had hitherto been the province of the propertied classes. Magistrates and local gentry deluged the Home Secretary with worried enquiries. While some authorities did not hesitate to harass the local Chartists in every possible way, others were anxious to remain within the law. *The Justice of the Peace* carried, as late as August, a letter of enquiry from a magistrate in the town of 'W', where

> there are a number of persons calling themselves Chartists, who hold their meetings three or four times, sometimes oftener, in the week in a building formerly used as a Catholic chapel. Their meetings are called together by a public bellman who goes through the streets giving notice 'that a public meeting of the Working Men's Association will be held at half-past eight o'clock in the Evening at the Chartists' Hall' and he sometimes states the purport of the meeting, such as 'to hear a letter read by Dr. Taylor, or a communication from Birmingham' etc. etc. At the time appointed, a drummer and fifer frequently go through the streets to assemble the Chartists, who proceed to the place of meeting in great numbers, to the terror of the peaceable inhabitants. Their meetings are addressed by some of the leaders in inflammatory harangues. At one of their meetings a police constable was present, when the speaker addressed the meeting as follows 'I don't advise you to arm, but I hope you all are so, and I hope when the time comes you will all fight to the last.' He then desired all who would do so to hold up their hands, when seemingly all did so. . .[28]

He asked for guidance as to the legality of these proceedings, in particular whether the drummer and fifer were acting illegally. The reply was that these activities appeared to be, in general, legal. As Lord Melbourne told the Earl of Wilton, who had asked about the legality of a Chartist placard on display in Bolton

> with the legal powers which exist in this country – with the privilege of free speech and free discussion which exists – in order to be extremely inflammatory and exciting, it is by no means necessary to break the law. On the contrary, it is not so entirely the breach and violation of the law which is to be dreaded, as the abuse of the law, and the pushing to the utmost of those powers and privileges which the people legally possess. . .[29]

At the end of the month, Russell circulated all magistrates with a clarification of the definition of a seditious meeting.

It was probably the ambiguities in the law which accounted for the slow response of many authorities to the massive presence of Chartists, and to the increasingly belligerent tone of many Chartist speakers in the weeks immediately after the rejection of the petition. Delegates discussing the proposal for the sacred month knew well that they were discussing the move towards confrontation, in an atmosphere in which talk of fighting, and actual arming and drilling, were widespread throughout the country. By the end of July, indeed, many delegates had given up the discussion and returned to their own localities to engage in local consideration of the next step. The placard issued by the Convention leaders to the local organisations in late July made no mention of the sacred month among the measures proposed, and it became increasingly clear that although most leaders felt that the strike was the logical next step, fewer and fewer were prepared to take the responsibility for calling it. After proposals to delay the start from the original 12 August had been defeated, together with proposals to begin immediately, the Convention compromised. On 6 August they issued a call, cancelling the proposed month, but proposing instead a three-day withdrawal of labour to begin on 12 August. Localities were instructed to hold meetings during the three days, and to forward petitions to the Queen, calling on her to dismiss her ministers.[30]

The abandonment of the plans for the general strike in 1839 represented the deliberate drawing back by the Chartist leadership as a whole from the advocacy of armed action. They had decided not to risk a nation-wide confrontation with the Government. The post-reform administrations were stable and confident, with none of the divisions which had characterised the pre-1831 political parties. There was no sign on the part of the authorities of the failure of nerve and insecurity which characterised many governments in Continental Europe during the first half of the nineteenth century, often in the face of far less numerous or threatening movements than Chartism. Nevertheless, this was undoubtedly a point at which Chartism might have taken a very different course. Throughout the country supporters were expecting to be called on to act. Colonel Napier, commander of the North, who has often been quoted as being calm and determined during the crisis of the summer, in fact veers sharply in his journals and letters between calm confidence and the awareness that it would need only a fairly small incident to change the balance of confidence. He urged continually that the soldiers should be kept in large groups and not spread through the manufacturing districts in small detachments. 'The Chartists are numerous, and should one detachment be destroyed the soldiers would lose confidence; they would be shaken, while the rebels would be exalted beyond measure. . .[31] Earlier, he had written to his brother William: '. . . the example of one rising might have been followed throughout England; for the agitation is so general no one can tell the effect of a single shot: all depended on avoiding collision'.[32] Napier is of course not a disinterested authority. He was concerned to maintain a particular strategy, and his biographer selected from his letters and journals material that justified his methods. Both brothers were, however, very much more sympathetic to the aims of the Chartists and much more critical of the Whig Government and of the local magistrates than might have been expected from men in their position. Charles James Napier wrote in June to William:

> Good God what work! to send grape-shot from our guns into a helpless mass of fellow-citizens; sweeping the streets with fire and charging with cavalry, destroying poor people whose only crime is that they have been ill-governed and reduced to such straits that they seek redress by arms. . .[33]

He certainly believed that the policy of the Government was encouraging armed resistance, and that the feeling in the country made an outbreak a real possibility throughout the summer of 1839. In September he was writing to the Duke of Portland: 'While the Chartists keep their arms we may suppose they intend to use them – they do keep their arms.'[34] The sense of anticipation, of waiting for a signal, was never to recur in quite the same way in the Chartist period.

It can be argued that had an outbreak of violence been a real possibility in 1839, it would have occurred with or without a signal from the Chartist leaders. The various brief eruptions, from the Bull Ring riots to the Newport rising, might each have sparked off outbreaks in other parts of the country, had the population as a whole been prepared for such actions. In fact, all the unplanned skirmishes of the summer were damped down deliberately by the leadership – Harney and Taylor were arrested in Birmingham while trying to calm the atmosphere, and Bronterre O'Brien and the local Chartist leaders locked the door of the Chartist meeting hall at Bury when the news was brought about the shooting of a boy by the police there, to prevent the active Chartists from rushing off to join the anti-police crowd. The Chartists wanted to avoid an unplanned rising, to continue with systematic arming and drilling rather than to encourage sporadic and continuing turbulence. If the Government were to be moved by the display of strength, it was disciplined numbers that would demonstrate such strength rather than riots. If they were to be moved by violence, then it had to be systematic armed action which could have the chance of defeating the armed force of the crown. It was this analysis which probably lay behind the decision to abandon the strike, since the inevitable result of a month's cessation of labour would have been local sporadic violence in the course of the acquisition of food, the resistance to police coercion and the employment of unworking hours by bitter and hungry people. Whether, however, the response would have been so great that this sporadic and localised violence would have coalesced into an all-out attack on authority can never be known. Popular revolutions do not as a rule begin by disciplined armed attacks on the centres of authority. The mass movement of poorly armed crowds has been the precipitant of nearly every popular uprising, with, as the main secondary factor, the possible adhesion of troops or at least their unwillingness to treat their fellow-countrymen in the same way as an enemy army. Whether a general strike called and determinedly encouraged by the leaders of the Convention in August 1839 would have precipitated a general rising in the manufacturing districts can never finally be determined. Clearly by the time a second attempt was made, in 1842, conditions were very different indeed.

The year 1839 was so important in the history of the Chartist movement that it could only be satisfactorily dealt with at the length of at least a volume. In a short account, many of the events must be summarised and inevitably foreshortened. The three days of the truncated National Holiday were themselves important, and resulted in more arrests throughout the country than any other period before 1842. It was then that the Government took the opportunity of rounding up local leaders in large numbers – or perhaps the initiative still lay largely with the local magistrates. Certainly the Chartist crisis was discussed by the Cabinet. A report on the state of the country from Lord John Russell on 1 August included some detailed descriptions of Chartist activities. On 10 August, James Cam Hobhouse recorded in his journal:

The so-called Convention, alarmed, perhaps, by the conviction of the Chartist rioters, had given up their project of assembling at some sacred mount and remaining there until their grievances were redressed. The advice was good enough, but it remains to be seen whether it would be followed by the masses, who were to have had three days of processions and speeches. The day fixed for this was August 12. 'God bless us' said Lord Melbourne 'why that is the day after tomorrow; 'tis time for us to be looking about us'.[35]

The arrested Chartists were brought before the magistrates in very large numbers. The tactic employed at this stage was to offer the majority the option of pleading 'guilty' to the charges – usually of conspiracy to incite the people to arm, seditious conspiracy, unlawful association or other such rather vague charges. Those who pleaded guilty were bound over in their own and others' recognisances, to keep the peace, usually for two years, and allowed to go home. This option was not offered to those offenders who were considered to be ringleaders, or who were arrested while carrying firearms. Clearly many hundreds of those held took the option of avoiding imprisonment. By treating them in this way the authorities ensured a period during which the local leaders and activists would feel constrained by the terms of their binding over, but at the same time were able to exhibit a degree of leniency. Although several hundred Chartists were tried and imprisoned, the numbers were small, given the scale of the demonstrations which had taken place.

The trials of the Chartists took place over the twelve months following the Convention. Stephens, although he had been arrested in December 1838, came up for trial at Chester only on 15 August 1839. By then he had moved away from Chartism, and his defence was an enormously long sermon in which he repudiated many of his former principles, and concentrated mainly on his opposition to the new Poor Law which he justified on Scriptural principles.

I am dragged here, my lord . . . as though I were a party to the Convention, and to the disturbances of Birmingham, to the Charter, to annual Parliaments, vote by ballot, universal suffrage and all the rest of that rigmarole, in which I never had a share. . . I declared my detestation of the doctrines of Chartism, and declared that if Radicals were in power . . . my head would be brought first to the block, and my blood would be the first blood that would have to flow. . .[36]

Stephens had, according to Place, been received by the Convention in

London in April 1839 with enthusiastic cheering that had lasted for several minutes. He was generally regarded throughout the country as the first Chartist martyr, and his arrest – the first of a major leader – had helped create a sense of crisis in the weeks immediately preceding the Convention. Many Chartists simply refused to accept his defection. £2,000 had been collected for his defence, a far greater sum than was available to most individuals when arrests became more widespread. His conviction and sentence of eighteen months' imprisonment seems to have wiped out for most of the Chartists the apostasy of his defence speech, and he remained a figure of respect in the speeches and publications of the movement. However, he had by then renounced his brief advocacy of radical politics, and came out of prison as a kind of traditionalist Tory, defending a paternalist attitude to questions of poor relief and the protection of factory children, and defending traditional institutions from the throne to the village alehouse.[37] It is perhaps significant that he was strongly influenced by German thought and literature. In many ways Stephens was an aberration in the general body of the radical leaders. He was much more the kind of charismatic, irresponsible demagogue that historians have represented O'Connor as being, than was O'Connor himself. Stephens was the man whose staring eyes and emotive language roused crowds almost to hysteria. Unlike O'Connor, Stephens never made jokes, never encouraged other speakers or leaders around him. He was the Savonarola of the early Chartist movement, and inevitably fell out of a movement which was not looking for an unquestioned moral and apocalyptic leadership. His trial and conviction, however, began a whole series which went on throughout the late summer and autumn of 1839.

At the same assizes as Stephens, Peter Murray McDouall stood his trial, to be followed shortly by the Stockport Chartists, arrested in August, and the Birmingham and Ashton men. James Williams and George Binns of Durham were arrested and speakers and demonstrators from all the major centres. Some were brought to trial in the autumn of 1839, others traversed to the Spring Assizes. The country was networked with Chartist organisations, and of the hundreds of Chartist local leaders awaiting trial, the great majority appear to have continued to travel, to speak and to organise whilst they were on bail. O'Connor himself and O'Brien were in the same position. Lovett and Collins were tried in early August, and both sentenced to a year's imprisonment. Stephens's eighteen months followed, and sentences of twelve months on Vincent, nine on Edwards and shorter ones on others who had been arrested in the West Country earlier in the year were passed in the early autumn. In September the Convention dissolved, and the few delegates who had remained to the end went back to their localities. Clearly the focus of action had returned from the centre to the opaque communities in which the great majority of the Chartists lived.

The *Northern Star* had already transgressed the libel laws by the publication of some of the speeches in the early months of the Convention. No further risks could be taken, and in any case, the more the Chartists themselves turned to illegal and conspiratorial activities, the less their press could record what they were doing. Police reports and spy and informers' reports exist for a few areas in these months, but for the most part the autumn of 1839 remains one of the most obscure periods of the history of Chartism. Those who remained in England after the events of those months were not anxious to reveal their part in any plotting that went on, while those who finally left the country either covered their tracks, or perhaps exaggerated the dangerous situation from which they had escaped in order to justify their own flight and the embarrassment this caused their bailsmen or supporters. From all the surging discontent, frustration and resistance to the closing in of authority, the only clear outcome was the Newport rising of November 1839.

CHAPTER FOUR

The Newport Rising

THE first Convention dissolved finally on 6 September 1839. By the time it dissolved, a large number of the most active delegates had already left for their constituencies, either because they were no longer being supported with funds or because by then they felt that the most important events in the movement were taking place in the localities. The decision to replace the national holiday with a three-day strike was probably one of the most momentous taken by the Convention. It was this decision above all which shaped the events of the rest of the year 1839.

The chief problem for the Convention to solve was how to make the most effective use of the Chartists' only outstanding strength – their numbers. The so-called 'ulterior measures' proposed by the Convention in May represented different proposals for bringing pressure on the Government and on national opinion by the use of this one source of influence. The proposals ranged from exclusive dealing (i.e. the patronage of only sympathetic shopkeepers) through the withdrawal of labour to the use of armed resistance if they were attacked. Measures such as exclusive dealing, abstention from excisable articles and the withdrawal of money from savings banks were practised, but could only have a limited effect, given the enormous inequalities in the distribution of property. As consumers, most working people lived so close to subsistence that the manipulation of the surplus constituted only an irritation in certain localities, rather than a threat. Their main weapon was of course their role as producers, or their mere presence as a large and threatening force. Both these ideas were present in the proposal for a national holiday. No one can say what the effect would have been if the call had been sustained for a national holiday of one month in the summer of 1839. The experience of 1842 showed that the idea was a powerful one, and that it could spread rapidly beyond the declared and countable supporters of the Chartists. In the tense atmosphere of 1839 the response could well have been greater. On the other hand, the response of the authorities to the limited actions that were called for in August 1839 may suggest that a national holiday would soon have developed into an armed confrontation with troops and police in the main manufacturing districts. What the outcome of such a confrontation would have been is impossible to determine.

As it was, the short three-day strike called for 12 August met with very varied responses in different parts of the country. Many of the most loyal districts followed the plan of leaving work and assembling for meetings – but some reported that many workers who supported Chartism were not prepared to sacrifice three days' pay for what was clearly no more than a token gesture. Where the response was on a large scale, as in Nottingham and parts of Lancashire, many local Chartists were arrested on charges of seditious speeches, riot, affray, threatening behaviour and obstruction. Of these, the rank and file who were not considered dangerous were given the option of pleading guilty with the near-certainty of being bound over to keep the peace for a year or two years and then being released. Only key people among the local leaderships were sent for trial. Many of these were sent to the assizes on the flimsiest of evidence, as O'Connor later recalled.

> I was present at the trial of Hoey, Ashton and Crabtree at York, when not a single act of conspiracy, riot, sedition or tumult was proved against them, when no evidence arose out of a public meeting which they were charged with having attended in the open air at mid-day, when the prosecuting attorney gave them a good character, and yet did Mr. Justice Erskine confine them to a felon's prison, hard labour and silence for two long years. . .[1]

Clearly most of the judges and all the juries felt like Lord Broughton, who told his cabinet colleagues that 'as the object of the Chartists was to knock us on the head and rob us of our property, we might as well arrive at that catastrophe after a struggle as without it; we could only fail and we might succeed' (to which Lord Melbourne replied 'Exactly so').[2]

By the autumn of 1839 nearly all the leaders of Chartism were either in prison or on bail awaiting trial. Vincent and O'Brien, Lovett, Collins and O'Connor himself were among them, while Frost, who was later to be charged with the most serious crime, was already charged with seditious speech and criminal libel for his activities as the leader of Chartism in South Wales and a leading figure in the General Convention.[3] The *Northern Star* spoke of 'a reign of terror', and clearly for many Chartists this was how the situation appeared.

After the ending of the Convention, delegates returned to their localities, and there is good reason to believe that a kind of duality developed within the movement. Open public activity continued, exclusive dealing was practised, the *Star* was read in public, education classes were held, and money was raised for the defence of arrested

Chartists, the support of prisoners' families and the construction of Chartist halls. But at the same time an underground movement developed, meeting secretly, gathering arms, and planning either an insurrection or armed resistance to an anticipated government attack. Such work as has been done on this 'underground' has of course met with difficulties greater even than those involved in recording the public or semi-public activities of the Chartists. Much remains to be discovered. Much may never now be discovered.[4] Of the existence of a national conspiracy there can be little doubt, although its extent and the involvement of national leaders remain to be teased out from a mass of contradictory evidence in English and in Welsh. The one event which has entered all the records was the Newport rising of November 1839.

Throughout Britain in the early nineteenth century, the approach of winter was heralded by the annual eruption of Guy Fawkes' Night celebrations. It was a rowdy and violent time of year and one that was feared by the authorities in an age which was becoming increasingly alarmed by the persistence of a rough impenetrable culture among many of the lower orders. On November the Fifth bonfires were lighted, effigies burnt, tar balls and tar barrels were ignited and hurled through the air by drunken revellers. The near-rioting of that time of year was the disturbance most often complained of by the respondents to the questionnaires sent out by the constabulary commissioners in the late thirties. In the tense atmosphere of the winter of 1839, the magistrates in South Wales admitted to some apprehension about the possible behaviour of the miners and iron workers in their districts. But that year, instead of the usual sporadic outbursts, colliers and iron men marched in military formation in columns of thousands strong across the hills from Nantyglo, Pontypool, Blackwood, Newbridge and Risca, converging in the early hours of a stormy 4 November on the town of Newport.

At the head of the columns walked well-known Chartist leaders, Zephenia Williams, atheist mine agent and Radical leader, William Jones, watchmaker and Chartist orator, and John Frost, former magistrate and one-time mayor of Newport, national leader among the Chartists, a chairman at the General Convention and one of the movement's outstanding spokesmen. This was no surreptitious adventure undertaken by a few hotheads or a gang of youngsters. It was clearly an event which had been planned with care over a number of weeks at least.

The stormy weather delayed some of the marchers, and there may have been some confusion as to the exact plans. When the columns arrived at Newport it was daylight, and the authorities, warned of the approaching crowds, had rounded up known local Chartists and put them under military guard in the Westgate Hotel in the centre of the town. The military contingent was small, and the Chartists, tired and drenched though they were, and depleted in numbers by the non-arrival of some of the columns, must have appeared a threatening presence as they crowded around the hotel. In the tense situation, the order was given to the troops to fire; a volley of shots was fired into the crowd, followed by another. Who ordered the shooting, and whether or not it was in response to initial shots from the Chartists, have remained in doubt. The crowd, however, certainly turned and fled in response to the fire from the troops, leaving at least twenty-two of their number dead.

The numbers involved in the march across the hills and in the confrontation in the square at Newport have been variously estimated at between several hundred and tens of thousands. Historians who have examined the evidence so far seem to agree on a figure of around five thousand in Newport, with perhaps as many as four times that number who remained in the hills or were prevented from starting out by the storm or the general failure of communications. Like so many aspects of the history of these years, the episode awaits its modern historian. Hostile press reports and cautious reports in the radical press have been confusing elements, as has the fact that the chief leaders were put on trial very soon after for high treason. The defence naturally tried to belittle the seriousness of the crime, and referred always to the 'riot' at Newport – since riot was a far less serious crime than treason. Those who took part remained as quiet as they were allowed to do; many fled to their homes, some hid out for a time in the districts around Newport, a few escaped to London or out of the country, but within a short time the three main leaders of the march, John Frost, Zephenia Williams and William Jones, were under arrest. Within two months they were under sentence of death.

In a short study there is no space to examine all the evidence about the events at Newport and the subsequent special commission at which the three leaders were tried. Much remains obscure, but one thing is clear, and that is the effect which the trial and condemnation of the three Welsh leaders had on the movement in the rest of the country. As long as the Chartist movement continued in existence, the return of the three from exile was a central demand; in the months immediately following their sentences, more signatures were collected on petitions for reprieve than had been collected for the first Chartist petition, and there is more evidence of genuinely insurrectionary organisation in connection with proposals for rescue or for risings in the event of the carrying out of the death sentences than at any other time. Had the three men been executed, as they were sentenced to be, the nature of Chartism would certainly have changed. Conversely, the reprieves which were granted – apparently in response to the massive petitioning which took place – appeared to indicate a responsiveness to pressure on the part of the authorities that went against their apparent indifference to the original Chartist petition.

Ironically, the commutation of the death sentences was probably not the result of popular petitioning at all, but of the very firm recommendation for mercy which was given by the Lord Chief Justice. When the special commission was appointed, it was originally announced that it was to be conducted by Mr Justice John Williams, a judge who was hated by the radicals for his conduct of the case of the Dorchester labourers, and for the draconian sentence he had passed on the six men. However, the Lord Chief Justice also decided to take part. He was Sir Nicholas Tindal, a cousin of the Chartist barrister W. P. Roberts, and one of the great lawyers of the nineteenth century. It was his patient hearing and conduct of the trial which succeeded to some extent in lowering the temperature of the proceedings, and it seems from his original charge to the jury that he wanted from the beginning to reduce the offence to one of riot. The Chartists were thus fortunate in their judge, and they were fortunate too in their counsel, paid for by funds raised by the movement. The two defending lawyers were Fitzroy Kelly, later to be Tory Solicitor-General, and Sir Frederick Pollock, later, as Tory Attorney-General, to be responsible for the prosecution of the Chartists in 1842. In 1839, the two represented probably the most highly-skilled legal team available in Britain. It was the jury of propertied gentlemen who ensured the verdict of guilty, in spite of the eloquence of the defence and the directions of the Lord Chief Justice. Even the jury, however, added a rider to their verdict recommending mercy, as Broughton recorded in his diary for 9 January 1840.

> At our Cabinet to-day we turned to the news which had just arrived, of the conviction of Frost, and the recommendation of the jury for mercy. Lord Melbourne said he saw little in that recommendation; the jury were frightened, so was the judge. For his own part he felt certain that some decided measures were indispensable to prevent anarchy. He added that as for himself he was prepared for them. . .[5]

At a later meeting, Broughton recalled that 'All . . . agreed that Chief

Justice Tindal pleaded like an advocate for Frost, so much so that when the jury went out, all the Crown Counsel retired to consider what they should do when Frost was acquitted, which they considered certain. . .' He reported that the Cabinet were unanimous in supporting the carrying out of the death sentence on the three leaders, but that at a further meeting Lord Normanby reported that Tindal had told him that 'it would be advisable for the government to consider whether under all the circumstances the lives of the criminals might not be spared. This opinion produced a great effect, and even Lord Melbourne confessed that it would be difficult to execute the men after such a hint. . .'[6] A reprieve was granted, and the sentences on the three leaders were commuted to transportation for life.

Discussion has continued as to the precise aims of the Newport Chartists. The view that they intended to rescue Henry Vincent from gaol is clearly untenable, since he was not, and had never been, held at Newport. The various other theories which imply a concerted effort to begin the conquest of Britain by Chartist forces have also been discounted, since no possible scenario could have been imagined which started with the taking of a small and, from the point of view of government and military control, entirely insignificant town. Professor Williams, the Welsh Chartists' most detailed historian, came to the conclusion that the idea at the back of the events of 4 November 1839 must have been simply the mounting of a massive demonstration. He discounts most of the talk about a Welsh rising as being both inconsistent with the facts and based on very dubious information given at the trial.[7]

If 4 November was simply intended as a 'monster demonstration', however, it was unlike any other Chartist demonstration. It had been preceded by secret discussions throughout the country. It was itself mounted with the utmost secrecy. The participants were exclusively men, and they carried arms – clubs, muskets and pikes – rather than banners.

The Chartists and those who sympathised with them always referred to the events as a 'riot'. This was, however, partly a legal point, since the crime of riot was a lesser offence than the treason with which the leaders were charged. But perhaps it is wrong to see the events of that bitter winter in too rational and logical a way. If the Newport colliers and iron workers saw themselves as embarked on something much more serious than a demonstration, and it is impossible not to realise that they did, it does not therefore follow that they were part of a consistent plan for a national revolution. There can be little doubt that many of the strongest

Chartist districts were considering projects for some kind of rising – Napier as commander of the north was aware of it, Harney recalled the 'concensus of opinion that force would have to be resorted to to obtain justice and the acknowledgement of rights,'[8] and the reports from magistrates of arming and drilling in Yorkshire, Lancashire, Nottingham and the Newcastle district were too widespread and consistent to be merely the imaginings of worried and frightened men. However, none of the evidence necessarily adds up to the positive existence of a coordinated plan. History did not, in fact, offer a model of a revolution started from cold in Britain. An attack by the authorities on a large demonstration, or the kind of harassment of the common people that had been practised in Ireland before the rising there of 1798, might have goaded a desperate population into armed resistance. No such provocation occurred. The Chartists lived in anticipation of such treatment, but the authorities were more cautious and more restrained than the rulers of Ireland. Arrests of local and national leaders were provocative and selective. But sentences were not over-severe, even though it is necessary to remember that a sentence of two years or even less in 1839 was a much nastier punishment for the prisoner and for his family than it would have been a century later. The advocates of armed force had to convince their followers that it was necessary to prevent an increase of repression. They also had to prove their often-quoted and firmly-held conviction that British soldiers would not fire on their fellow-countrymen. Perhaps the Newport attack was meant simply to demonstrate the power of a formidable armed attack on a centre of authority, deliberately chosen because it was not a great centre of military and administrative power. Perhaps, like the attack on Harper's Ferry during the anti-slavery campaign in the United States, it was intended to give the signal to Chartists in other towns to take over their cities and proclaim the Charter as law. Perhaps some among its leaders hoped it would be simply a demonstration of the seriousness of the movement and the scale of its support among the people of South Wales, whilst others hoped that it would be the spark that would fire the rest of the country. The *Manifesto* of the Convention had perhaps hinted at this kind of demonstration of force.

> The mask of *constitutional liberty* is thrown aside, and the form of despotism stands hideously before us. Shall it be said, fellow-countrymen, that four millions of men, capable of bearing arms and defending their country against every foreign assailant, allowed a few domestic oppressors to enslave and degrade them? . . . If you longer continue passive slaves, the *fate of unhappy Ireland will soon be yours*, and that of Ireland more degraded still. . . .[9]

Ironically, the provocation which was lacking before Newport very nearly occurred after it. Had Frost, Williams and Jones been executed, there might well have been more significant risings in the manufacturing districts than the rather badly-organised and small-scale ones which occurred in the West Riding of Yorkshire between the sentence and the announcement of its commutation.[10] Napier, who found little to commend in the Government's handling of the condition of the people in general, praised them for commuting the death sentences and for using restraint in punishing sedition.

> . . . so far as falls within my limited sphere all shall be done to assist the poor, for they are ill-used and suffering. I must however give my approval of government for having avoided bloodshed by executions: it is cruelty to do so, and useless for changing men's opinions. . . . It is not law but barbarity to slay men for political opinions, in which thousands of honourable men agree with the condemned person! It is not justice, it is the vengeance of a dominant party.[11]

So far from encouraging violence, the result of the petitions in tempering the response of the authorities gave additional strength to the moderate Chartists, to those who advocated petitioning rather than fighting. Many of these moderate men withdrew from Chartism after Newport, perhaps convinced that the threat of a reign of terror had receded, perhaps warned by Frost's fate of the dangers of putting themselves at the head of a popular movement in which no holds appeared to be barred.

There do remain a number of documents relating to the Newport rising which throw some light on it. The strange Scottish radical, Dr John Taylor, chose William Lovett to be the recipient of his apologia, and sent a series of letters to Lovett to offer his version of the events.[12] Taylor was a romantic with Byronic pretensions, and although he was undoubtedly deeply involved in the events which took place after Newport in the North of England, he escaped punishment and died in his bed soon after.[13] William Ashton, of Barnsley, who was arrested and sentenced on very slight evidence, offered two contradictory versions of the events. Ashton was suspected by his fellow-Chartists of having been bought by the Government, since he accepted funds to emigrate after his release from gaol. His appearance before the Chartists of Barnsley to argue his case, in 1842, that O'Connor had known about the proposed risings and had betrayed Frost by not relaying an important message about the delaying of plans for supporting action, was credited neither by his fellow-Chartists nor by O'Connor, who offered to appear in person to answer Ashton's charges.[14] As Professor Williams pointed out, the final answer to this particular charge was the unbroken friendship which existed between Frost and O'Connor. Although it may well have been the case that some of the rank and file Chartists had hoped for a more vigorous lead towards armed action from O'Connor, it seems highly improbable that any of his friends would have expected support from him for actions of a kind which went against all his teaching. To his credit it must be stated that O'Connor spared neither time, energy nor money in the defence of Frost and the other arrested leaders, and never condemned them in public, or ceased to agitate for their pardon and return from transportation.

A great deal of mystery must remain surrounding the Newport events. Although on balance it seems unlikely that there was a widespread plan for a national rising, of which the Welsh march was the only part actually to go into action, it is also fairly clear that the Welsh march did not come as a complete surprise to the active Chartists in the manufacturing districts. Some kind of rising was clearly expected, and would perhaps have occurred in Newcastle or the West Riding if it had not happened in Wales. The successful occupation of a provincial town was probably intended to act as the inspiration for similar acts in other parts of the country, rather than to form the first of a series of inter-connected risings which had already been planned. Had there been no soldiers at Newport, or had they been taken by surprise at night, the result would have been very different. Devyr spoke of the total change of attitude on the part of the police in Newcastle when the first incorrect story arrived in the town that Frost had successfully taken Newport.[15] Undoubtedly the failure of the Newport attempt nipped in the bud a number of more or less vaguely-formed insurrectionary plans in various parts of the country. The trial and condemnation of the Welsh leaders took place in an atmosphere of tension which would certainly have erupted into more serious outbreaks if the death sentences had been carried out. As it was, however, the complete failure of the attack – failure brought about by the resistance of a handful of troops – brought the insurrectionary plans to an abrupt halt. O'Connor had always insisted that an unarmed crowd, however determined, must always crumple before trained troops, and the events at Newport bore this out. The troops had not hesitated to fire on the crowd, and the crowd, although partly armed, had fled at the first burst of fire. The energies of the Chartists turned, firstly to somewhat vaguely-planned rescue attempts, and then, after the commutation of the death sentences, to a sustained campaign for the pardon and return of the transported men.

Against armed and disciplined troops, the forces of the Chartists had demonstrably failed.

The main body of the Chartists and their leaders never disowned Frost and the other Newport Chartists. The demand for their return remained a central part of the Chartist programme, recurring in speeches, resolutions and petitions until a pardon was finally granted in 1855.

The tone of the Chartist response to the events at Newport was both elegiac and defiant. A lament sold in the streets in 1840 emphasised the pathos in the fate of the transported men and their followers.

Many a heart will beat in sorrow,
Many an eye will shed a tear
Many an orphan and its mother
Will lament in Monmouthshire;
For the third of last November,
When their fathers went astray,
Tens of thousands will remember
The sad disasters of the day.
. . . .

We will conclude our mournful ditty,
  Which fills our aching hearts with pain
Shed a tear for us of pity –
  We never shall return again;
And when we've reached our destination,
  O'er the seas through storm and gales,
O may you live at home in comfort,
  While we lament in New South Wales.[15]

The same tone informed Thomas Cooper's reference to Frost in his prison-poem, *The Purgatory of Suicides*.

Poor victim! sold, trepanned
By hirelings of the minion whose spite planned
Thy death, and built thy gallows, – but, through fear
Of Labour's vengeance, stayed the hangman's hand;
Victim of thy heart's thirst with bread to cheer
England's lean artisan and Cambria's mountaineer![17]

From Newport itself, however, a more militant tone was reported by a correspondent in May 1841.

Sunday week, being Palm Sunday, the graves in our churchyard were decorated with flowers and evergreens. The most conspicuous were those in which the men who were shot in the late Chartist riots were buried; and at the head of each grave were placarded the following lines written on a large sheet of paper.

Here lie the valiant and the brave,
That fought a nation's rights to save;
They tried to set the captives free
But fell a prey to tyranny!

Yet they shall never be forgot,
Though in the grave their bodies rot;
The Charter shall our watchword be
Come death or glorious liberty![18]

PART TWO:

WHO WERE THE CHARTISTS?

CHAPTER FIVE

Leaders and Followers

THERE'S colliers and miners and labourers too,
Gun-makers, stampers and casters a few,
All bravely united, courageous and true,
    Stand firm to Lovett and Collins,
    For Lovett and Collins, huzza.

There's tailors, shoemakers and masons likewise,
The plasterers and bricklayers strongly do rise,
The great nobs of this town are struck with surprise
    At the speeches for Lovett and Collins,
    For Collins and Lovett huzza.[1]

So a Birmingham balladeer anticipated the crowd that would turn out in his city to welcome the Chartist leaders from prison in 1840. The roll-call of trades to which known Chartists belonged in Britain amounted to nearly two hundred, while the occupations given by members of the Chartist Land Company were nearer three hundred. Grouped into a smaller number of general categories, they seem to cover all the occupations followed in the manufacturing towns and districts of Britain, together with a few from the lower professions and small businesses. Modern historians have rightly shown an interest in the occupations from which radical politicians came, and a number of generalisations have been made on the basis of the information available. It has been suggested that 'dying' trades were the most likely to encourage Chartism, and that conversely the 'new' working class in the factories or in the developing sector of industry, particularly engineering and metal working, had less interest in radical politics. A close study of the make-up of the movement suggests a number of modifications of this accepted wisdom.

The first thing that emerges in a detailed study of the attitudes of various trades towards politics is not the disparities but the great similarities between different trades and occupations. The political ideas which we have been looking at affected most areas of the country. The dogma of the political economists and free traders was being applied in all industries. Although the amount of competition for jobs could differ according to the level of skill demanded, nevertheless the philosophy of the free market in labour was as damaging to the skilled as to the unskilled workman – more so in fact. The apparent preponderance among the Chartists of certain trades could mean more than one thing. It has to be remembered that the textile trades, in all their branches, were still Britain's main productive industries, both in the home and export markets. It is not surprising therefore to find a great many spinners, combers, weavers and workers in a variety of textile ancillary trades among the Chartists. Certain trades, however, were also rather more free from restriction and supervision than others, so that the operative who allowed his name to be published as a delegate or committee man might be taking advantage of his greater freedom from victimisation rather than indicating a high level of political awareness in his trade. We are unlikely ever to know the names and occupations of more than a small fraction of the Chartist membership, and we must beware of drawing too many conclusions from those we do know.

Very few of the Chartists left enough material behind them to enable biographies to be written. A handful of autobiographies provide valuable historical sources, but they have also distorted the picture by their very existence. A few Chartists who gained prominence in later life as literary or political figures have been the subjects of biographies or biographical sketches, but here again, the type of person of whom it has been possible to make such a study has usually been an un-typical member of the movement. The very ordinariness of the majority of Chartist members and supporters has led to the temptation to record them simply as statistics. Nevertheless, although the material is accidental and fragmentary, some picture of the men and women who made up the movement can be put together, and certain tentative conclusions drawn about them. In this study, apart from a brief consideration of O'Connor himself, I shall devote very little space to Chartism's national leaders. Instead I shall try to fill in some of the details about the men and women who made up the organisation throughout the country.

The information is patchy and thin. Radical journals, and in particular the *Star*, had a deliberate policy of printing names, occupations and addresses of local speakers and officials. In many districts names are very localised, and the same ones occur again and again. This may have been the reason for the addition of occupations – an addition which the editor of the *Star* continually stressed to branches of the National Charter Association when they sent in their committee lists.[2] Members of the Land Society in those lists which have survived also always gave their occupation as well as their name and address.

Thus there are several thousand Chartists and Land Plan members for whom we have this basic information. A close study of radical and local papers enables us to build up some picture of quite a large number of local leaders, and local studies have been able to add information from the census enumerators' notebooks, ratebooks, Poor Law records and other sources. Local papers provide invaluable information since in these years local news was beginning to have sales value, and in the post-Chartist years reminiscences of local experiences were very often carried.

A major source of information about ordinary Chartists is the record of those who were arrested, tried or imprisoned. Here again, records are patchy and their survival partly accidental. A report was called for in the winter of 1840 on prisoners held for 'Chartist offences', and although the list is almost certainly incomplete, it contains the names of some 470 men and women, with their occupations and their offences.[3] A more detailed investigation carried out by the prison inspectors later in the year on those remaining in prison contains some of the most interesting personal information we have about one small group of local and national leaders.[4]

The only actual membership list of a Chartist locality to have survived is that of the Great Horton locality of the National Charter Association, from 1840 to 1866. Members' names and subscriptions were carefully entered in an exercise book, scribbled on by later generations of children, but nevertheless preserved by the family of a secretary. It shows, as would be expected in the district, a membership made up of woolcombers with a sprinkling of weavers and building workers and one schoolmaster. In this case the actual occupations of the members parallel closely the published occupations of the committee.[5] Nevertheless, out of a total membership listed of nearly two hundred, without the list we should have known only about a dozen at the most. This may be taken as fairly representing the ratio between known and unknown Chartists – although clearly some committees represented very much smaller and some probably very much larger memberships.

The Chartist Land Company started in 1845, and in the proceedings connected with its closure in the late forties, two membership books have survived in the Board of Trade papers at the Public Record Office.[6] Several thousand names and occupations are listed, with addresses. There are, however, considerable problems in using these as indications of Chartist membership. The most obvious is their incompleteness. After the company was wound up, about 70,000 people claimed for money invested.[7] This is about the figure usually agreed to have made up the membership – perhaps a slight understatement to allow for some loyal Chartists who did not claim, or others whose holdings were not big enough to warrant claiming. The committee of enquiry seems to have worked on an assessment of 'over 60,000' members,[8] while the company's historian mentions both 70,000 and 60,000 at different points.[9] In any case, it is clear that the surviving lists represent only a fraction of the total. What is more, the lists are full of repetitions and overlaps, so counting them can produce only a notional idea of the number of individuals who enrolled even in the years represented, 1847 and 1848. Apart from the incompleteness of the record, there is the problem of the degree of overlap that may be assumed between Land Company members and Chartists proper. That there is more overlap than has sometimes been suggested is certainly true. As Thomas Frost recalled, the establishment of the Plan often led to the re-establishment of Chartist localities[10] – the Appendix shows a strong correlation between branches or members of the Land Company and Chartist localities in the late forties. Information and propaganda for the plan were spread only through the *Northern Star*, and clearly no one who was not to some extent involved in and sympathetic to the movement was going to show the kind of confidence in Feargus O'Connor that membership of the plan demanded. However, it may be argued that there were important sections of the movement or parts of the country which were not represented, or were under-represented in the plan and its membership. Where I have used the lists, I have counted the names individually and checked for overlap. I have not felt justified in making any kind of detailed quantification or generalised analysis from a source which is so incomplete and so problematic in its significance. It is worth stressing, nevertheless, that in the districts of which I have some detailed knowledge, many of the best-known Chartist names do turn up among the members listed.

In the following sections I have indicated the information that the sources yield about individuals rather than about statistical trends. In order to avoid repeating some of the sources, and to avoid unnecessary footnoting, it may be taken that the quantification of London trades is taken from David Goodway's *London Chartism*, unless otherwise indicated; material about Land Company members is abstracted from the membership books, and has been arranged by me according to localities, except for an interesting list drawn up by David Jones in *Chartism and the Chartists* of occupations, in all parts of the country, of members with names beginning with the first three letters of the alphabet. The reports of the prison inspectors are from notes and *pro forma* reports on 73 Chartist prisoners between 1840 and 1841, and the list of imprisoned Chartists is of 470 arrested Chartists listed as the result of questions asked in Parliament in 1840 and 1841. Other sources are indicated as they are used, but these four recur throughout the discussion.[11]

An accurate occupational analysis of the whole movement may be taken to be an impossibility. The information is too heavily weighted by its sources to have general validity. The best analyses have been made, and will continue to be made, in local studies, where information can be cross-checked, and local detail examined. I have raided many such studies, published and unpublished, to try and make some kind of a national picture. For factors which further define a person's identity – membership of a religion or sect, family traditions of non-political kinds, and so on, information is usually so scanty that one can do no more than suggest that such factors may be relevant, and indicate such information as it is possible to obtain. It is clearly desirable to try and see individual Chartists in their own communities, and to look for the qualities that made them into leaders and members, but there are bound to be very large areas of doubts and uncertainty.

This study is mainly concerned with Chartism in its provincial and crowd aspects; the national leadership will not be looked at closely. Much remains to be found out about many Chartist leaders, not all of whom have yet found biographers.[12] But there is no space here to fill these particular gaps.

The history of Chartism has in the past been seen too much in terms of its leaders or would-be leaders. Those men who wrote their own accounts or edited their own journals were not necessarily those whose influence on the movement was greatest. Some figures who were widely respected and followed in their lifetimes have only recently begun to be noticed at all in histories of Chartism.

One indication of the real importance of Chartist leaders could be the attention paid to them by the authorities. Governments rarely needed detailed or specific proof of treasonable action to put dangerous men out of the way for a term of imprisonment. O'Brien, Benbow, Lovett, McDouall, O'Connor, Roberts, Cooper and Ernest Jones were all put behind bars for a year or more in the course of their careers, and hundreds of less well-known but locally influential men were also incarcerated. But some of the best-known names managed to avoid imprisonment. It could have been administrative inefficiency, but it seems strange that both George Julian Harney and Dr John Taylor were released after their arrests without being sent for trial, although both were speakers who employed a strong revolutionary rhetoric. General Napier indeed regarded Taylor as the most dangerous of the Chartist leaders, and feared that if O'Connor were to be imprisoned in the winter of 1839, Taylor's influence would be unrestrained.[13] Even his involvement in the Bradford attempted rising in January 1840, however, did not lead to Taylor's arrest, although his fellow-conspirator, Peddie, served a term of imprisonment with hard labour, and several Bradford Chartists were awarded the same punishment.[14] The immunity of Taylor and Harney remains one of the minor mysteries of the Chartist movement, but it may perhaps indicate that some of the men whose writing has survived, or who have left a picturesque or romantic image, may have been treated less seriously by those in authority than those whose leadership met with a greater response in the more troubled districts.

Of the importance of Feargus O'Connor as a national leader, there can, however, be no question, and even a brief consideration of the question of leadership must begin with an examination of his role.

By most of Chartism's historians, O'Connor has been seen as the evil genius of the movement.[15] Only recently has this distortion begun to be redressed, but it is a judgement which will die hard. In fact, so far from being the exploiter and distorter of the Chartist movement, O'Connor was so much the centre of it that, had the name Chartist not been coined, the radical movement between 1838 and 1848 must surely have been called O'Connorite Radicalism. Remove him and his newspaper from the picture, and the movement fragments, localises and loses its continuity.

O'Connor was a politician rather than a theoretician. Throughout his career he held to certain political principles, above all to the principle of universal (manhood) suffrage. The corollary of this principle was a belief in the worth and dignity of every individual in the country, a belief that provided an acceptable credo for the popular democratic movement which no other principle could have united. What was more, O'Connor believed firmly in the need for working people to form their own organisations, trade societies, schools, reading groups and land colonies, through which they could develop their own ideas, control their own lives and resist the exploitation and the cultural dominion of the higher classes. Such ideas, in a society still dominated by influence and patronage at all levels, had revolutionary implications which may not seem so fundamental today. The response to O'Connor's politics and speeches by members of his own class, even many who considered themselves to be politically extremely radical, is significant of a fundamental difference of approach. One of his bitterest opponents in the House of Commons declared:

> . . . my experience of the hon. Member out of this house, and of the spirit and manner in which he has tried to array the working classes against every man who could effectually assist them in carrying forward the objects in which the hon. Member himself professed to wish them success, convinces me that he has done more to retard the political progress of the working classes of England than any public man that ever lived in this country.[16]

The speaker was Richard Cobden, to whom the working people were at best an argument *ad terrorem* to be invoked by the Anti-Corn-Law League in support of its arguments. O'Connor's continual emphasis on the need for independent working-class organisation, on the need for self-activity of all kinds, and his hostility to all exploiting classes, whether landowners or industrialists, provoked hostility above all in those middle-class radicals who saw themselves as the natural leaders of society. If, as part of his rhetoric, he presented himself as a self-sacrificing popular leader who had abandoned everything to plead the cause of the people, he did so with more justification than he has usually been given credit for, since there is ample evidence in his early career in Irish politics and in the law that he could have pursued a successful and very much more comfortable career at the bar or in conventional politics than the one which he undertook in the Chartist movement.

Much of the dislike shown by historians for O'Connor's leadership is based on the distaste felt for the character of the demagogue. But, as James Epstein has shown in his study of O'Connor's leadership, this character was a traditional one in British popular politics, and even here O'Connor did in fact change its nature, making himself at least nominally far more accountable to his followers than figures like Hunt or Cobbett had ever been.[17]

But O'Connor retained his unquestioned leadership of the Chartist movement above all because he kept the matter of the suffrage in the forefront of his arguments. His political stance was simple, and the fact that he did not spend a great deal of time on questions of longer-term social and political aims gave him an ability to hold together supporters whose views on the question differed. His conduct of the *Northern Star* has already been discussed, and this clearly contributed to his popularity. But in the end, the qualities of leadership which keep a man at the head of a mass movement for ten years and more are not to be found in his political philosophy or his administrative ability alone. Too many historians have credited O'Connor with only the charismatic qualities of leadership, and it must be pointed out that he was a shrewd and capable politican and a not inconsiderable organiser and administrator in addition. Nevertheless, his power did also consist in the much less easily defined leadership qualities of the demagogue. Not only are these qualities difficult to define, they have the additional problem for the historian that they operate at levels which are often not amenable to exact documentation. Those who are most affected by them are often ashamed to acknowledge in later life the power of such subjective factors. Thomas Cooper has already been mentioned. It is clear from letters in 1842 that he was completely under the spell of O'Connor's personality in the summer of that year. His later disavowal to Gammage, and the tone of his autobiography, reflect a rational embarrassment at his own attitude. George Julian Harney has often been pointed out as one of O'Connor's critics in the later forties. Working on the *Star*, Harney found himself increasingly at odds with Feargus as he himself became more absorbed in the Continental nationalist and socialist movements. His correspondence, however, illustrates both the attractions of O'Connor's personality and the frustration of trying to organise a cabal against a figure whose personal qualities seemed to be able to win back even his most bitter opponents. In an interesting letter to Frederick Engels in 1846, Harney spoke of the qualities which made O'Connor the leader of Chartism. Engels had apparently suggested that Harney's writing in the *Star* was better than Feargus's, and that Harney would make a better leader of the movement. Harney replied:

I must next notice what you say about my '*leadership*'. First let me remark that you are too hard on O'Connor. You find fault with his 'leaders', but you say the 'weekly summary' affords you entertainment – fun. You speak as though you credited me with the 'summary', but the 'summary' is prepared by O'Connor as you might have known by the Irish jokes and the very Irish poetry continually introduced into the Commentary. You are wrong in supposing that he prevented my continuing remarks concerning Cabet. The discontinuance was the result first of my own neglect and second that Hetherington has never completed the translation . . . I must do O'C the justice to say that he never interferes with what I write in the paper, nor does he know what I write until he sees the paper. . .

As to his own qualities as a popular leader, Harney again is doubtful.

A popular chief should be possessed of a magnificent bodily appearance, an iron frame, eloquence or at least a ready fluency of tongue. I have none of these. O'C has them all – at least in degree. A popular leader should possess great animal courage, contempt of pain and death, and be not altogether ignorant of military arms and science. . . . From a knowledge of myself and all the men who live, and do figure in the Chartist movement, I am convinced that even in this respect, was O'C thrown overboard, we might go further and fare worse. . .[18]

The correspondence in the Harney papers shows O'Connor as a generous and easy-going employer to Harney. The few letters and personal papers that remain all indicate the same characteristics.[19] In his personal relationships, he evinced charm, good humour, energy and a total commitment to the movements with which he was associated. Had O'Connor been the brutal braggadocio, self-important figure that so many historians have presented, he could not possibly have maintained his leadership of the Chartists for ten years, years in which it was never seriously questioned or challenged. The organisation of the movement was carried on in the localities by hundreds of men and women with standing in their own communities, and by a smaller number of dedicated and talented men working full-time as organisers, journalists and lecturers. O'Connor was the national figure whose visits were the occasion to organise massive demonstrations, to exploit every theatrical device, from the unhitching of his carriage outside the town to the massive display of numbers, banners, tableaux and music at the gathering point of the rally. Napier spoke of mass meetings at which the crowds melted away once O'Connor had finished speaking,[20] and there is no doubt that no other figure ever produced the same turn-out. He played on this function of the figurehead, dramatising his personality and using the demagogic rhetoric of the sacrificial leader. O'Neil Daunt pointed out that 'he addressed the people more in the style of a chieftain encouraging his gallant clansmen than of a commonplace agitator talking down to the level of an unenlightened auditory'.[21]

He was always the gentleman demagogue making no attempt to present himself as 'ordinary'. John Hugh Burland remembered his first encounter with O'Connor when he visited Barnsley shortly before the beginning of the Chartist movement.

His figure was tall and well-proportioned, and his bearing decidedly aristocratic. He wore a blue frock-coat and buff waistcoat, and had rings on the fingers of each hand. In a graceful manner and in emphatic language, he told the Radicals of Barnsley that he had sold off his horses and dogs, greatly reduced his establishment, and come weal, come woe he would henceforth devote his whole life to promote the well-being of the working classes. . . . The language of O'Connor, to ears accustomed to little else than the Barnsley dialect spoken by pale-faced weavers and swart cobblers, sounded like rich music.[22]

O'Connor may be criticised for the manner in which he led the Chartist movement, but his promise was kept, and the Chartists remembered it. Adam Rushton recalled 'Feargus O'Connor, with his herculean form, majestic head, sandy hair and splendid voice . . . husky with constant use. . .'[23] Samuel Fielden described his father as 'a Chartist and an earnest champion and admirer of the principal advocate, that noble but unfortunate Irishman, Feargus O'Connor'.[24] W. H. Chadwick, 'the last of the Manchester Chartists', wore the O'Connor medal round his neck until the day of his death in 1908. Charles Wilkins, radical historian of Merthyr Tydfil, considered that 'few men have been worse maligned and less deserved it'.[25] There was no other leader who came anywhere near O'Connor in the respect and following among the main body of Chartist supporters.

Both Whig and Tory governments in the Chartist period paid O'Connor the tribute of regarding him as the most dangerous of the leaders. The conspiracy trial of 1843 was mainly concerned to involve O'Connor. The Attorney-General wrote to George Maule: 'I mean to indict O'Connor as a conspirator generally, and put him in the same category as the operatives and shew up him and his mischief and his companions together – this will be the best way to secure a conviction and set forth the offence in its truest light.'[26] On that occasion the plan failed. O'Connor was an able lawyer, and conducted his own and his fellow-prisoners' defence with skill. On the occasion of his earlier arrest, however, for seditious libel, he was imprisoned for a year in York Castle. Clearly some of the Government's advisors considered that this would end the Chartist movement. Napier wrote to the Duke of Portland in September 1839, warning him against this kind of optimism. 'A man who pretends that such a general movement of the working classes as we have lately witnessed can depend upon the freedom or imprisonment of Mr O'Connor must be actuated by some sinister motive, or have very little perception of what is going forward. The Chartist spirit is not broken. . .' A few days later he elaborated: 'I did not say O'Connor's imprisonment would have *no effect*, but that it could not arrest the general movement . . . so far from that arrest stopping violent proceedings I have no doubt it would increase them'.[27] The authorities, however, proceeded with the trial, and O'Connor was sentenced.

In York Castle, O'Connor had a far better time, after the first few weeks, than any of the other Chartist prisoners. True, his offence was civil rather than criminal, and he had money for comforts that many others could not afford. But it was partly also a matter of class and of personality. When the inspector of prisons called to make his report, Feargus soon reduced him to the inferior partner in the dialogue, by declining to be interviewed except on his own terms. Even Stephens, who enjoyed many privileges and was clearly not short of money, never managed to alter the relationship in this way. No other leader or would-be leader in those years had the energy, ability, physique or charisma of Feargus O'Connor. For good or ill, he was the main inspiration and guiding force of the movement.

William Lovett and the London Working Men's Association represented not so much an alternative leadership to the Chartist movement, as a different sort of movement altogether. Whether, in the absence of O'Connor and some of the provincial leaders, such a movement would have become nation-wide is one of the many unanswered and unanswerable questions about the period. But there is one other figure who saw himself as the potential leader of a national movement, and as the originator of Chartism, whose claims need to be briefly examined. This is the enigmatic Bronterre O'Brien. He has had, on the whole, a better press from historians than O'Connor, partly simply because of the quarrel between them. But he has also always appeared to be more of an intellectual and less of a demagogue than his fellow-Irishman, and his willingness to cooperate with the middle-class Complete Suffrage Movement has seemed to show someone with a less intransigent attitude than the main body of the Chartists. O'Brien left a small band of followers in London who provided a link between Chartism and the modern labour movement, and who did not become absorbed in popular Liberalism in the later years of the century as did so many Chartists.[28]

W. J. Linton described O'Brien as 'perhaps the cleverest man in our party',[29] and Belfort Bax recalled that Engels, although he disliked O'Brien, considered that he 'had in some respect a wider range of views than the others'.[30] He was probably the nearest thing to an intellectual that the very activist movement produced, was indeed dubbed by O'Connor 'the schoolmaster of Chartism'. His influence was largely exerted through the printed word, however, and was at its greatest in the very early years of the movement. By the mid-thirties, as editor of the *Poor Man's Guardian*, and as a contributor to many other journals, stamped and unstamped, he was held in the highest regard by most London radicals. When he began the first of the several journals that he floated during the Chartist years, early in 1837, an admirer wrote urging him to make the connection with his earlier writing.

Bronterre should have stated at the outset of his paper, that he was '*Late editor of the Twopenny and London Dispatch, and the Poor Man's Guardian*' etc. etc. Great numbers would then have hailed the publication as that of an old friend with whom they had been long acquainted, and to whose writings they were much indebted.[31]

Apart from their friendship and their political agreement, there was clearly a strong commercial reason for O'Connor's anxiety to associate O'Brien with the *Northern Star*. Bronterre wrote his own column in the paper during the first year of its publication. O'Connor always referred to him in the most eulogistic terms in those months, and indeed always recognised his considerable qualities as a journalist and sought to retain them for the *Star*. There is no suggestion in the published or unpublished material that the 'quarrel' between the two men originated with Feargus, as so many historians of Chartism have suggested. Bronterre was clearly a very difficult personality, and was, at the beginning of the Chartist movement, past the best of his radical period. The inspector of prisons who interviewed him in 1841 considered him 'a mere trading agitator of no great power except in name', and considered that he could quite easily be persuaded to emigrate.[32] By 1841 he had quarrelled with Hetherington, not the easiest man with whom to quarrel, was highly critical of O'Connor, with whom he proceeded to quarrel when he left prison, and whom he accused, untruthfully and unfairly, of failing to take care of his (O'Brien's) wife whilst he was in gaol. When John Watkins wrote to him in prison, seeking his support for a new journal, O'Brien wrote accepting the role of advisor in the project, but warning Watkins that

> neither . . . the knowledge-mongers, nor O'Connor, nor the rag-money radicals, nor the Cobbettites, nor the Socialists will ever be (as a body) friendly disposed towards me, for this simple reason – that I am opposed to the *trading* or *profitable* part of all their schemes. Friends and followers I have among all these parties; for there are honest as well as dishonest men in all parties. But the leaders and principal men in all of them are my sworn enemies.[33]

It is possible to present O'Brien as a perfectionist who was not prepared to make political compromises, and to explain his quarrels with every other major leader in this way. But both his published comments and his private correspondence indicate a more personal explanation. There seems little doubt that he was an extremely unstable personality, probably an alcoholic, and quite incapable of holding down any kind of job. Not only did all his publications fail – something which was not unique to Bronterre – but every other enterprise with which he was associated foundered. His friends and admirers made many attempts to help him, but he seems to have ended his days in poverty, earning a few shillings a night at working men's clubs by opening the drinking and debating sessions. There is a note of paranoia in his complaints that does not go with a purely political account of his failures. In a series of letters to Thomas Allsop, who tried in the late forties to reconcile Bronterre and Feargus, O'Brien outlined his complaints.

When O'Connor came into the movement I was rising in name, fame and circumstances – the just reward of long and disinterested service in the cause – at the time of the convention thirteen of the largest constituencies of the Kingdom spontaneously selected me to be their representative . . . and several other convention members owed their election simply to the fact that they were recommended as 'friends and disciples of Bronterre O'Brien'. . .

He blamed O'Connor for the loss of that popularity, but not O'Connor alone:

At a time when he knew Hetherington had robbed me of large sums of money – of £375 in one swoop – . . . he joined Hetherington openly in a crusade against Bernard, Bell and myself – treacherously pretending to be neuter. . .[34]

Not only Hetherington, but Smith and Carpenter, who had been associated with him in the production of the *Southern Star*, were accused of having conspired against him in a personal way.

Carpenter's conduct to me has been of so cruel, and at the same time so villainous a nature that I cannot describe it – to him mainly I attribute Smith's conspiracy to degrade and destroy my poor family, and to blast my reputation with the public. . . I am the victim of a cruel and heartless conspiracy on the part of Smith and Carpenter. . .[35]

This is the tone of paranoia. On at least one occasion O'Brien's accusations became so embarrassing that the Chartist leaders answered some of them in public. At a time when Hetherington was accused of having robbed him, Hetherington, with his books in his hand, showed that he had been paying O'Brien five pounds a week – a handsome salary by any standards. In 1847, Allsop made every possible effort to reconcile Feargus and Bronterre. From the one-sided correspondence which survives, it would seem that even the ever-optimistic Allsop lost patience at one point with his friend. O'Brien replied in his usual accusatory tone.

You tell me of O'Connor's 'joyousness' and 'activity' and of my indolence and brooding over imaginary wrongs and you upbraid me with '*appearing to derive pleasure from representing myself as an injured man*' and now my dear Sir this is so unjust and ungenerous a comparison on your part, that I can hardly persuade myself it comes from the same Thomas Allsop I ever knew in Regent St. . . .[36]

On more than one occasion O'Brien was accused of coming drunk to meetings, and on the occasion of his public challenge to the Chartist leaders, when he claimed that he had at one time been forced to 'tear the ear rings from his wife's ears' to sell before he could buy food for his family, it was shown that his income at the time was a very comfortable one, and he was accused of needing the money to buy drink. He was often referred to by people who knew him as 'moody' and 'irritable', and he certainly carried his propensity for quarrelling well into the fifties, when he engaged in a pamphlet war with Ernest Jones. His break with main-line Chartism occurred over the question of the Complete Suffrage Union, and it was clearly this episode which led to the loss of confidence in him by provincial Chartists. There is something simplistic in crowd politics, and what to Bronterre looked like a continuing O'Connorite conspiracy to silence him and to prevent the sale of his papers, was in reality the response of a loyal and perhaps somewhat fixated crowd to attacks on their most respected leader. None of the alternatives to the National Charter Association ever achieved a mass local following. The NCA was the organisation of the Chartists, as the *Star* was their paper. Neither was monolithic or totally consistent, and had Bronterre joined the NCA in its early days he would have had more opportunity to present himself as an alternative leader, or as a modifying influence on the leaders. As it was, he retained a small but loyal following, and continued to engage in a dialogue, and to issue manifestos in association with a group of largely metropolitan ultra-radical intellectuals, men like Linton, Cooper, Thornton Hunt and G. J. Holyoake who were tangentially connected to Chartism through small radical journals, but were not involved in the continuing provincial activity. O'Brien undoubtedly provided a great deal of the rational argument for ultra-radicalism and Chartism in its earliest months. Had he remained in its central councils, he might well have influenced its later development, but his personality and his delusions made that impossible.

There were very few other candidates for alternative leadership to that of O'Connor. Most of the other nationally-known figures worked either intermittently or consistently as part of a second-level national leadership. Men like Peter Murray McDouall, Thomas Cooper, John Tavlor and George Julian Harney all achieved a certain national status and some kind of national following. There were a number of popular speakers who could draw crowds of reasonable size when they toured the country, and many more who were known mainly in their own localities. Every district contained men who were able to provide lectures or speeches and who could be relied on as supporting speakers to national figures on the platforms of mass rallies. Quarrels were common among all these leaders. Historians have noted that many of them quarrelled with O'Connor. It should be noticed, however, that they quarrelled among themselves even more. The conditions under which they worked – the continual shortage of cash, the need to raise funds from people who could ill afford it and who naturally regarded its laying out with intense interest, the harassment of the authorities, the temptations of more comfortable and rewarding work, and all the other discomforts of the day to day political action, intensified the sensitivity of individual leaders, and perhaps enhanced the tendency to elevate political differences into personal vendettas. George White wrote to Thomas Cooper in July 1842: 'Cooper, I am sick of the horrible vanity of our *leaders*! save the mark. When in Scotland I have been ready to vomit at the little paltry jealousies between Collins and McDouall. . .'[37]

So far from O'Connor being the instigator of squabbles among the leadership, he was sometimes criticised by his loyal followers for going too far in 'propping up doubtful customers' in the interests of unity. There seems to me to be no doubt that O'Connor's influence was far more unifying than divisive. Adulation of O'Connor can be found in all the Chartist journals, by no means only in the *Star*. In spite of his subsequent disavowals, Thomas Cooper was, in his period as a Chartist leader, well to the fore in this adulation. He wrote, in the *Midland Counties Illuminator* of 17 April 1841:

> Working men feel an ardent devotion to the names of Vincent, and Lovett, and Collins, and O'Brien, and Moir, and McDouall and Pitkethly – and a host of others that might be mentioned; but while they know how to appreciate the stirling honesty, the active intelligence, the indomitable perseverence, the glorious enthusiasm, in brief the true patriotic qualities which distinguish, severally, the individuals in the front phalanx of the army – in *no one name* do they discern a *combination of qualities* so commanding in their influence, so magnetic in attracting an unswerving attachment, as in their brave O'Connor. . .[38]

CHAPTER SIX

The Manufacturing Communities

THE Chartist national leaders worked through the press and the platform, bringing to a high point of organisation methods that had been operating since the days of Henry Hunt. It was to this tradition that O'Connor constantly referred and he was often presented on banners and in speeches as Hunt's successor. The main work of the movement was carried on in the manufacturing districts throughout the British Isles, districts which shared a range of problems, a variety of cultural and working traditions, and a similarity of size and scale. The importance of this latter point is considerable. J. C. Coombe, editor of the *London Democrat*, complained in 1839 that London was 'too huge a place to carry out the details of organisation in a business-like or satisfactory manner; and besides, the people are not sufficiently known to, nor have they the necessary confidence in each other'.[1] This alone may account for the lesser importance of London and other large cities, or for the fact that in the cities, organisation was often by trades rather than by locality. The main strength of Chartism always lay in the manufacturing districts. Here the experience of the half-century leading up to the Chartist period had produced a common sense of exclusion from the political system and a common alternative radical and politico-religious tradition which could be nourished by the press and the platform of the radical leadership.

The introduction of steam power in the last quarter of the eighteenth century was only a part – although an important one – of the changes which affected the life and work of the manufacturing districts of Britain in the half-century before the Chartist movement. During that period the outstanding fact was the expansion of production rather than the changes in technology. A great deal of this expansion took place in the non-mechanised industrial processes. Steam affected cotton-spinning and then cotton-weaving, worsted-spinning, some worsted-weaving, the operation of the heaviest hammers in iron and steel forging and the pumping of water from some coal mines, by the Chartist period. In some other processes, such as the grinding of cutlery and edge-tools, steam-driven wheels replaced water-driven ones in these years, changing the pace and location of the work but not essentially the technology of the individual craftsman. But in agriculture – by far the largest sector of employment, with just short of a million workers listed in the 1841 census – building, employing more than 300,000 male workers, tailoring and shoemaking, mining, road-building, cutlery and tool-making and a vast range of other productive occupations, work-patterns were barely affected by changes in the source of power. Changes that were occurring were in response to increased demand, and consisted of the application of ingenuity to traditional processes and the erosion of institutions and customs which impeded expansion. There was a considerable increase in the tendency which had been going on slowly for a century and more, for workers to be gathered together in workshops and factories where there was increased supervision, increased standardisation of products, a greater control over the use of raw materials, but where work was often carried on with traditional tools and equipment, and where payment was still made by the piece rather than by the hour. The rapidly-expanding carpet industry of Kidderminster is a good example of this process. By the 1830s the weavers were working for one or other of three or four large manufacturers, each of whom owned large weaving-sheds. Weavers, however, worked in their own time, and 'sold' the results of their work to their employer. Industrial conflicts were over 'prices' rather than 'wages', though they were none the less bitter for that.[2]

Chartists and radicals were very much aware of the changes which the introduction of machinery was making in working conditions. On occasion they blamed machinery for creating unemployment and for the worsening conditions of those who had to work with it. The cotton factory operatives were among the most active and consistent Chartists. But most trades sensed a worsening of their working conditions which could not be attributed to the introduction of machinery. The cotton handloom weavers were the only ones whose trade had been completely taken over by machines. Yet hand-weaving in all branches of textiles was a depressed trade. A Scottish weaver, Allan Hogg, pointed out in 1847 that the decline in standards of the weavers was not due to machinery alone.

> The fabrics which are generally wrought on the handloom cannot be wrought to an advantage on the power-loom; and there are a number of them, from the fineness of the yarn, the variety of colours, complication of patterns etc. that probably never will be attempted to be wrought with machinery. As regards the fabric that I am employed at, there has been no material improvement made in my time by which we can facilitate our production. . . .

Nevertheless, in his thirty-seven years as a weaver, he had seen the trade decline from a prosperous one, paying one shilling a yard for the cloth, to a depressed and impoverished one, paying one and nine-tenth pence for the same work. He recalled the good life of the weavers in his youth, when weavers were 'reckoned as men'. Now, 'we have to take work through agents . . . the most part of whom keep truck shops and who give out the work at any price,' and the result was the descent into poverty and degradation, a loss both material and spiritual.[3]

Like many others, Hogg saw the deterioration as being due to financial and political factors. Like many other Chartists, he looked to government intervention to curb the power of the merchants and bankers and to protect the standards and wages of the working people.

Nearly every trade in the pre-Chartist period had seen industrial conflict, concerned with wages, prices, methods of payment, working hours and apprenticeship regulation. Such conflict had occurred in trades which were technically advanced, like cotton spinning, as well as in those, like tailoring and shoemaking, where technological change was minimal. Almost every trade produced leaders for the Chartist movement, with the outstanding exception of the largest occupational group in the country, for very few Chartist leaders came directly from working as agricultural labourers.

Most of the accounts we have of the manufacturing districts in the Chartist period were written in the late nineteenth century, where the descriptions were often counterposed to the more rational and modern communities of the later industrial period.[4] In examining the trades or occupations of the Chartists, we shall look at some evidence about the social composition of these industrial areas, and at the differences and similarities between them. Certain generalised points may, however, be made about all these districts in the 1830s and 1840s.

In the first place, most of the manufacturing industry in Britain at this time was located in townships and industrial villages, usually clustered around a main centre. Nottingham had its cluster of surrounding stocking and lace-making villages, Leicester its frameworking and glove-making communities, Halifax, Huddersfield and Bradford were centres for worsted and stuff weaving, with villages and out-townships on the moors around. South Wales and Tyneside were centres of iron working and coal and iron mining, again with the population grouped in industrial villages around the main towns. Lancashire was networked with cotton towns, centred around Manchester which was the main centre for cotton merchanting, but also contained cotton mills and textile ancillary manufacturers. In Leeds the woollen industry was made up mainly of a few large employers, but in the countryside around were villages to which the Leeds manufacturers put out work. Gloucester and Stroud were old woollen centres, and the country around housed villages of weavers, as did the neighbouring county of Wiltshire, where the villages also included hatters among the weavers and textile workers.

Although by Chartist times very few of the workers in the main manufacturing trades of Britain would be described as independent artisans in the strict sense that they worked with their own tools on materials that they themselves owned, very many of them worked in trades which had originally been organised as artisan trades. What is more, there was no alternative to the old 'model' of artisan training. Skill could only be passed on by a system of training by skilled workers. If this system was allowed to lapse, half-learnt skills and the division of labour into semi-skilled strata must result. Many skills – notably the textile trades – really did not require a traditional seven years' apprenticeship. Woolsorting might remain a trade learnt only by lengthy application and experience, but weaving and combing could be learnt in a matter of months, particularly in the coarser branches of the trade. The simple fact of the population increase may have been a factor in the great increase in the pressure for entry into the traditional trades in the years after the Napoleonic wars. Habits and customs which had for generations protected the skills of the apprenticed trades were being attacked and undermined in the new industrial expansion. A few highly skilled trades retained control over entry, but the main body of middle-ranking skilled trades were under continuous pressures which were forcing them to relinquish the control which they had hitherto exerted over their conditions of work. William Brown's account of the flax dressers in Dundee in the 1820s described a state of things which was already on the way out by the late thirties: 'The workmen in some measure controlled the trade, dictating as to their rates of wages to be paid, number of journeymen and apprentices to be employed, and the stocks of dressed flax to be kept up. . .'[5] By the Chartist period, the flax dressers had lost a major strike in 1834, and heckling machines were encroaching on the skills of the operatives. The hecklers were avid readers of the *Northern Star* which was read aloud in the heckling houses in the 1840s.[6] The disputes in the linen trade in Scotland in the years immediately preceding the Chartist movement were led by men who were to be leaders of Chartism. They soon associated their disputes over wages and conditions with wider political questions. Leader in Dundee in 1834 was James Gow, a young weaver-poet, soon to be the town's leading Chartist. Appealing for support in the strike in 1834, he wrote:

Brethren! We are determined to resist to the uttermost this liberty-destroying edict of our employers. Were the laws of self-preservation to compel us to submit to it, our feelings would be little different from those of the seaman who is impressed, or those of the free African when he is seized and dragged into slavery. . . . None of you can fail at once to perceive in the present measure of our employers a blow aimed not at the linen weavers of Dundee alone, but at the existence of Unions throughout the empire, and none of you who perceive this will hesitate to fight with us shoulder to shoulder for the principle of the Union – the principle of liberty and civilisation. . .[7]

Such experiences, the erosion of traditional controls, the attack on wages and conditions of work by employers, the response of strike action and its defeat by the importation of cheap labour or the extension of machinery could be paralleled in most areas and in most industries in the British Isles.

Although most Chartists respected the protective institutions in principle, many of them were in fact slop or unapprenticed workers of various kinds, and many, working in factories, lacked the freedom which the out-worker or artisan still retained to organise his own working hours. By 1840 many Chartist localities were reluctantly calling their public meetings on Sundays, so that members who worked in factories and did not therefore have the right to take Monday off, could attend. But the freedom to organise their time was strongly defended, even where the hours to be worked in order to earn a livelihood were so long that little actual freedom was experienced.

Other traditional forms of behaviour included many associated with drinking. 'Footings' – the introduction of ale into the workshops to celebrate special occasions – were common still in many trades, although in some they had already been commuted and 'foot-ales' had become contributions of cash to society funds. Middle-class attacks on the habits of the working people usually included the accusation of drunkenness, as did Disraeli's account of Wodegate, and associated this with the undisciplined work hours and the retention of out-dated apprenticeship regulations. For the Chartists, however, the things were not inseparably bound up. Many Chartists criticised the excessive drinking that went on in some trades. In his autobiography Lovett described the way in which his own entry into the cabinet-making trade had to be eased by alcohol.[8] Joseph Gutteridge recalled the ubiquity of alcohol in the Coventry ribbon-weaving shed where he served his first apprenticeship. The foreman who should have instructed him, although 'a talented and capable workman', was too often drunk to do his work properly. Every newly-initiated workman in this factory had to buy a gallon of ale, to which the other workmen added a pint apiece, and all work stopped until the lot had been drunk.[9] In the pottery where Charles Shaw worked as a child, the potters stayed away from work at the beginning of the week to drink, and made up the time by working at night at the end of the week, forcing their child assistants to do the same. On working days they would resort to subterfuges to get drink brought into the workshop, usually by women and child workers.

> Drinking away at the beershop was bad enough, and this was the commonest course taken, but drinking on the works was far more horrible, being accompanied by jollification and devilry unnameable. Then the young women were persuaded to join in the indulgence. . . . The night was a revel of lust and beastliness. . .[10]

But 'St Monday' was not invariably spent at the alehouse. Traditionally a day of rest for the artisans, it was also used for political meetings and 'rational recreations', visits to museums, outings and excursions. It was the most popular day for theatrical performances until the middle of the century, and for working women it was wash-day and house-cleaning day.[11]

The modernising drive of larger-scale industry required the elimination of irregular hours, the establishment of discipline in factory and workshop, and the clearer demarcation of work and of rates of pay. The middle-class temperance movement stressed the wastefulness of traditional drinking habits, and the growing movement against 'cruel sports' among the working people can also be seen as part of the same process of 'modernisation'. Of course it is a crude over-simplification to see all these moral onslaughts on traditional work and leisure patterns as being motivated by simple economic self-interest on the part of the employers. Clearly cock-fighting, badger-baiting, bull-running and others of a large variety of 'sports' involving cruelty to animals evoked genuine horror and revulsion on the part of many cultivated people. The same horror was not, however, evoked by fox-hunting, deer-stalking or by the many ways in which horses were constrained and mutilated to comply with fashions in carriages or riding style. Some of these questions will be looked at again later, but the point should be emphasised that the working people themselves had in many cases proposals for change and improvement which did not involve the abandonment of cherished customs, and above all did not involve the total relinquishment of control over their own work and environment. The ideology of the free market and the jungle laws of competition did not succeed purely because no alternative was offered. Chartism represented both the defence of certain existing values and proposals for change which were not the same as those of the political economists.

The outstanding case of a traditional occupation under stress was the case of the handloom weavers. Long before the displacement of any but a minority by power looms, the weavers were complaining of continual reductions in their rates of pay and loss of status generally. In constitutional fashion they petitioned Parliament for redress, and in the early Chartist period they were the subject of Parliamentary Commissions of enquiry.[12] In Parliament John Fielden and John Maxwell proposed trade boards to regulate wages and prices, but their proposals were overwhelmingly defeated.[13] The Royal Commission ended its report in 1840 with the famous advice to the weavers to 'flee from the trade, and . . . beware of leading their children into it, as they would beware the commission of the most atrocious crimes'.[14] The system under which the weavers worked was unable to offer them a living from their trade. It was not in most cases under-employment or unemployment which caused their poverty, but the fact that a full – or over-full – day's work, sometimes by a whole family, did not produce a subsistence wage. As the handloom weaver Philip Warner complains in *Sybil*, 'It is not vice that has brought me to this, nor indolence, nor imprudence, I was born to labour, and I was ready to labour.'[15] The Rev. Humphrey Price told the Kidderminster carpet weavers in 1830 that their only hope was to obtain the suffrage if they were to protect their trade and their standards.[16] The same message was being preached throughout the weaving communities as the thirties advanced. Many of the early Chartist leaders were men who had given evidence to the commissions of enquiry – Rushton and Crossland in Halifax, Charleton in Kidderminster, Marsland in Preston. Others had been leaders in strikes like linen weavers William Ashton and Frank Mirfield of Barnsley who served sentences of transportation for their part in the strike of 1829.

By far the greatest occupational group in Chartism, as in the country as a whole, were weavers of various kinds. Britain's major industry was textiles, and it was among the textile workers that the political, social and industrial conflicts took their sharpest form. It was also above all among the weavers that alternative social philosophies were canvassed. Owenism proper with all its alternative forms of social institutions did not take hold in the main manufacturing communities, although there were pockets of socialist influence, like the silk weavers of the Colne valley who were said to be strongly Owenite in the 1830s.[17] But elements from Owen's teaching, particularly the emphasis on cooperative production and marketing, were very strongly influential on the Chartism of the textile districts, as was his emphasis on education. The last producers' cooperative in Britain seems to have been among the fustian cutters of the upper Calder valley,[18] who had been strong Chartists, and the areas in which the first consumer cooperatives started up in the 1840s and 50s were these same Chartist strongholds in the textile districts, where the first shareholders were almost invariably Chartists.[19] The same districts were usually also centres of the Chartist Land Company in the latter part of the 1840s, which suggests that the dichotomy between Owenite or Socialist solutions and the Land Scheme which some writers have suggested may be too hasty an analysis. The desire for self-sufficiency and freedom from the dictates of merchants and employers could lead either to involvement in petty landholding schemes or to cooperative ventures, often much closer in practice than in theory.

The inhabitants of the manufacturing districts included many people who wanted change and improvement. They were not static, 'pre-industrial' quagmires, opposed to all ideas of enlightenment and progress. To most of the inhabitants, however, enlightenment and progress were not seen as emanating from the middle classes of society. Their employers, like the clergy of the established church and the magistrates who enforced the Master and Servant Acts, the Game Laws and the licensing laws, were seen as inimical to the kind of advance that the working people were after. The worst abuses of traditional drinking habits, for example, were reinforced by employers who insisted on paying wages in public houses. In the Potteries,

> The custom was to pay three or four men, with their helpers in one large sum, say a five-pound note, and some odd sovereigns. . . The wages were fastened up in one lump until loosened at some public house. Men, women and children had to go there for their wages. The publican took good care to be in no hurry changing the money given him. . . When all were paid, the women and boys were sent home, the night's booze properly set in, and towards ten o'clock, poor wretched women would appear and entreat their husbands to go home.[20]

In Stockport d'Eichthal recorded in his diary the evidence of a cotton operative whose employer paid his workmen in the public house, again on the pretext of getting change for his banknotes.

> The publican alone was in possession of small change. Mine host used to insist, on every transaction, that each worker should buy a pint of beer. After the first pint a second would follow, and so on until the majority of workers would get drunk, so that the most frightful disorders broke out.[21]

The problem here was not drink so much as the place of drinking. Home-brewed ale was a regular part of the diet of working men and women, as the historian of Pudsey in Chartist times recalled. Here it was referred to simply as 'drink', and it came in two kinds, 'small' and 'strong'.

The hospitality of Pudsey people is well-known, and as regards this drink it is boundless. One can scarcely put his head into a house, or look in at a door or window, but he is asked to take a 'sup of drink'. On a winter's night, when neighbours meet to chat in all but total darkness, the host is certain to draw them mugpots of drink. If one is extra pleased or grieved he gets an extra 'drop of drink'. It is drunk by all, rich and poor, old and young, parson and cobbler, made extra strong for weddings, Christmas and feasts, and sometimes warmed and sugared and rum put in. People have no idea a person's health would be safe without it, and some Methodist class-leaders say they could not lead their classes without getting a mugpot of drink. . .[22]

Thus drinking could be an essential form of neighbourliness or an extension of the exploitation practised by employers and merchants. A general attack on the consumption of alcohol as being a root cause of poverty among the working people could hardly be acceptable to the people themselves.

The workers in the industrial districts were acutely aware of the effects of falling wages and prices on their ability to care for their children and to supervise their education. In 1838 the Barnsley Chartists, a group of weavers, miners and shoemakers, appealed in their manifesto to their 'fellow-workmen':

. . . have you ever felt those glowing pleasures that rise in a parent's mind at seeing his little child neatly attired with its basket in its hand, and with a cheerful gait, repairing to a place of instruction, where its little mind would be expanded and stored with profitable learning? Did you ever feel that holy pride, that parental tenderness, that inward adoring of God for having made you a father which arises in a father's breast at hearing his little boy read the Scriptures, or any other pleasing book to his little brothers and sisters? . . . if you have, can you ever after allow the idea to enter your minds that others of your children and those of your friends and kindred are doomed by poverty to be brought up like the wild ass's colt, and as ignorant as the Indian's brood, and to become the dupes and slaves and victims of their oppressors, who go prowling about like a wolf after its prey to rob your daughters of their virtue and chastity?[23]

The motif recurs throughout Chartist writing. The women of Newcastle complained that '. . . our husbands are over wrought, our houses half furnished, our families ill-fed and our children uneducated

– the fear of want hangs over our heads; the scorn of the rich is pointed towards us; the brand of slavery is on our kindred, and we feel the degradation'.[24] The Chartists – of all sections – wanted the right to supervise their own children's education, and certainly did not look to the middle classes to take over the function for them. Temperance, self-education, community improvement by cooperative and mutual organisations, were all important ideas found among the Chartists. The individual who got ahead and pulled himself out of the community was the exception, and his account must be viewed with caution. Robert Lowery and William Lovett are two writers whose work has been important in the recovery of the history of Chartism. They were, however, exceptional not only in the range of ability which they possessed, but also in the motives which drove them forward. At least as typical of the Chartists, and probably much more so, were figures who have left no apologia, like the shoemaker Abram Hanson of Elland[25] or the other shoemaker, Thomas, who accompanied Lowery to France in 1838. This man taught himself to speak several European languages, and spoke them well enough to travel easily – indeed, Lowery records that in France he was taken for a Frenchman. But to Lowery's indignation, he did not use these abilities to 'better himself'. 'He lacked energy and ambition' was Lowery's comment.[26] Other Chartists who refused opportunities to 'better themselves' included the silk weaver John West and tailor Robert Crowe, who were both offered the chance of using their abilities in paid positions by members of middle-class professions, but whose radicalism, rather than the lack of 'energy and ambition', kept them at their trades and in their own class.

Chartism was a political movement, demanding political rights and political participation. It was not, however, one among many such organisations. If we except the Owenite movement, whose claim to be called political is dubious, there were no other political organisations in which working people could take part. They were either Chartists or not concerned with political action, accepting that this was something exclusively reserved for members of the higher classes. An organisation for the achievement of political rights for the lower orders was without precedent on a national scale, and it produced its own unique forms of organisation. It is dangerous, therefore, to project backwards later political developments, and too readily to assess the Chartists simply as precursors of the modern labour movement – as dangerous in the organisational assumptions that this implies as in the political and social.

Chartism was important to its participants for the social and community life it offered as well as for its political programme. Only Disraeli among contemporary upper-class commentators recognised the extent to which Chartism was a way of life. The memories of former Chartists, however, abound in such recollections. Writing of a dull period in local activity, when members were leaving the Association and when attendance at meetings and lectures was low, Benjamin Wilson recalled that 'the rent of the room, the printing and posting of bills, together with the travelling expenses and small remuneration of the lecturer had all to be paid by us, and this kind of business had to be done for one thing or another for a good many years, yet no part I have taken since I became acquainted with the movement gave me so much pleasure as at this time for the memory of those men will ever be kept dear to me'.[27] This quality of association was not that of an out-group of sectarians, but was based on local community and occupational ties. Such information as we have suggests that in any area the Chartists were mainly members of the dominant trade of their district, adhered to the main stream of religious organisations in their area, and took part in the cultural and educational activities in which their neighbours were involved.

The question of religious affiliations illustrates in important ways the social nature of the Chartist movement. There was no specific Chartist religious outlook, although a general Christian rhetoric can be found throughout the movement. There were always many Chartists who were opposed to established religious institutions, and some responded to questions about their religious affiliation with replies like 'has his own ideas about religion', which may be taken to indicate agnosticism or scepticism, but in the main there seem to have been Chartists in most of the groups and sects. In any case, religious differences were rarely divisive. Of the 73 prisoners questioned in 1840-1, 9 professed no religion and the rest disclosed between them 15 different affiliations. The largest number were the 26 who belonged to the established church, a figure that may well have masked a certain number of sceptics. 15 were Methodists of various kinds, 7 were Baptists and 6 Catholics. The rest belonged to a variety of smaller sects. A similar spread of allegiance is to be found in the reports of baptisms of young Chartists, which took place in Catholic, Anglican, non-conformist and democratic chapels. Adhesion to Christian congregations, moreover, did not seem to impose any restriction on the violence of Chartist rhetoric, and it is noticeable that a great deal of the most fiery language was to be heard from Chartist pulpits. Arthur O'Neil preached in his chapel at Birmingham about 'The imbecility of the ravenous

Hanoverian hyaenas who live upon the flesh and blood of the industrious millions'.[28] He wrote to McCrae, the Scottish Chartist preacher and schoolmaster:

> I am delighted with what you state in your reference to the progress of Chartist Christianity (which is primitive Christianity) against the long-faced hypocritical pharisees of the day, whose religion consists in making long prayers, devouring widows' houses and preaching slavery to the poor under the name of humility, and dutiful submission to the 'powers that be', which powers, they would fain make us believe, are 'ordained by God', although the sleek vagabonds well know that, without the devil and his works, such 'powers' would never have been heard of. By all means get rid of the 'black slugs'; by all means protect the consciences and the cabbages of the poor from the 'black slugs'.[29]

In some districts Chartists set up their own chapels, or radical preachers gathered around them their own congregations. In this, as in other activities which were only marginally political, they were often preserving customs and institutions which were under attack by the forces making for conformity and respectability in early Victorian Britain.

The popular theatre was another institution which was usually defended by the Chartists, although it was frowned on by many contemporary moralists. One newspaper editor wrote:

> If the march of intellect has done nothing else, it has well-nigh marched the players out of the English counties. . . Few respectable people are ever found within the walls of county theatres. When any are there, they avoid recognition – a fair criterion by which to estimate how much additional respectability they obtain within the walls of the playhouse. . .[30]

Throughout Britain the gulf between the popular theatre and the small enclaves of the fashionable theatre in a few large cities was immense and was increasing. In Cheltenham Spa, where the Theatre Royal was burnt to the ground in 1839, the Evangelical anti-Chartist incumbent, Francis Close, succeeded in preventing its rebuilding or replacement. Chartist W. E. Adams recalled that as an apprentice in the town he spent his pocket money after the burning of the theatre on performances by travelling companies who performed in booths in inn yards.[31] Although there were some Chartists who shared the Evangelical dislike of the stage, the great majority seem to have supported the popular theatre. Dr Arthur Wade, vicar of Warwick and delegate to the first Chartist Convention, spoke and agitated in support of the unlicensed theatre in London. In many ways the battle with the licensing regulations paralleled that of the unstamped press agitation.[32]

Throughout Britain Chartists performed and promoted plays as well as attending the theatres. Fund-raising performances of the trial of Robert Emmett were especially popular. In the winter of 1839-40 these were given in the Nottingham area, the West Riding of Yorkshire and in several parts of Scotland. Democratic dramas like *William Tell* were put on by local groups. Thomas Cooper filled the theatre in Leicester for two nights with a performance of *Hamlet* with himself in the lead, while the egregious John Watkins wrote a five-act drama on the trial and condemnation of John Frost, which was more to be praised for its intentions than either its dramatic power or its historical accuracy. But just as the unstamped press had brought together the radical and the cheap theatrical press, so the tradition of popular drama remained a radical cause for many of the Chartists.

W. E. Adams became a liberal newspaper editor in the latter part of the nineteenth century. In his autobiography he presents a picture of a childhood and youth spent in a radical family which was humane and decent, but very far from 'respectable'. He recalled the street games played by the children of Cheltenham, the un-liturgical carols and mumming plays with which Christmas was celebrated, the Morris dancers at Whitsuntide and the sweeps' Jack-in-the-Green on May Day. His washerwomen grandmother and aunts who brought him up were staunch Chartists, as was the grandfather of his fellow-apprentice, Thomas Willey. Willey, whom Adams refers to as 'our local Catnach', was a printer of ballads and broadsheets who, as well as publishing anti-Poor-Law ballads and Chartist manifestos, produced the last dying speeches of all criminals executed at Gloucester – 'generally', as Adams recalled, 'the same speech altered to suit the name and circumstances of the new culprit' and 'invariably adorned with a ghastly woodcut'. Among the traditional ballads and nursery rhymes which have survived with his imprint are to be found nationalist songs dating from the days of the United Irishmen, presumably particularly aimed at those Irish who came to the annual Cheltenham races.[33]

In the towns and villages of Britain thousands of anonymous men and women organised the Chartist movement, using traditional forms of processions, carnivals, theatrical performances, camp meetings, sermons and services to put across the message of the six points. Flags, banners, caps of liberty, scarves, sashes and rosettes appeared on public occasions. Slogans from the Bible, from literature and from earlier radical movements decorated the banners and placards they carried. Hymns and songs were written and sung, poems were declaimed. Every aspect of the religious and cultural life of the communities was brought into service to press home the Chartist message. The result was a movement whose local characteristics were determined by the nature of the communities in which the branches were organised, but in which a national programme and a national rhetoric were able to hold together the disparate local components, and to provide a sense of national purpose which was its most important element.

CHAPTER SEVEN

The Women

At its height, Chartism was a movement which involved whole communities. Families took part, men, women and children demonstrated shared values. In the townships and villages of the manufacturing districts there is ample evidence in all the accounts and reports of the active participation of women. The leaders who appealed to the movement throughout the country, following in the tradition established by Henry Hunt, made a particular point of appealing to the women as well as to the men.

> Let every man, woman and child sign the petition. . .
> Go on, good men! Go on, virtuous women! . . . we are engaged in the cause of justice which is the cause of God. Sign the petition![1]

– wrote Feargus O'Connor from the first Convention. John Collins reported to the same Convention that of Birmingham signatures to the petition, 24,000 were those of women.[2] Women's radical associations were soon publishing addresses and manifestos. Elizabeth Neesom signed one from the London Female Democratic Association in May 1839, making a point that was often repeated up and down the country:

> To those who may be, or may appear to be, surprised that females should be daring enough to interfere with politics; to them we simply say, that as it is a female that assumes to rule this nation in defiance of the universal rights of man and woman, we assert in accordance with the rights of all, and acknowledging the sovereignty of the people our rights as free women (or women determined to be free) to rule ourselves. . .[3]

Although they seldom spoke on public platforms, these women presented banners, made and presented gifts to visiting speakers, and invariably marched in the great processions and demonstrations, usually at the head. Yet their presence has been virtually ignored by Chartism's historians.[4]

There are certain obvious reasons for this rather surprising omission. One is, simply, that the rank and file of the movement has still not been closely studied for most parts of the country. The extent of Chartism was so great that historians have been compelled to concentrate on what appear to be the most important characteristics of a national movement, essentially therefore on leaders, journalists and those involved in one or two major confrontations with authority. Since women were not among such people, they have not been studied. Most local studies have reproduced at a local level the framework set up by the historians of the movement nationally, and have therefore usually overlooked important features. The second reason is that the difficulty of tracing individual Chartists is far greater for the women than for the men. Men's occupations were given in certain circumstances. If they were arrested or imprisoned more information sometimes came to light. Women were almost invariably recorded merely by their marital status, and were, in any case, rarely arrested. The named Chartist women who have been traced are mainly members of Chartist families. This suggests that to appear in public, or to allow her name to be published, a woman needed the protection which membership of a well-known family gave. Women of all classes were much more liable to harassment and embarrassment if they took part in too much open public activity than were men. So the majority must, like the majority of the Chartist crowd of both sexes, remain anonymous.

There is, however, a third and more important reason for the lack of subsequent interest in these Chartist women, and this lies in the preoccupations of historians. In the later nineteenth century, the presence of women in a movement, or at any occasion, was seen as somehow lessening the seriousness of the event. The early historians, from Gammage to the Fabians, were concerned to present Chartism as a serious political movement. They played down all aspects, such as social occasions, tea parties, Sunday Schools, processions and other picturesque or ritualistic elements which belonged to an older tradition, contrasting them unfavourably with the rational and modernising aspects of the movement. In the same way, most contemporary observers, with the notable exception of Disraeli, saw the irrational and the decorative, in which they mostly included the female, parts of the movement as lessening and demeaning it. Historians of women's movements, on the other hand, have discounted the Chartist women since they have not perceived them as being specifically feminist.

The presence of women among the Chartist membership and the Chartist crowd is an important fact about the movement. It would seem to indicate that divisions of sex and gender did not, any more than divisions of religious adhesion and ethnicity, inhibit the prevailing class loyalties, at any rate in the earlier years of the movement.

The pattern of women's participation is interesting. I have stressed the early years of the movement, and it does seem that when the agitation against the Poor Law became absorbed into the wider agitation, and when, indeed, some of the worst predictions about the administration of the new law were not fulfilled, some of the steam went out of the women's protests. From some time around the middle of the forties women seem to become less prominent in Chartist demonstrations and organisations. Although there were women's localities of the National Charter Association, and women members of ordinary localities, the number of purely female radical and democratic societies declined dramatically. So also did the participation of women in demonstrations and outdoor meetings. Whilst a few outstanding women emerge as lecturers, women in the crowd seem to have declined in numbers.

The reasons for women's withdrawal from politics remain unclear. Probably a combination of different reasons affecting different groups added up to the overall picture. The rationalisation of the crowd, the reduction of the role of the mass demonstration, the replacement of participatory politics by the politics of committee and representative delegations, all certainly limited the role of women, as they limited that of migratory and unskilled workers. The change in the tactics of the authorities in handling crowds may also have kept some women away from meetings and demonstrations. The decade of the 1840s saw the introduction of police forces in many areas under the provisions of the Rural Police Act of 1839. It may seem contradictory to suggest that women, who had been notoriously defiant of authority in the crowd politics of the food riot and the anti-Poor-Law movement, were more affected by the presence of a local police force than were the men, but there is no doubt that the introduction of local forces did alter the nature of the supervision exercised, and it could be that mass demonstrations began to assume a generally rougher nature. The photograph of the crowd on Kennington Common in 1848 – the only surviving photograph of a Chartist demonstration – seems to suggest that very few women were present.

Changes in the attitudes of women towards political action were often brought about more by changes in the style of politics than by changes in political programmes, and they are therefore difficult to locate precisely and still more difficult to quantify. For one thing, the meeting-place for most Chartist activities, as for trade and friendly society meetings, was the inn or alehouse. But even in the early years, some women's groups were uncomfortable in such surroundings. Changes in drinking habits were certainly taking place among women. In Nottingham, for example, there was a long tradition of women's trade and friendly societies; the women there took an active, public and often turbulent part in street demonstrations, and set up their own organisation in 1838. But even here they were pleased to be able to move from their original meeting-place in the Hope and Anchor Inn to the Chartist meeting rooms in Halifax Place when these were acquired.[5] Women's groups and mixed groups that continued to meet in alehouses may have found their membership dropping away with the growth of temperance among Chartists throughout the forties.

Money spent on ale and tobacco by the men must always have been a point of contention in the working-class family. Benjamin Wilson, recording his own adoption of temperance and non-smoking in 1849, associated it characteristically with an anecdote about 'A politician in Leeds, a moulder by trade, who used to visit public houses to discuss politics, and one night whilst speaking on Lord John Russell, who, he said was unfit to govern the country, was interrupted by his wife entering and suggesting that he should take his money home to her and his starving children, make his own home as comfortable as he possibly could, and then find fault with Lord John Russell. . .'[6] Political leaders who advocated meeting in premises other than public houses were welcomed by the women. One of the few women's groups to surface in the late Chartist years wrote to Ernest Jones's *Notes to the People* in 1851 supporting his campaign to 'remove the Charter from the Pothouse'. . .

> . . . did our brothers but admit our rights to the enjoyment of those political privileges they are striving for, they would find an accession of advocates in the female sex who would not only raise the Charter from those dens of infamy and vice from which so many of us have to suffer, but would with womanly pride strive to erase that stigma, which by the folly of our brothers has been cast on Chartism, not only by exercising their influence out of doors, but by teaching their children a good political education. This, sir, will never be done while men continue to advocate or meet in pot-houses spending their money and debarring us from a share in their political freedom.[7]

Once, it seems, the urgency of the attack on the new Poor Law had subsided, and traditional forms of protest, the procession, the mass demonstration, even the riot, became less frequent, the wives of the Chartists dropped into the background, leaving the routine work of running the localities of the National Charter Association to their menfolk. The NCA was open equally to men and women, and many women certainly took out membership cards. In 1843 the *English Chartist Circular* said that 'hundreds of women had enrolled in the NCA'.[8] But information about these women Chartists is very scarce.

Among the papers confiscated from Thomas Cooper when he was arrested in 1842 are a few class lists for the Leicester district. Some of the classes included women members – class 69, for example, consisted of George Caunt, Dorothy Caunt, George Bott, John Stanton, Elizabeth Stanton, John Whitmore, William Dalton, John Slater, Robert Green, William Wigfield and Joseph Clarke. The ratio of women to men is low – few classes have more than one woman member – and in any case the sample is very small. But paid-up membership of the NCA was not necessarily a measure of support for Chartism, particularly amongst women, who may have felt that a husband's subscription was enough for both.

Support for the idea of women's votes was always widespread amongst the Chartists. In 1842 John La Mont suggested that it was time to 'suggest . . . such changes as the probable extension of the Suffrage to sane minded males of 18 years of age instead of 21, already provided by our Charter; and the enfranchisement of females – notwithstanding the amount of blackguardism, folly and coercion which will be arrayed against this extension by the aristocratic *debauchés*'.[9] In a famous footnote in his autobiography, William Lovett stated that 'the first draft of the Bill, afterwards called the People's Charter, made provision for the suffrage of women, but as several members thought its adoption in the Bill might retard the suffrage of men, it was unfortunately left out'.[10] Lovett's memory does not seem to have been quite accurate here, however. What actually appears to have happened is that the Charter was circulated to all the working men's associations and other radical groups with whom the LWMA had contacts, and then re-published with some of the proposed amendments. It was at this stage that the proposal to include women's suffrage was put forward, presumably by groups from the provinces. The LWMA commented:

> Among the suggestions we received for improving this Charter is one for embracing women among the possessors of the franchise. Against this reasonable proposition we have no just argument to adduce but only to express our fears of entertaining it, lest the false estimate man entertains for this half of the human family may cause his ignorance and prejudice to be enlisted to retard the progress of his own freedom.[11]

The London Working Men's Association did not include women among its own members, and in London it was the seceders from the Association, Harney, Ireland and Neesom, who actively encouraged women's organisations, Mrs Neesom being perhaps the leading woman Chartist in London.

Two pamphlets supporting women's rights were written by prominent Chartists. Both proposed the extension of the franchise to include unmarried and widowed women. R. J. Richardson, whose *Rights of Woman* was written whilst he was a prisoner in Lancaster Castle, presented a strong case for women's participation in politics and blamed the men in the movement for not paying sufficient attention to political and social rights of women. For him, as for most of the Chartists who mentioned the subject, no serious questions of philosophy were involved. The right of women to vote was as obvious as the right of working men, and based on the same principles:

> 'it is a duty imperative on women to interfere in political affairs'. I think, nay I believe, that God ordained woman 'to temper man'. I believe from this reason, that she ought to partake of his councils, public and private, that she ought to share in the making of laws for the government of the commonwealth, in the same manner as she would join with her husband in the councils of his household.[12]

The vote, however, should go to unmarried and widowed women only. The sentiments he expressed in his concluding paragraph – 'bad laws will never cease to be, nor wicked legislators cease to rule until every man of twenty-one years of age and every woman of twenty,* obtain . . . a voice in the election of those whom reason and honesty qualify for law-makers. . .[13] – were qualified by the footnote 'Spinsters and Widows'. John Watkins, the other Chartist who addressed himself to the specific question of women's rights, wrote in his *Address to the Women of England*: 'So far from being excluded from taking part in politics, women ought to be allowed to vote; not wives – for they and their husbands are one, or ought to be as one – but maids and widows. . .'[14]

The *Scottish Chartist Circular* included many appeals to women to join in Chartist activities, and stressed the importance of their educative and social function.

> By *politics* we mean the *science of human progression*; and this requires the elevation of woman as well as man in the scale of society – the increase of her happiness as well as his – the social equality of woman with man, as a man with his fellow – and the improvement of the physical, moral and intellectual condition of all individuals which compose the great human family.[15]

The politicians of the 'new move' included women's suffrage among their aims, although they had no women among their members or their sponsors. But by the early 1840s it seems to have been one of the main reforms which most Chartists expected to follow from the gaining of the

Charter. It is interesting, however, that most of the references and discussion of the question come from men. The women seem much more concerned with immediate issues such as the operation of the Poor Law, the low level of wages, or the threat of the press gang. When the suffrage is mentioned it is almost as an afterthought. One of the most vivid of the female *Addresses*, that of Ashton-under-Lyne, an area whose women were well to the fore in the action of the early Chartists, began with a list of grievances connected with the state of their homes and the suffering of their families, but went on: 'we are determined that no man shall ever enjoy our hands, our hearts, or share our beds, that will not stand forward as the advocate of the rights of man, and as the determined enemy of the damnable New Poor Law . . . we do not despair of yet seeing intelligence the necessary qualification for voting, and then sisters, we shall be placed in our proper position in society, and enjoy the elective franchise as well as our kinsmen'.[16]

Many Chartists made what was perhaps an obvious point for the time, that England was ruled by a queen and yet women had no political rights. James Hyslop was a Scottish weaver, living and working in Lancashire, who regularly sent back political tracts to his native Wigtownshire. He annotated them with remarks and comments, including this point, that 'If a woman can rule, surely women could and should have the vote'.[17]

The question of the vote for women was not only of less importance to the Chartists than the vote for working men; in some ways it could be seen as standing in the way of the working-class franchise. If women had been granted the vote on the same terms as men, the voting strength of the propertied classes would have been strengthened. Writers and journalists hostile to universal suffrage used the example of propertied women to attack the Chartists' arguments – pointing out, for example, that Miss Coutts paid very much more tax than any working man, and yet did not have the vote.[18] No Chartist would ever have put the question of women's franchise before the Charter, and a great many, including many of the women, do not seem to have put it as a very high priority afterwards. The women at this stage did not see their interests as being in opposition to those of their husbands – or if they did, they did not see any solution to such conflict in political action. Chartist women seem for the most part to have worked together with their husbands, sons and brothers in a joint opposition to oppression perceived as coming from employers and administrators. Those Owenites who attacked marriage and the family met with little response among working women.[19]

What perhaps did divide the women from the men increasingly as the decade of the forties continued was the question of temperance that has already been mentioned, combined with increasing activity by chapel and Sunday school movements. The women who took part in the demonstrations of 1842 were reported as singing hymns as they marched,[20] and many accounts of Chartist camp meetings in the early days show a combination of political and religious rhetoric. At a joint demonstration of the Sheffield and Barnsley Chartists late in 1839, William Thornton preached a sermon, hymns were sung, prayers were offered for the success of the Chartist movement and tea was provided for the 'females, who attended in great numbers'. 'The moon lighted them on their journey home, and the silence of the road was broken by the singing of hymns. The countenances of the people wore the impress of peace and gladness. . .'[21]

As the urgency of their situation seemed to relax, with the relaxation of the tensions associated with the new Poor Law and the increase in the regularity of employment in the mid-forties, many women turned towards the chapel rather than the political groupings. The foundation in 1840 of the National Charter Association with its national executive, weekly membership payments and elected officers marked the beginning of a generally more structured kind of working-class organisation. Trade unions of the 'new model' kind emerge in the mid-forties; cooperative stores with large memberships and committees also appear at this time. Organisations like these relied upon a membership that could attend meetings regularly and pay an assured weekly contribution. Women and unskilled workers would find this most difficult. Certainly the typical working-class organisation of the third quarter of the nineteenth century was an all-male one, whether trade union branch, mechanics' institute, friendly society or mutual improvement society.

Much of the activity in the later years of the decade centred round the Chartist Land Company. Here again, the subscribers needed to be able to contribute a regular weekly sum, and of course a subscription by a man would have led to an allotment to which his whole family would have moved, so that there was no reason for man and wife to hold separate shares. The vast majority of names in the surviving lists are of men, although a few women had shares on their own account. The 189 female members in Lancashire and the West Riding who had their own shares gave as their occupations:

Housewife (or Domestic duties)	35
No trade	39
Spinster	26
Housekeeper	16
Servant	14
Minor	8
Widow	7
Innkeeper	6
Sempstress	5
Dressmaker	5
Cardroom hand	4
Weaver	3
Shopkeeper	3
Labourer, Woolcomber, Rover, Overlooker	2 of each
Draper, Milliner, Bonnet-maker, Cook, Confectioner, Baker, Tripe Cleaner, Piecer, Tuler, Farmer	1 of each

This list is less informative than a similar list of men would be.[22] The great majority of these women do not indicate their occupations – even the description 'no trade' does not make clear whether these are working women who have no particular skill, or whether they are women living at home and not earning. Housewife as a description may be taken to indicate a married woman, but the description 'domestic' or 'domestic duties' may be used to describe either a married woman or a daughter housekeeping for a parent. Are the housekeepers paid servants, or is this another way of describing the woman who works full-time at keeping house for a member of her family? The fact that all these women have independent shares in the Land Company suggests some source of income other than a husband's wage, but for the majority this is all we can say. Those who do list trades list the main occupations of self-supporting women in working-class communities; but there is a notable shortage of full-time textile operatives in two districts largely given over to cotton and stuff manufacture. It may, however, be assumed that some of the twenty-six spinsters were textile operatives.

The comparatively minute number of independent women shareholders in the Land Company is mirrored by the almost total absence of women in the early committee and shareholders' lists of the cooperative societies which started up in so many Chartist areas in the mid-forties. It remains something of a mystery why more women did not take part in their founding and running. Many of the active Chartist women had been shopkeepers and innkeepers, and could have brought a great deal of practical experience to these ventures. The fact remains, however, that they do not appear in leading roles. The co-ops could not have succeeded without the women's participation in the role of purchasers, but the leadership and organisation of these consumer stores was as firmly in the hands of the men as was the organisation of the trade unions.

We end the general consideration of the role of women in the local Chartist movement, therefore, with many questions unanswered. Their presence in the early years of the movement cannot be questioned. In the opposition to the Poor Law, in the early demonstrations, processions and social organisation of all kinds they played a central part. Somewhere around the mid-forties, however, the nature of their participation changes. The later years of Chartism see the appearance of a number of women lecturers, a small number, but more than were around in the early years. The number of women in their audiences and in the Chartist crowd seem to diminish, the rough confrontational action which occurred in the early years, especially in 1839 and 1842, disappears. This is partly a change in Chartism itself. The desire for a rational and orderly image led many groups to abandon mass demonstrations and popular street activity. Feargus O'Connor wrote in 1843:

> Much indeed of what was called enthusiasm has apparently subsided – the glare of the torch has gone out. Processions and demonstrations, instead of being necessary 'to keep up the steam', are abandoned with the feeling that they are but little worth – and flags and banners perhaps may yield to what seems to be a general necessity. Be it so – they have done their work – and well![23]

Although this may have been a political reflection in support of a particular argument, nevertheless it represented a trend in Chartist thought and organisation towards more structured, less open and 'spontaneous' politics. Bronterre O'Brien, by 1847, was dismissing this older style as incompatible with 'true Chartism'. In a typical attack on O'Connor, he accused him of taking good care 'that all the public should know of Chartism was through the medium of torchlight meetings, and senseless processions two or three miles long, and demonstrations of tens and hundreds of thousands of people, congregated they knew not why, and dismissed as impotent and ignorant as they came, and thousands of pounds of hard-earned money squandered upon flags and banners, and coaches and triumphal cars, – and such like trumpery.'[24] But the large demonstration and the flamboyant procession gave the opportunity for all members of the community to participate. Women's banners were to be seen in all the processions and demonstrations, and women themselves were an important presence.

The dropping out of the women may also have been symptomatic of changes in the work and in the social life of the industrial districts. Many of the female crowd members were workers in the early factories and workshops – glove-makers, button-makers, lace workers and cotton operatives. Towards the end of the forties many of these trades were becoming rationalised, hours of work were being limited for women and young children, and some hitherto exclusively female occupations were being undertaken by men and boys. Among the artisan trades – and most of the named Chartist women were members of artisan families or the wives of small shopkeepers – work was moving into workshops and factories and out of the home, even where mechanisation was still delayed. Since most working people of all levels spent the greater part of their time at work, the major preoccupations in their conversation and in their leisure were related to work and workmates. As long as the place of work was the home, women and children shared these preoccupations with the men to some degree, whether they themselves worked or not. Women were able to help out at their husband's trade, and they were sometimes allowed to inherit even an apprenticed trade if their husband died. Thomas Cooper's mother inherited her husband's trade of dyer,[25] and John Bedford Leno spoke of the help his wife gave him in his trade as a printer: 'How she laboured at the press and assisted me in the work of my printing office, with a child in her arms, I have no space to tell, nor . . . the many ways she contributed to my good fortune.'[26] A carpet weaver's poem about the Christmas rush says:

The 'missus' the bobbins must 'fettle',
  Neglecting her household affairs;
The 'Draw-boy' must show his best mettle;
  While I scuffle down for 'repairs'.[27]

Even in the most depressed trades, as long as they remained attached to the household, men and women worked together. Many of the Bradford Chartist women would have been from the families of woolcombers, the predominant trade in the district. A contemporary described the last years of the hand-combers.

. . . The whole family of sometimes six or eight, both male and female, worked together round a combpot heated by charcoal. . . As for their houses, they were necessarily filthy, it being impossible for the good wives to keep them clean, reeking as they were with oil and other abominations had they been at liberty to make the attempt, but they had too often to stand at the pad-posts and work from six o'clock in the morning till ten at night like their husbands. . .[28]

Changes in the nature and organisation of Chartist activities, changes in the work-place, and changes in the family nature of work all help to explain the changes in make-up between the early and later Chartist crowd. These changes did not happen suddenly or uniformly, and they are not enough to account for the almost total disappearance of women from working-class organisations in the immediately post-Chartist period. There must also have been changes of perception on the part of both sexes. The 'modernisation' and 'rationalisation' of popular politics led to men assuming a different view of the 'woman question'. It is perhaps significant that when articles appear in Ernest Jones's *Labourer* or Bronterre's new *National Reformer* on the subject of women in the late forties, either they take the form of revelations from enquiries into women's labour, particularly the 1842 *Commission on the Work of Women and Children in Mines*, or they are written in a thoroughly middle-class manner, complaining that women are taught only to embroider and sing and not to exercise their minds, or even that a lack of female education lowers the quality of domestic servants. It seems hardly possible that a Chartist journal could publish such statements as the following account of domestic servants:

They are constantly about us in our dwellings; and our domestic comforts almost entirely depend upon them. They tend our children and guard our property. . . . Domestic servants are, in a great measure, the models of all children; and, if vitiated or ignorant, they will inevitably become contaminated by the contact. . . [29]

A year earlier O'Brien's readers had been apostrophised:

As long as you continue to rear up your daughters as mere dolls for admiration; as long as you are content to educate them after the present doltish system, with a little dancing, a little French, a little sampler work and other little etceteras . . . with a great deal of attention to curls, the looking-glass, and fine clothes . . . so long will you find [man] content with his supremacy. . .[30]

One wonders how the woolcombers' and shoemakers' wives of the Chartist areas received such addresses. Certainly neither paper shows the easy familiarity with the women of the manufacturing districts and the radical organisations which characterised the rhetoric of Vincent, Harney and O'Connor in the early years.

But perhaps the women too were gaining a changed perception of themselves and of their social role? 'Respectability' has been much talked of as a concept governing social behaviour in the Victorian period. In certain aspects of working-class life there can be no doubt that changes took place around the middle years of the century.[31] Such activities as smoking and drinking, indulged in when funds permitted by both sexes in the early industrial communities, became increasingly frowned on as relaxations for women. The growth of temperance, the increasing attempt to reclaim the working population for organised Christianity, and the spread of 'provided' education for both sexes, all helped to impose a less rough, more domestic, more genteel image of female behaviour. Women became a proportionately smaller part of the full-time workforce in all trades but domestic service, an occupation which expanded considerably throughout the nineteenth century. The qualifications for a good servant, of course, included an awareness of the canons of respectability which would not have been required in a woolcomber or a glovemaker.

Perhaps the last occasion on which a female Chartist crowd behaved in a 'traditional' manner was on the occasion of the visit to Britain of the Austrian general, Heynau. Chartist journals protested against the official welcome given to the man who had suppressed the 1848 revolutions in Europe, and had earned a reputation for brutality as well as for reaction. The high point of popular protest was the famous incident which occurred when the general was paying a visit to Barclay and Perkins' brewery, when the draymen and other workers attacked him physically and forced him to run for his life. All observers commented on the part played in his discomfiture by the women brewery workers, and *Reynolds's Weekly* described with delight how 'a large portion of females took part in this glorious manifestation, and tore the fellow's grisly moustachios until he roared again and again with pain and fury'.[32] Clearly, as late as 1850, radical women were still capable of direct and immediate action.

In spite, however, of the problems of getting close to individual women in the Chartist crowd, there is plenty of evidence of their presence and of their actions, as groups as well as individuals, particularly in the early years. Many Chartist autobiographies refer to the part played in the passing on of radical ideas by women. James Watson's mother read Cobbett, Benjamin Wilson's aunt was a Chartist, W. E. Adams, whose parents had left home to look for work, was brought up as a thorough-going radical by his washerwoman grandmother and her daughters. John Vallance, linen weaver and leader of the Barnsley Chartists, was another of the many radicals who was brought up by a widowed mother, who had passed on her own radicalism. She had appeared as early as 1819, on a platform at a meeting in protest against the Peterloo massacre.[33] John Bedford Leno, Uxbridge Chartist and later a poet and publisher, recalled that he had received his earliest education from his mother.

> The sources of my mother's contribution [to the family income] were needlework and a dame school. I am afraid her scholastic qualifications would fail to commend her to the School Board authorities of to-day. In those days, however, a little education among the extremely poor went a long way, and as all her scholars were of tender years, the chief thing required from her was the power to interest them in all she professed to teach, and this power she possessed to a remarkable extent. Moreover she had full control over her temper, and no matter how dull or stupid the child she was teaching, she never impressed or advertised to her scholar a sense of her impatience or weariness. To my mother I attribute my love of learning, and under her care I made considerable progress.[34]

In Ashton-under-Lyne, perhaps the most radical and Chartist of all the factory towns, many young people were introduced to radicalism through the celebrations organised by the women on the anniversary of the Peterloo demonstration.[35] All these women worked in communities which were small enough for them to be known, and to spread their ideas through their families and through their daily work. This may well have been another important difference between the Chartist period and the later years of the century. In the politics of a township or large village, women could take part in meetings and demonstrations because they were well-known to most of the other participants. In a large city women would have been more liable to be harassed or insulted by strangers. Certainly the strength of the women's participation was in their own communities. When Henry Vincent toured the country in 1838 and 1839 on behalf of the Working Men's Association, he was welcomed by the turning out of whole populations. He wrote enthusiastic letters home, describing his experiences, and in particular commenting on the interest and enthusiasm of women. In some places, as at Bath, he organised meetings for women only, at which hundreds, even thousands, attended. He helped to set up female radical associations in many districts, and when he was arrested in 1839, much of his support, moral and financial, came from women's organisations.[36]

By May 1839 the women's presence was sufficient to elicit a comment from the *Annual Register*, whose account of the great Kersal Moor demonstration of that year found 'the presence of several female political associations'[37] the most noteworthy thing about it. In a letter written from prison to the women of England and South Wales, Vincent started with the same point: 'The formation of political societies amongst the women may be justly ranked as one of the most important features in the present political movement; for on no other occasion have women been aroused to a just sense of their social and political importance. . .'[38]

Well over a hundred female radical associations have been recorded in the first few years of the movement, and there is strong evidence of independent activity by women in centres where no separate organisation seems to have existed. In Halifax, for example, no separate women's organisation is mentioned until the late forties, but the women were prominent in the social and political activity of the radicals. In the neighbouring village of Elland a female association dated from before the Charter, and at least one female friendly society donated money to the first Chartist Convention.[39] Here one of the leaders was Elizabeth Hanson, described by her husband as a Xanthippe to his Socrates, and others were wives of leading Chartists.[40] The group formed in the winter of 1837-8 as a Female Anti-Poor-Law Association, and held a series of public meetings which received some coverage in the northern press. In February 1838 the Elland women met Thomas Power, the unpopular Poor Law Commissioner who was attempting to establish the new regulations in Yorkshire, and 'rolled him in the snow'.[41] They organised a petition against the new law, and argued their case in the press with considerable sophistication and verve.

Another West Riding town with a long record of female radicalism was Bradford. Georg Weerth, the German writer, was impressed in the 1840s by 'a wonderfully pleasant people! Robust Yorkshire wenches in colourful clothes, in lacquered shoes with small straw hats on their heads'[42] when he met them at a radical fair. He considered that 'the clothes of the girls who worked in the worsted mills were, at that time, far better than those of the German mill girls'.[43] The Bradford Female Radical Association, formed in March 1839, included workers from the factories as well as woolcombers, weavers and wives and daughters of male Chartists in other trades.[44] It had a continuous existence until at least the mid-forties, changing its organisation to conform with the NCA system after 1841. When a meeting of delegates was held in York on the occasion of the release of O'Connor from York Castle in the late summer of 1841, the stirring address issued by the delegates was signed by, among others, Elizabeth Simpson and Elizabeth Ellis of

Bradford.[45] This was a rare example, for few women attended mixed delegate meetings, even in years when there were a great many active women's groups in existence. Like the other early groups, the Bradford women began their activity with agitation against the Poor Law, and the raising of money and support for Joseph Rayner Stephens after his arrest. They met monthly, hearing talks and lectures from women and men speakers, and they started groups in some of the outlying districts. In August 1839, the *Northern Star* reported: 'The female radicals of the Bradford district, amounting to upward of 600, walked in procession through the principal streets headed by a band of music and banners . . . at the head of the procession there was carried by a woman a large printed board with the words "exclusive dealing". . .'[46]

The organisation of exclusive dealing to put pressure on shopkeepers to vote for radical candidates or to donate to Chartist funds was a job for which women were particularly suited. As the family marketers their support was essential for this activity, and in most of the active Chartist areas the support of the women could be deduced, even if we had no other evidence, from the widespread success of this tactic.

The Bradford women did not shun publicity, and we have plenty of evidence of their existence as a group. Nevertheless, it is difficult to find out much about them as individuals. Some, like Elizabeth Ellis, were related to leading men Chartists – she was probably the wife of George Ellis, temperance leader and coffee-house proprietor – while the Miss Rushworth who was a member of the committee of the female section of the National Charter Association in 1841 must have been related to David and Francis Rushworth, both active Chartists. David was on the West Riding Council in 1840, while Francis, at the age of twenty-one, took part in the abortive rising in Bradford in January 1840, and was among the prisoners interviewed by Major Williams. Martha Holmes was one of a group of Chartists arrested in December 1848 for assaulting and robbing Robert Emmett. Emmett was an ex-soldier who had associated with the Chartists in Bradford early in 1848, and had helped them train and drill. Later the same year he became a police informer and gave names to the authorities. He was attacked one night by a crowd of Chartists, beaten and thrown into the beck. In the course of the struggle he lost four shillings, and brought a case against the four ringleaders of the crowd for assault and robbery. Although, he said, a hundred people watched the attack, he could get no one to come forward as a witness to speak for him. The magistrate accepted his account, in spite of some damaging evidence about his past activities which was elicited in cross-examination by the Chartists, and all four were sentenced to two months' imprisonment with hard labour, including Martha Holmes.[47] Martha was in her mid-thirties, and may have been the wife or sister of Chartist woolcomber Joseph Holmes who had served four months' imprisonment in 1842, and was still an active Chartist in 1848.

One woman radical in Bradford did leave some account of her life, as well as a strong impression of her personality. In the report of the meeting in 1845 to consider the question of the Bradford trades joining the recently-formed National Association of United Trades for the Protection of Labour, after several men had spoken on behalf of their trades,

> Miss Ruthwell, treasurer to the Power Loom Weaver's Society was loudly called for and on making her appearance was received with three rounds of cheers. . . In addressing a meeting composed of hundreds of thinking men, she keenly felt her situation and was aware that among the ranks of the middle and upper class she would obtain the unenviable epithet of a bold and forward girl: but, should that be the case, they who would thus charge her should remember that the blame lay at their own door. The persecution of herself and her family had caused her to reflect and that which to her was a mystery and buried in obscurity was now clear and plain before her mind's eye. Had Mr Trimble not discharged her brother, sister and herself for the high crime of attending a meeting on Good Friday 'to take into consideration the means of bettering the condition of the Power-Loom Weavers', she would still have been the unreflecting slave of the power-loom without the cause being ascertained why she was a slave. Her father was discharged because her brother was chairman of the meeting alluded to, and her sister was discharged because she had accepted the office of treasurer; but she was thankful to Mr Trimble for that circumstance. . . The time was approaching when the mind of the Power-Loom Weavers would arise above their thraldom; and she now warned the employers that the day was fast approaching when the tyranny practised on them would end forever and the sun of freedom and virtue rise to shine refulgent to the end of time. . . While she had a tongue to proclaim the wrongs of sisters in slavery; while a drop of British blood flowed in her veins she would strive for the emancipation of her class and ere long they would find that the female workers in Bradford would be a powerful auxiliary in the onward march to 'a fair day's wage for a fair day's work'. Miss Ruthwell sat down loudly cheered.[48]

The report is worth quoting at length, for it contains clues to problems of public activity by women. Many of the unmarried girls in the textile districts were employed in the factories, and the kind of direct victimisation shown here would be a common risk. The fear of being dubbed a 'bold and forward girl' might be almost as inhibiting for many as the fear of victimisation, and clearly a family association with radical activity was a source of strength.

The women of Nottingham had been involved in radical and trade-union activity since well before the publication of the Charter, and were among the first to organise a female radical association, in 1838. Like Bradford, Nottingham was an area in which a great many women worked in the local industries. It was also a district in which social and educational activities were an important part of the Chartist programme.[49] The first secretary of the Female Political Union in 1838 was Mary Savage, who signed the manifesto on behalf of the members. The manifesto opened with a description of the poverty in which the members lived, and urged women to support their menfolk in the fight for better conditions. It then went on to attack the shopkeepers for their lack of concern with the popular movement.

> . . . no persons are so well qualified to bring these very important personages to their senses as the women of England upon whose minds we would impress as a public duty the necessity of expending their money only with the people or shopkeepers friendly to the cause of freedom, justice, Universal Suffrage etc. . . . Let every shop and shopkeeper be noted in a book kept for the purpose, stating name, residence, trade and whether Whig or Tory; also another book containing the names of those friendly to the cause of the people. . .

The detailed instructions and the defence of exclusive dealing were followed by the declaration that women should be expected soon to help in actual battle: ''Tis better to die by the sword than by famine, and we shall glory in seeing every working man of England selling his coat to buy a sword or a rifle to be prepared for the event. . .'[50]

The *Northern Star* agency in Nottingham was held by Mrs Smith, whose husband had been imprisoned in 1836 for selling unstamped newspapers. The Nottingham women did not hesitate to pass resolutions commenting on the political events of the day, and also to agitate locally on many questions, above all on the administration of the new Poor Law. Nottingham was in 1838-9 undergoing a severe depression, and a local observer commented on the active opposition to the law: 'Females in particular are against it; and when, through long deprivation of food the husband could not bear any longer to see his family in such a state, the wife has refused, and they then bring up their children in destitution and wretchedness.'[51] In November and December of 1838 the Female Political Union took up the case of Susan Robinson, an elderly woman who had been set to stone-breaking by the

Poor Law authorities. They called meetings of protest and collected money to help her. But even here, though the initiative was clearly with the women, it was William Lilley, a Chartist shoemaker, who spoke at the meeting of protest, at which he said that her fate 'might be the case of every workman's wife or sister in the country'.[52]

When the Nottingham female branch of the National Charter Association was started in 1843, and the names of its council were published,[53] at least one member appeared from among the leaders of the earlier organisation: Mrs Hannah Barnett, who had proposed the adoption of the first manifesto. Others had the same surnames as some of the leading men in the Nottingham Chartist movement, and two, Mrs Jane Abbott and Miss Mary Ann Abbott, may have been mother and daughter. Mary Ann was responsible for the organisation of the Chartist Sunday School. The Nottingham women received their share of obloquy from the local newspapers, and, like the women of Lancashire and the West Riding during the 1842 disturbances, earned the hostility of the respectable press by their rough manners and militant behaviour. After the demonstrations in August 1839 in support of the National Holiday, the *Nottingham Mercury* spoke of 'these harpies, whose expressions on every occasion, whose oaths and blasphemy, groans and yells, really made us blush for the feminine sex of England. . .'[54]

Another strong Chartist centre in which the women played an important part was the Northeast. Here again was a district in which many women worked outside the home. In the winter of 1838, a notice appeared on placards throughout Newcastle:

> Persecution by Employers. A public meeting will be held on Tuesday evening November 27 in the New Lecture Room to take into consideration the conduct of Messers Cookson in discharging Mr Thomason, one of the secretaries of the Northern Political Union, and one of the most active Apostles of the movement for Equal Rights. Those employed at Messers Cookson's Plate Glass Factory, and more especially the females in that employment, are earnestly invited to attend. . .

The next day some three hundred women were among the crowd who followed the Winlaton band to the meeting, to hear the case in support of Thomason. He described a number of occasions on which he, an overlooker in the factory, earning seventeen shillings a week, had been summoned to answer to his employers for political actions outside the factory. His collection of funds in support of the Glasgow cotton spinners, his sale to fellow-employees of copies of *The Radical's Remembrancer* and finally his acceptance of the elected post of secretary of the Northern Political Union, had all in turn led to a summons and a 'harsh rebuke' from his employer. Then the employers had begun to change the day and method by which the women glass workers were paid for their work. The women had twice come out on strike, and had been supported by Thomason. His dismissal followed. A resolution condemning the employers' behaviour was proposed by Robert Lowery and seconded by Edward Charlton – both leading Chartists – and carried unanimously. The second, also unanimously passed, declared: 'That whilst this meeting is resolved to resist such persecution to the uttermost, and to cherish and support those who may be marked out for its victims, they are deeply convinced that labour can never be adequately protected till it is adequately represented in the Commons' House of Parliament'.[55] The meeting then declared its intention not only to thank Mr Thomason for his past efforts, but to pledge itseif to 'take care of his future welfare', before departing in procession behind the band.

Women glass workers from Cooksons were probably enrolled in the Female Political Union of Newcastle on Tyne, which published its manifesto in the *Northern Star* in February 1839,[56] for a contribution to the national rent was sent by 'The women in the employ of Messers Cookson and Co's manufactory' in January of that year.[57] Like the women of Bradford and Nottingham, the Newcastle women organised exclusive dealing. They passed a resolution in January agreeing to issue cards to all their members for the collection of contributions to the national rent from the tradesmen they dealt with, and another at the same meeting pointing out that 'a shopkeeper who will not admit the claims of their fathers, husbands and brothers is an enemy and ought not to be supported'.[58] In December 1839 they were busy raising funds for the defence of John Frost and the other Welsh leaders. At a tea party held for this purpose at the Andrew Marvell Tavern in Botchergate, they displayed their banner, which was white, with 'on one side the keeper of the Bastile about to part the mother and her children, with the motto "Tyrants beware – think ye a mother's love is not stronger than your laws?" on the other the same inhuman monster parting man and wife with "Whom God has joined together let no man put asunder"'.[59]

At their Democratic Festival in June 1839, Julian Harney told the Newcastle women that 'Good as the men of Cumberland were, the women were the better men of the two'.[60] He had a special relationship with his constituents in the district, and recalled many years later the welcome he always received from the people, and the 'singing hinnies' the women baked for him.

Birmingham has sometimes been given the credit for initiating female Chartism, and certainly the women's organisation started by Thomas Clutton Salt at the end of 1837 must rank among the very first. In a letter to Ebenezer Elliott in April 1838, Salt spoke of a meeting of 12,000 women, an extraordinarily large number.[61] When Henry Vincent visited the town later in the year, to speak at a huge meeting at Holloway Head, he commented in his letters home on the large number of women who were part of the crowd.[62] Although the Salt initiative might be said to have emerged during the brief period of middle- and working-class collaboration in the early months of the Chartist movement, it seems as though many of the women remained with the Chartists after Salt and his friends left. The police spy, Wilson, reported that one of the meetings he attended in the tense period after the Newport rising consisted of between thirty and forty Chartists, and 'half of them was women'.[63] While these clandestine meetings were taking place, the female Chartists continued to meet openly. Later it is clear that some of them joined the Chartist Church of Arthur O'Neil. But in the summer of 1842 the National Charter Association and the Birmingham Chartist Church, which divided between them the city's membership, seem to have been working closely together. It was at this time that Arthur O'Neil was arrested and sentenced for seditious utterance for his speeches to striking coalminers outside the city. He called a meeting in Birmingham, and signed a placard announcing it which he sent round the town:

> Men of Birmingham! – The crisis is now arrived. Britain and Ireland are aroused. The nation's voice declares, in the loudest tones, the noble struggle must now be made. The days of tyranny are numbered. Shall Birmingham once the polar star of liberty, now slumber? Arise! Awake![64]

The placard-bearers were arrested, but later in the afternoon their place was taken by four women carrying more copies of the placard. When they were arrested they behaved, as the local paper reported, with 'indifference'. They jeered at the police who arrested them. One of them proposed that they appoint a chairman and hold a Chartist meeting then and there, and another seconded the proposal. Even before the magistrates they were more inclined to argue their case than to make the required promise to refrain from exciting the people in such a manner again.[65]

But the women of the north of England had no need to wait for an example from Birmingham. Lancashire, in particular, had a tradition of women's radical organisations going back to the early decades of the century. The activities of the different groups related more to the kind of actions carried on in the localities than to any national pattern of specifically female activities, so it is perhaps not surprising to find a delegate at a Lancashire meeting early in 1839 reporting that in his area 'women were now in a state of progress, and were purchasing pikes in large numbers'. At the same meeting, the delegate from Hyde declared that his society had 300 men and 200 women, and all he could say was that the women were the better men.[66]

Although it was not the custom for the authorities to hold women on political charges, some of them were arrested at each of the periods of Chartist activity. Whether because of the problems of establishing the guilt of married women under the law of *femme couverte*, or whether because the facilities available for imprisoning women – especially 'respectable' women – were limited, it was unusual for women to go for trial. A certain number of women Chartists did, however, serve prison sentences. Of the fifty Chartists arrested in Mansfield during the demonstrations in support of the National Holiday in the summer of 1839, the only one to be armed was Elizabeth Cresswell, a 43-year-old framework knitter. She was carrying a loaded revolver and spare ammunition for it. When she appeared in court, she was carrying a young baby, but she was nevertheless sent for a month's imprisonment with hard labour for 'unlawfully assembling with five hundred other persons marching and parading on the public highways'.[67] In Wales three women, Margaret Meredith, 'single woman', Ann Williams, 'servant', and Elizabeth Lucas, 'widow', all served terms of six months' imprisonment, the last-named with hard labour, for their parts in the Llanidloes riot – an occasion on which observers commented on the participation of the women.[68] Amy Meredith, a collier's wife, was arrested and charged with her husband for stealing a gun to take part in the Newport events.[69]

Life could be very hard for women whose husbands were imprisoned. Left to support their children by themselves, they relied either on the cold charity of the Poor Law or on the support of their fellow-Chartists. In the winter of 1839-40 hundreds of men were imprisoned, some for long terms. In Sheffield, Mary Holberry, a loyal and spirited Chartist, was arrested with her husband and interrogated by the police. She was released without being brought to trial, but during her husband's imprisonment their baby son died and a year later Samuel Holberry himself died as the result of his treatment in prison. James Burton, a whitesmith from Stockport, told the prison inspector that his wife's health had become so bad since his imprisonment that there was little chance of her survival. 'If she dies,' he said, 'I would as well remain here – I am beggared and ruinated.'[70] As the arrests of the men continued, difficult decisions sometimes had to be made by those left at liberty. In Sheffield, 'The keys to the Chartist committee room were kept by a woman and the women, being apprehensive that the entries in the books might affect their husbands, got the keys through her and destroyed them at the time when enquiries were being made by the police.'[71] In Barnsley the Chartist leader John Widdop recalled that a proposal was made there to burn the books of the local Northern Union, which contained the names of all the members and the minutes with the names of movers and seconders of resolutions. The proposal was overruled, but the problem of what to do with the books remained. Widdop was given charge of them.

I walked down the town, called at a gentleman's house, asked to see a servant girl there whom I knew, gave her the books and asked her to keep them safely in her box until I asked for them again. They remained in her keeping seven months. Before the night was over, the gentleman went down into the kitchen and told the girl that the authorities had got to know all about the Chartists now, as they had seized their books and papers. Their custodian smiled, and said to herself, 'No, they are perfectly safe over your head. . .'[72]

Clearly, in many such areas women were trusted supporters of the movement. Nevertheless, although they were encouraged to join the National Charter Association, it seems that only in their own female branches did they act as officers or committee members. At least, I have found only one example of a mixed NCA branch, in Craig, which had a woman, Mrs Charles Eastwood, as secretary. The rest of the council members were men, and their occupations, mostly in textile trades, are given. Mrs Eastwood is recorded only by her name.

Of the novelists who wrote about Chartism, only Benjamin Disraeli pictured the political importance of the women in the movement. Not only is the heroine of his Chartist novel, *Sybil*, the only character who makes what the author considers a 'correct' assessment of the tactics necessary to achieve its aims, but the factory girls too are presented as intelligent and articulate characters. Dandy Mick complains in the dark days of the summer of 1842 that 'The gals is the only thing what has any spirit left. Julia told me just now she would go to the cannon's mouth for the Five Points any summer day.'[73] In a discussion between a group of women, the factory girls argue their case cogently.

'Life's a tumbleabout thing of ups and downs,' said Widow Carey, stirring her tea, 'but I have been down this time longer than I can ever remember.'

'Nor ever will get up, Widow,' said Julia at whose lodgings herself and several of Julia's friends had met, 'unless we have the Five Points.'

'I will never marry any man who is not for the Five Points,' said Caroline.

'I should be ashamed to marry any one who had not the suffrage,' said Harriet.

'He is no better than a slave,' said Julia.

The widow shook her head. 'I don't like these politics,' said the good woman, 'they bayn't in a manner of business for our sex.'

'And I should like to know why?' said Julia. 'Ayn't we as much concerned in the cause of good government as the men? And don't we understand as much about it? I'm sure the Dandy never does anything without consulting me.'

'It's fine news for a summer day,' said Caroline, 'to say we can't understand politics with a Queen on the throne.'

'She's got her ministers to tell her what to do,' said Mrs Carey, taking a pinch of snuff. 'Poor innocent young creature, it often makes my heart ache to think how she is beset.'

'Over the left,' said Julia. 'If the ministers try to come into her bedchamber, she knows how to turn them to the right about.'

'And as for that,' said Harriet, 'why are we not to interfere with politics as much as the swell ladies in London?'

'Don't you remember, too, the last election here,' said Caroline, 'how the fine ladies from the Castle came and canvassed for Colonel Rosemary?'

'Ah!' said Julia, 'I must say I wish the Colonel had beat that horrid Muddlefist. If we can't have our own man, I am all for the Nobs against the Middle Class.'

'We'll have our own man soon, I expect,' said Harriet. 'If the people don't work, how are the aristocracy to pay the police?'

And thus the conversation continues, making the point that the girls in the factory districts were as concerned with politics as the men – a point that the experience of 1842 in Lancashire bears out, although it has largely been overlooked by the historians of the movement.[74]

Our information shows that most active Chartists were in their twenties, thirties or forties, and that most for whom we have the information were married. Arrest and imprisonment meant hardship and harassment for their families, and it must have been very much easier to stand if their political convictions were shared ones. Julia Goulborn, whose death was announced in the *Star* in February 1843, was described as an 'affectionate wife, a kind mother, a faithful friend and a sterling Chartist . . . by her death the Association together with her family, have sustained a severe loss.'[75] The names of other wives appear as beneficiaries of victim funds, or as petitioners for improved conditions during their husbands' imprisonment, but little remains apart from their names to identify individuals. One Chartist leader, Ernest Jones, was a convert from the upper classes, and was already married when he became a Chartist. He endured imprisonment, poverty and ill-health as a result of his life as a Chartist. His wife shared the hardships, but not the convictions.

Better much [she wrote in 1851] to be the wife of an itinerant pedlar – for then I might probably be fitted by birth and habits to tramp after him, with our children at our backs, and our sentiments being in unison could still enjoy the pleasure of his society – but to be the wife of an itinerant Chartist lecturer! Who could endure it? . . . .[76]

A similar tone is heard in John Doherty's complaint in the 1830s, suggesting that working-class women could also resent the time and money spent by their husbands in political action.

. . . there is the almost incessant complaints, if not reproaches, of the wife at home. From the very nature of things, he who becomes a leader among his fellow-workmen must of necessity, be often out at a late hour. The same circumstances render it necessary that he should expend more money than others of his fellows, as all the meetings, or nearly all, are held in the public house. Of this the wife soon becomes acquainted, and indeed, probably, as soon feels the effects. Her complaints and too often reproaches, for what she chooses to call inattentions to her, follow almost as a matter of course; and every meal is embittered by her incessant and almost irresistible entreaties to quit a course which requires such a course of life and causes her so much pain.[77]

William Carrier, outstanding leader of the Wiltshire Chartists in 1838 and 1839, emigrated soon after he was released from gaol in 1842, possibly because, as the prison inspector noted, his wife had been unfaithful while he was in prison. George White, on the other hand, wrote to a friend after his release from Kirkdale in 1849:

I am at home, surrounded by the love and affection of my wife and children. . . I am blessed with as good a wife and as intelligent dutiful and loving children as ever fell the lot of man . . . I have spent nearly four years out of the last ten in gaol for Chartism. My wife is a glorious trump and seconds my views. She would perish of starvation rather than degrade me in my absence. . . Is this not happiness to a man like me?[78]

One index of women's involvement in Chartism may perhaps be seen in the habit of naming children after Chartist and radical leaders. Writing to his brother-in-law in 1838, Henry Vincent claimed:

I have lots of sweethearts, married and single. Some of the ladies joke and say

> they are afraid there will not be *a bit of me left* . . . I should tell you that when I leave Bath I shall leave at least *three Henry Vincent's behind me!* Now, don't *laugh!* I don't mean to say, to use a holy phrase, *bone of my bone and flesh of my flesh* but made namesakes by the aid of a little *holy water* and a few mystical words pronounced by one of God Almighty's Lambs *the parsons!* There's Henry Vincent England, Henry Vincent Jones and Henry Vincent Young.[79]

Vincent was one of the most popular of Chartism's early leaders, and had many 'young patriots' named after him. Among these was Henry Vincent Millsom, infant son of plasterer William Millsom of Cheltenham, who named his son so that 'When he grew up he might enquire why he was so named after the great radical compositor who fought the Government.'[80] Alas, by 1843, Millsom found himself publicly attacking his hero for 'political betrayal for having left the ranks of O'Connor's party'. History has no record of whether he changed his son's name after Vincent's apostasy.[81]

Those Chartist babies who were not baptised in Chartist chapels could find some resistance among established clergy to the names they were given. When David Black and his wife of Barnsley gave their son's name as George Washington Hoey, 'the man of God looked wonders and asked if George would not do. However, finding himself at bay by the parents, the child was christened'.[82]

John Frost Hurst was baptised in February 1841, as was Joseph Frost, the baby son of Joseph and Grace Phillips of Bradford. Many other boys and girls had the name Frost included, while young master Greensmith of Nottingham was christened Zephenia Williams Frost. Thomas and Ann Walton of Dalston had their family of four children baptised at the same time with the names Adam Henry Vincent McDouall Walton, George Arthur Feargus O'Connor Walton, John Frost Walton and Margaret Lovett Collins Walton. It is to be hoped that the young Waltons showed more amity in the family circle than was shown by their namesakes in the world of politics.

Inevitably the most popular names for 'young patriots' of both sexes were Feargus and O'Connor, names which still persisted in non-Irish families in Lancashire and the West Riding well into the present century. John Johnson, weaver, of Macclesfield and his wife Sarah, Thomas Clarke, stonesmason, and his wife Mary of Lancaster, Hugh and Ann Smith of Carlisle, John and Mary Haswell, Methodists, of Bradford were among the many couples who gave Feargus's name to their infant sons. When David and Nancy Brear of Birkenhead offered young Henry Vincent O'Connor Brear for baptism,

The man in office, who is paid for his work, asked several questions as to the reason of their giving the above name? Having been answered he said he would not have called him after an Irishman. We suppose that no questions would have been asked if he had been named 'Marcus' or after the framer of the New Poor Law Bill.[83]

The *Northern Star* recorded with delight the dialogue which took place between Mrs King, of Manchester, and Richard Webb, registrar for the district:

Mr Webb – What is the child to be called?
Mrs King – James Feargus O'Connor King.
Mr Webb – Is your husband a Chartist?
Mrs King – I don't know, but his wife is.
Mr Webb – Are you the child's mother?
Mrs King – Yes.
Mr Webb – You had better go home and consider of it again; for if the person that you are naming your child after was to commit high treason and get hanged, what a thing it would be.
Mrs King – If that should be the case, I should then consider it an honour to have my child called after him, so that I shall never have him out of my memory so long as the child lives; for I think Feargus O'Connor a great deal honester man than those who are punishing him.
Mr Webb – Well, if you are determined to have it named after him, I must name it; but I never met such an obstinate lady as you before.
Mr Webb then registered the child by the above name.[84]

The Chartist movement throughout the country was made up of radical families like these. People like Abram and Elizabeth Hanson of Elland were clearly respected by their neighbours for a variety of qualities and contributions to the life of the community. But they were certainly not 'respectable' in the sense in which the word came to be used in the mid-Victorian years. They valued education highly, for example, and sought it for their children and for themselves, but they did not use it to ape the manners or style of members of a higher class. Many Chartists, indeed, saw provided education, and the values it attempted to instil, as inimical to their beliefs. George Mart, Stoke Chartist, giving evidence to the Commission on the Employment of Children and Young Persons in 1841, said that he had educated his five children at his own expense, since he 'did not like the system of education pursued in the national schools, where they instil the principle of paying deference to superiors, when we are all of the same flesh and blood.'[85] This was hardly a 'respectable' attitude, and the commissioner found him to be a dangerous character to be in charge of young people. Elizabeth Hanson was certainly not behaving 'respectably' by engaging in political activity with the other women Chartists in her village, speaking at meetings and writing to the press. *The Times* made a famous attack on such 'hen radicals' and considered them fair game for suggestive sneers.[86] *The Essex Standard* went further and declared that the idea of a female radical association must 'stink in the nostrils of all decent people' and apostrophised its readers with a column of doggerel:

Mothers for Radicals who train
  Their babes – not for the Lord –
May live to reap, in rebel sons,
  Their bitter just reward.

Women may influence great possess
  But on certain conditions
And one of them is – they must ne'er
  Set up for politicians. . .[87]

The women who organised the Chartist schools and Sunday schools were setting up educational institutions in deliberate opposition to those on offer by church and charitable bodies. In the words of Sarah Foden, wife of a leading Sheffield Chartist and herself secretary of the Sheffield women radicals, the purpose of their schools was to 'instil the principles of Chartism into their children'.[88] All the Chartist advocates of education, including Lovett, Collins and Linton, as well as the local and provincial educators, stressed the importance of education in the principles of the Charter, and of political rights generally. In his attack on the female Chartists who occupied his church in Cheltenham, the Rev. Francis Close regretted the influence of these ideas in the home.

A bad mother of a family is far more mischievous in the country than a bad father, because the infant children are entrusted to her.

. . . What a curse are such women to the country! Their children must grow up revolutionists, for they have been taught revolution at home![89]

There is a certain correlation between areas in which there is strong evidence of women's participation in Chartism and areas with records of educational provision. The Scottish branches had a higher average of schools, Sunday schools or Chartist churches and of women's associations than either England or Wales, at least according to the published record. But it is very probable that many short-lived Chartist schools never got mentioned in the press. Enthusiastic groups like Elland kept the *Northern Star* informed, and in their small village recorded a radical school which met on three nights a week with 104 scholars. We know from a worried report from a magistrate that Bedlington boasted its own Chartist school, run by an Irishman, Henry Cronin, who had been dismissed from his work at the ironworks for his political activities.[90] Engels spoke of there being Chartist schools in all the manufacturing districts, and it seems likely that most areas made some attempt to provide education for their members and their members' children, and that the women took a leading part in the organisation of these schools. 'Talk of putting down the Chartists, forsooth, why every kitchen is now a political *meeting-house*; the little children are members of the unions and the good mother is the political teacher. . .'[91] as Henry Vincent rejoiced to observe.

The Chartists often repeated their demand that there should be no female labour except in the hearth and the schoolroom. In general they regarded women's work outside the home as a burden, certainly for married women. There may have been an ideological connection between this programme and the rather surprisingly small number of women speakers produced by the movement. It is more likely, however, that the women speakers hesitated to address mixed audiences, or to travel far from their homes, and so never developed national reputations, or got sufficient practice to become expert orators. There were a few exceptions to this generalisation. The female associations invited men speakers, but meetings were usually chaired by women, and some women spoke in their own neighbourhoods. Mrs Anna Pepper, secretary of the Leeds women, spoke in other parts of the West Riding,[92] and at a large meeting in Marylebone on the eve of the presentation of the 1842 petition, an audience of men and women heard a lecture from Bairstow, after which 'Mrs Godwin ably addressed the females assembled, and urged upon them the necessity of swelling the procession on the following morning. . .'[93] In 1843 Mrs Fields spoke to the Manchester Chartists at Carpenters Hall,[94] and women speakers occasionally seconded resolutions at mixed meetings. In the mid-forties a few women speakers are reported who clearly went outside their own branches and regularly spoke on Chartist platforms, though again often to female audiences. Susanna Inge, of the City of London Female Chartist Association first appeared as a speaker in 1843, and had by then already published a fairly long letter in the *Star* 'To the Women of England'. In this she urged support for the Charter, but went further, questioning women's exclusion from 'The more rational enjoyments of life, [since] women are gifted with a mind to which in point of delicacy of taste, depth of feeling and devoted affection even proud man himself must bow. . .'[95] Miss Inge, like Mary Wollstonecraft before her and like many later women writers, questioned the whole idea of a purely domestic role for women. Although the Chartists read and re-published Wollstonecraft, they very seldom admitted this kind of discussion into their journals. It may have been that the basic idea of greater equality between the sexes was assumed to be accepted by them all, or it could have been that to the working-class women this was not at the time the most burning issue. Certainly Susanna Inge was almost alone in putting the case, although there was no opposition at the time, nor is any contrary case to be found in Chartist journals. Unfortunately Susanna became involved in a series of quarrels, beginning with some kind of disagreement within the City Females branch, and going on to a fairly mild criticism of O'Connor's intervention through the *Star* in Chartist elections. The latter elicited an editorial defence: 'Miss Inge thinks the people would sooner elect a man on Mr O'Connor's recommendation than on their own judgement. We do not think them quite such fools'[96] which was a trifle disingenuous. Nevertheless, it would not have seemed a sufficient reason for her withdrawal from Chartist politics, and it is more likely that the disagreements within the City organisation were the real reason. For whatever reason, she does not seem to have taken an active part after the autumn of 1843.

Mary Anne Walker was another speaker at the meetings of the City Female Chartists. She was one of the 'Hen Chartists' attacked by *The Times* and vigorously defended in the *English Chartist Circular*. Unfortunately the defence is made on general principles, and does not add to our knowledge of Mary Ann. From her reported speeches she seemed to be in the direct line of mainstream Chartist speakers, dealing with the poverty and exploitation of workers, particularly women, the evils of the Poor Law and the need to end 'class legislation'. The *Annual Register* considered that 'Miss Walker's oratorical powers and style of ratiocination will sufficiently serve the purpose of confirming the Chartist faith in those who make the six points their creed, but it is by no means calculated to make new converts from the thinking and intelligent'.[97] This is in line with what we know about the activities of women Chartists in other parts of the country. Those who concerned themselves with problems of women as opposed to those of men, rather than with the general miseries of society, are few. Women speakers might, like Mary Ann Walker, illustrate the particular sufferings of women as workers and as victims of the Poor Law, or like Mary Grasby at Elland insist that 'women had more to fear from the Bill than men',[98] but their solution was the enfranchisement of the working people as a whole and not a change in the relative social and legal position of the sexes. When Emma Miles, president of the City of London Female Chartist Association, wrote to the *Northern Star* in 1843, proposing that a women's petition be drawn up and sent to the Queen, asking her urgently to consider the current state of the working classes, the letter ended: 'Be assured that love of country will not lessen in any woman's heart the love of home.'[99] The care of home and children, the hearth and the schoolroom remained the chief concerns, even of working women.

Throughout the forties a few women continued to appear as speakers, mainly still members of Chartist families. Mrs Caroline Blatherwick of Nottingham was a committee member of the female NCA in that town, and Miss Eliza Blatherwick spoke at meetings, and occasionally, as at the celebration of Thomas Paine's birthday in February 1847, performed songs and recitations.[100] John Blatherwick, framework knitter, was a leading Nottingham Chartist, and the ladies were almost certainly of the same family. After the middle of the decade, the number of women reported as speaking dies away.

Tantalisingly, it should perhaps be admitted that the increasing rationality and respectability of the movement which has already been mentioned could mean that the radical papers ceased to mention women, rather than that women dropped out of the movement. Certainly by the middle fifties the *People's Paper* is lamenting the absence of women from Chartism, but as late as 1848 the chief constable of Leicester reported to the Home Office that he calculated at a conservative estimate that he had 5,035 men and 1,748 women Chartists in his district, and that they possessed considerable supplies of firearms.[101]

Women in the Chartist movement, then, were important, particularly between 1838 and 1843. Their presence emphasises the community base of the movement, and it is difficult to conceive Chartism without their participation. They set up many separate organisations, and a considerable amount of organising, speaking and demonstrating was done by these women. In the course of this activity a general commitment to the inclusion of women in the suffrage and the improvement of women's education can be seen to have been accepted by most radicals.

The active presence of these Chartist women, and their occasional boldness in addressing mixed meetings, were in direct contrast to the behaviour of even the most radical middle-class women of the time.[102] It may, indeed, have been this freer attitude towards the participation of women in the Chartist and Owenite movements[103] as well as the muted but nevertheless very present support for the idea of the extension of the suffrage to include at least some women which engaged the interest of some of the more adventurous of the young radicals of the dissenting middle class. In a letter to Wendell and Ann Phillips, American abolitionists, written in 1842, Elizabeth Pease regretted her inability to answer all their questions about the Chartists, 'notwithstanding that I reckon myself one of their body'. Although a friend and supporter of Joseph Sturge, she considered that he and his friends were wrong to reject the name of Chartist for the organisation they were trying to build: '. . . why succumb to the prejudices of the middle classes by rejecting an appellation which tells you their principles at once?'[104] In a letter written from Darlington during the plug riots, she showed that even these events did not change her allegiance: 'One's whole sympathies go with the disorganisers – driven as they are almost to desperation, by insult and injury heaped upon them by those who, if actions be right interpreters of feelings, consider they are but chattels made to minister to their luxury and add to their wealth.'[105] Miss Pease had clearly read Richardson's pamphlet but was not sure whether he fully represented the Chartist view. 'I *believe*,' she wrote, 'the Chartists generally hold the doctrine of the equality of women's rights – but, I am not sure whether they do not consider that when she *marries*, she merges her political rights with those of her husband.'[106]

William Shaen, a Unitarian and later a Christian Socialist, declared that he was glad to hear that his sister had become 'a regular Chartist', in 1841. 'As it is perfectly unnatural for any lady to be anything so ungenteel, Miss C— thinks you call yourself so because you think it pleases me!'[107] From the Chartist standpoint, these young dissenters probably seemed very much part of the middle class, but it is interesting to see that, for them, Chartism represented a challenge to orthodoxy in the area of women's rights as well as of the suffrage.

CHAPTER EIGHT

Traders and Professional Men

THERE was not a very hard line in the early nineteenth century between the employed workman and the small self-employed or freelance trader. Many craftsmen and women like shoemakers, tailors, masons, dressmakers and milliners, hired their labour directly to their customers, or worked from their own homes. Many artisans who would have preferred to be employed spent time when work was short in making up scraps of material into saleable articles and hawking them in the streets. The law allowed such unlicensed hawking in one's own parish.[1] The self-employed man, even some small employers and garret masters, might be lower in status and reward than the fully-employed workman.

Many of the shopkeepers and small traders among the Chartists were certainly of this kind. Or they came into the other category described by Allen Davenport:

> Almost every individual when he is kept out of employment by machinery or any other contrivance, turns his attention towards merchandise and becomes a trader or a little middleman; others again, finding their income or wages too small to provide for an increasing family, take a shop for their wives to manage, while they follow their regular employment. . .[2]

A few came from shopkeeping or merchant families and carried on rather more substantial businesses. Others again were either forced or encouraged into trade by the needs of the movement itself or by the victimisation which kept so many local Chartists out of their proper employment. Their comparative independence, provided by the support and custom of the local Chartists, only rarely put them into a true 'middle-class' social or economic group.

The most powerful economically were the publishers and larger booksellers. The thousands of Chartist readers enabled a considerable living to be made from the production and sale of books and journals. In London Hetherington and Watson were already by 1838 established as radical publishers, while John Cleave had interests in radical and theatrical publishing, as well as a considerable agency for the distribution of radical journals. Cleave became London agent of the *Northern Star*, a very profitable business which enabled him to underwrite some less financially successful ventures such as his *English Chartist Circular and Temperance Record*, which probably never broke even financially.[3] In Manchester the main agency was held by Abel Heywood who had also begun in a fairly small way as a rebel publisher and distributor of unstamped journals. During the Chartist years he acted for a time as O'Connor's business manager, and during O'Connor's imprisonment the prison inspector spoke of Heywood as having 'the management of his money affairs'. Like Cleave, who was in many ways his London counterpart, Heywood acted for a time as treasurer of the National Victim fund which raised and distributed money for the families of imprisoned Chartists. Major Williams reported that O'Connor in prison received £10 a week from his publisher which far exceeded his own needs, and that he passed most of it on to Heywood – probably for this fund. Cleave and Heywood also had in common service as treasurer of the National Charter Association. These radical publishers were very important figures in the Chartist movement – they were visible, their names appeared every week on numbers of journals, and they had records which included imprisonment for the cause of radicalism in the unstamped period, which had laid a basis of trustworthiness before the temptations of mass sales made radical publishing and bookselling potentially profitable. In the Chartist years they had enough financial independence to enable them to act as treasurers of national funds, with the necessary political experience to make them trustworthy administrators. Heywood made no compromise with his radical beliefs, and was prosecuted in the Chartist period as well as earlier for publishing and selling forbidden books. Nevertheless he ran a very successful business, which outlived him by a century, and he became a prominent politician in his native city. He became a town councillor in 1843, and went on to become an alderman and twice mayor. He worked with Ernest Jones in the years before the Second Reform Bill, helping to found the Manchester Manhood Suffrage Association in 1858. The firm he founded for producing cheap newsprint prospered as well as his publishing and bookselling, and his widow was able to bequeath £10,000 to Owen's College, the forerunner of Manchester University, for female education.[4]

The equivalent of Cleave and Heywood in Yorkshire was Joshua Hobson, Heywood's exact contemporary. Both were children of handloom weavers with little formal education, both became involved in radicalism and in the unstamped press agitation, both were imprisoned for their activities. Both became involved in municipal politics. But whereas on his side of the Pennines Heywood gravitated towards Liberalism after the Chartist period, Hobson grew up in a Tory-radical tradition, and after the end of Chartism returned to a generally Tory position. Hobson was born in the neighbourhood of Fixby in Huddersfield, and worked closely with its Tory radical steward Richard Oastler in the factory and anti-Poor-Law movements before Chartism. He was one of the working-class men who made the famous Fixby Hall compact with Oastler on 19 June 1831, by which Oastler agreed to work on the factory question in cooperation with the operatives. At the time Hobson was a cotton handloom weaver, but he had been trained as a joiner, a skill which enabled him to knock together the wooden frame for his first printing press. From 1831 onwards he worked in the radical movement, publishing his unstamped *Voice of the West Riding* in 1833-4, serving a term of imprisonment for publishing it, and becoming intensely interested in political radicalism and Owenism as well as in the factory and anti-Poor-Law movements. By the time O'Connor was considering the publication of the *Northern Star*, Hobson was well-known as a leading Yorkshire radical, and it was to him that Feargus entrusted the acquisition of the presses and the setting up of the paper. He continued to publish it until 1843, when for two years he took over its editorship. He also published Owen's *New Moral World*, and a series of radical almanacs. He became a member of Leeds town council in 1842, having moved to that city in the late thirties, and having been one of the founders of the Working Men's Association there in 1837. He remained a leader in the Leeds Chartist movement, and the most prominent figure in the group of Chartists who took part in local government. He fell out with O'Connor over the administration of the Land Plan in the late forties – a quarrel which Oastler tried unsuccessfully to patch up. When Chartism declined, Hobson returned to his native Huddersfield and worked on the local Tory newspaper. He interested himself in model lodging-houses and other social issues, and died in 1876.[5] A local historian described him as 'a tall man, of good figure and carriage, of genial temperament and a good speaker'.[6]

Watson, Hetherington, Cleave, Heywood and Hobson were all established in business and ready to help forward the radical press as Chartism got into its stride. Their importance can hardly be overestimated in a movement which depended so much on communications. Other publishers started during the Chartist period, some carrying on into the next stage of radical publishing like G. W. M. Reynolds, whose newspapers picked up the radical tone of the late Chartist years and continued it in a form of popular weekly journalism which laid the foundations for the mass newspapers of the last quarter of the century. In the provinces many former Chartists were associated with the growth, from the 1860s onwards, of a vigorous Liberal weekly press. Among these were Thomas Lingard with his *Barnsley Chronicle*, Thomas Frost, who worked on several Liberal newspapers in Liverpool, Shrewsbury, Barnsley and Sheffield, and W. E. Adams, under whose editorship the *Newcastle Weekly Chronicle* in the years 1864–1900 became one of the most interesting and lively of the Liberal provincial journals. These were all young working men in the early days of Chartism.

Essential for the distribution of the Chartist press were the men and women who ran newspaper agencies throughout the country. Some of them had begun with no intention of making a business of selling journals. Thomas Dunning, shoemaker and shoemakers' leader, recalled that when the *Northern Star* started in 1837, he and a dozen of his fellow-workmen decided to take it every week. They asked the only newsagent in their town of Nantwich to order copies for them, offering if necessary to pay a quarter's money in advance. 'He declined taking the order in a most contemptuous manner, with "Oh! Ah! a radical paper I believe. I am a stamp officer and will not order it, etc.". . .' Dunning therefore wrote directly to the *Star* with his order, 'and from that moment, thanks to Mr Tory Griffiths, I became a newsagent'.[7] Joseph Lingard of Barnsley, another shoemaker, started selling unstamped newspapers from his shoemaker's shop and by the Chartist period had a regular book and newspaper-selling business. His wife took an active part, and when their son Thomas, also trained as a shoemaker, married in 1839, the parents handed over the Barnsley business to him and went to Sheffield, where they took over the local *Star* agency. Joseph Lingard had come originally from Sheffield and had settled in Barnsley after serving for some years in the army. He was described by a contemporary as 'A tall man, who wore a frock coat and had a genteel carriage. His eye was penetrating, his oratorical action graceful, and he could speak words which kindled enthusiasm in a crowd. . .[8]

Reginald John Richardson of Salford was a master carpenter. His wife carried on a newsagent's business, selling radical journals and becoming the agent for the *Star*. When an accident prevented him from working at his own trade, Richardson joined his wife in the business.[9] James Watson of Newcastle upon Tyne was one of the first people to set up as a full-time newsagent in that district. A cork-cutter by trade, he came north from London in the 1830s in search of employment. He started a stall in the market selling radical and temperance literature, including unstamped journals. He was an early adherent of the Chartist movement, became an agent for the Land Company and represented the local NCA locality at the meeting on Kennington Common on 10 April 1848. By the early 50s he was clearly a man of some substance, and was able to help Ernest Jones raise money for the *People's Paper*. He was a well-known speaker in Newcastle on Chartism, Temperance, Barkerism and later Unitarianism, and helped to organise a Chartist reading-room and lecture room in Nun Street. Like a number of old Chartists, he was an active campaigner for the Second Reform Bill and a member of the Northern Reform Union.[10] Thomas Brown Smith of Leeds, another Chartist newsagent, ran a Chartist Sunday school, and with his wife was a leading propagandist against the new Poor Law and against alcoholic drinks and tobacco. In 1841 he became a national vice-president of the Anti-Tobacco and Temperance Association, of which his wife Mary was a keen supporter.[11] James Leach, former factory worker and the leading Manchester Chartist, also made his living by running a bookseller's and newsagent's shop, described in 1842 as 'a very respectable business'. In Sunderland the bookshop run jointly by George Binns and James Williams provided a living for its proprietors and a centre for the organisation of Chartism in the district. As well as selling books and journals, Williams and Binns, until their imprisonment for sedition in the summer of 1840, published tracts, handbills and poems from the shop. Binns emigrated to New Zealand soon after his release from prison, where he died an early death from consumption in 1848. His obituarist in the *Star* recalled him as 'a handsome, high-spirited talented true-hearted man – every inch a democrat'.[12] As a speaker and as a writer of Chartist hymns and poems he was a very popular figure in the north-east. James Williams, his partner in the booksellers' business, and fellow-prisoner in 1840, came to the attention of a wealthy lady prison visitor while he was serving his sentence. They fell in love and married, and it was with her help that he was able to extend the printing side of his business, and eventually, in 1857, to buy the Tory *Sunderland Times* and transform it into a Radical paper. He became and remained an active Liberal politician, being elected to the town council in Sunderland while still a Chartist in 1847, and going on to become an alderman. Like many former Chartists he managed to combine a strong interest in the practical side of local government, being prominent in pressures for sanitary reform of all kinds in the district, with a continuing participation in cultural and educational work. He was a leading figure in the Literary and

Philosophical Society, and helped to establish public libraries and parks.[13]

Thomas Cooper earned his livelihood as agent and correspondent for the *Northern Star* during his period of intense activity as a local leader of the Leicester Chartist movement. From his correspondence one can gain some idea of the way a Chartist agent worked, and an idea too of the more shadowy network of local agents who took the journals out into the smaller centres. Most of these men and women would not expect to make a profit from their activities, but would be pleased to cover the cost of the collection and distribution of journals. Such loyal supporters did not hesitate to offer Cooper political advice as well as ordering newspapers. When Cooper quarrelled with his colleague and fellow-shoemaker John Markham, Gideon Cooke, who distributed radical literature in Melton Mowbray, warned him: '. . . this must not continue, it is a shout of Triumph to our opponents. . .'[14] Supplies of the *Northern Star*, of his own journals and of a variety of radical publications went out from Cooper's house to newsagents, some of whom combined a newsagent's business with that of a coffee-shop or alehouse. Jeremiah Yates, potter and coffee-house keeper of Shelton, ordered 100 copies of *What is a Chartist?*, 50 *Hints to the Army*, 50 *Calumnies Refuted*, the second part of Thomas Paine's *Rights of Man*, 2 *Red Books*, 2 *Poor Man's Companion*, and 6 copies of *Feargus O'Connor on the Land* as well as the *Northern Star* and the *Commonwealthsman* 'as usual', in the summer of 1842.[15] Cooper himself ran a coffee-shop as well as a bookshop, and depended, as did many of his customers, on sales of the *Northern Star* for a regular income. He also sold bread, and had several rooms in his house which were used for meetings and committees. His account of Chartist activity in Leicester is valuable for the information it gives about the less formal side of Chartism – the reading-rooms, coffee-shops, Sunday and evening classes which formed the regular social activity of provincial Chartists.[16]

Those among the Chartist book and paper sellers who made a substantial living from the trade were probably a minority. Bills were often unpaid – both Thomas Cooper and John Watkins fell behind with the payment for copies of the *Northern Star*, and valuable stock could be impounded by the authorities. Mrs Edwards, wife of the Welsh Chartist baker, had £20 worth of newspapers seized after her husband's arrest in 1839.[17] Politically and organisationally, however, these small distributors were very important. Two of the imprisoned Chartists in 1841, Charles Davies, cotton-spinner of Stockport, and Thomas Howarth, factory overlookers from Hyde, kept small shops for the sale of books and pamphlets. Neither ranked very high on the tests for literacy, although the inspector noted that both had taken advantage of their imprisonment to improve their education.[18] Nearly every town had its agent for radical papers, or its radical bookseller, ranging in status from large concerns like that run in Leeds by Alice Mann, widow of James Mann, the pioneer of radical publishing, and her nine children, to individuals like 'Radical Jack' Dennis, hawker of cheap publications whose 'ready wit and great command of language made him an especial favourite with the multitude'.[19] People like Dennis were often harassed and prosecuted for minor infringements of regulations governing street sales, or for drunkenness, rather than for directly political offences. Dennis certainly found himself in gaol on more than one occasion. He may have been the prisoner with the same sobriquet who interrupted a sermon on the virtues of Jesus Christ being preached in Durham county prison in September 1839, by standing up and exclaiming in a loud voice:

> Sir, Jesus Christ was the first Chartist. He was the best man that ever came into the world. He taught the doctrines of humility and equality and even instructed men to sell their garments and buy a sword.[20]

He was rewarded for the interjection with three days' solitary confinement.

The booksellers' shop was a centre for radicals to gather around and in many districts the bookseller was an important political leader. Men like Christopher Tinker of Huddersfield, James Arthur of Carlisle, John Fraser of Edinburgh, John Cook of Ipswich, John Seal of Leicester and James Ibbetson of Bradford appear as NCA committee men, as speakers and occasionally among the lists of those arrested. In Ashton-under-Lyne another Joshua Hobson, who has sometimes been confused with the Yorkshire publisher, kept an agency for radical literature going until his death in the early months of the Chartist movement in 1838.[21] He was a member of a long-standing radical family in the town. Another of the influential local bookshop keepers, Joseph Linney of Bilston, had a namesake in the same locality whose radical career has sometimes been conflated with his own. Linney was born in Macclesfield and began work in the local silk-weaving industry at the age of four and a half. He later moved to Manchester where he worked as a cotton powerloom weaver. His wife Mary came from the cotton town of Blackburn. By the time of the Chartist movement, the Linneys had opened a radical bookshop in Manchester, and Joseph was among the leaders arrested in August 1839. When Christopher Doyle, arrested the same night, heard of the other arrests, he said 'What! Jackson and Linney? Poor fellows, they don't know it as I do; I know what it is, I've had a taste of it before.' 'He was then', as the *Star* reported, 'taken down and locked up with his comrades; and thus in less than three hours five of the principal leaders of the people in Manchester were arrested. . .'[22] Linney moved into the Black Country some time before the events of 1842, and was among the most prominent Chartist leaders during the colliers' strike and the turbulent events connected with it. His support for temperance did not prevent him from taking on the White Horse Inn in Bilston High Street in 1845, and he appears to have remained a total abstainer in spite of his new avocation. As George Barnsby has shown, Chartism in the Black Country persisted throughout the 1850s, and Linney was among its leaders throughout the decade.[23] There is some confusion, however, since a working miner, of the same name, emerged as a local leader in the political and industrial movement during the 1850s.[24] Linney is a very good example of the local leader who used the basis of a bookshop, and then an alehouse, to obtain the independence to act freely as an organiser and speaker, but who, reciprocally, had to satisfy his local supporters that he was acting in the interests of the movement in order to keep his livelihood.

Few Chartists lived in houses with room enough to accommodate meetings or even large committees. When meetings were mentioned 'at the house of' local Chartists, these were usually alehouses which were built with large rooms which could be lent or hired out. Nearly every locality had a dream of building its own Chartist hall for meetings and social events, and a number of them did manage to rent or buy their own premises. In Halifax the friendly society of Odd Fellows, to which most of the male Chartists belonged, built an enormous hall in 1840, with a large meeting hall, several good-sized rooms and a warren of smaller committee rooms. The building survived to serve the trade union and labour movement of the town for more than a hundred years. Where they had no room or chapel of their own, however, most Chartist groups met in alehouses. The 1835 Act allowed licences for the sale of beer and ale under less stringent supervision than was required for a licence for other alcoholic drinks, in order to encourage the drinking of beer rather than of spirits. The Act was unpopular with many people in authority, as it was held to encourage precisely the kind of meeting that the Chartists held – informal and unsupervised. As well as alehouses there were in the manufacturing districts inns which were the haunts of radicals, but whose landlords nevertheless managed to retain their licences. A number of leading Chartists throughout the country were keepers of inns or alehouses. For some of them this was, as with the newsagents, a resource when they were excluded from their trades for political reasons. For others it was a deliberate choice of a vocation which allowed for the maximum of political activity. For others again, keeping an inn or alehouse was subsidiary to their regular trade, and was entrusted to their wife or other family members. Women alehouse keepers were common, and many Chartist wives helped out in this way. Probably the most famous of all Chartist innkeepers was Zephenia Williams, one of the leaders of the Newport rising, landlord of the Royal Oak at Coalbrookvale in Monmouthshire. A mine agent by profession, Williams relied on his wife and daughters to run the inn, which was the meeting place both for the local Working Men's Association and for the Female Chartist Society in 1838 and 1839. After he was transported for his part in the Newport events, Mrs Williams kept the licence and made a good living from it.[25] The miners and iron workers of South Wales continued to meet at the remoter alehouses in the district in the quieter years following 1839. Reports by the spy, William Philips, on the Merthyr Chartists in 1842 and 1843 spoke of regular meetings in the Three Horseshoes, Georgetown, where the language spoken was very much stronger than any reported in the radical press. The landlord was described as 'a sound Chartist' as were three other local landlords, James Horner of the Queen Adelaide, Newport, William Williams of the Prince of Wales, Newbridge, and Abraham Evans of the Rolling Mill, Merthyr.[26]

In Yorkshire there were a number of radical inns and alehouses. When Thomas Vevers of Huddersfield, landlord of the Dog Inn, died in 1843, the *Northern Star* recalled that '. . . for half a century he has known what it is to brave the "battle of the breeze". He was a Jacobin in the days of Church and King mobs, a reformer in the days of Horne Tooke and Hardy, a Radical in the days of Hunt and Cobbett and a Chartist in the present day of Whig and Tory persecution. . .'[27] Vevers served on the NCA committee, and was elected as a possible reserve delegate in 1839, when there was a fear that the members of the Convention would be arrested.[28]

Joseph Crabtree's Freeman's Inn in Barnsley was an important centre and meeting-place for Barnsley Chartists, but the best known of the Yorkshire beerhouse-keepers was 'fat Peter' Bussey of Bradford, landlord of the Roebuck Inn. Bussey had been a radical all his life, and had been a leading figure in Bradford working-class politics for many years before the beginning of Chartism. Born in the North Riding and apprenticed as a carpenter, he transferred to the worsted trade, first as a comber, then as a merchant. By the time of the Chartist movement, he was running a merchant's business as well as his alehouse, and was a man of a certain substance. He was a leader in all the radical activity in Bradford, going as one of a delegation to present the case for the Dorchester labourers to Lord Melbourne, collecting money to aid the Canadian revolutionaries, and always appearing on platforms and hustings as the spokesman of ultra-radicalism in the city. In 1839 he was described as

. . . exceedingly corpulent and in height about five feet nine or ten inches. His countenance is indicative of much thoughtfulness, albeit there is an expression of restlessness and of stern resolve that cannot be mistaken. His manners are somewhat rough and his address blunt, though by no means offensive. . . As a member of the Convention he is punctual in his attendance and exemplary in the discharge of his duties. Without ostentation he is one of the most effective delegates who have seats in that assembly. . .[29]

Bussey attained notoriety, and assured himself a place in the histories of Chartism, by his flight to America in the autumn of 1839. Most accounts agree that the West Riding was prepared for an operation of the Newport kind, and that Bussey was to have led it. A letter from an informer in Halifax claimed that the Halifax Chartists were armed and that 'had not Peter Bussey been taken badly they would of commenced the same day that Frost did'.[30] Bussey's illness has been assumed to have been strictly diplomatic, and may well have been so, although the story which Devyr tells of the Newcastle preparations at the same time suggests that there was a lack of certainty about the exact plan they were intended to execute which cannot be laid at the door of a single leader. However that may be, Bussey was certainly missing when the local Chartists expected to receive his summons to action, and he made his way to the United States. Reuben Holder, the Bradford balladeer who had earlier sung Bussey's praises in radical broadsides, produced a famous rhyme which was still remembered forty years later, slanging the radical leader for twenty-four doggerel stanzas.

I've heard Peter B--ss-y has fledged and flown
And pack'd up his wallet and left Bradford town;
And if all is true what I've heard I protest,
He's lined well his pockets and feather'd his nest.[31]

When, in 1840, he left for the United States, many of his former associates felt that he had betrayed an important trust, and abandoned the Yorkshire radicals at a crucial moment. For this reason, some of the reminiscences have an acid edge to them. Thomas Frost recalled that Bussey had used his position as Convention delegate to drum up custom for the Roebuck, and that he had sent back daily reports to be read aloud to the customers by his wife, but 'not . . . till the factories closed, when the slaves could have an opportunity of receiving the intelligence of their independent representatives. The beer-house was like a theatre; there was a rush for early places, and all paid for admission. . .'[32] When Bussey set up in New York as a lodging-house keeper, his enemies implied that he was doing very well out of it. 'He has been accused', Thomas Cooper wrote, 'of receiving moneys as a government spy, and escaping to America, opening a dram shop in New York whose very front cost £1,000 and becoming a reckless renegade to Chartist principles.' The accusations, Cooper maintained, were groundless.

> . . . a Leicester Chartist, known and respected for his veracity, has just returned from America and completely refutes much of these malicious statements. Peter Bussey rents a tavern – but it is in no shape a building of the kind just described. His heart is open to every Chartist, and his purse is open to their wants. Many who have been unable to find employ when they have gone over have received his free hospitality in the most generous manner for months. His rooms are hung with the Star portraits, he constantly defends and maintains Chartist principles – manifests an eager enthusiasm for the brave Feargus and a deep sympathy with the exiled Frost and displays the deepest interest in all he can learn and hear of the advance of Chartism. . .[33]

In 1842 an advertisement in the *Northern Star* recommended a 'Private Boarding House' in New York, America, kept by Peter Bussey from Bradford and Benjamin Worswick from Clayton, offering board and lodging on reasonable terms, and also 'every information . . . to Emigrants Etc.' Like many emigrants, Bussey was disillusioned by his experience of American political life. He spent about fourteen years in the United States, working as lodging-house keeper, farmer, tavern keeper and pedlar, before returning to the West Riding to his old trade of innkeeper. He died in 1869.[34]

In Gloucester, the Chartist movement was kept going by the Sidaway family. Thomas Sidaway was a master chain and nail maker and kept the Magnet Inn with the help of his wife, son and daughter. The family were Unitarians and long-standing radicals, Thomas's interest in politics dating at least from the days of Peterloo. He had taken part in demonstrations against church rates, and been prosecuted for his refusal to pay, had organised a meeting to protest against the sentence on the Dorchester labourers, and had been a member of the town's political union in the reform agitation of the early thirties. During the later part of the 1840s their radicalism led to a loss of trade for the family, and they moved for a time to France, where they set up one of the French branches of the Land Company, and each took out a share. Soon after they returned to Gloucester in 1848, the old man died.[35]

Martin Jude, leader of the miners in the north-east of England and an active Chartist, was earning his living as an innkeeper by the time the Chartist movement began. Like many other trade unionists, he had little chance of employment at this trade.[36] For men of this kind, the keeping of an alehouse could mean earning less money than they would have gained at their trade. James Mitchell, the 27-year-old cotton spinners' leader from Stockport, told the prison inspector that he had earned twenty-five shillings a week as a cotton spinner, but that the beerhouse which he and his wife ran barely afforded them subsistence; 'I have not derived much benefit from Chartism since I became a member of its body' he added.[37]

The alehouse or the newsagent's shop provided a meeting-place between formal meetings, and also provided a filter through which strangers in a neighbourhood could gradually be introduced to the councils of the local Chartists. Most towns had their well-known radical pubs and alehouses, and the *Star* agent, whose name appeared in the paper, was an obvious figure for a newcomer to a town to approach to be put in touch with the local radicals.

There were other radical shopkeepers whose premises provided a port of call for travelling radicals. One of England's best-known radicals in the Chartist period was Lawrence Pitkethly, draper, of Huddersfield. Patrick Lloyd Jones, the Owenite and Cooperative lecturer, recalled the atmosphere of Pitkethly's home many years later.

> Lawrence Pitkethly I knew very well. He was for many years a woollen draper in Huddersfield. . . In the old coaching days, after a cold ride over Stanedge from Manchester, the first place I used to make for was Pitkethly's and there in his first floor room over the shop he was sure to be met with, if at home, and in nine cases out of ten he was surrounded by a small group of the most thorough Radicals. . . I remember with pleasure these old kindly faces and the many warm discussions held by the parties assembled. . . There was no man better known in the West Riding than 'Old Pitt'. . .[38]

Pitkethly was a lifelong friend of O'Connor, and always closely connected with the main line of Chartism. He was in comfortable circumstances and could afford to employ as shopman John Leech, also a committed radical, which meant that he was able to take time off from his business concerns to travel or to organise meetings or campaigns. He spent many weeks stumping the country raising money and support for the Glasgow cotton spinners in 1837, and he was a supporter and colleague of Richard Oastler in the short-time movement. He was not an impressive speaker, nor did he do a great deal of writing in Chartist periodicals, but his name crops up in almost every major area of activity. He stood as a candidate in the 1841 election, and, with Harney, won the show of hands for the West Riding. In 1842 he visited the United States, and made contact with some of the exiled Canadian rebels and emigrant Chartists. When he returned he wrote a series of articles on emigration for the *Star*. Gammage characterised Pitkethly as a radical of the Cobbett type, but he was much more of a mainline or O'Connor Chartist. He was never concerned, as was Cobbett, to respect the niceties of conventional politics. Although he stood as a Chartist candidate, it was never with the view of becoming a Member of Parliament, and he was always on the wing of the radical movement which anticipated armed conflict with the authorities.[39]

One of the most consistent radical shopkeepers was Samuel Cook, another draper, in Dudley. In the local library there are still a large number of Cook's pamphlets, posters and handbills which he distributed from his shop in the main street of the town. A strong universal suffrage man, he also consistently supported women's suffrage and women's rights generally, and appealed to a participatory popular democracy which went well beyond the programme of the Chartist six points. From his draper's shop he had supported striking nailers in 1826, and was arrested in that year for seditious libel. A few years later, as chairman of the Dudley Political Union, he was again considered as a candidate for prosecution, although in the heat of the reform agitation the magistrates decided not to prosecute. In the post-Reform Bill period, Cook, like Bussey in Bradford, led the local campaign for the extension of parliamentary reform and for universal suffrage. When Chartism drew together provincial radical groups throughout the country, Cook was one of its natural leaders. He was again arrested after speaking at a meeting in 1839 called to protest against the behaviour of the Metropolitan Police in the Birmingham Bull Ring clash. He was convicted and sentenced to six months' imprisonment. He remained in the forefront of the local movement. His shop windows had been smashed in 1834 when he had displayed radical posters. In 1842, when striking miners marched through the street his were almost alone in not being damaged. He was again arrested in the autumn of 1842 for inciting the population to tumultuous assemblage.

He served as an officer of the NCA and of the Chartist Land Company, and after the Chartist movement had subsided nationally, he remained a proponent of universal suffrage, women's rights and participatory democracy. He also retained a strong concern with international affairs, and was in the process of raising a fund to support Garibaldi when he died in 1861.[40]

Neither Pitkethly nor Cook were figures who have made much impact on the historiography of Chartism. Yet they and others like them up and down the country were much more influential than some of the more picturesque and self-indulgent figures who saw themselves as leaders of an English revolution. Chartism was a movement whose strength lay in the localities, and the consistent work of a core of convinced and self-sacrificing people in all parts of the country gave it the staying power which was its unique quality. No other European radical movement in the first half of the century had the same continuity of personnel and organisation.

In Morpeth and Newcastle upon Tyne, shopkeepers also gave stability to the organisation and to the publications which sustained one of the most lively Chartist districts. Robert Blakey of Morpeth was a furrier whose business was substantial enough to provide funds for the purchase, jointly with Thomas Doubleday, a member of a local Quaker business family, of the influential *Northern Liberator* in 1838. Blakey had been mayor of Morpeth in 1837, and is an example of the ultra-radicalism of some of the smaller self-made businessmen of the period. Both Blakey and Doubleday had been associated with Cobbett, Blakey having written for his *Register*. Both were intellectuals as well as active local leaders, both were arrested during the Chartist period, and both published substantial works during those years – Blakey a pamphlet on the Poor Laws, and Doubleday a substantial volume in refutation of Malthus.[41] They were able to employ a group of talented radical journalists on the paper, including Thomas Ainge Devyr, who also acted as organisers for the Northern Political Union. One of Blakey's apprentice furriers also achieved some prominence in the Chartist movement. This was Charles Junius Haslem who is best remembered as the author of *Letters to the Clergy of All Denominations*. The sale of this booklet led to the prosecution under the blasphemy laws of Abel Heywood, John Cleave and Henry Hetherington, part of the rearguard action still being fought against free thought in the 1830s and 1840s. Haslam was active in Manchester as a Chartist and radical.[42]

John Blakey was another Newcastle Chartist shopkeeper. He was a master shoemaker and clogger, whose premises, according to Devyr, were used for the manufacture and distribution of pikes during the summer of 1839.

I was present in some part of nearly every Saturday at the pike market to take sharp note of the sales. The market was held in a long garret room over John Blakey's shop in the side. In rows were benches of boards supported on tressels along which the Winlaton and Swalswell chain and nailmakers brought in their interregnum of pikes, each a dozen or two, rolled up in a smith's apron. . .[43]

The comparative independence of the shopkeeper in a sympathetic local community meant that many more names of such people have survived than of those with more vulnerable occupations. As well as Pitkethly, Cook and Frost, Chartist drapers included Robert Cochrane of Paisley and Hugh Craig of Kilmarnock, both important figures in the early years of Scottish Chartism, although both left the movement early. Craig resigned as delegate for Ayrshire to the first Chartist Convention in July 1839, in protest against the proposed ulterior measures, and rapidly moved from radicalism to confirmed Toryism. His main contribution to radicalism was in the immediately pre-Chartist period. He was one of the Jacobin-type radicals, followers of Paine and Cobbett, who became more cautious politically when the Government's response to the Convention appeared more restrained than they had feared. When weighed in the balance, the evils of the Whig post-reform politics seemed less dangerous to such men than the potentially uncontrollable mass action which Chartism appeared to be encouraging. Robert Cochrane was a very important figure in the early months of the founding of the movement in Paisley. He later moved into the orbit of the Complete Suffrage Movement, which he saw as less likely to arouse dangerous elements in society. Unlike Craig, Cochrane remained an associate of the Paisley Chartists, and an active supporter of the Ten Hours agitation and of Richard Oastler, its leader; after the end of Chartism he continued to support radical liberalism including the Scottish National Reform League at the time of the Second Reform Bill. His draper's shop grew into Paisley's largest department store.[44]

Thomas Allsop, one of Chartism's few wealthy supporters, was also a draper in the early days of his business career. Allsop was a very important figure, if only because he was the one man of means who remained a staunch supporter of mainline Chartism throughout its existence, helping with money and advice on many occasions. It is strange that his name does not appear in the index of any of the histories of Chartism. The entry in the *DNB* by Holyoake is an affectionate account by someone who knew Allsop and had been helped by him, and rightly stresses the importance of his relations with Feargus O'Connor. In the collection of Allsop's papers at the London School of Economics[45] are some of the very few surviving letters of O'Connor, as well as letters from Bronterre O'Brien, Richard Oastler and Robert Owen. It is clear that Allsop and his wife were on terms of close personal friendship with all of these, as they were with Lawrence Pitkethly and many of the other Chartists. Allsop was an almost exact contemporary of Feargus, and had been involved with radical thought and radical politics since he was a young man. Holyoake, with his simplistic Whig view of history, characterised Allsop, as he also characterised Owen, as a 'conservative' because both put more emphasis on the need for social change than for political reform. It is perhaps this description, since Holyoake is the only historian of the movement who gives him a mention,[46] that has led to Allsop's omission from the enquiries of Chartism's other historians. However, there are clues to be found throughout the period. In 1838, the *Operative* published in full a paper by Allsop on his response to a summons for jury service. The Recorder had refused to read the paper, but had excused Allsop from jury service on the grounds of his conscientious objection to finding anyone guilty on a capital charge. The paper gave the reason for this objection, and made an impressive argument. It began by pointing to the known existence of 'seminaries of crime' in districts of London in which children were instructed in thieving, and which the Government was making no attempt to suppress or counter; it went on to summarise the inadequacies of the criminal law ('not unfitly named') to deal with crime and its causes, to point out the unsuitability of violent punishment for crimes against property, and the total lack of provision for the rehabilitation of criminals, and ended by saying that 'I do not consider myself justified in sending for punishment any prisoner arraigned at the bar.'[47] Allsop's name occurs on various occasions at meetings, not as a speaker but as a contributor of ideas for funding and controlling funds. He acted as bail for many arrested Chartists, provided money and credit for the Chartist Land Plan (by this time he had given up his connection with the drapery trade and was a stockbroker and property owner) and he provided O'Connor with the title to freehold property worth £300 a year to enable him to qualify as Member of Parliament when he was elected for Nottingham in 1847. To the end of his life he remained in correspondence with the old Chartists – Harney and Holyoake among others – and was also in touch with Marx and Engels, apparently on terms of friendship.[48] His letter to Feargus on the eve of 10 April 1848 is important and interesting, not only for its indication of Allsop's own ideas, but for the fact that it shows an assessment of O'Connor which is not at all in line with the dismissive attitude taken by so many later writers.[49]

As well as booksellers and drapers, there were a number of Chartist grocers, including John Leach, the 'red cat of Hyde', who played a leading part in the plug riots of 1842, and was among those arraigned in the conspiracy trial. At the trades conference on 15 August, he represented the factory workers of his district, so may well have been another of the active Chartists who found a small shop a better basis for organising in his district than working in a factory. He played a prominent part in the meetings during August, and was one of the defendants found guilty on the fourth count of the indictment. In his summing up the judge singled out Leach for 'using the most inflammatory and vulgar language, as to the quantity of provisions used by the Queen etc.'[50] Thomas Powell, the Welshpool Chartist, kept an ironmonger's shop, Alexander Taylor of Oldham, a former powerloom weaver, was a shopkeeper and flour dealer, Nathaniel Whimper, one of Ipswich's leading Chartists, was a wine merchant, and Peter Foden of Sheffield was a confectioner. At least two prominent Chartists, James Sweet of Nottingham and David Pilmore of Barnsley, were hairdressers, and there were also a certain number of druggists and apothecaries. These included William Potts, of Trowbridge, who displayed in his windows in 1839 bullets labelled 'Pills for the Tories',[51] and John Ruecastle of Tyneside, who skipped bail with T. A. Devyr in 1839 and emigrated to America.[52] James Scholefield was also described during the trial of 1843 as an apothecary, although he was probably more correctly to be called a herbalist. He was born in Yorkshire, but towards the end of the Napoleonic wars he took over a small congregation in Manchester of Cowherdites or Bible Christians, whose chapel was built beside the apothecary's business of their founder. Here Scholefield carried on practising as a herbalist and vegetarian, as well as minister of the chapel and master of the school which was held on the premises. By the Chartist period his eldest son William was mainly responsible for the school. Scholefield was a supporter of Henry Hunt, and had been present at the Peterloo massacre. His house remained a centre for radicalism in the Ancoats area, and Feargus O'Connor often stayed there when he visited the city. In 1842 a meeting there of the Chartist executive and a few others to organise the erection of a memorial to Hunt was the centre around which the conspiracy trial turned. Scholefield's chapel was watched by the authorities and his letters opened by the Home Office in 1842. He was connected with the development in Lancashire of non-denominational Sunday schools, at which an all-round education was provided. Both he and William were arrested and included in the conspiracy trial in 1842-3, although all the charges against William were dropped before the trial ended and his father was found 'not guilty' on all counts. They remained among the leaders of local Chartism, and James Scholefield was a speaker with O'Connor at the opening of the Manchester Chartist Hall in July 1846.[53]

The small businessmen and shopkeepers who cropped up in the committee lists of the National Charter Association were always in a minority in the whole lists; it is interesting, too, that it was by no means the case that where a shopkeeper or even a businessman was a committee member, he held the position of greatest responsibility. The seven members of the Wellingborough committee in January 1842 were all shoemakers except for Mr George Gibbons, a butcher. But both treasurer and secretary were shoemakers. In Chelsea in the same month, the treasurer was William Martin, a victualler, while the secretary was John Dowling, a bricklayer. In Rochdale all the committee members except the treasurer were members of working trades, but the treasurer, George Morton, was a blacking manufacturer. The secretary was a joiner. It seems to have been the case that the very small number of men who belonged to slightly more 'middle-class' occupations did not stand out as superior in organising skills or clerical abilities to the working men among whom they lived, with the possible slight exception of the choice of such people for the role of treasurer. The vast majority of committee lists, of course, contained no names which belonged to even a notionally middle-class occupation.

The genuinely middle-class Chartists were very few in number, and usually did not take part in the actual running of the Association. There were a small number of sympathetic clergy, the odd surgeon or lawyer, and a sprinkling of schoolmasters, some of whom, like many of the shopkeepers and small manufacturers, had lost their jobs at their own trades, or found the restrictions on political activity too great.

The best-known of the Chartist clergy was fat Dr Wade of Warwick. He combined membership of the Established Church with strong support of Owenism, and particularly of trade unionism. He had been forbidden to preach in his parish during the early thirties, when his association with the Grand National Consolidated Trades Union became too distasteful to his ecclesiastical superiors, and in the early Chartist years he was a free-flowing ecclesiastic, available to take part in processions, or to lead a prayer at the opening of Chartist meetings or demonstrations. He was, however, never very happy in the mass movement, and in fact wrote to the authorities warning of the danger of some of the 'physical force' advocates in 1839. He resigned from the Convention even before the Birmingham delegation, and reappeared later only as a forceful and eloquent pleader for clemency for John Frost, and as a supporter of the Complete Suffrage Union.[54]

A more consistent and influential clergyman, whose name was widely known during the Chartist years, has been left out of the history books in a rather surprising way. The Reverend Humphrey Price was born in Kidderminster, and although his incumbency was at Needwood, near Burton-on-Trent, he retained a lifelong interest and concern for the carpet weavers of his native town. During the long strike in 1828, Price wrote and published anonymous ballads and open letters to the manufacturers. He spent a year in Stafford gaol for criminal libel as a result. When Thomas Cooper spent a year in the same prison, he, like most of the Chartist prisoners, agitated constantly for better conditions. He recalled that the governor congratulated him.

> 'I admire your pluck, Cooper,' said the dear old governor . . . in an undertone . . . 'your day-room was the day-room of the Reverend Humphrey Price, the "good parson of Needwood Forest" as he was called. He was a clergyman who sympathised, like you, with the poor; and for defending the poor wretched carpet-weavers of Kidderminster, had to pass a year in this prison. But he was never allowed a single privilege. . . What he might have gained if he had shown as much spirit as yourself, I cannot tell; but he never seemed to have the spirit to ask for anything. . .'[55]

Unlike the more spirited Cooper, however, Price came out of prison with his views unchanged. In 1836, when the weavers were again on strike, led by the men who were soon to become leaders of the Chartist movement, Price circulated a handbill entitled *The Reverend Humphrey Price to his Native Townsmen, the Kidderminster Carpet Weavers*, urging the weavers to press for political rights, without which a man 'is a slave without a vote in the state, or even in the petty place in which he lives. He must work as ordered and take what he is offered or starve.'[56] Price issued a series of leaflets and pamphlets in support of the Charter, and remained sympathetic in spite of the Newport rising and in spite of the turbulence of 1842. In fact in the latter year he went bail for the Irish Chartist lecturer John West of Macclesfield, and was publicly thanked for this by the Leicester Chartists. He acknowledged their thanks, and reiterated his support for universal suffrage.

> To make every man's vote good is in the power of God only; but to secure the

man his vote, and to counteract its tendency if bad is within the power of man and may be greatly promoted by passing into law . . . the document called 'The People's Charter', a document in perfect accord with the purest principles of the British Constitution.[57]

A very different kind of clergman was William Vickers Jackson. A shoemaker by trade, he had his own congregation of supporters who had followed him when he seceded from the Methodists and set up his own society. He was one of those arrested at the same time as Doyle and Linney in Manchester in 1839, where, although he told the inspector of prisons that he had never been a member of any Chartist organisation, he had been a very prominent figure on Chartist platforms. He continued to speak and preach in favour of the six points for many years after he was released from gaol, and it can only be supposed that his disavowal to the inspector was deliberately misleading, if, as it may well have been, technically correct. Jackson was a friend of another famous shoemaker turned agitator, William Benbow. A gossipy letter addressed to Jackson by Benbow when they were in different prisons was confiscated by the governor, presumably because of criticisms it contained of prison treatment and prison food; at the time both men were strongly in support of Stephens and consequently critical of McDouall. Even in prison the followers of the two leaders squabbled, and Benbow and Jackson seem to have taken the side of Stephens. Major Williams characterised Jackson as

a very ignorant man, but by intense reading of the scriptures [he] has obtained a facility of quoting passages from them and also a readiness and propriety of applying them. . . He states he was first induced to embark in politics from opposition to the New Poor Law. . . I believe him to be a man of great religious feeling. His great failing, like many of the others, is personal vanity.[58]

David John, the Chartist minister at Twyn yr Odyn, Merthyr, was also the centre of a loyal congregation. A Unitarian and a working blacksmith, he held a Sunday school and night classes at his smithy, and with his sons, Matthew and David, produced a local Chartist newspaper, and played a leading part in the Chartist activity of Merthyr and district throughout the thirties and forties.[59]

Barnsley had the rare distinction for a time of having a Catholic priest who was a Chartist. When Fr Ryan returned to Ireland in 1841, he became a member of the Irish Universal Suffrage Association, and a letter was sent signed by 109 of his former male parishioners, congratulating him on doing so. Peter Michael Brophy, secretary of the Association at the time, tried to get similar letters from other groups of

Catholic Chartists, but there is no evidence that he succeeded.[60]

There were some chapels which were organised and run by the Chartists – a system which Stephens found distasteful when he discovered that he was to preach at a Democratic Chapel in Hebden Bridge.

> Alas – he declared – that the Church, in any part of England can thus drive her children from her path! I am certain there never would have been a *Democratic Chapel* in Hebden Bridge if the *Theocratic Church* had done her duty.[61]

In Scotland in particular many districts had their own chapels which served also as schools. The Birmingham Chartist Church, led by Arthur O'Neil, which earned O'Connor's condemnation, did so not because it was a Christian Chartist organisation, but because it was set up at the time of the 'new move' in opposition to the NCA, and its members did not join the main Chartist organisation.[62] The atmosphere of ultra-dissent in the Chartist chapels, however, was always seen as something of a problem in districts like Birmingham in 1842, in which attempts were being made to win the cooperation of the immigrant Irish. In other districts, some nonconformist congregations must have consisted very largely of Chartists, like that of the Rev. Mr McPhail, Baptist minister of Uncoat, which was reported in 1844 to have been made up of 'only colliers and Chartists'.

Independent tradesmen and professional men were an important element in the Chartist movement. They did not, in the main, make up the leadership, but rather provided a network of premises, communication centres and meeting-places, and on occasion helped to supply certain skills and certain kinds of understanding which were of service to the movement. The great mass of the membership, however, and the majority of leaders, both national and local, came from among the working members of the trades and crafts of the manufacturing districts.

CHAPTER NINE

Labourers and the Trades

AN examination of the known trades and occupations of Chartists suggests that throughout the towns and manufacturing districts of Great Britain the distribution of Chartists' trades was fairly close, on the whole, to the general distribution throughout the population. There was, however, an outstanding exception to this pattern. More people were employed full-time in agriculture in the first half of the nineteenth century than in any other occupation, but agricultural labourers rarely appear in either the NCA committee lists or among arrested Chartists. Their views on political matters are rarely heard, and many writers have assumed on their part a deferential acquiescence in the *status quo*.

How far can a study of Chartism help to understand the attitudes of agricultural workers? Clearly there are very large silences. Chartism occurred at the beginning of the years during which the countryside was becoming depopulated. Improved communications and the changes in marketing habits were causing the decline of the rural artisan, villages were becoming ever more pastoral, and every year thousands of men and women voted with their feet by leaving behind the life of the village and migrating to the industrial centres and the towns. It is probably true that this migration took with it many of the most restless and dissatisfied of the rural workers. A number of Chartists had been born in villages and into agricultural families. Of the forty Brighton Chartists examined by T. M. Kemnitz, nine had been born in rural villages and had come to Brighton in childhood or early youth. No similar study has been done of a major manufacturing district, but some prominent Chartists we know came from a country background. Robert Meek Carter began work at the age of six as an agricultural labourer, but by the age of sixteen he had moved into the city of Leeds and work in a cotton factory. He became an overlooker, saved some money with which he set up in business as a coal merchant, and eventually became a noted figure in the town's radical politics and a Member of Parliament for the borough.[1]

That there was a potential response in the countryside to the message of Chartism is shown by a number of incidents. The Loveless brothers, leaders of the Tolpuddle labourers, returned to Essex in 1836, and by the time the Charter was launched several of the leaders, including

George Loveless, were settled in south-west Essex. George Loveless was elected to the first Convention in 1839, but was able to spend only a short time there, as he could not afford to leave his small holding.[2] He seems, however, to have gathered round him a very lively movement at his home.

> . . . Chartist newspapers were quickly seen in active circulation. The beer shops in which they were to be found became more frequented and more noisy than heretofore. A Chartist Association was formed at Greenstead and, by the combined or alternate influence of persuasion and of terror, nearly the whole of the agricultural labourers in that and the adjoining parishes were induced to join it. . .

The report goes on to chronicle a remarkable increase in numbers and in activity throughout the spring and summer of 1839. But the 'persuasion and terror' were not all on one side, and the farmers took action.

> The effect of these proceedings was to diffuse a general sense of insecurity throughout that part of the country and so far to disturb the habitual relations between the farmers and labourers that the former thought it necessary to adopt a system of hiring for the last harvest different from their previous practice and to engage their labourers on such terms that, in case of desertion from their work, they might be liable to summary punishment.[3]

If the actions of the employers subdued the activities of the Chartist labourers, the Loveless brothers themselves continued to be part of the movement. In 1847 William Loveless was writing to his brother, by now established in Canada, with news of his membership of the Land Plan and sending him the words of Chartist songs, including the hymn 'Britannia's sons, though slaves ye be'.[4]

Membership of the Land Company was, indeed, one of the few ways in which a farm worker could associate with Chartism without fear of dismissal. Names among the surviving lists suggest a participation much greater than the known participation in NCA branches. But here there is the problem that the designation 'labourer' is a broad one, and it is not usually possible to know the proportion of farm labourers. To take part in the plan, a regular access to the *Northern Star* was essential, and membership in isolated villages suggests a very wide diffusion of the paper. But even subscription would not have been easy in the countryside. In 1841 the problem was noted.

> Many have been dismissed from work for reading the *Star*. Many, very many, in country districts, walk, on a Saturday night, after a week's toil, as many as three, four, five or six miles to the country town, fearful of taking the *Star* from the village agent, under the nose of the village tyrant.[5]

In spite of this, there were Land Company members in places like Caythrop Lambey, Bishops Itchington, Iveston, Lytchett Maltravers, Powick and Shebbear.[6]

The countryside was by no means devoid of class antagonisms in these years, and farmers and landowners were far from being complacent about the situation. Many reacted strongly to any attempt by urban Chartists to speak to their labourers – indeed their alertness made the Chartists' task of penetrating the countryside with any kind of organisation almost insuperably difficult. Elliot Yorke, MP for Cambridgeshire, voiced the unease of many when he said:

> If gentlemen think there is nothing to be dreaded from our rural labourers, I fear they are greatly mistaken. I do not believe there is any village in my neighbourhood that would not be ready to assert by *brute force* their right (as they say) to eat fully the fruit arising from their own labour. . . . Every parish in this neighbourhood is . . . ripe for any outbreak.[7]

When Henry Vincent toured the West Country in the summer of 1838, he met with some success in attracting agricultural workers to his meetings. The difficulty of following up such success, however, was illustrated by the experience of the villagers of Steeple Ashton, where William Carrier, Trowbridge Chartist leader, spoke in April 1839. The day after the meeting a local farmer dismissed all those of his workpeople who had attended the meeting. Such dismissal meant the loss of their houses as well as their livelihoods, and when one of the dismissed men was re-hired by the farmer, the others gathered to demolish his cottage, and a riot ensued.[8] A magistrate from the district wrote in alarm to the Home Secretary that thousands of members were being enrolled by the Working Men's Association of Trowbridge and district, including his own gardeners and farm hands.[9] In East Anglia the tactics of the gentry were perhaps less brutal than those of their Wiltshire counterparts. At Friston, in 1838, one gentleman laid on a feast for his labourers to coincide with a Chartist rally, whilst a local farmer bribed his hands with a bushel of potatoes apiece to stay away. In spite of these inducements, however, a meeting of one thousand was held and a Working Men's Association formed.[10]

The reform agitation in the towns and cities in 1830-2 had laid the basis for the Chartist movement, and the resistance to the imposition of the new Poor Law had added experience and enthusiasm to the growing movement. In the countryside, however, the thirties had been a decade of defeat. The 'Swing' riots and their draconian suppression had left a demoralised population able to do little more than organise sporadic resistance to the hated Poor Law, or to demonstrate by arson and cattle-houghing their resentment and disaffection. Recent studies have shown that such disaffection was more widespread than has always been recognised,[11] and observers as varied as Charles Kingsley, Benjamin Disraeli and Alexander Somerville were agreed in finding the atmosphere of the countryside as alienated and class-divided as that of the towns.[12]

For the Chartists, the plight of the labourers was always an issue. The Dorchester case of 1834 had been one of Chartism's starting points. Another was the almost-forgotten incident of the Battle of Bossenden Wood in 1838. When Robert Lowery was speaking at a meeting in Newcastle, and a group of soldiers was seen approaching, he launched into a fierce attack on the military and was loudly cheered when he urged his audience to 'remember Peterloo and Canterbury!'[13] John Thom, alias Sir William Courtenay, had been slaughtered, with eight of his followers, on 5 June 1838, at a small village outside Canterbury. Thom was a man with a history of madness, who had built up a following among the labourers and small farmers in the district. His rhetoric was religious – he sometimes presented himself as the Messiah at his second coming – but also strongly opposed to the new Poor Law, and with overtones of democracy. 'If Courtenay was mad,' Feargus O'Connor wrote, 'how woeful must be the condition of those men who will follow a mad man in the hope of change.' But Courtenay's rhetoric and publications were by no means incoherent.

> The poor are the great sufferers in every age of the world, but does poverty abrogate the liberty of the subject? God forbid! It is . . . this class from which all blessings flow to those above them – it is . . . the poor labourers and working mechanic, who are the real riches of a country, and never more so than when virtue and morality are the companions of their daily toil. . .[14]

He attacked the Established Church, the tithe laws, and the 'present ignorant House of Commons, which is a mock Parliament, not being the voice of the people'. When he shot a constable who tried to arrest him, he and his small group of followers were surrounded by the military, and he and eight others, unarmed except for sticks, were killed. O'Brien wrote in the *Star*:

> An event has occurred which has filled all virtuous minds with horror, and which makes me look with dismal forebodings to the future. Need I say that I allude to the recent bloody tragedy enacted in Bossenden Wood near Canterbury? Now I say that while this tragedy is before my sight I can think of no other subject. Nine of my countrymen have been assassinated and there is to

be neither vengeance or redress! Redress did I say? Alas! It is the murderers who have taken cognizance of the crime, and the murdered men who are at this moment *branded as murderers*! Not all the waters of ocean will ever wipe this stain from our country's annals.[15]

In retrospect the incident can be seen as an isolated event, but at the time, coming soon after similar events in the tithe war in Ireland, it had reverberations which heightened the tensions throughout the country.

The Chartists never wrote off the country workers, in spite of the difficulty of reaching into the villages. In his defence in the 1843 trial, James Leach linked agricultural workers, factory workers and out-workers together when he declared that

. . . in proportion as we increase our productions, the working people sink down into wretchedness and want. At this very moment the agricultural labourers are pining and getting a very scanty portion of food, in the midst of the vast accumulation of the produce of their own labour. In proportion as they have thus multiplied what ought to have given blessings to all, they are themselves in want, woe and sorrow. Is it not a truth that while the warehouses of Manchester are at this moment ready to break down with the superabundant weight of the goods piled in them, the result of the slavery of the industrious classes of England, those who produce the cloth have not themselves a decent suit of clothes to put on their backs, and cannot attend a place of worship on Sundays because they are in rags and would be despised by the better classes?[16]

The starting of O'Connor's Land Plan in 1845 brought a practical form of radical action within reach of the labourers. Although they seldom appear in Chartist committee lists – a Mr Powell of Birmingham seems to have been the only committee man who gave his occupation specifically as 'farm labourer' – labourers form one of the largest groups in the lists of Land Company members. Of course, the description 'labourer' covers many different types of work, and there is no way of telling how many who gave this as their occupation were agricultural workers. But it is probable that Adam Rushton, 'Farmers Boy, Factory Lad, Teacher and Preacher', spoke for many of them when he wrote of his Chartist period:

What interested me most at these meetings was the question of the Land, which was earnestly discussed. My father had always the earth hunger upon him, and so had I. Should I ever be able to possess a few acres of freehold to make an earthly paradise? This was a question I pondered over frequently and long. . .[17]

Aspects of land questions had been discussed in the radical press before 1845, and country grievances like the decline of gleaning which had caused riots in some districts had been given something of an airing.

Gleaning is not *now* a matter of right but courtesy. All the old customs and wholesome conversations of merry England – our country so-called some years ago – are banned. Plague of the economists![18]

With the Land Plan, however, something more than protest became possible. Whereas the labourers had of necessity to keep their heads down in any public action, they were able to take out shares in the company without risk of persecution. In Yorkshire, outside the main cities and manufacturing towns, 146 of the 1,437 members were labourers, second only in numbers to weavers. In Gloucestershire outside the towns, 38 members gave their occupation as labourer, of whom 2 specified farm labourer, of a total of 102 members. In Halifax where farm labourers made up 2·88 per cent of the employed males over twenty, 52 of the 502 Land Plan members were labourers – more than 10 per cent – though not necessarily farm workers.

Chartists in areas near the countryside set out to take the Land Company material into the labourers' houses. In 1848 an anxious gentleman in Tewkesbury wrote to his Member of Parliament, enclosing a copy of *Liberty or Bondage or a Voice from the Oppressed*, a twenty-six-stanza poem by the balladeer and printer, Thomas Willey.[19] 'They were found in the cottage of a labourer, and I understand they have been extensively circulated, which fact taken in conjunction with frequent meetings of Chartists from all quarters in this neighbourhood is making politicians of the agricultural labourers, many of whom have joined the "land scheme".'[20]

Many thousands of agricultural workers emigrated in the later years of the nineteenth century, and those who remained were often alienated and dejected. For a small number a radical alternative may have seemed possible, at least for a time, but for others the radical press itself served only as a vehicle for the expression of their hopelessness. A Suffolk labourer wrote in 1847:

These mushroom great people have all grown up since I remember, and if I speak to them of the hard times, they tell me to look at the great improvements, the new docks, the cheap postage, the fine railways; really, say they, this is a grand and glorious country; Sir Robert has repealed the Corn-laws and Lord John will drain our streets and erect baths. Oh! What a blessed land this is. Well, well, Say I, very good, but what benefit has it conferred on me? Here I am working harder than ever, poorer than ever, with no remedy for want and no hope but death.

The railway whizzes past my door, but I never had my foot in a railway carriage. I have no correspondence but with my neighbours . . . my brown bread is dearer, my wages are no higher. The great docks with their many ships, the great railways and fast-running mail carts, have added not a stone to my cottage, nor a crumb to my table. . .[21]

A smallholder or small farmer, like the master workman in the towns, had a lot more freedom to follow his political inclinations. But, although one of the often-neglected precursors of the Chartist movement, the Central National Association, was based on a cooperation between the London radicals, including O'Connor, O'Brien and most of the leading members of the LWMA with the Cambridgeshire Farmers' Association, in the years 1836 and 1837, not many farmers or smallholders were prominent among the Chartists; not at least until the drawing of an allotment in the Land Company turned some of the Chartist stalwarts from other trades into agriculturalists. Among the Welsh Chartists arrested after Newport was Jenkin Morgan, a small farmer who also traded as a milkman and tallow-chandler. In the West Midlands the Feckenham representative to the Birmingham and Worcester delegate meetings was a Mr Bolton, farmer, in 1844. Feckenham was a small town in the middle of a rich agricultural district, whose main industry was pin and needle-making, but there is very little evidence in the national press of much activity among radicals there in the Chartist period. Another farmer who made a brief appearance in the records was 'A public-spirited wealthy farmer, of the name of Brown, of Burton Bradstock who, when the six Dorchester labourers were arrested, had hired a post-chaise and four and hurried up to London to procure the ablest counsel to defend them, and to arouse public opinion in their defence. . .' This gentleman gave Henry Solly a generous donation towards the cost of producing his radical-Christian pamphlet *What Says Christianity to the Present Distress?* in 1842, but Solly records that 'He was much annoyed, on the last occasion when I met him, by my outspoke denunciation of Feargus O'Connor. . . Mr Brown thoroughly believed in O'Connor and I never saw or heard of him again.'[22]

After agriculture, textile manufacture and building, the leather trades, of which shoemaking was the most widespread, were the largest employers of male labour in Britain in 1851.[23] However, even given their very large numbers, most people at the time, and since, have considered that shoemakers were over-represented among radical and Chartist activists.

The general denomination 'shoemaker' covered a wide range of trades and many different levels of skill. Shoemaking, like all artisan trades, saw many changes during the Chartist period. Although it was as yet totally un-mechanised, the trade had been rationalised, and many who took part in it would have been hard put to it to make a whole shoe or boot. In some areas, like Northampton and Kettering, shoemaking was organised as a manufacturing industry, with some of the work being put out into homes or small workshops, some being carried on in larger workshops. Bespoke work was still carried on all over the country, and a skilled man seems to have been able to get work in this branch without much difficulty. At the other end of the scale, the snob – the slopworking shoemaker – used more ingenuity than skill, and turned out work of which he was himself ashamed. John James Bezer gives a hilarious account of his year's training in the dishonourable calling, after which 'in less than a year I became a snob, but not a *shoemaker*; not a tradesman. No; it would be harder for me to learn to make a *good* shoe than perhaps if I had never learned how to make a bad one.[24]

The radicalism of the shoemakers may have arisen from their general resistance to discipline and control. They had the reputation of being particularly irregular in their working hours, and particularly rowdy in their leisure.

> Shoemakers of forty years ago were characterised by great slovenliness of dress and dissoluteness of habits. Of this there can be no manner of doubt. . . Nor were these objectionable features confined to the shoemakers of any given place or number of places. They were tarred with the same brush in both London and the country. This possibly, in part resulted from the freedom which shoemakers then enjoyed, a freedom that has not materially diminished. Freed from the eye of the master, there was nothing to hold them in check, and as it was customary to make up lost hours by trespassing on those of the night, the propensity to fuddle was less restricted than in other trades. . .[25]

So wrote an old shoemaker, looking back from 1879. His judgement coincides with that of many contemporaries. A Bolton newspaper editor told Gustave d'Eichthal that 'The journeyman boot and shoemakers and tailors are just as disorderly as the textile workers'.[26] Shoemakers shared with textile outworkers the lack of discipline, the right to organise their own time and the system of piece-work which enabled them to control the amount of work and the speed of work. In parts of the country St Monday was known as 'Cobblers' Monday' for this reason. They had an additional advantage of working at a trade which was not noisy or physically very tough. The shoemaker's 'seat' produced poets, writers and radicals.

The truth is, I could never think off the seat, and if this history had not been thought out in days long gone by, when I stuck to the seat as close as wax it would never have been written. I veritably believe that Drew composed his 'Immortality of the Soul', Cooper his 'Purgatory of Suicides', Bloomfield his 'Farmer's Boy' and Gifford his 'Baviad' on the seat, and I know that MacKay framed his model of the planetary system, and O'Neill wrote his great Bacchanalian song while sitting on it. . .[27]

Thus another old shoemaker, recalling his youth and his involvement with the Cato Street conspiracy. The shoemaker's seat had been occupied by many of the Cato Street conspirators, and was later the source of inspiration of several of the members of the Chartist Orange Tree conspiracy. Shoemakers' shops and garrets sheltered army deserters, refugees from political trials and Irish confederates during the Chartist years, as well as serving as distribution centres for unstamped journals, Chartists pamphlets and the *Northern Star*.

Chartist shoemakers belonged to all sections of the trade. Some were village cobblers, making and mending shoes in the community and providing a centre for discussion of politics and other questions. Others were small masters, journeymen working on one process in a workshop, or outworkers performing one part of the manufacture in their homes. A few, like Bezer, were snobs. Some areas had separate shoemakers' localities of the NCA, but apart from these, there were at least thirty-three other localities which had shoemakers as their secretaries. Some of the best-known figures in the movement were, or had been, members of the trade. The names of William Benbow, Samuel Kydd, Thomas Cooper, Allen Davenport, John (Daddy) Richards and William Cardo appear in all the histories. Others were well-known to their contemporaries in the movement; John Mitchell, first president of the Aberdeen WMA, was a journeyman shoemaker who became the leader of 'moderate' Chartism in the city until his early death in 1845. He had had a leg amputated, and was never strong physically, but he became an outstanding speaker and writer for the movement, publishing a volume of poems, and editing two radical journals, the *Spectator* and the *Aberdeen Review*. Towards the end of his life he gave up his trade and earned a living by bookselling.[28] The Rev. W. V. Jackson of Manchester was a shoemaker turned minister, John Skelton a London shoemaker who became a naturopath. William Martin and Thomas Clarke were Irish shoemakers who travelled the country agitating and gaining a living by their convenient trade. Many in the trade served terms of imprisonment, including some of those mentioned, and five members of the Orange Tree conspiracy in London in 1848, Thomas

Fay, William Lacey, William Burn, George Greenslade and William Gurney.

Like the innkeeper or the blacksmith, the village shoemaker could be an important local figure. 'As regards intellectual power and ability,' claimed one writer, 'go into any village in England, and you may safely take odds that the shoemaker will be found the most prominent member of the little community.'[29] James Fenney, delegate from Wigan to the 1839 Convention, was clearly an influential figure among the handloom weavers of his district. He had been the chairman of the meeting at which Joseph Rayner Stephens made the speech for which he was arrested in 1838. He was forty-two, and had been a leading radical since he had attended the Peterloo meeting twenty years earlier. A contemporary described him as 'Tall, almost ungainly' and 'fierce-looking'.[30] Another village shoemaker was Abram Hanson of Elland. His name appears in the *Star*, and as secretary of the Elland Radical Association in the list of organisations to which the LWMA sent the first draft of the Charter.[31] His biographer described him as 'shoemaker, politician, dramatist and medical practitioner'. Almost entirely self-taught, he was a wide reader, and was respected for his knowledge of many subjects. When a brother of Charles Dickens came to Elland to make enquiries into the sanitary conditions of the town, Hanson attended his meeting and made an intervention.

> Mr Dickens lifted his head from the book in which he was taking notes, and was astonished at the apparition of a tall, thin and not overclean person, in a leather apron, just as he had left his seat. 'Are you a medical man?' says he, to which our friend answered with the most imperturbable gravity, 'I am!' 'Where did you study?' 'In the College of Nature sir,' was the reply.

The writer of the memoir was clearly from a higher class and was in many ways rather condescending and patronising about the shoemaker. On the matter of his medical advice, however, he was respectful and defensive, declaring that Hanson fulfilled a valuable service for the neighbourhood, and had effected cures where 'regular' doctors had failed. As well as being a doctor, Hanson was a popular actor. When the players came to the district, he would leave his shoemaking and take a part in the production. He was particularly famous for the part of a shoemaker in the travelling players' version of Ali Baba, when he would be billed as 'Abram Hanson of Elland, the political cobbler'. 'And to the credit of Abram, it must be mentioned, that the manager was sure of a full house on those occasions.' On one occasion the players were persuaded to stage a performance of Cobbett's anti-Malthus play,

Surplus Population, in which Cobbett's own views are put in the mouth of the character of Last, the village shoemaker, Hanson's part of course. The production went off well, and may have been the only occasion on which the play was actually staged outside Cobbett's own village.[32] Like many of the chief speakers in the Chartist movement, Hanson used the technique of preaching.

> Ruminating with grief at the apathy of the people as regards 'their rights', and turning the matter over in his mind, our friend bethought him of Cromwell and his regiment of unconquerable Ironsides. . . To think was to act with Abram. He laid down his lapstone, and went directly to his wife. 'I say lass, thah mun find me a white handkerchief for my neck ready for next Sunday; I am going to preach.' 'What, ar'ta going to turn Methody na?' 'Noa' says he 'but I'm going to preach for all that. I've just fun aght that t'Charter is to be gotten by preaching and praying.'

But although he was prepared to preach, he always took with him a friend 'to do the singing and praying matters, which I don't understand'. At the Whitsun meeting on Peep Green in 1839 this friend may have been local preacher William Thornton, who opened the meeting with a prayer 'that the wickedness of the wicked may come to an end'. Feargus O'Connor clapped him on the shoulder and said 'Well done, Thornton, when we get the People's Charter I will see that you are made the Archbishop of York.'[33] The sermon preached by Hanson, however, was very far from episcopal. He urged his hearers to keep away from sectarian preachers who

> preached Christ and a crust, passive obedience and non-resistance. Let the people keep from these churches and chapels (we will!). Let them go to those who preached Christ and a full belly, Christ and a well-clothed back – Christ and a good house to live in – Christ and Universal Suffrage.[34]

As well as the workshop, pulpit and stage, the other main institution in the industrial village, the alehouse, was also frequented by Hanson.

> His company was much sought after, and, unfortunately, this led to his frequenting the public-house too much, but he never became what you would call a sot, and he managed to bring up a family in decency, considering his station in life.

His wife Elizabeth was a political leader in her own right. The Elland women had a Radical Association before the Charter and Elizabeth chaired many of the meetings and spoke at others. The women were attacked by the local press, and it was perhaps the secure place the Hansons held in their community which enabled Elizabeth to respond with spirit to these attacks. Another member of the family, Feargus O'Connor Hanson, was born in 1838, and named in honour of the leader to whom the Hansons remained loyal throughout their lives.

Probably the majority of Chartist shoemakers were journeymen, like Thomas Dunning and Thomas Lingard. Both these men are examples of shoemakers who left their trade almost by accident as the result of their political activities. Dunning became a newsagent in order to get copies of the *Northern Star* and pursued that occupation for the rest of his life. Lingard, whose parents had combined newspaper selling with shoemaking, found himself blacklisted by the master-shoemakers in his district as the result of his trade-union activities, and so returned to the family's other occupation, and ended his life as a successful newspaper proprietor.[35]

The self-employed cobbler, bespoke shoemaker, or skilled journeyman had considerable freedom of movement, as the history of these Chartist shoemakers shows. Thomas Frost, coming into Chartism as a young man, was much influenced by the local leader, Jem Blackaby, bootmaker and poet.

> He was a spare man, about the middle height, with a slight stoop at the shoulders, contracted probably by constantly bending over his work of boot-making, which might also be chargeable with a marked narrowness of the chest. His face was one of those strongly-marked countenances which, once seen, are never forgotten. He was far from being even ordinarily good-looking, yet both his aspect and his manners were prepossessing. . .

Frost retained his friendship with Blackaby, who moved several times during the Chartist years, and was in 1848 living in Finsbury 'where he made gentlemen's boots for a first-class shop in Cheapside'. Frost always used to drop in to the shoemaker's 'garret' for a talk when he was in London. Like some of the other skilled members of his trade, Blackaby seems to have been able to move around and find work without too much difficulty.[36]

The aristocrats of the bootmakers' trade were the 'dons' – skilled workmen who made specimen boots and shoes for exhibition and for competitions. The trade in the Chartist period was one in which Britain had gained a world-wide reputation, and the famous dons achieved a popularity commensurate with that of famous sporting figures. The biography of one, Walter McFarlane, recorded that he was born in Wigan, apprenticed in Preston, where he witnessed the Chartist riots of 1842, worked in Oxford and London, and in 1849 exhibited a prize boot in the City, the proceeds of the prize and exhibition going to help the

Chartist prisoners. This small example perhaps illustrates the commitment of shoemakers to Chartism, which seems to have been for many a kind of 'house charity' and an obvious object to which funds should be directed.[37]

The historian of London Chartism has suggested a participation by shoemakers in metropolitan Chartism which is second only to that of stonemasons.[38] London shoemakers were traditionally ultra-radical, but similar figures are to be found in almost all the centres for which any kind of estimate can be made. Of the 470 Chartist prisoners listed in the parliamentary return in 1840, shoemakers, with thirty-one prisoners, came behind only cotton spinners, labourers, weavers and colliers. The smaller group interviewed by the prison inspectors in 1840-1 included 6 shoemakers, their number exceeded by weavers (10), colliers and cotton spinners (9 each), and woolcombers (7).[39] In Essex, among known Chartists were four shoemakers; they included Robert Blatche, who at twenty-one had helped to form the Colchester Working Men's Association, became the secretary of the National Charter Association when it started in the town, and was still a leading radical in 1866, when he took part in the local branch of the Reform League. The secretary of the Colchester WMA was another shoemaker, 'young' George Frederick Dennis, son of a veteran reformer in the district. Dennis became a master shoemaker, but always retained an active interest in the shoemakers' union, and would only employ society men.[40] There were 7 shoemakers among the 40 Brighton Chartists whose biographies were reconstructed by T. M. Kemnitz in his work on the town.[41] Of the 66 Chartists arrested in Sheffield in August 1839, four were shoemakers, tying with stonemasons as the most numerous group after members of the dominant local cutlery trades. In South Wales, an analysis of 231 known Chartists at Merthyr showed shoemakers, with 11, second only to miners. David Jones's count of Land Company shareholders whose names began with the first three letters of the alphabet showed that of the 2,298 names, 235 belonged to shoemakers, exceeded in the listings only by textile workers and labourers. In individual towns, the Land Company membership figures bear out this finding. In Cheltenham, for example, where the majority of the 152 members belonged to artisan trades, only labourers, with 30 members, and tailors with 14 exceeded the number of shoemakers, 13. Of Sheffield's 312 shareholders, only labourers exceeded in number the shoemakers among the non-cutlery trades. Lancashire's 3,650 shareholders in 1847 included 149 boot and shoemakers. Barnsley had 10 shoemakers among its 457 members, Leeds 20 out of 198 – with only cloth dressers, labourers and mechanics ahead. Huddersfield had 8 out of a total membership of 264 and Bradford 30 out of 792. London had nine shoemakers' localities of the NCA between 1841 and 1844, while Manchester, Stafford, Northampton and Nottingham had shoemakers' localities at some time. Wellingborough, although not a shoemakers' locality, had six out of its seven committee men in the trade in January 1842.

Shoemakers, like weavers, often moved into other trades and professions. R. G. Gammage, a coach-builder by trade, worked as a shoemaker during part of his years as a Chartist, and then studied to become a physician. John Skelton, a leader among the London Chartist shoemakers, also studied medicine and moved from being a political dissident to being a medical one and editor of a nature-cure journal. Samuel Kydd qualified for the bar, and Thomas Cooper became a minor member of the literary establishment. All of them retained their radical beliefs in the post-Chartist period, as did other less well-known figures. Henry Vincent reported on his return from a visit to the United States in 1868.

> Who should walk into my room, dressed in the comfortable garb of a farmer, but French of Banbury. . . He was then a journeyman shoemaker, and was literally starved out for the crime of believing that working men were the children of God and had souls and intellect and feeling. . . Here he is a farmer with 160 acres of good land; his wife in cosy comfort with him, and seven children all doing well.[42]

Another Chartist shoemaker who left for the new world was Tom Philips, who emigrated in 1852, and helped to form the Boot and Shoe Workers' Union in the States. He had been apprenticed to his brother-in-law, and recalled: 'My boss was an active Chartist and an ex-Methodist local preacher, and with him I attended Chartist and other meetings and became interested in all the reforms of the day.' Although he was only nineteen when he left the country, he was already a member of the National Charter Association, his card having been made out personally by Ernest Jones on the occasion of a visit to Bolton where Philips was working, and he carried a lifetime's commitment to radicalism and trade unionism with him across the Atlantic.[43]

The journeyman shoemakers in Britain, too, remained a radical lot. When John Plummer, staymaker of Kettering, launched into the anti-trade-union verse and pamphlet-writing that was to earn him the patronage of Lord Brougham and other members of the aristocracy, it was the striking shoemakers of Northampton who aroused his particular ire. In the winter of 1857-8 their code of rules still had a strongly Chartist rhetoric.

It is high time that the employed should have a fair share of the benefits arising from the productive industry of the country, as well as the employer, and not to be obliged in his old age to finish a life of labour in a poor-law bastile, and a pauper's grave, while those for whom he has toiled hard, are allowed to revel in luxury, through their assumed rights to dictate their own terms to the workman, and the carrying out of their favourite dogma of unrestricted competition.[44]

It was their insistence on the limitation of apprenticeships and their refusal to admit his brother to the trade that enraged Plummer. His writing, welcomed by the employers who provided the money for its publication, led to his being burnt in effigy by the shoemakers. He was, however, on the winning side, for the strike was defeated, and the shoemakers entered the next stage of the devaluation of their trade with the admission of machinery to the workshops.

Charles Kingsley based his fictitious Chartist, Alton Locke, on the character of Thomas Cooper, the Chartist shoemaker poet. Instead of being a shoemaker, however, Alton was a tailor. The two trades shared many characteristics in the Chartist period, and members of both trades were to be found among Chartists in all parts of Britain. Like shoemaking, tailoring was not confined to one part of the country. It was a trade with long traditions, not affected by machinery, but also subject to the pressures of change in its organisation.

It is perhaps surprising that there were considerably fewer tailors listed in the 1851 census than shoemakers, 139,219 as against 243,935. Dudley Baxter, in 1867, included tailors with shoemakers in the lowest category of skilled workers, and calculated that around 83,000 tailors were earning wages of between 21 and 23 shillings a week. Throughout the Chartist period and for some time afterwards there were no mechanical aids to tailoring. There was thus no cheap, machine-made clothes trade, and every coat and suit had to be made by hand in the tailor's shop or in the mass-production workshops. Although tailoring proper was mainly a male trade, there were very many women working in branches of sewing who do not appear in the tailoring figures. There was also a great deal of sewing and mending done in individual households. Many people, at this time, men as well as women, went through life without wearing any new tailor-made garment. A description of a Yorkshire textile village in the 1830s said:

As for the working men of the village, they were almost universally dressed in fustian, even on Sundays. If any of them managed to secure a good cloth suit for Sundays it was made to last almost a lifetime; a large 'checker brat' being worn to protect it when in use. As for the children, the parents of that generation were not so particular in putting their boys early into suits as parents are at this day. In fact, both sexes were dressed in frocks up to the age of seven, and sometimes even ten; and when the coveted suit was gained at last, it had often to be protected by a leather budge.[45]

Unlike the shoemaker, the tailor was not essential to every citizen. Many coats and suits were passed on between families, and the clothes of the richer members of society worked their way down through markets and pawn shops to the poorer.

The tailors were organised in strata not dissimilar to those in the shoemaking industry. The high-class bespoke tailor was a man of some considerable skill and status. But even more, perhaps, than the bespoke shoemaker, the tailor was a servant of fashion and of the personal whim of his customers. Francis Place, one of the best-known of radical tailors, described the way in which he had been forced to lie and dissemble to please finicky customers. 'In short, a man to be a good tailor should be either a philosopher or a mean cringing slave, whose feelings had never been excited to the pitch of manhood.'[46] Below the most skilled and independent were the members of the 'honourable trade'. These were time-served journeymen who worked in the better class of shop, who were responsible for the production of whole garments on the master's premises. Many provincial bespoke tailors would be small masters employing a few such apprenticed journeymen. Alton Locke's first employer was an old-fashioned West-End tailor in London, who kept 'a modest shop . . . paid good prices for work . . . and prided himself on having all his work done at home. . .'[47] Robert Crowe's brother, to whom he was originally apprenticed, was a skilled journeyman, 'considered one of the best coatmakers in London', who with his wife's help in sewing and pressing, seems to have earned very good money in the late thirties.[48]

The tailors had been defeated in a major strike in London in 1834,[49] and the result of the defeat was to hasten the decline in conditions of work which the strike had attempted to arrest. As with other artisan trades, the main grievances of the tailors were the decline of apprenticeship regulation, the employment of unskilled and cheap labour, and the great increase in sweating – the proliferation of small masters, family workshops and 'home work', the latter often done at the cheapest of rates by women and children. *Alton Locke* used descriptions of the tailoring trade taken from the investigation made by Henry

Mayhew for the *Morning Chronicle*. The findings of Mayhew, together with the scandal of the spreading of typhus into the house of a member of the upper class through the agency of a coat made in a sweater's workshop, fastened public attention on the tailoring trade at the end of the forties. Charles Kingsley published one of his first tracts in 1849, *Cheap Clothes and Nasty*,[50] based on Mayhew's writing but making very strongly the political point, which he later re-emphasised in *Alton Locke*, that the whole degeneration of the tailoring trade was speeded up and encouraged by the wealthy people, army officers and clergy who, as customers, demanded the cheapest possible work from their tailors. Slop shoemaking was largely the manufacture of low-quality and cheap shoes for working-class customers. Slop tailoring, however, was employed just as much on government contracts and on high-quality garments, the savings being made on the cost of labour and not of materials.

Throughout the Chartist period, tailors were among the most active radicals for two reasons. One was that, like other non-factory trades, there were members of the better branches of the trade, particularly in the provinces, who had the degree of independence needed for public activity. The other was that the tailors, like the handloom weavers and many other trades, had tried to protect their conditions of work through traditional means – trade societies, petitions and so on – and had found it impossible to do so. They were therefore looking to government regulation as their only hope. At the end of the Chartist period and in the immediate post-Chartist years, tailors were one of the trades in which cooperative production was attempted.

Among the best-known Chartist tailors was William Cuffey, a leader of the London Chartists from the movement's beginning. His father had been a slave in the West Indies, where his grandfather had been taken from his native Africa. Cuffey himself was, like many tailors, physically deformed – 'a good spirit in a little deformed case', as a fellow-workman described him.[51] He was known in his own trade as an excellent workman, a reputation he maintained until the end of his life. He was also extremely meticulous and outstandingly honest and reliable. 'I have known some thousands in the trade,' his contemporary observed, 'and I never knew a man I would sooner confide in: and I believe this to be the feeling of thousands in the business to this day.'[52] By the time he became involved in radical politics, Cuffey was already forty-six years old, and a late convert to trade unionism. The strike of 1834 which had made him a supporter of his society also led to the loss of his job. From 1834 onwards he worked partly at his trade, but increasingly was involved in radical political activities; he served as Westminster delegate to the Metropolitan Chartist council, and was a member of the National Executive of the NCA in 1842 and of the Democratic Committee for Poland's Regeneration in 1847. His reputation for integrity and scrupulous attention to detail is shown by his repeated election as auditor of the National Land Company from 1845 onwards. In 1848 he was an acknowledged leader of London Chartism, and a member of the National Convention. In that year he was involved in the Orange Tree conspiracy, and was sentenced to twenty-one years' transportation. As a convict and ticket of leave man he continued to be respected as 'a sober and industrious man',[53] and in Australia he again took up radical politics. He died in poverty at the age of eighty-two in 1870. He was clearly an amiable and balanced character, and was rarely involved in personal squabbles among the leadership. An accomplished musician and singer, he was in demand at social functions as well as at meetings as a speaker. He was three times married; his third wife, who worked for some time as a servant in Richard Cobden's household, had to be removed from the court during his trial for interrupting the proceedings. She joined him in Tasmania in 1853.

Another tailor who entered the trade because of physical infirmity was Robert Lowery. Originally trained as a seaman he became lame during his early voyages, and was forced to look for work which made fewer physical demands. He became apprenticed to a tailor, but balked at doing another full seven years' training, and so worked sometimes alongside society men in a tailoring shop, but on other occasions was employed making up 'slop-jackets', cheap ready-made clothes for sale in shops, for which he earned around two shillings a day.[54] He was one of the chief opponents of the old exclusive organisation of the trade society in Newcastle, where he lived and worked. He was associated with the revival of general unionism in 1834, and was victimised for his part in organising the local branch of the Grand National Consolidated Union. Lowery was unusual among the early Chartists in always having seen political reform as more important than the mutuality of trade society or community. Although one of the outstanding working-class leaders and orators in the early years of the movement, he was much more motivated by individual ambition than most of the men of his kind. He was already in revolt against the theatricality of traditional skilled working-class organisations and friendly societies in the early thirties, if his autobiography is to be believed, and it is therefore not very surprising that his period as a Chartist leader was short, or that he soon became a full-time worker and lecturer for the middle-class temperance movement. However, it should be remembered that he wrote his memoirs for a temperance journal, and that perhaps some of his recollections were coloured by this fact.

Many of the most violent Chartist rhetoricians were later at pains to disavow any serious intention of being involved in armed action, and whereas Cuffey, a mild and unassertive man, when he was caught up in the partly police-inspired conspiracy of 1848, rejected the chance to escape and waited to be arrested with his fellows, Lowery, the rhetorician of violence, was thrown into a great terror when he discovered that his name had been mentioned in a letter to Wales; fortunately for him the sensible Mrs Frost had put the letter on the fire as soon as she realised its content. Lowery was most certainly, in spite of subsequent denials, one of the speakers who sailed as close to the wind in the advocacy of armed insurrection as was possible in the heated atmosphere of 1839 without actually asking to be arrested immediately.

> He knew he was liable to transportation did he advise the people to arm – he knew it would implicate the Chairman and all the men who got up the meeting, if he said anything of the kind; but surely there could be no harm in asking them were they armed? (loud cries of 'yes, yes' 'we are, we are.') It was no harm for one neighbour to ask another whether he had a good musket as he was ordered to have by the constitution – the law and the Bible. When a man went to ill-use Moses, he turned round and knocked his brains out . . . he knew that if driven to it by unconstitutional acts of the Government they would take up their arms, and never lay them down till justice was done them or till the members of a treasonable Government had their heads fixed on Temple Bar.[55]

In January of the same year, Lowery took part, with Harney, in a meeting at Winlaton, where

> a splendid moonlight meeting was held, amid the firing of cannon, upwards of 3,000 men and women were present, in fact the whole population *en masse*. At the conclusion of the proceedings, Mr Harney was presented with a pike of real Winlaton manufacture, for the defence of the constitution.[56]

Like a number of those among the early Chartist leaders who changed direction after 1840, Lowery presents, in his autobiography, a picture of a movement in which all the violent rhetoric and mistaken tactics are to be blamed on the leadership of O'Connor. In July 1840, however, O'Connor was praising Lowery for his oratorical skill: 'Lowery is a man of the very highest order of impassioned eloquence. I never felt so much afraid of speaking after any man as Lowery. . .'[57] Lowery swung from a sentimental violent rhetoric of a dangerous and rather irresponsible kind, to a sentimental faith in the power of temperance to solve the world's problems. His was a humourless and self-centred world in which 'bettering oneself' was the aim. He was only for a short time a working tailor, and his history does not shed much light on fellow-members of his trade. What above all he lacked was any sense of solidarity with his fellow-workmen, or pride in the trade which he abandoned for the trade of paid propagandist at the first opportunity.

Another Chartist tailor with a great belief in the power of teetotalism was Charles Hodgson Neesom. He was a Londoner of the same generation as Cuffey, a small master who had become involved in Metropolitan radical politics in the days of Thistlewood and the London Spenceans. After working at his trade for over thirty years, his eyesight failed and he turned to radical bookselling, together with his wife, who was also a radical of some standing. During the early years of the Chartist movement, Mrs Neesom kept a school, and also organised the East London Female Democratic Association, while her husband was a leading member of the London Democratic Association and a book and newspaper seller for the London radicals. Neesom later became a follower of William Lovett and so appeared to be a 'moderate' among Chartist leaders. But in the confused weeks after the Newport rising, when there were plans afoot in various parts of the country to rescue the Welsh leaders, or even to follow the Newport events with risings elsewhere, Neesom was sent by the London Democratic Association into the country, in his own words, 'for the purpose of ascertaining how far the working classes are disposed as regards numbers to unite to obtain the People's Charter. That Committee . . . delegated me to Yorkshire.'[58] Neesom was among the London Chartists arrested in January 1840,[59] and spent some months in prison before he was released on bail. Clearly up to this point he had been associated with the conspiratorial end of the movement, strongly represented in the older London artisanal tradition. He was delegate for Bristol at the first Convention, voted against the dissolution in September 1839, and supported the proposal for a sacred month. After his release from prison, he turned, with his wife, more towards temperance than political reform, and became a founder member of the 'new move'. When he and his wife joined Lovett's National Association, the Chartists not only deserted the school and the bookshop, but actively harassed them, forcing them to close both enterprises. In later life they became involved in temperance, free-thought and vegetarian movements: C. H. Neesom died in 1861, at the age of seventy-seven.[60]

Robert Cranston, one of the foremost Edinburgh Chartists, took up tailoring after he lost a leg in an accident and had to give up his original trade of printer. By 1843 he had a shop in the High Street, and was an established master tailor. He too was a keen temperance supporter, and opened a series of temperance hotels and coffee-shops, all of which seem to have flourished, and to have provided centres for the spread of Cranston's brand of ultra-radical and temperance politics.[61]

Two of the Ipswich Chartists, William Rushbrook and Henry Lovewell, were working tailors. Both were foundation members of the Working Men's Association and were members of the Chartist Association in 1847. Both took part in the establishment of the Young Men's Literary and Scientific Society in the early fifties, and remained interested in parliamentary reform after the demise of Chartism in their localities.[62]

Master tailors were prominent among the small traders who took leading parts in local Chartist organisation. At Bradford John Hinchcliffe and Joseph Alderson were both employers with their own premises, and were both staunch Chartists. Hinchcliffe emigrated with his brother Robert, also a leading local Chartist, to the United States in 1847, where they continued to take part in working-class and radical movements.[63] Joseph Alderson was a leading figure in Bradford Chartism, serving as treasurer of the Chartist Cooperative store, and of the local branch of the land society. In 1842 he was arrested and charged in connection with the clashes of that year, but accepted the option of being bound over. He was still serving on the West Riding Chartist council in 1852, and walked at the head of the Bradford procession attending the funeral of Benjamin Rushton in Halifax in 1853.[64] Like almost all the other tailor Chartists of whom we have any detailed knowledge, he was a keen temperance supporter.

Although tailors were not as well represented among the known Chartists as shoemakers, they were probably as numerous *pro rata*. Many NCA districts had tailors among their officers, including Bradford, Huddersfield, Oundle, Bilston, Bristol, Birmingham and Cheltenham.[65] Many more included tailor committee-men. There were five different branches of Chartist tailors in London in the early forties, and in Manchester in 1841 a branch made up entirely of tailors and shoemakers. The Birmingham Chartist tailors' locality in 1843 announced itself as 'a political society, independent of the trade society'.[66] There were 5 tailors among the sample of 68 Suffolk Chartists,[67] and in the membership of the Land Company in 1847, tailors represent one of the largest occupational groups in nearly every district.

Of David Jones's sample, 104 were tailors. In some areas in which there was not a major manufacturing industry, tailors comprised a considerable proportion of the members. In Cheltenham, for example, they were second only to labourers, with fourteen of the Land Company's 152 members. Of the 29 leading members of the Cheltenham NCA, 4 were tailors.

Although tailors figure prominently in most Chartist lists, the showing of the trade amongst those arrested is very low. One of the few who did go for trial was Albert Wolfenden, from Ashton-under-Lyne, who was a leading figure during the events of the summer of 1842. He was among the conspirators in the 1843 trial, and defended himself, although, as he said, 'I labour under considerable disadvantage, both from poverty and want of learning, in contending against the array of learning and talent against me'.[68] He was acquitted on all the charges.

Robert Crowe was a young Irish journeyman tailor who was arrested in 1848. He had come to London in 1837 to be apprenticed to his brother, a skilled tailor. But after three years, he found the position intolerable. His brother, although 'one of the best coatmakers in London', was a compulsive drinker, and the good money he made, with the help of his wife, he immediately spent on drink, leaving his wife and young Robert to run the household and care for the children on very little money. These years were remembered as

> Three years of bitter persecution, during which time I became a mere domestic drudge, far more expert in cooking and nursing than in tailoring. . . . At last I mustered courage enough to snap the bonds and fling myself into the arms of the London sweating system, where, with all its repulsive features, I became more proficient in six months than I had been during the three years of my apprenticeship. . .[69]

The extra time gained by his move allowed him to become an active member of the temperance movement, which at that time enjoyed a particular influence among the Irish under the inspiration of Father Matthew; he also renewed his family's concern with repeal, and joined the Chartist movement. In 1843, at the age of nineteen, he was spending all his evenings on these three movements.

> In the bewildering whirl of excitement under which I lived during these years, I seemed almost wholly to forget myself. Night brought with it long journeys to meetings and late hours, though the day brought back the monotony of the sweater's den.[70]

An active Chartist and repealer, Crowe saw no conflict between the two movements, nor indeed between both and the temperance movement.

When O'Connell and Young Ireland parted ways, he went with the latter and became a confederate, but it is worth noting that the anti-Chartist attitude of O'Connell did not until then prevent Crowe from being both a Chartist and a repealer. He was arrested after 10 April 1848, in the second wave of arrests. Ernest Jones, 'a barrister and our leader', Fussell, Sharp, Williams and Vernon were arrested in May, and a few weeks later a second batch of thirty-two arrests included Crowe. After his two years in Westminster House of Correction, mainly spent working in the tailoring shop, he left prison and was invited to join the Christian Socialist tailors' cooperative. This had been set up by the group, led by Charles Kingsley, Frederick Denison Maurice and J. M. F. Ludlow, who had been inspired by the events of 1848 and by the revelations in Mayhew's *Morning Chronicle* articles, to set up cooperative workshops in the printing and tailoring trades. Crowe remembered that it was the death of Sir Robert Peel's daughter from typhus fever on the eve of her marriage which had caused a short-lived scandal, and had aroused the conscience of some of the charitable members of the middle class. The young woman had apparently contracted typhus because the riding habit which was being made for her by a fashionable West End tailor had been made up in the home of a tailoring worker, where the skirt had been used as a bed-covering for a child dying of typhus. The Christian Socialist workshops were short-lived, and subject to continued pressure from their patrons. For example, the Christian gentlemen tried to prevent Gerald Massey, the Chartist poet who was book-keeper of the organisation, from publishing his poems in Harney's *Red Republican*.

Several other Chartist tailors were involved in the cooperative association. Walter Cooper, the manager, was a Scot in his middle thirties. He had become disillusioned with the Methodism of his early life, and had become a freethinking radical soon after he came to London in 1834. Like many members of his trade, he lived in great poverty – he told the story that when his child was born there was neither food, fuel nor bedclothes in the house, and he was working desperately to finish a pair of trousers, for the completion of which he was paid sevenpence.[71]

The Chartist tailors were notable for their concern with temperance, and for the determination with which they tried to protect their declining trade. Because they appear less often than many trades amongst those arrested we know rather less about them as individuals than we know about some local Chartists. Certain names recur – for example F. and C. Goodfellow are recorded as speaking and lecturing for Chartism in various parts of the country, and also as speaking for the journeymen tailors. At a meeting in Exeter Hall in 1850, where the working conditions of the London tailors were again exposed, and a petition adopted to Parliament for legal intervention to abolish sweating, F. Goodfellow demanded 'what the parsons were about'.

How will Exeter Hall saints *dare* to stand forward in May next and ask for money to convert heathens thousands of miles off while the white slaves of England stand in such awful need of emancipation? What account can the bloated church give of its twelve millions a year, when such diabolical oppression is practised in this *Christian* country which has the benefit of such a Church?[72]

Like members of the other trades, Chartist tailors were agitating for political rights and for the protection of their trade society and its standards. They are well represented among the most consistent of local Chartist leaders in the metropolis and in the provinces.[73]

Although they were not so numerous, blacksmiths shared with tailors and shoemakers a fairly even distribution throughout the country. Farriers and iron workers were required in all communities, and although the level of skill and the amount of space and equipment required meant that the smith's trade was not threatened to any great extent by unskilled workers, there were nevertheless many blacksmiths who shared the radicalism of the people amongst whom they lived and worked.

As might be expected, the political colour of a blacksmith often showed in his attitude to the manufacture of pikes and other weapons. Police reports during periods of arming give us some insight into the activities of radical smiths. In 1839, for example, the deputy constable of Bolton described a visit to two local smithies. The first was that of John Matthews in Crook Street, where pikes were reportedly being made. Although the door was locked, the constable was admitted without question when he knocked, and Matthews went on unashamedly with his task of shaping files into pike heads. He admitted that he was regularly employed at making them, and had made a hundred the day before. The constable knew the smith, but did not recognise the other men who were present in the smithy, who appeared to be 'weavers and spinners'. When he left Matthews, he went immediately to the smithy of Daniel Cowle, another local Chartist.

I said 'Well Dan, I've come to look at you making pikes', he laughed and said 'are you going to give me an order for one?' . . . I went through the front cellar to the back cellar and there was a man and a boy at the anvil making a pike and there were two other men at the grinding room grinding a pike, Daniel Cowle came into the back cellar, he had a pike in his hand. He said 'I'm making mine out of good stuff, they will bend and come again'. . .

Cowle said that there were thousands of pikes in Bolton, and several smithies working on them. 'Cowle', the constable reported, 'is a speaker at the Chartist meetings, I have known him for several years and he knows me.'[74]

Blacksmiths tended to be better-paid than the majority of workmen, and were often outstanding as leaders in the community. Joseph North of Shipley had been reported in 1839 for making pikes in his smithy, but had avoided prosecution. He was still a leader of the Chartists in 1842, when he was described as 'a fine-looking person [who] had a good address, was bold and self-possessed, had a clear and distinct expression, was very fluent in speech, and just the man to fill his followers with confidence'.[75] He avoided arrest in 1842 after taking part in the plug riots of that year, by escaping to America.

Isaac Johnson, blacksmith of Stockport, was also in fairly comfortable circumstances. At the time of his arrest for sedition in 1839 he had been earning on average thirty shillings a week, and also owned some small house property. His radicalism went back to his childhood, for he claimed that his schooling had ended 'at Peterloo time' when he was expelled from school 'in consequence of his father obliging him to go to school in a white hat with crape and a green riband'. He took advantage of his time in prison to make up some of the deficiencies of his early education, and studied arithmetic. The inspector found him 'a shrewd man – a republican I suspect upon principle. . .'[76]

Joseph Capper was another blacksmith whose Chartism did not arise from personal poverty. In 1842 he told the court that he had a vote, and had two tenants that had votes but 'he thought it wrong that men had not votes instead of houses'. Capper was a Primitive Methodist preacher, and had been a leader of radicalism in his home town of Tunstall since at least 1830. His shop was 'one of the most prominent places in the town in those days'; he was 'a stout man with a round, placid face, a sort of saintly-looking John Bull . . . on Sundays he wore a white cravat, such as was worn by the early Methodist preachers, and some Quakers'.[77] In the association of the smithy with dissenting preaching, Capper resembled David John of Merthyr, and this similarity seems to have extended to the influence which the two men had in their localities. Capper was arrested after the 1842 riots and served two years in prison. Although it was clear from the evidence that he had not been personally involved, his violent biblical rhetoric was held to have been instrumental in setting off the crowd violence of 1842. His case was not helped by the fact that, when a group of special constables arrived to arrest him, his blacksmith son floored one of them with a single blow, and had to be restrained from treating the others in like manner. This tendency of blacksmiths to use their traditional physical muscle against the authorities is epitomised by the activities of Isaac Jefferson, the Bingley blacksmith who rallied the local forces in 1848 under the nickname of Wat Tyler, and whose brawny wrists proved too large for the handcuffs with which the police tried to hold him.[78]

Ten blacksmiths have been identified among London Chartists, three in Merthyr; there were two among Gloucestershire Land Company members, six among the Barnsley membership, two in Leeds, two in Sheffield and one in Cheltenham. In the sample Land Company list of members in 1847, 54 blacksmiths, smiths and farriers appear. Clearly in many districts the smithy provided a meeting-place, or its occupant leadership.

Blacksmiths were employed in many trades other than farriery and iron forging. One of these was the trade of coach building, where the smiths played a vital part in the construction of springs and axles. Several of the local Chartist leaders were employed in this branch of the trade, including William Glenister of Cheltenham and Robert Booley of Ipswich. Booley was an autodidact whose radical activity made him a natural choice as a leader when the movement got going in the late thirties. He went as delegate from Ipswich to the Palace Yard meeting in September 1838, having been a founder-member of the Ipswich Working Men's Association and one of its earliest speakers and propagandists. In May 1839, when the missionaries from the Convention visited Ipswich to hold a public meeting, Booley, as leader of the local WMA, was summoned by the mayor to discuss the matter. He left the foundry when he got the message, and appeared before the mayor in his working clothes. He defended the peaceful nature of the proposed meeting, and insisted that the women of the town had the right to attend as well as the men. Booley continued as a leading radical in Ipswich until the late forties, when he emigrated, as many Chartists did, to Australia. There he helped to found the Geelong People's Association, to agitate for the six points of the People's Charter. A contemporary described him as 'Standing there with uplifted arms, for to him the hustings are a pulpit'. In Australia he continued to press for parliamentary democracy, and also for the legal eight-hour day, and was one of the many Chartist emigrés who helped to mould the tone of Australian democracy.[79]

Other smiths – like James Burton, whitesmith of Stockport – also appear among named Chartists. Burton was in his fifties when he was arrested for conspiracy to incite the people to arms. Like many others, he was offered the option of pleading guilty and being bound over, but, he told the prison inspector, 'I did not come forty miles to tell lies in court.' The inspector found him 'most formidable in appearance', but considered him less dangerous than his associates.[80]

Whitesmiths, silversmiths and machine smiths occur among Chartists and Land Company members in many parts of the country. James Cantelo, who took the chair for Bronterre O'Brien at Portsmouth's first Chartist meeting, was a machine smith.[81] Edward Brown, one of Birmingham's leading figures, who served a term of imprisonment in 1839-40, was a journeyman silversmith, and had been earning good wages before his arrest. Sheffield's Land Company membership, as one would expect, was made up of a large proportion of cutlery and other metal workers. Among them were a fender smith, a job smith, a metal smith, two scythe smiths, four sickle smiths, three whitesmiths, five file smiths, two blacksmiths and six who described themselves simply as 'smiths'. As Robert Sykes has shown,[82] the smiths in the Manchester district were, as organised trades as well as individuals, among the most political of the working people in the late thirties and early forties. Alexander Hutchinson, secretary of the biggest trade society, the National Associated Smiths, presided over the important trades' meeting that preceded the outbreak of the strikes of 1842. Clearly, then, these skilled metal workers were more involved in Chartist activity than many historians have allowed. Nevertheless, it is true that very few of them appear as national leaders. The only national figures who emerged from among the metal workers were John Ardill, an iron-moulder from Burley-in-Wharfdale who became cashier and book-keeper to the *Northern Star* and a leading figure in the movement,[83] James Adams, the Chartist preacher from Glasgow, who had originally been a mechanic, John Collins of Birmingham who was a toolmaker by trade, and William Jones, watchmaker, one of the three Welsh leaders condemned to death in 1840. For the most part the mechanics, engineers and smiths whose names occur are local officials, Land Company members, or among the ranks of the arrested Chartists.

Why metal workers are so under-represented among the national leadership presents an interesting problem. For one thing, of course, although there were plenty of them, they were still a very small minority of the total workforce. Although it is clear that in districts like Sheffield and Manchester, where they were numerous and organised, they played a full part in the movement, most parts of the country would have had only a few smiths and mechanics among the population. Leaders tended to emerge first from among the people they worked with, having gained their followers' confidence in trade and community questions. These skilled metal workers often worked alone or in very small shops. It is also likely that the comparative rarity of their skills meant that they were not as likely to be permanently excluded from employment in their trades as members of overstocked trades like weavers, shoemakers and tailors. Mechanics, therefore, who were active in the high point of Chartism, even those who served terms of imprisonment, were probably able to get work again while weavers and factory workers might be forced to look for a living in the movement, as speakers, writers and organisers.

More than a hundred members of metal-working trades occur as committee men in NCA districts, or among the lists of arrested Chartists from both old and new trades. Among the Chartists in the traditional trade of watchmaking was 28-year-old John Broadbent of Ashton-under-Lyne, sentenced to a year's imprisonment in 1840 for conspiracy to excite people to arms. He was described as 'a country watch-maker and repairer of arms, and one of Thompson's agents for arms'. When he was arrested a number of firearms were found at his home. The prison inspector considered him to be 'of some mind'. 'He has been in the United States where he says he imbibed his political principles. He did work there, but his brother persuaded him to return . . . ' Among the questions Major Williams discussed with Broadbent were the latter's ideas for a more efficient was of putting out fires. George Thompson, the Birmingham gunsmith referred to, served sixteen months of an eighteenth month sentence for conspiracy in 1839-40. He was described as 'doing considerable business' at the time of his arrest, which business included supplying Chartists with arms, particularly in Lancashire. In 1839 he was forty-two years old, married with three children, and clearly a man of some substance.[84] Daniel Ladbrook of Chelmsford, a leading figure throughout Chartist years, was another watchmaker, and, as would be expected, Coventry, the centre of the English watchmaking trade, contributed several representatives, including George Allen, Samuel Knight and William Mayo. London and Sheffield also included watchmakers among the local leaders, and at least one other, Evan Edwards of Monmouthshire, was sentenced for his part in the Newport rising.

Many Black Country Chartists belonged to the older metal trades of nail and chain making, although perhaps not as many as the wide distribution of these trades in the area would suggest. The best-known Chartist nailer was John Chance, one of the district's three most important leaders. A nailer from a family of nailers – his parents and his ten brothers and sisters worked at the trade – he took a leading part in the political radical movements from 1830 onwards, and in various attempts in the same period to organise the nailers into trade unions. In a speech in 1848 he indicated that he had suffered nine prosecutions for his various activities.[85] Thomas Sidaway of Gloucester, who has already been mentioned as the town's leading Chartist, was a master chain-maker by trade, although his radical activities deprived him of custom, and led him to become increasingly dependent on the family second string, the Magnet Inn. In Wolverhampton and Bilston a number of representatives of the local light metal and hammer-making trades appear among the committee-men.

In the Land Company lists metal workers and mechanics are rather better represented than they are among either committee-men or arrested Chartists. Among the 198 members in Leeds were 20 who gave their trades as 'mechanic' as well as 9 others in a variety of metal trades. Gloucestershire had no mechanics, but did list 5 shipwrights. Cheltenham listed 2 watchmakers and a coppersmith, Barnsley 2 engine tenters and 3 mechanics, while David Jones's list includes 80 practitioners of metal trades as well as 37 engineers or mechanics and 6 watch or clock-makers. In London Goodway has identified 23 engineers and millwrights, 11 coppersmiths, 7 tin-plate workers, 10 blacksmiths and 12 other assorted metal workers.

At this distance it is difficult to identify all of these metal-working trades precisely. The words 'smith' and 'mechanic' are ancient words, and in these years they may be applied to traditional crafts or to workers in the most modern departments of mill machinery or railway rolling stock. Wood workers, on the other hand, who formed a large proportion of the Chartists, were probably for the most part engaged in fairly traditional occupations. Cabinet makers, joiners and carpenters took part in the movement in all parts of the country, and several of the leading Chartists were members of the highest artisan branches of the trade. W. J. Linton was a wood engraver, Richard Moore and George Mantle were wood carvers. Linton was probably the leading engraver of his day, and incidentally provided an interesting link with the modern labour movement, since Walter Crane, the associate of William Morris and the designer of so much of the material associated with the socialist revival of the late nineteenth century, served as his apprentice.[86]

Probably the most famous Chartist wood worker was William Lovett. A Cornish rope-maker who left his native county to seek his fortune in the metropolis, he left in his autobiography a vivid account of the problems which faced a member of a trade which had ceased to provide employment for its members, who tried to transfer to another trade. Lovett managed to make the transfer, and indeed to become a leader in his new trade. He also gives incidental glimpses of the working life of the London artisan, before he became entirely occupied with political and educational activities. On one occasion, when he was working in a small workshop, he had intended to go to a radical meeting, but was asked by his employer to stay and put in extra time to finish a set of dining tables for a customer. 'My employer,' he wrote, 'being himself a radical and an earnest and good man, would have gone with me to the meeting at the time specified, but for this pressing request about the tables.'[87] Among the artisan trades there are many examples of such small masters who shared the radical views of their journeymen, and were able to provide employment for active Chartists. Abram Duncan, leader of the Glasgow Chartists, was a skilled wood-turner who was enabled to take the time he needed for his Chartist and trade-union activity in the city partly by the fact that his employer, Daniel McNaughten, was also a strong radical in his views. McNaughten, however, has gone down in history for quite a different reason. In 1843 he shot and killed Edward Drummond, secretary to the Prime Minister, Sir Robert Peel, mistaking him for the Prime Minister himself. In one of the most famous trials in British legal history, McNaughten was found not guilty by reason of insanity, and the definition of legal insanity was established for over a century.[88] Whether McNaughten was indeed insane, or whether his was simply, as he claimed, a politically motivated assassination, the episode has rather curiously been missed from most accounts of the Chartist movement. In many ways the Glasgow wood-turner was a typical Chartist artisan. Self-educated in literature and in the French language, he was among the most skilled and valued members of his trade in the city. His admission notes to Bethlem Hospital, where he spent most of the rest of his life, record him as being of temperate habits, fair education, with a shy and retiring manner, and indicate his insanity only by the entry 'Imagines the Tories are his enemies'.[89]

William Cordukes, leader of the York Chartists,[90] R. J. Richardson, Lancashire anti-Poor-Law leader and member of the first Convention, Benjamin Lucraft, London Chartist active in the 1850s and a leading radical publisher after the movement's end, were all carpenters or cabinet makers. Richard Spurr, one of the first Chartists in his native Truro, was the owner of a carpenter's shop in the town and had established a reputation as a leading radical in the years immediately preceding Chartism. In an episode called the 'Church rates riot' in May 1838, a group of dissenting small tradesmen who had refused for two years to pay church rates organised resistance to the forcible seizure and sale of goods to cover the debt. The resulting public comedy provided a starting point for the group of protesters to establish themselves as the town radicals, soon to become town Chartists. Spurr led the Truro Chartists until he left for London in late 1839. In London he continued his activities, and was among the Chartists arrested in January 1840.[91] William Garrard, founder and first secretary of the Ipswich WMA, was a carpenter by trade. He had a radical history well before the publication of the Charter, and remained prominent in all radical activity until he moved away to London in 1852, supporting not only the six points, but trade unions, women's suffrage, the Land Company, and the campaigns against the Poor Law and the 1844 Master and Servant Bill. He was a member of Goodwyn Barmby's short-lived Communist Propaganda Society in 1841, and was a Chartist delegate to the CSU conference in December 1842, at which he of course voted with O'Connor.

Whether a man described himself as 'joiner' or 'carpenter' seems to have been to some extent a matter of local variation. In Manchester members of the trade were organised in a 'Carpenters and Joiners' locality of the NCA. The Leeds Land Company membership included seven joiners, but no carpenters or cabinet makers. Cheltenham's 150 members included 21 carpenters or cabinet-makers but no joiners. Cabinet-makers usually saw themselves as practising a specialised and highly-skilled branch of the trade, but all three designations have been included in the same group for the purpose of counting. Other wood-working trades have not been counted, or the few such as 'turner' which, at this period, could have been either metal or wood. There were no national leaders who came from among the smaller wood-working trades, although there were a sprinkling of sawyers and wheelwrights among the NCA committee-men up and down the country. The secretary of the Croydon Chartists for several years was a sawyer called Hodges, described by Thomas Frost as 'a fine, sturdy example of the best portion of the English working classes'.[92] Young Frost learned his politics from Hodges and the shoemaker Jem Blackaby. Another sawyer who achieved some fame was John Charles who was sentenced to three months' hard labour for his part in the Newport rising. Wheelwrights and coopers occur among NCA officials, including the cooper Henry Summerskill, secretary of the Dewsbury Chartists in 1848, and Thomas and William Selby, wheelwrights, who served together on the committee of the Newark NCA in the early forties.

Carpenters of various kinds contributed about 100 NCA committee-men recorded in the *Northern Star*, and 91 carpenters and joiners and 25 cabinet-makers have been identified among London Chartists – the second largest occupational group after shoemakers. Among arrested Chartists, wood-workers of all kinds figure in much smaller numbers. In this way they resemble tailors rather than the more trouble-prone shoemakers and textile workers. There were eight cabinet-makers and two carpenters among the full list of arrested Chartists in 1840, and only two among those interviewed by the prison inspectors. Two of the Orange Tree conspirators in 1848, thirty-year-old Henry Small and thirty-two-year-old James Snowball were listed as joiners, and Thomas Railton, joiner and one of the leaders of Manchester Chartism, was among the defendants in the 1843 conspiracy trial.

The census returns for Halifax in 1851 list 1.74 per cent of the men over twenty as being carpenters or joiners by trade. Land Company lists for the town show 6 carpenters out of 502 members in 1847. Manchester had 42 carpenters or joiners among its 1,516 members, whilst there were only 44 among the 4,193 members in the same lists for the rest of Lancashire. It would seem that the trade was probably represented fairly much as would be expected. In towns like Cheltenham, where 21 of the 150 members were cabinet-makers or carpenters, they represented the largest single trade. But here there was no large local industry, and apart from the 30 labourers, the members were spread among fifty different occupations. In the textile, mining and stocking-making districts the trades were concentrated around the main industry, and the older artisan trades were represented by proportionally smaller numbers. In London and Manchester there were larger concentrations of artisans engaged in manufacturing as well as on building and maintenance. In prosperous and expanding provincial centres like Cheltenham, the artisan trades were still stable and well-patronised, both in the production of goods and in building.

One of the best-known of the Chartist carpenters was Henry Ross of Hammersmith, a leading figure in London throughout the Chartist years. He was a member of the short-lived Central National Association and of the East London Democratic Association in 1837, and graduated naturally into the metropolitan Chartist movement. He was a delegate to the 1843 Convention among others, and was chairing meetings of the Fraternal Democrats in 1850. William Westoby of Croydon, who appears as a Land Company shareholder in 1847, was described in Thomas Frost's recollections as 'an elderly operative carpenter . . . who was an old and respectable inhabitant of the town'.[93] Like many of the carpenters we can identify, he had been a radical before the movement began, and was able to gather support for the Charter rapidly as the movement took off. Brighton had a number of carpenters among its founding members, as had the London district of Chelsea, where the leadership seems to have been mainly in the hands of wood-workers and building workers.

A significant number of the local and national Chartist leaders worked in departments of the building trade, which employed in its different branches some 398,756 workmen in this period. Stonemasons, and others engaged in shaping, trimming and building with stone, brickmakers and bricklayers, painters, tilers, plasterers, and other trades concerned with the preparation of building materials and the erection of houses and public buildings were in great demand in an age of expanding population and increasing urbanisation. Housebuilding was an industry in which men with comparatively small amounts of capital could make a start, so that employers ranged across a wide spectrum in the scale of their operations. Like other trades, building workers were struggling to maintain standards of work and wages; their success varied in different branches – the masons, for example, in spite of some bitter strikes, managed to maintain their society, but among the lower trades there was considerable dilution by unskilled labour, and an apparent increase in casual work in most trades. There is no mistaking the similarity between the grievances of the building workers and those of tailors, shoemakers and weavers. There was almost no problem of technological change involved in building. Like the other trades, the problems arose from the intensification of competition, the influx of untrained but willing labour and the vagaries of the market. Whereas in the past houses had been constructed more or less to order, in building as in other forms of production, speculation had taken over by the 1830s, especially in the great cities. The increase of brick over stone building, for example, was alleged by the building workers to be in the interest of cheap and rapid production, and represented nothing new or improved in building techniques.

Grievances in the trade paralleled those in other trades, and were well summed up for the Chartists by two letters from 'John the

Workman' – obviously a London building worker – in the *Democratic Review* in February 1850. The slop-master had his equivalent: '. . . the trade has been taken out of the hands of those large and respectable firms – where at least one was sure to be at work with men bred to the trade – and has fallen into the hands of unprincipled, uncharactered, and incapacitated men, who will take a job at any price and "make it pay" . . . ' Standards of work had fallen, especially in the big cities, materials had declined and standards had plummeted. In addition the skilled workmen, who could still command high wages, complained of increasing casualisation.

High wages? Do you call it high wages when a man is 'horsed' to death four months in the year for thirty shillings a week, and travels about, weary and hungry, the other eight months, glad if he can pick up a day's work anywhere at any price? Plasterers, painters, carpenters, is not this correct?[94]

The response of the building workers was the same as that of other trades. They attempted to maintain wages and standards of work through their societies, and through the traditional method of petitioning. Like the other trades, they met opposition that was both practical and ideological. One of the most bitter strikes among the skilled workers was that of the stonemasons who were engaged on the building of the Houses of Parliament and Nelson's Column. By the time of this strike, in the winter of 1841-2, the masons had come round, as the textile trades had done before them, to the need for a political solution to their problems. In June 1841 they had issued an address to members of other trades, calling for support for the Charter and the setting up of a committee of trades to work for it. In the address they stated:

At length we have opened our eyes and seen the errors of the whole system. For many years we struggled by our associated unions to protect ourselves, but the giant which has destroyed all the institutions of our country was able to destroy those also which we vainly hoped would have given protection to our body. This, to a certain extent, was class legislation, and perhaps our appeal may come with a better grace for having tried all methods of protection before we joined, as a body, for the great organic change which we now seek . . . [95]

Building workers provided both local and national leaders. Christopher Dean, Manchester delegate to the 1839 Convention and for many years a full-time Chartist lecturer, was a stonemason, as was Henry Candy of Wolverhampton. Skilled men of this kind could re-enter their trades, as Candy did in the mid-forties, when he gave up full-time lecturing, took a job in his home district, and organised the movement in his out-of-work hours. Robert Knox, delegate to the Convention from the county of Durham, was twenty-four years old and a slater who had been working at his trade since the age of eleven. He was a member of the Mechanics' Institute in Sunderland, and a keen temperance worker. Bath's leading radical in the early Chartist years was the plasterer Anthony Philips, and George Alexander Fleming, former editor of the Owenite *New Moral World* who joined the staff of the *Northern Star* in 1844, had started life as a journeyman housepainter. Committee-men in London and in some provincial centres included a number of building workers. Newcastle-upon-Tyne had the stonemason Edward Charleton as its chairman, and Jamie Ayre, a bricklayer, as one of its leading figures. Edward Burley of York, another plasterer, served as correspondent to the *Northern Star* during the forties, and several of the leading figures in Cheltenham, including the long-serving secretary of the NCA, William Millsom, a plasterer, were building workers. The founders of the Sheffield WMA in 1838 included bricklayers William Barker and David and Joseph Waller, while Charles Bird, master-painter, helped in the establishment of the WMA in Ipswich.

Among building workers to fall foul of the law were two of the Orange Tree conspirators, James Richardson and Joseph Ritchie, and the Lapish family of Bradford, Francis, stonemason, and James and Samuel, painters, who were arrested after the abortive rising in that town in 1840.

David Goodway has identified 103 building workers among 1,158 London Chartists, and they figure prominently in Land Company lists. Halifax, where there were 1,022 masons in a working population of 31,023, had 9 from a total of 445 members. There were in addition 3 painters and 3 plasterers. Of Cheltenham's 150 members, 10 were masons, 1 a stonecutter, 2 bricklayers and a brickmaker, 3 painters, 3 plasterers and 2 plumbers, making 14 per cent of the total. The four masons and three bricklayers among the arrested Chartists and the single painter and plumber in the same list, bear out the evidence from local studies, which suggests that, for whatever reason, building workers were either law-abiding or adept at avoiding arrest.

Shoemaking, tailoring, wood-working and the building trades provided members of the Chartist movement in all parts of the country. The metal trades of all kinds were very much better represented than has always been realised. Printers, engravers, bookbinders and other trades of a similar level of skill provided officers and leaders in many places, and a network of shopkeepers and inn and alehouse keepers provided bases for the organisation of membership and communications for the national movement. But undoubtedly the largest number of known Chartists worked in various branches of the textile industry.

The production of cloth – wool, worsted, fustian, linen, cotton and silk, cloth by the piece or in the form of shawls, blankets, carpets, rugs, hosiery and other finished articles – occupied well over a million people in Britain in 1851. Textiles were still Britain's major exports, and sectors of the industry were the most highly mechanised of any in the country. It was the industry most susceptible to fluctuations in the market, to changes in fashion and to the experiments in capitalisation which were changing the nature of British industry and finance. When the mechanised parts of the textile trade were doing well, other industries such as coal and transport were stimulated. New inventions in textiles kept the engineering industry busy. Above all, the textile operatives had seen their industry expand and their employers grow wealthy, while their own conditions had worsened in almost every way since the end of the Napoleonic wars. A recession in textiles threw more people out of work than any other disturbance in trade, and whereas a bad harvest or a recession in agriculture left labourers dependent on charity, or handouts from employers, the textile districts had no machinery to cope with the apparent irrationality of the trade cycle. Textile districts were made up of large single-industry villages or small townships, with few wealthy or charitable people to provide resources in bad times. They tended to have strong networks of mutuality and community among the workers, but not much in the way of either authority or paternalist care from employers or traditional authority.

Engels suggested that the leading force in the Chartist movement was the cotton factory operatives.[96] Later historians have stressed the role of the outworkers, particularly the handloom weavers. The figures of Chartist occupations which are available suggest that this distinction is misleading. In factory districts, like Stockport and Ashton-under-Lyne, there is no doubt that the majority of the Chartists were connected with the factories. If they were not disqualified by being trade unionists or radicals, the probability is that they or their children would work in the mills. Because factory owners were not as likely to have the monopoly of employment in their own districts, there may have been rather less victimisation of trouble-makers in the factory districts than in the mining districts. However, many well-known Chartists did find themselves kept out of employment – Richard Marsden told the first Convention that 'not in one mill out of twenty would a man be received who was known to be a Radical; he instanced a number of cases of tyranny, and one of revenge'.[97] Factory workers were more restricted in their working hours than out-workers, which meant that factory districts were often represented at delegate meetings and conventions by out-workers or artisans, and which also accounted for the change during the Chartist period from Monday as the day for meetings and rallies to the Sabbath, a change which occurred most rapidly in the factory districts. But among the arrested Chartists, the Land Company members and, above all by the evidence of the level of activity in their districts, the factory workers are at least as well represented as out-workers and artisans. There was, in any case, in these years, less of a hard and fast division between factory and non-factory employment in most divisions of the textile industry than has sometimes been suggested. Before the middle of the century much of the work in the factories was carried on by women and children, so that many families would contain both factory workers and out-workers. When they were too old to be employed as juvenile labour, factory workers would often return to domestic industry, and even those men who stayed at work in the factories were usually dismissed through failing eyesight or other infirmities in their forties, and returned to labouring or other outside work.

Weavers by hand or powerloom were the largest occupational group recorded among the Chartists. If combers, spinners, cardroom operatives, dyers, block-printers, fustian-cutters, framework-knitters and lace hands are added, together with the considerable number of other textile or ancillary trades, a great proportion of the Chartist support is accounted for in very many parts of the country. It is important to remember, however, that in the textile districts – in Lancashire, the West Riding, Nottinghamshire, Leicestershire, Carlisle, Dundee, Paisley and the rest, textile workers made up the leadership as well as the crowd. The picture of the brains of the London artisans providing a programme and leadership for the mindless mass of textile operatives is totally misleading. *Pro rata*, weavers and other members or ex-members of the textile trades provided a larger number of branch officers, local lecturers, speakers, journalists and national leaders than members of any other trade, with the possible exception of shoemakers.

My father's name was Abram Fielden, he was one of a family of four sons and three daughters. They were of a very powerful physique; my father stood nearly six feet in height; they were a family of handloom weavers, until the application of steam to weaving. This occurred when my father was barely out of his teens, and then they became steam-loom workers. My father became a foreman when quite young in the mill of Fielden Brothers, where he worked until incapacitated by infirmities and age. He was a man of more than ordinary intelligence, and was generally acknowledged to 'know a thing or two'. . . . I remember when I was quite young, he and a few more of the intelligent of the factory kind of the place, instead of going to church on Sunday, would meet at our house and discuss politics, religion and everything else. These discussions used to become quite warm, and carried on as they were in the rich Lancashire accent, they contained a peculiar charm. I used to wonder how they could know so much. . . . [98]

Samuel Fielden's memories of his father are of an untypical mill worker only in that Abram's politics did not prevent him from becoming a foreman in the Fielden works at Todmorden. In other respects, in his leadership in the locality of the short-time and cooperative movements, as well as of the Chartist movement, in his life-long admiration for Feargus O'Connor, and in his later attachment to the radical end of the Liberal party he was typical of hundreds of such local leaders in the factory districts.

The textile districts of Lancashire and Yorkshire had been the heartlands of operative radicalism for more than twenty years by the time Vincent and the other London Working Men's Association speakers made their tours in the late thirties. Vincent was impressed by the enthusiasm and the high level of political commitment that he met with everywhere.[99] Not least militant among the textile workers were the cotton spinners. Although in no sense a dying trade, or one threatened by mechanisation as such, spinners faced the same pressure to reduce wages and to dilute the labour force with female or juvenile labour as old artisan trades. The cotton spinners' strikes of the decade preceding Chartism had been very similar, although conducted by a factory-based union, to those of the carpet-weavers, the shoemakers, the tailors, and the woolcombers.[100] The leaders of the spinners, both nationally and locally, were increasingly preaching political measures, above all the suffrage, to influence national policy at a higher level than could be reached by appeals to their local employers.

Timothy Higgins was a cotton spinner and secretary of the Ashton-under-Lyne Chartists. He was arrested in 1839 and charged with conspiracy. At his trial he was shown to have been involved in collecting arms and in drilling, as well as in the general organisation of the movement in his locality, and he received an eighteen months' prison sentence. An Irishman by birth, Higgins was thirty-five at the time of his imprisonment, married with four children. He professed no religious beliefs, and was clearly both literate and widely-read. He complained that he had read all the books that were available in the prison library – 'Scott's novels and common history works' – outside prison, 'where I read everything I can find', and said he was spending his time writing poetry. He told the inspector, who considered him 'a man of considerable intelligence':

I was brought up a cotton-spinner – it was a very agreeable calling when I first followed it, but they have got into the habit of applying self-acting machinery and *man* is of no use. I know of some of the most intelligent in [the] Society who cannot get bread. They take a man now for his muscular appearance, not for his talent. Machines have become so simple that attending them is commonplace labour.[101]

Charles Davies of Stockport was another cotton spinner interviewed by Major Williams. At the time of his arrest he had been keeping a newsagent's shop since 'in consequence of having taken an active part against the masters on the subject of wages, and being a delegate from the working men, [he] has been unable to get work for two years'. Williams considered him to be 'a man of considerable energy and talent', and noted:

This man's political agitation seems to have emanated from the failure of his attempts to increase the wages of the working man which he says only political power can accomplish. I find among the notes of a long conversation with him the following words – 'The great distress is the cause of our discontent – if the wages were what they ought to be we should not hear a word about the suffrage. If the masters will only do something for the workmen to get them the common comforts of life, we should be the most contented creatures upon earth'. I have no doubt this man would go to any lengths to carry his own feelings with regards to the working classes.

Davies returned directly to activity when he left prison, and was a leading figure among the cotton spinners in the events which led up to the 1842 strike. His signature appears on several of the trade-union placards issued in 1841 and 1842.[102]

William Aitken, another of the leaders of Ashton Chartism, began life as a piecer in a cotton mill, graduated to being a spinner, but left after giving evidence to the 1833 factory commission. 'I took an active part in the shortening of the hours of labour, and I had some unpleasantness with my employer and I commenced teaching in consequence of being out of work. . . . '[103] By the time Major Williams interviewed him in prison in 1841, Aitken, then aged twenty-nine, had been running a school for some years, an occupation which brought him a respectable income of about £3 a week. Major Williams considered him to be 'rather of a superior order and of stronger mind' than the other prisoners. Aitken had been introduced to radical politics through being invited to take part in the annual Peterloo celebration at the house of 'owd Nancy Clayton' who with her husband had been at the massacre, and who celebrated annually with a pie supper and the display of a black flag and a cap of liberty. He soon became a leader among the Ashton radicals, and his school, which in 1840 had 120 day pupils and 40 evening, must have been an important centre of radicalism in the district. In the early summer of 1839 a letter from Richard Oastler to the *Northern Star* described an argument between Aitken and the deputy commander of the North, Colonel Wemyss, which took place at the end of a Chartist demonstration.

William Aitken: The present Government have suspended the constitution of Canada, and now they are introducing a Bill to suspend the constitution of Jamaica.

Colonel Wemyss: What have we to do with the blacks? I care nothing about them; it is only the other day since they emancipated them.

William Aitken: I care for the blacks, and every human being, whether black or white, and, as far as emancipation is concerned, they have given them leave to get something to eat for hard working for – nice emancipation that. (Loud laughter, in which the colonel joined.)[104]

He was arrested in August 1839, charged with sedition and conspiracy and sentenced in March 1840 to a term of imprisonment, of which he served nine months. He continued after his release to lecture, write and organise. At the time of the 1842 strikes he was a leading figure in the Chartist movement, and he was one of the fifty-eight charged with O'Connor in the conspiracy trial. Like many of the others, he was found guilty on one count but not called up for sentence. He was arrested again in 1848, but on this occasion was released without being brought to trial. After 1843 he was one of the many Chartists who emigrated to the United States, where he joined a Mormon colony in Illinois. He only stayed a year, however, and returned to Ashton to lead the Chartists and to organise friendly society and educational activities in the town. He remained in Ashton for the rest of his life, running his school until forced by ill-health to give it up in 1868. He died by his own hand a year later.[105]

The trial of the Glasgow cotton spinners had been an important precipitant of Chartism. The cotton spinners' leader, John Doherty, was one of Britain's leading radicals, widely respected and followed throughout the manufacturing districts for his support for general unionism, for universal suffrage, factory reform, opposition to the Poor Law and to the Act of Union with Ireland. Several of the most impressive leaders of Lancashire Chartism were spinners or ex-spinners, including Timothy Higgins, William Aitken, James Duke, John Allinson, James Mitchell and Charles Davies. There were, however, very few cotton spinners in the published lists of NCA committee-men, even in the cotton factory districts. The interesting thing about those cotton spinners whose names have been traced in the Chartist movement is the high percentage whose names have been obtained from among arrested Chartists. There were also large numbers of spinners in the Land Company lists. Of the eighty or so known Chartist cotton spinners apart from the Land Company members, half have been identified from lists of arrested or imprisoned Chartists – a higher proportion than for any other trade except mechanics and colliers. Of the Chartists interviewed by the prison inspectors in 1840-1, seven were spinners or ex-spinners – the largest occupational group except for miners. Of the arrested Chartists listed in 1840, 32 were cotton spinners, the third largest group after weavers and labourers – ahead of shoemakers and miners, each of which trade had 31 representatives in custody. In the Land Plan lists again they show up in large numbers, although here it is sometimes not possible to separate cotton from worsted spinners. In Yorkshire, apart from Leeds, Halifax, Bradford, Huddersfield, Hull and Sheffield, of the 1,425 members listed, spinners, with 84, came sixth in numbers after weavers (286), labourers (146), combers (144), clothiers (109) and shoemakers (96). In Huddersfield, of 264 members, spinners came third with 13, after weavers (93) and clothiers (58); in Lancashire outside Manchester, after the 785 weavers, spinners made up the largest group, with 290 members. In Manchester itself they again came second with 83 after the 101 weavers, and just ahead of the 81 mechanics. If the 5 piecers in Manchester and the 53 in Lancashire are added to the spinners, the numbers are even greater.

What seems to emerge from these figures is that, although the spinners may have been part of the 'modern' section of their industry, they were, by the nature of their employment, more liable to be dismissed or otherwise victimised for taking too prominent a role in the local radical movement than workers in the 'unmodernised' sector. Their commitment is not in doubt, since they took part in crowd action which led to their arrest in some numbers, and since they also subscribed to the Land Company.

Apart from the spinners, other cotton operatives occur frequently among the identifiable Chartists. Powerloom weavers of both sexes were involved, although, apart from Miss Ruthwell, the women are impossible to identify by name. In the strikes and meetings of 1842, though, they were well to the fore, and often appeared more determined and aggressive in their behaviour than their male fellow-strikers. Among powerloom weavers who became national figures was Christopher Doyle. He was twenty-nine years old when he was arrested in Manchester in August 1839. He told the magistrate that he was 'a powerloom weaver, a single man and a lodger'. The magistrate asked, 'Are you in work?' to which Doyle replied, amid laughter in court, 'I was yesterday evening.'[106] When he was interviewed by Major Williams in prison, he said that he had been earning 12*s*. a week at his trade, but that he had little hope of getting work when he left gaol 'from being so well known as an agitator'. He had already served nine months in prison on an earlier occasion on a charge of conspiracy to raise wages, in that case with hard labour. Doyle was an Irishman and a very popular speaker – the *Northern Star* called him 'the Cheshire favourite'. Something of his cheerful nature comes through in the interview – the inspector reported that he had acted as a nurse in the prison hospital for three months, and had been allowed to receive letters and books. Doyle declared: 'I have improved myself much – I would not take £50 for what I have learnt. I have lately been reading Watt's *Logic and Improvement of the Mind*, also Locke and Bacon's essays.' Major Williams considered that Doyle possessed 'a mind of great astuteness', but that 'He is still resolved to pursue the career of agitation.' In this he was quite right, for Doyle, who never seems to have returned to his trade, became a full-time lecturer and then an official of the Land Company. After the end of Chartism he earned his living as an insurance agent.[107]

There were a number of other powerloom weavers amongst the Lancashire and Cheshire Chartist leadership, but there is always a problem with finding an exact figure, since so many people simply gave 'weaver' as their occupation. Of the 785 Land Plan members in Lancashire who gave their occupation as 'weaver' only 94 specified 'handloom', but it is likely that many more were in fact handloom weavers. Among the leaders of the 1842 strikes, however, a number of the Chartists were clearly identified as powerloom weavers. Two of the most prominent were Richard Pilling and Alexander Challenger. George Cooper described 'Dickie Pilling and Sandy Challenger' as the leaders of the 1842 events in Stockport,[108] and it is clear that both were men with considerable influence among the working people of the district. At his trial as one of the 58 other conspirators in 1843, Pilling made a defence speech which has become one of the most famous documents of the Chartist movement. It has, however, given rather a misleading image of the man. Edouard Dolléans, for example, read the speech as that of a simple, unsophisticated working man, swept into a political movement of which he understood little, and motivated purely by a gut reaction to the hardships suffered by his family. In reality, it does nothing to detract from the sincerity of Pilling's statement to point out that it is an extremely sophisticated speech, carefully constructed to fill the purpose of a defence structured around the insistence on a limited 'economic' explanation of the events of 1842. Pilling, although he was clearly the most influential of the local leaders of the strikes, was found not guilty on all counts by a jury that had been moved deeply by his defence speech. Challenger, although clearly less prominent than Pilling, was, like most of the leading Chartists in the trial, found guilty on one count.

The two men were leaders of the powerloom weavers and of the local Chartists. A local constable, giving evidence at the trial, was very anxious to make clear Pilling's political activity. The judge asked whether Pilling had ever spoken about anything other than wages, and the constable replied:

> O yes, he was one of those that were sent for trial at Chester.
>
> *The Judge*: – we don't want to hear that. Did he ever speak about anything but the wages question? Yes.
>
> *Pilling*: – My Lord, the constable and I have been together on a committee for years for the ten hours bill; we are *chums*. (Laughter). . . .
>
> *The Judge*: – was Pilling long anxious about the wage question? I am not aware of that; but, in 1839 he was agitating for the Charter very much, my Lord . . .
>
> *The Judge*: – Were you a *chum* with him? Never, my Lord. Explain yourself a little more – What do you mean by a chum – Where is Pilling?
>
> *Pilling*: – Here my Lord.
>
> *The Judge*: – He says he never was a *chum* with you.
>
> *Pilling*: – My Lord, I was anxious to get a ten hours bill; a committee was appointed; I was one of that committee, and we chose him as another.
>
> *Witness*: – With regard to that my Lord, I was working at a mill some years ago, and I took, twice, some money from the rest of the men to the committee, but I did not stop, my Lord.
>
> *The Judge*: – You were subscribing money to carry out the objects of the ten hours bill? When was that? It would be about 1834 or 1835, my Lord.[109]

Pilling had, it was clear, been prominent in every kind of radical activity in his native Ashton as well as in Stockport, where he was working in

1842. He continued to be a leader of Ashton radicalism. In the summer of 1843 he was a speaker at a meeting of striking operatives along with his fellow 'conspirator' Albert Wolfenden.[110] He represented Ashton at the Leeds Convention in 1846[111] and in March 1848 presided over a meeting at Oldham Edge, at which 13,000 people heard Chartist and Irish speakers welcome the French Revolution.[112] Later that year he was a member of the Chartist National Assembly meeting in the John Street Institute in London, and was elected one of twenty commissioners by the Assembly. In the summer of 1848 Ashton was the scene of a violent outbreak in which the local Chartists overpowered the police and a policeman was killed. Before events had reached this crisis, Pilling was on his way to the United States. Challenger was either there already or went over at about the same time. Challenger worked in the cotton mills of Fall River, Massachusetts, in company with many other Lancashire and Cheshire emigrés, and died there some time before 1858. Pilling, however, soon returned. He wrote back in December 1848 that although conditions in the States were rather better than in Lancashire, wages were low and unemployment high.[113] By 1850 a local magistrate was reporting his return to Lancashire,[114] where he spent the rest of his life in a variety of radical activities, including participation in the Reform League, and support for Liberalism, in the 1860s.[115]

Several cotton factory workers were among the imprisoned Chartists interviewed by Major Williams. Compared with the out-workers, most of these men were less literate and generally impressed the inspector less favourably. George Wareham, a 26-year-old powerloom weaver, was described as 'a poor weak creature', who had serious abcesses on his legs when admitted, which had been unhealed for six or seven years. He was quite illiterate and had been earning 14*s*. a week before he was arrested. His wife continued to do the same work for 10*s*. a week, although she was within a week of the birth of her second child. Another factory worker, Thomas Howarth, overlooker from Hyde, was also illiterate when he entered prison, but had learnt to read from his fellow-prisoners. Both he and Wareham were rank and file Chartists who had been offered the chance of release if they had pleaded guilty, but had refused. Howarth said 'I am a Chartist on principle, but I have done nothing.' He did not think he had much chance of getting sureties if he were to be offered his release, since he had 'never had the chance of keeping property men's company'. Daniel Ball, a Catholic – probably Irish – spinner from Bolton was also low in the literacy scales, being able to read a little but not to write. William Barker, a Manchester powerloom weaver, was described as 'very ignorant'.[116]

It would be dangerous to read too much from such a small sample, but there is certainly nothing here to support the view that the factory workers were more sophisticated or progressive in outlook than the domestic workers. The leaders of Chartism in the factory districts as in the mining districts were usually people from other trades, like Albert Wolfenden, the Ashton tailor, and John Leach, the grocer from Hyde. Mill workers were subject to greater discipline and control than out-workers – as for example is illustrated by the occasion of the great West Riding meeting at Peep Green in October 1838, when a message was read from 'the operatives employed in several factories near Huddersfield', signed 'for and on behalf of the prisoners' by John Powlett. It conveyed their greetings, and said that their employers had threatened with dismissal anyone taking time off to attend the demonstration.[117] Such direct control was easy for employers to exert, but it is also probable that political ideas were developed in many of the older trades by the kind of discussion between individuals and small groups which would be quite impossible in a mill. The reading aloud of the *Star* in the Dundee heckling sheds, or the ardent discussions around the Bradford comb pots were a kind of shared activity not available in the noise of a spinning or powerloom shed.

The great majority of the Land Company members in Yorkshire and in Lancashire were engaged in textile manufactures, many of them clearly in factories. Loom jobbers, overlookers, picker makers, strippers, twisters, warehousemen and engine tenters were among the 2,536 members of the textile and ancillary trades in Lancashire. They included 691 weavers and 94 who specified handloom weaver, 290 spinners, 127 block printers, 44 dressers, 31 dyers, 71 overlookers and 53 piecers. The remainder were spread among another seventy or more trades, including some who simply wrote 'operative'. In Manchester 772 of the 1,516 members belonged to these trades. In Yorkshire outside the main towns, the 1,428 members included 778 textile workers, 286 of them weavers, 109 clothiers, 10 specifying handloom weaving, 144 woolcombers, 84 spinners, 19 flax dressers, 30 silk workers and 17 carpet weavers. Towns like Halifax, with its 204 weaver members, and Barnsley with 286, Huddersfield with 58 clothiers and 93 weavers, and Bradford with 406 woolcombers and 44 weavers out of a total membership of 792 men and 14 women, added to the picture of a membership in the West Riding very largely made up of textile workers. In Sheffield and Leeds, however, with far smaller memberships listed, the numbers were nothing like as great; Leeds had only 8 weavers in a membership of around 200, and Sheffield only 2. The local distribution of textile workers was very different from that of the artisan trades like shoemakers, tailors and blacksmiths, who tended to make up a similar proportion of the membership in all Chartist centres. Like miners and heavy metal workers, textile workers were concentrated in particular districts. Thus, David Jones's list for the whole country shows only 344 weavers out of a total of 2,289 with 63 spinners and 87 woolcombers. The same kind of analysis can be applied to the framework knitters and stockingers. In David Jones's list there are only 89 of them, but in the Nottingham area, as James Epstein has shown, they made up 34 per cent of the NCA committee members in the town, and up to 76 per cent in some of the out-villages. This kind of local concentration shows the dangers of taking national samples of occupations, since, however powerful these textile workers may have been in the centres of their industry's strength, they can have had little influence directly in the many areas in which they were not represented at all. Having said this, however, one has also to add that these textile areas had the most consistent and long-lasting Chartist organisations. It is interesting, incidentally, that the list of London trades includes only silk weavers as a textile trade, of whom there are only 57 identified among the Chartists.

It has already been suggested that the textile trades were not amongst the most highly-skilled. For this reason, there is still another trap to be avoided in making an occupational breakdown of the Chartists. Many people will have done a bit of weaving when the trade was busy, and might be entered as weavers in membership lists, but have abandoned the trade when the busy times ended. With the possible exception of shoemakers, no other trade produced as many ex-members as the weaving trade. Benjamin Wilson, who never left his native Halifax, worked as a weaver among other jobs. 'From 1842 to 1848 I should not average 9/- per week wages . . . I have been a woollen weaver, a comber, a navvy on the railway and a barer in the delph that I claim to know some little of the state of the working classes.'[118] Benjamin Rushton, who was for most of his life a fancy worsted weaver, was entered in 1847 in the Land Company lists as a tea dealer, although he was soon back at his loom and was seen working on intricate patterns in his home by Ernest Jones a month or two before his death in 1853.

Benjamin Brierley, famous later in the century as a writer of folksy dialect sketches, was born into a radical family in the silk and cotton weaving district outside Oldham in Lancashire. He started work in a factory, but it was considered bad for his health, and he was removed and put to work on a velvet hand-loom. He received his education in a four-loom shed, with one of the looms working while lessons were going on. Nevertheless, he learned enough to be able to read the *Northern Star* aloud to his parents' friends and neighbours on Sunday mornings. In 1842 he had another weekly task. 'Besides reading the *Northern Star* on Sunday mornings, my Saturday afternoons were occupied by more arduous work. I had to turn my grandfather's grindstone whilst rebelliously-disposed amateur soldiers ground their pikes . . .'[119] Like other reminiscences of weaving districts, Brierley's stress the ubiquity of Chartism and the *Northern Star*, 'the only newspaper that appeared to circulate anywhere'.

Elijah Dixon was another factory worker who left when his health was affected by the work. He had been trained as a fine cotton spinner, and worked at his trade in the Manchester district. He had been at the Peterloo massacre, and in 1817 served a sentence of imprisonment for radical activity. He found the prison 'palatial' compared with his factory, and when he started spitting blood soon after he returned to the mill, he left the work, determining that neither he nor any of his family should work in a factory again. He was a strong supporter of the factory reform movement and of radicalism generally, and for a time he earned a rather precarious livelihood through a number of small enterprises. In 1841 he abandoned the small-scale manufacture of pill boxes in favour of making matches, and this business succeeded so that he eventually became quite a prosperous manufacturer. In 1869 he was one of the four Peterloo veterans who acted as pall-bearers at the funeral of Ernest Jones.[120]

Like the Scottish weavers and the Lancashire cotton operatives, the linen weavers of Barnsley were a community whose leaders and chief spokesmen were Chartists. Almost without exception the men who came to the fore in the early years were already established as leaders of the weavers during the strikes which took place in the 1820s and 1830s. Two of the most prominent, William Ashton and Frank Mirfield, had been transported for their parts in the bitter strike of 1829, and returned to the town just at the beginning of the Chartist movement, as the result of a petition from the townspeople, who raised a fund to pay for their return fares from Australia. Ashton was the son of a Barnsley linen weaver and an Irish mother. He was a Catholic with strong Irish loyalties, a good speaker, and a leading, if controversial, character in the district. After the events of August 1839, and the demonstrations which replaced the sacred month, he was one of the Chartists arrested and sentenced to imprisonment for sedition. He had attempted to avoid arrest by going with his wife to France in October, but they ran out of money and were forced to return. The three Barnsley weavers, Crabtree, Hoey and Ashton, were tried together and sentenced to two years' imprisonment. Joseph Crabtree and Ashton seem to have felt extremely resentful about their sentences, considering, with some justice, that they had been singled out because of their status in the community rather than because they had acted treasonably. In the case of Crabtree, the resentment went so far that he actually wrote to the Home Secretary offering to give information about Chartists who had genuinely been engaged in treasonable activity. The offer was refused. Ashton came out of prison still full of resentment which in his case took the form of a vehement campaign against Feargus O'Connor, whom he accused of having failed to prevent the Newport rising, although it had been in his power to do so. Ashton's accusations – which were eventually printed in the *Northern Star* in a long letter in May 1845 – were repeated by Gammage in his *History*, and have been perhaps treated with more credence than they deserve. Gammage did not print any of the subsequent refutations by O'Connor and others, nor did he mention the fact that much in Ashton's accusatory letter was in direct contradiction to the contents of another letter published in the *Star* just before his imprisonment. The full story of Ashton's strange behaviour may never be fully teased out, but as far as the main line of his attack on O'Connor goes, it may be set aside as being irrelevant to the history of Chartism. O'Connor offered to come to Barnsley to answer the accusations, and clearly convinced Ashton's fellow townsmen, including Francis Mirfield, who remained the secretary of the weavers' association for many years.[121] What is more, the accusation implied the deliberate betrayal of John Frost by Feargus, an accusation which Frost never made, and which, if it had been credible, could have been the one thing to have punctured Feargus's popularity with the Chartists. Ashton was accused by Mirfield of emigrating to the United States 'at the expense of his former persectors,' since Ashton had accepted the offer, made, it would seem, to all the political prisoners interviewed by Major Williams, of free travel to the States. However, he stayed only ten months. He seems to have renewed his contact with the Chartists when he returned to Barnsley, although the quarrels which his accusations aroused in 1845 probably isolated him from many of his former associates. In 1850 he emigrated to Australia with his family, where he gave up weaving for various shopkeeping ventures which seem to have afforded him a reasonable livelihood until his death in 1877. Mirfield remained in Barnsley as secretary of the handloom weavers association, when his obituarist recorded that he was 'generally resorted to as their confidential advisor in all cases of doubt or difficulty'.[122] Like many of the weavers, Frank Mirfield was not a native of Barnsley, but had been brought up in the London foundling hospital, was apprenticed in Otley, and moved to Barnsley some time in the early 1820s. Joseph Crabtree had been a parish apprentice from Dewsbury, who had also moved to Barnsley in the 1820s. He was almost the exact contemporary of his fellow-prisoner Ashton, and in spite of the episode of his letter to the Home Office, he seems to have been welcomed back into the Chartist group when he left prison. His wife and children had managed to keep the household going during the father's imprisonment, and his son James remembered working all day at winding yarn when he was barely nine years old. As a result, though, Crabtree returned from prison to a comfortable home – 'a hearty welcome, a quiet fireside, a loving family and a fair chance for a new start in the world'.[123] In 1845 he left Barnsley and went back to the heavy woollen district, spending the rest of his life as a schoolmaster in Heckmondwyke. His son, James, was a founder member of the cooperative store in the district, and a leading cooperator throughout his life.

Another leading Chartist and linen weavers' leader was John Vallance. Born in Lancashire in the 1790s, he came to Barnsley with his widowed mother, herself already an active radical, in about 1813. He was almost exactly the same age as O'Connor, and had been actively concerned with politics since his childhood. The family radicalism passed on to his children, two of whom appear as Land Company members. Vallance was associated with every radical and Chartist event in the district throughout his long life, but managed to escape being sent for trial. He helped with the formation of the Land Company and of the Barnsley Cooperative Society, and in his old age was a strong supporter of liberalism. He lived to the 'patriarchal age' of eighty-seven, dying in March 1882. Thomas Frost wrote a series of articles in the *Barnsley Times* under the title of 'The Life and Times of John Vallance', which read like a history of Barnsley radicalism and Chartism.[124] Other Barnsley leaders included Peter Hoey, a weaver and leader of the weavers until his imprisonment left him crippled, and he was unable to carry on his trade. With his wife, who had supported herself by the trade during his imprisonment, he turned to innkeeping for his living.

Arthur Collins, Catholic weavers' leader who had represented the mourning weavers in the Peterloo memorial procession in 1819, continued as an active Chartist, with his son Henry Hunt Collins, by then of an age to take part in political activity, although his much younger son Feargus O'Connor Collins, born in 1840, was too young even for the Young Chartists. Vallance was a Methodist, Mirfield had been brought up in the Church of England, as had Crabtree; Hoey, Ashton, the Collins family and several of the other Chartist weavers were Catholics. There seems to have been no time at which these denominational differences presented any kind of problem, or any at which divisions of opinion on policy occurred on denominational lines. The non-Catholics were as ardent in their support of the repeal of the union as the Catholics, and on questions such as education the whole Chartist group seems to have been unanimous.

Linen weavers were among the leading Chartists too in Dundee, the other main centre of the industry in Great Britain. James Gow was only twenty-four when the Chartist movement began, but was already established as a leader of the Dundee weavers. The son of a regular soldier – one of a number of radicals who came from this background – he had served his apprenticeship to the weaving trade, and combined it with an interest in literature which led to the publication of a number of poems. Many of the Scottish weaver radicals were poets, others were journalists or preachers, and again they call into question the facile identification of handloom weaving with violence and desperation. Gow was a leading figure among the Dundee Chartists until his early death in 1849.

William Thomson, editor of the *Chartist Circular* from 1839 to 1842, also began life as a handloom weaver. While still working at the loom, he edited the *Weavers' Journal* from 1835 to 1837, and acted from 1834 to 1836 as secretary of the General Protecting Union of the Handloom Weavers of Scotland. He was always on the side of moderation and regularity of organisation, and was a great advocate of cooperation, participating actively in the setting up of early cooperative stores in the West of Scotland. From the beginning of the Scottish Chartist movement until 1842 he held the influential position of secretary of the Universal Suffrage Central Committee for Scotland.[125]

Another Scottish weaver who achieved more than local fame was Willie Thom, friend of Harney and Cooper. Lamed in childhood, he started work in a hand-weaving factory at the age of ten. He taught himself to read, write, read music and play the flute. He wrote verse, some of which appeared in local papers and later in Chartist journals. In

1837 he was earning five shillings a week at his trade, a figure very much the same as that given by Richard Marsden for the Preston cotton weavers' earnings at the same time. To support his family Thom was driven to play his flute in the street, and to beg for money. He began a small and short-lived journal, the *Inverury Gossamer*, and in 1845 his poetry began to attract wider attention. When a second edition of his verses was published he was invited to London to supervise the further publication of his work, and to be introduced to literary circles. A sympathetic account of Thom is given by Thomas Cooper, who recalled one particular evening.

> We had a merry meeting, for there were a round dozen of us; and as Willie Thom *mellowed* he began to pour out his wondrous words of thought till Miller grew silent . . . and fixed his eyes on Thom in amazement, till he broke out with –
>
> 'Why the d—— don't you write such talk? It would bring you gold!'
>
> 'I dinna think it's e'en worth siller' said Willie very innocently.[126]

Money was found to set him up as a linen merchant in London, but the atmosphere there, which Cooper found so stimulating, was unbearable to the Scot. The business failed, and he found himself unable to write in the metropolis. He returned with his family to Dundee, from where he wrote to Harney in 1848:

> For four years gone I was encased in a carpeted room – with a fire and sound windows – Lord man, how it contrasts with the dank dark den – the fireless – hopeless hell of a Dundee weaving shop! Such is the destiny of your ruined friend – a feeble body encountering an ill-paid occupation is paying pretty well for the errors of an ill-directed mind. . .[127]

A few weeks later he died, leaving his wife and children destitute.

There were many other radicals and Chartists among the shawl weavers of Paisley, and linen and jute weavers of Dundee and the cotton weavers of Glasgow and district. Many accounts confirm the general radicalism of the weaving workshops. In Dunfermline, for example, the respondents to the Chartist Convention's questionnaire in 1839 reported that 'Among the weavers there are 1800 who pay for newspapers – these go into the workshops and are read by all the men and boys in them so that a man who does not read newspapers is rarely met with. . .'[128]

The most depressed weavers were the handloom weavers in cotton. By the Chartist period they were mostly located in the Carlisle district, and in that part of the country a number of Chartist leaders were still working at the handloom. In parts of Lancashire a few handloom cotton weavers were still working within the factories, but most of the former workers at the trade had moved into powerloom weaving, like Abram Fielden and Richard Pilling. Probably best known of the cotton hand weavers in the Chartist movement was Richard Marsden, delegate from Preston to the first Convention, and one of the only four of its delegates also to be present at the 1848 one. Marsden's speech at the Convention describing the condition of the weavers has taken its place with Pilling's defence in 1843 as an outstanding document from the working population of the cotton districts.[129]

Marsden was associated with a rhetoric of physical force, and may indeed be partly responsible for the violent image that history has given the weavers. But his violence was of language only, as Gammage, never one to sympathise with the wild men of the movement, noted.

> Perhaps of all the men elected there was not one more sincere in purpose than Marsden; he belonged to the extreme school of Harney and Rider, and seemed ready to adopt the most forcible measures in order to effect the object of his wishes . . . but there was nothing in the nature of Richard Marsden which savoured of ferocity. As a private man he would not have crushed a worm. Whoever looked into his mild blue eyes and gazed upon his placid open countenance, was forced to conclude that in his breast at least there flowed abundantly the milk of human kindness.[130]

Marsden spent a life of radical activity in a town in which confrontation between employers and workers was endemic in the first half of the century.[131]

The weavers, more perhaps than any other workmen, were constantly aware of the continuing degradation of their trade. Speeches and reminiscences recall the days when the trade had produced a good living, and weavers had been the leaders of their communities.[132] Mechanisation proceeded slowly during the Chartist period, but each process that was mechanised threw more workers into the unmechanised branches. The Bradford weavers complained that the introduction of power looms made more worsted weavers turn to combing – so that that profession became more and more overcrowded and underpaid until the introduction of workable combing machines in the late forties drove the hand combers to emigrate or to leave the city. The silk weavers of Spitalfields pointed out that the mechanisation of silk winding had forced the women winders to look for looms, and that the introduction of the Jacquard process had eliminated the need for draw boys in the weaving of figured silks, and turned them into would-be handloom weavers. Nevertheless, throughout the period the great majority of textile operatives were still employed on hand processes, whether these were carried out in factories or in their homes. John Hartley, Hebden Bridge Chartist, who had been born in 1821, recalled:

When I was a boy, nearly every house . . . on the hillsides had its hand-looms and the principal industry of the district, beside the factories, was hand-loom weaving and small farming. . . The masters had their places of business where they kept their warps and weft, also their piece-goods when the weavers returned it. . .[133]

The Chartists were asking for the regulation of machinery, but many were also trying to preserve a way of life which they saw as superior to the crowding and regulation of factory industry. The Land Plan owed much of its popularity among textile workers to the prospect it seemed to offer of a combination of work at a trade with the cultivation of a smallholding. As one writer put it:

A leading feature of Mr O'Connor's plan is that it is well adapted to be of the greatest advantage to the most oppressed. Shoemakers, tailors and handloom weavers are the most oppressed and most intelligent of the operative classes, and the very men of all others best fitted to live on the land. The shoemaker and the tailor can work at their trades, the weaver also if provided with a loom; shoes, coats, towels, shirting etc. must be had, and when the rain falls in Spring, and during the long terms of winter, profitable, pleasant and useful employment may be found in indoor work. . .[134]

Very many leading Chartists had begun their working lives at the handloom. Jonathan Bairstow, stirring orator and colleague of Thomas Cooper's period of leadership of the Leicester Chartists, had started work at the age of ten at a loom, Peter Michael Brophy, secretary of the Irish Universal Suffrage Association in 1842 and later an organiser for the Miners' Association, started life as a woollen weaver, and a majority of the leaders of the West Riding movement were weavers or former weavers. The treasurer of the West Riding Chartists was Halifax fancy worsted weaver, Benjamin Rushton. When he died in 1853, at the age of sixty-eight, Ben Wilson recalled that he had been 'a reformer before such as myself were born, and a leader among the Chartists since its commencement'. Although he died, as he had lived, a poor handloom weaver, his funeral saw bigger crowds than those who attended the funerals of national leaders. Benjamin Wilson, without guessing at the numbers, said that he saw more people in Halifax that day than he had seen before or since, and five extra trains were put on to bring people in from Bradford. Ernest Jones in the *People's Paper* estimated that a quarter of a million people were present.[135] Rushton epitomised the type of the W. Riding local leader. Although some may for a time have been supported by Chartist localities as full-time lecturers, they mostly, like Rushton, earned their living at their trades, often low-paid trades. But time was always taken to attend, and in his case very often to chair, great demonstrations or local gatherings, even though the time had to be made up by night or Sabbath work. Ernest Jones recalled having seen Rushton a few weeks before his death, working on intricately-patterned cloth on his loom, although near the end of his seventh decade. He was, as Wilson remembered, 'a good speaker, although using rather broad language'; and was also a popular preacher, firstly among the Methodists, but later as a non-denominational deliverer of numerous Chartist sermons. One writer, forty years after his death, still remembered hearing 'that rare old man, Ben Rushton, commence a speech from a waggon at the bottom of the market with the words rung out with his strong voice "Fellow slaves!"'[136] Another, drawing on local reminiscences, re-created an account of the Chartist chapel in Littletown in the Spen Valley. He described the chapel as an adult school during the week, when those who could read and write instructed those who could not. At weekends, and increasingly on the Sabbath, political speeches and sermons were delivered to audiences which packed the chapel to suffocation. John West and Benjamin Rushton were the most popular speakers, and it was Rushton who was the preacher on the day described, when the chapel was crowded.

The opening hymn was a lively melody by a Chartist poet, commencing –

Hark! listen to the trumpeter,
  He sounds for volunteers!
Rise, helots, rise, unite your strength,
  Shake off your slavish fears!

Many of the congregation were without coats, some perhaps because the room was warm, and others because they had no coats to put on that were decent. The band was there, of course, in full force. . . The other preliminaries followed, and when the sermon was reached Mr Rushton announced as his text, 'The poor ye have always with you'. He pointed out that there were three distinct classes of poor. There were the halt, the maimed and the blind; these were God's poor, and they might trust the all Merciful to look after his helpless ones. Then there were the men who made themselves poor by their reckless or careless manner of living – men who might be well-to-do or at least comfortable – these had deliberately placed themselves in a dependent position, and deserved only to be left to look after themselves. Then, thirdly, there were the poor who had striven and worked hard all their lives, but had been made poor or kept poor by the wrong doing and oppressions of others who had deprived them of their God-given rights. Then with fiery eloquence he went on to denounce the men who refused political justice to their neighbours, and who held them down till their life was made one long desperate struggle for mere existence. As he depicted in glowing language the miseries of the poor man's lot and the sin of those who lorded it so unjustly over him, the feelings of his audience were manifested by fervid ejaculations which gradually culminated until at last one, carried away by Mr Rushton's strong denunciations of oppressers, cried out, 'Aye, d——n 'em, d——n 'em.' Strange as the outburst may seem to us, it created no scandal and the service went on to its close without any one thinking that aught blameworthy had occurred.[137]

Many, probably most, of his congregation were wool, worsted or blanket-weavers, and such communities produced strong, radical groups of Methodists and other nonconformist congregations which often seem to have passed over almost entirely to the Democratic or Chartist chapels. By the time of his death, Rushton was sufficiently estranged from church and chapel to have left the request that no paid priest should officiate at his funeral, but he never abandoned the rhetoric of Christianity. It was indeed the common rhetoric of the Authorised Version of the Bible that made it possible for orators speaking in many different dialects and accents to communicate throughout Britain.

As has already been shown,[138] weavers predominated in Chartist localities in Lancashire and most parts of Yorkshire. They appear not only among the lists of arrested Chartists and Land Company members, but also as secretaries, treasurers and committee-men of the localities of the National Charter Association. Many of the shopkeepers, schoolteachers and journalists in the north were also ex-weavers, including James Leach and John Campbell, first chairman and secretary of the National Charter Association in 1840, Joshua Hobson, publisher of *Northern Star*, William Grocott, secretary of the Miners' Association, William Hill, first editor of the *Northern Star*, linen weaver William Carnegie, secretary of the Dunfermline Chartists and father of the American millionaire, powerloom weaver Joseph Linney, leader of the Black Country Chartists, and John West, perhaps the most noted orator in the movement, apart from O'Connor himself.

John West was an Irishman by birth, and like many of his countrymen had come to England in the 1820s after the collapse of the Irish textile industry. He worked for sixty years as a handloom silk weaver in Macclesfield, and was always associated with the political movement in the north of England. He was an eloquent and accomplished speaker, and had more than one offer from middle-class organisations to become a professional speaker in their causes. But unlike Lowery and Vincent, and a number of other able speakers, he never became a professional speaker, although he was very much in demand at meetings of parliamentary and factory reformers and anti-Poor-Law agitators as well as Chartists. He spoke in support of William Cobbett at the Oldham election in 1832, defeated the free trade lecturer Timothy Falvey at a public debate in the town hall at Macclesfield, and contributed regularly to the columns of the *Northern Star*. He was always ready to defend the cause of Irish independence and to speak and write in favour of the repeal of the union, and he was also famous for his stirring oratory in support of Poland. He was a Chartist parliamentary candidate for Stockport in the election of 1847, and won decisively at the hustings. He was a delegate at more than one Convention, and was several times arrested and imprisoned. He was one of the Kirkdale prisoners from 1848 to 1849, one of his children being born whilst he was in gaol. He was always a mainstream Chartist, a member of and eloquent spokesman for the Land Company. He was working at his trade until his death in 1887, and one of his sons became a designer in William Morris's firm. Although West was clearly a man of above-average gifts of oratory and intelligence, he was also, in his way, typical of many of his fellow-craftsmen in the movement.

The other textile trade that contributed a number of leaders to the movement, especially in the West Riding, was that of woolcomber. For the production of yarn for worsted spinning, the fibres must be combed into one direction, and the work was, until around the middle of the nineteenth century, performed by hand with the use of metal combs, heated in charcoal-fired comb-pots, in the houses of the combers or in small workshops attached to their houses. The work was not highly skilled, it could be done by men or women and it could be easily learned. Although machinery did not become a serious threat until nearly the end of the Chartist period, the trade had become very overcrowded, as workers forced out of other branches of textiles took it up. The woolcombers' strike in Bradford in 1825 had seen the end of any kind of protection for the trade, and by the 1840s the combers were among the most depressed workers in the country. In addition to the low wages brought about by competition, the particularly dirty and unhealthy nature of the work itself contributed to their depression.

Thomas Martin Wheeler, London Chartist, Land Company officer and member of the national executive, had begun life as a woolcomber, as had John Snowden, leading Halifax radical and Chartist, and George White. White is probably the best-known of the Chartist combers, and one who, like West, returned regularly to his trade throughout his life. He too was an Irishman by birth and had probably also come to England as a child, since his father was a stationer and newsagent in Bradford. White was associated with the beginning of Chartism in Leeds, and with its earliest period in Bradford. For some time he worked as *Northern Star* agent in Birmingham, acting as agent and correspondent for the paper and also as organiser for the NCA in the city. He was a loyal supporter of O'Connor and a friend and supporter of Harney. He was a competent journalist, speaker and organiser, and his letters show him to have been literate and very articulate.[139] He spent many years in prison for his activities – perhaps as long as any Chartist leader – but he was clearly not someone who sought violence and confrontation for its own sake. He seems to have retained the respect of both Gammage and Holyoake, neither of whom had much time for the more violent and rhetorical end of the movement. His numerous arrests may indeed be an index of the seriousness with which the authorities regarded his activities, and in this connection his Irish origins and connections would certainly have made him appear more dangerous. He was associated with attempts to renew trade union organisation amongst the combers, being their representative on the council of the United Trades Association for the Employment of Labour in Agriculture and Manufacturing in 1845, an organisation which tried to promote cooperative production among unemployed members of various trades. White has sometimes been presented as intransigent and confrontationist in his politics – it is easy to see the consistent Chartists who were always suspicious of middle-class overtures in this light. It is, however, anachronistic, and White himself provides an illustration of the extent to which even the most class-conscious Chartists were always looking eagerly for support and genuine sympathy among their social superiors. The *Morning Chronicle* investigations, and the reports of various royal commissions on social and working conditions were welcomed in the Chartist press, and were genuinely believed by most of the Chartists to provide ammunition for their case. In 1845, under White's leadership, the Bradford Chartists, from a base in Bussey's old inn, the Roebuck, set up their own commission of enquiry into the conditions of life and work among the combers. The committee was appointed by 'a numerous meeting of woolcombers' on 5 May, with George White as secretary, and Chartists as its members. Their eighteen-page report, based on a door-to-door investigation by the committee members of the woolcombing areas of the city, was presented at a public meeting on 3 June of the same year, presided over by the Vicar of Bradford, the Rev. W. Scoresby. It is worth reading as a precursor of many later social investigations, and for the information which it contains. In 1847 and 1848 White was again organising and speaking on behalf of Ireland and Poland as well as in the general Chartist cause. He was imprisoned in Kirkdale for a year in 1849-50, and on his release remained an active Chartist until the movement finally collapsed completely. He edited his own paper briefly in Birmingham, and was one of the speakers at the funeral of Benjamin Rushton in Halifax in 1853. He died in poverty in Sheffield workhouse in 1868, at the age of sixty.[140]

Woolcombers tie for sixth place in the national count of Land Company members. In Halifax the combers are the second largest group, with 79 out of 502 members (one comber being a woman). In Bradford, of 806 members, more than half, 406, were combers. In Huddersfield there were 10 among the 264 members, and in Yorkshire outside the main towns there were 144 combers among the 1,425 members – the third largest group after weavers and labourers. In the lists of arrested Chartists in 1840 were 10 woolcombers, nearly all of whom had been arrested in Bradford after the abortive rising in January 1840. Seven of these were among the prisoners seen by the inspectors, and given that the weavers were divided between wool, linen, silk and cotton, the woolcombers make up the biggest single trade. They were prominent in the worsted manufacturing area. Their number included John Snowden, leader of the Halifax Chartists, who spent nearly sixty years in various forms of radical activity, but throughout those years made his income from his trade, until in his old age he was given a small pension by his former employer.[141]

The only surviving membership list of a Chartist association comes from the small Bradford out-township of Great Horton, an area largely occupied in textile manufacture. The book covers the years 1840 to 1866, but if we take the members who joined between 1840, when the NCA was founded, and 1842, we find in those two years 50 weavers, 35 combers, 5 coalminers, 4 dyers, 3 masons, 2 warehousemen, 2 engine tenders and one each of shoemaker, tailor, labourer, dresser, whitesmith, mechanic, joiner, turner, gardener, corn miller, surveyor and schoolmaster. It is in fact a near profile of the male workforce of such a community.

I have stressed very much in this book the community of interest between working people in a variety of trades and many different parts of the country. This is certainly the remarkable thing about Chartism and accounts for the wide spread of its following and organisation.

Nevertheless, it did gain colour and style to some extent from the communities in which it was strongest, and there can be no doubt that in the textile districts of Lancashire, Yorkshire and Nottinghamshire it took its most characteristic form, and did represent the hopes and aspirations of whole communities to a remarkable degree.

Much more could be written about the participation of various trades in the movement, and more detailed and local studies will still have a great deal to tell us. Two other working groups should be briefly mentioned, however, although many must be left aside. One group which inspired particular fears among respectable people was the miners. Towns like Wakefield and Newcastle, which were at the centre of coalfields, were always on edge at times of high social tension, fearing an 'invasion' by the colliers. In fact, the isolation of many mining communities, and the control exercised by a small number of powerful employers in many coalfields, meant that theirs is one of the trades which seems not to have contributed to Chartism in proportion to its numbers in the country. This many, however, be another misconception. As with some other trades, the low profile kept by miners among the local leadership is compensated for by a much fuller representation in the Land Company and among arrested Chartists. In David Jones's Land Company list, miners are exceeded in numbers only by weavers, labourers, shoemakers, tailors, stockingers, combers and spinners.[142] There were forty of them amongst the arrested Chartists in 1840, more than either shoemakers or cotton spinners – indeed, they come second only to weavers in this list. It is, of course, a list that includes many of those arrested as the result of the Newport rising, and this may partly account also for their large numbers among the prisoners interviewed in 1840-1, where they tie with woolcombers as the second largest group after weavers. They certainly played a very important part in the disturbances of 1842, and it is in the year preceding these that most miners appear among the committee-men of the National Charter Association. They form the largest occupational group among those transported for their part in the 1842 disturbances.

The picture of the miners' participation in Chartism to be drawn from these figures might perhaps suggest that they were the shock troops for the more violent actions. It should be remembered, however, that the Miners' Association of the 1840s was one of the most important early attempts at the formation of a national trades union, and that some of the miners' leaders of this period were outstanding for their ability and intelligence. Men like Thomas Hepburn and Martin Jude were convinced Chartists, and they brought into the organisation of the union some of the ablest of the Chartists, including W. P. Roberts, who became known as the Miners' Attorney General, the Lancashire Chartist, William Beesley, and the former leader of the Dublin Chartists, Peter Michael Brophy. The presence of miners in the Chartist crowd is born out by the figures of arrests and Land Company membership. The strikes in the coalfields during 1842 and 1844 had a strong political flavour, and the leaders whom they elected and followed were for the most part committed Chartists. At one of the first Chartist rallies in Newcastle, on 28 June 1838, Hepburn proposed a resolution in support of the Charter, and claimed in the course of his speech that 'The stewards of Lord Ravensworth had offered his colliers three quarts of porter a man, if they abstained from marching today with banners belonging to their order, but the brave colliers laughed the brute to scorn, and he now saw before him the banner floating in the breeze.'[143]

If the miners were, to some extent, apart from the mainstream of political and cultural life in Britain, the printers were among the most metropolitan and sophisticated of workers. As an 'aristocratic' trade it has been suggested that they were not very well represented among active Chartists, and it may be that their conditions of work, in an expanding market for the printed word, may have set them apart from the more depressed traditional artisan trades. Printing, however, also faced problems of mechanisation and technological change, and as W. E. Adams found, tramping the country with his composing stick and his apron in the winter of 1855, could also feel the effects of economic recession.[144] Compositors have played an important part in radical working-class movements throughout Europe, and the British Chartists were no exception. Among the autodidact Chartist leadership were many printers or ex-printers, including three of the signatories to the original Charter, Hetherington, Vincent and Watson, while, apart from W. E. Adams, Chartist autobiographers included Thomas Frost and John Bedford Leno, both of whom began life as journeyman printers before turning to journalism.[145]

Apart from well-known names, there were six printers among David Jones's list of Land Company members, six among the arrested Chartists in 1840, and 50 named London Chartist printers.[146] In Cheltenham, Thomas Willey, printer and balladeer, was a stalwart of the local Chartist movement and his grandson Thomas Hailing was one of the small group of young republican printers who joined W. J. Linton at Brantwood in the early fifties to publish the *English Republic* and the *Northern Tribune*.[147] Among the imprisoned Chartists was John Livesey, son-in-law of the veteran Manchester Radical, James Wheeler;

as a jobbing letterpress printer Livesey had been earning between fifteen and sixteen shillings a week at the time of his arrest, a wage which was about on a level with that of the ordinary cotton spinners. He seems to have kept his head down during the interview, for his replies are laconic and non-committal, in spite of the fact that he had been acting as agent for the sale of arms in the Manchester district. The inspector considered him 'a man of little ability or energy'.[148]

The trades which have been discussed are only a few of those to be found among the Chartists. Carpet weavers and potters have been described elsewhere, and local studies will no doubt continue to give a fuller picture of the occupations of provincial leaders and members.[149] The multifarious occupations have in common, however, the fact that all branches of each trade, from the skilled society man to the slop worker, can be found among the Chartists, and indeed among the leadership. It is not true to see the movement as having been led by the skilled stratum in each trade, which was then bought off or in some way diverted from politics in the post-Chartist period, leaving the mass of the working people leaderless. Chartism revealed the enormous amount of skill and ability which resided in all sections of a working population confined by custom, education and location, from among which very few members rose into the class above.

PART THREE:

1842–1850

CHAPTER TEN

The Chartists and the Middle Class

THE passionate loyalty and emotional commitment felt by so many working people towards Chartism was clearly fired by more deeply-felt motives than the simple wish for political enfranchisement. To the upper classes of society the marching plug rioters or the huge crowds that flocked to Chartist demonstrations represented a threat to far more than their political exclusiveness. Although the demand for the vote hardly constituted a revolutionary threat to British society, there were very many people who agreed with Macaulay's statement in the House of Commons that universal suffrage was 'incompatible with the very existence of civilisation'. What they feared was the lack of respect for property, the lack of respect for authority, and the lack of dignified behaviour which they perceived in these Chartist demonstrations, as well as their avowed purposes. There were, indeed, a certain number of radicals among the middle classes who supported in principle the idea of manhood suffrage. But these middle-class politicians never made common cause with the Chartists for more than a fleeting moment.

Many historians have blamed the Chartists for not winning the support of such valuable allies. Chartist impetuosity and lack of control, the violence of some of its leading advocates, and the people's attachment to jealous demagogic leaders have been given as some of the reasons for this lack of strategic wisdom.[1] Much of the discussion about relations between the political parties of the middle and working classes in this period, however, has been distorted by a lack of understanding of class attitudes, particularly of the attitudes of members of the middle class.

A number of differing interpretations of the class nature of Chartism have been made in recent years. Two which continue to be cited should be mentioned. One, set out by Renee Soffer in 1965, claimed that 'the mass of working men, particularly in the industrial North, were not class conscious, and through the 'thirties and 'forties they remained uneducated, inarticulate, unskilled and unaware of any "identity of interests as between themselves"'.[2] She argued that the unskilled workers – by whom she appeared to mean everyone except factory workers – were unreasonably opposed to the middle classes and to the Whigs, whom she considered to have been 'better reformers than the Tories'. Their actions were not those of an independent class, but of a deferential people, who looked to the Tories for leadership. Two years or so later David Rowe, in *Past and Present*, was putting the opposite view – that the Chartists were totally dependent on the middle classes, and that both Julius West and Mark Hovell had placed too strong an emphasis on working-class elements in early Chartism. He too, though, agreed that 'the growing working-class political consciousness was not strong enough by the mid-1830's to formulate its own ideas and programme'.[3] Most social historians of all schools, though, have agreed in finding Chartism strongly informed by a sense of class and by class-determined stances on a whole range of questions. They have, however, found contradictory evidence, some of which may account for the confusion in the interpretations of Soffer and Rowe. It is not always easy to trace the source of the confusion, which clearly derives partly from the sort of evidence we have to use, and partly from the class attitudes of most of the earlier observers.

A very great deal of our information about the 1830s and the 1840s must come, by definition, from middle-class sources. Observers, journalists, parliamentary commissioners, moralists, novelists, all who were showing an interest in the 'condition-of-England question' in these years came from the upper orders. Even accounts written by men and women who had lived through the period and had participated in the movement were written later in the century, in a mellower Liberal atmosphere, for journals and publishers anxious to cater for a large, mainly middle-class, reading public. The culture shift which is generally reckoned to have occurred around the middle decades of the century affected people's views of their own past as well as their words and actions in the changed atmosphere of Mid-Victorian society. Thus, to recover the strengths as well as the limitations of the environment in which Chartism flourished, we have to get behind the screen of prejudice and moral judgement which came between it and even the most sensitive and apparently sympathetic members of the professional and business classes who recorded most of the information.

To a certain extent this problem of sifting applies even to the Chartists' own journals, for the style and within certain limits the subject matter of mid-century journalism had already been set by the time the *Northern Star* was started in 1837, by an existing tradition of upper-class newspaper production. The radical journals made innovations in style and content, but they re-wrote speeches and contributions from demotic into standard English, for example, and for reasons of style or to avoid prosecution, ironed out militant, local, blasphemous and overly idiomatic references – as can occasionally be seen by comparing police reports of speeches with those printed in the Chartist journals. The occasional demotic phrase that creeps in to the standard English adopted by working-class correspondents suddenly brings the press to life – as in the letter from a Welsh Chartist collier, complaining of a report published from the *Morning Chronicle* about the colliers of Glamorgan, based on information given to their reporter by the local clergyman.

> Sir – on perusing the columns of the *Star* of Saturday week, I observed an extract from the *Morning Chronicle*, treating at some length on the morals of the working men of the iron and mining districts of Glamorganshire, and also on their extravagant mode of living. . . Probably I am better acquainted with the morals and the mode of living of the working men of this district, being one of that order myself, than the Reverend John Griffiths, the Vicar of Aberdare who furnished the commissioners with this false and calumnious report. . . I am of the opinion this said Reverend J. Griffiths is in the habit of living rather greasy himself.[4]

Henry Candy, a stonemason and a very popular speaker in the West Midlands, was regularly reported in the columns of the *Star* as speaking decorously in support of the Chartist programme. In a private letter to Thomas Cooper, however, the secretary of the Leamington Spa Chartists complained of Candy's 'somewhat coarse and vulgar style of language accompanied by denunciatory remarks against the Wesleyan Methodists and in general against the middle class'.[5] Clearly, what went down well in Wolverhampton was not suitable for the more decorous atmosphere of a spa town, but the newspaper reports give little hint of the problem.

Demotic speech is spoken speech, of course, and any attempt to indicate it by phonetic spelling, or even by printed variations of grammatical forms invariably sounds patronising, and usually is. Even modern 'oral historians' who consider themselves to be presenting a genuine version of working-class spoken recollections often distance the speakers by phoneticising their local speech, when they would not dream of doing the same thing to evidence spoken with – say – an American or an Oxford accent, both of which deviate phonetically from written English. Thus when radical journalists do occasionally use phonetically written demotic forms, it is either in humorous passages, or occasionally actually as a form of putting down middle-class characters – millowners or foremen, for example. Only accidentally can one find out from contemporary sources about the extent to which speakers used local forms. Some later accounts, like those of the later nineteenth-century dialect poet Ben Brierley, used dialect forms to trivialise and make slightly comic the figures from the earlier part of the century.

The problem of recovering the form in which the Chartists actually spoke is not the greatest one, however. Their own publications do allow them to speak for themselves to a certain extent. A bigger problem in the writing of their history has been the attitudes of observers and historians. In his introduction to the reprint of R. G. Gammage's *History of the Chartist Movement*, John Saville cites a review of the book which appeared in the *Leader* in 1855. This was a journal which published work by some Chartists, and whose editor, Thornton Hunt, was very close indeed to the movement in its later days.

> Mr Gammage, [the anonymous reviewer wrote] one of themselves has compiled an honest and intelligent account of the Chartist agitation from its beginning to its close, and this narrative should set the unrepresented classes on their guard. It is a deplorable story in many respects, but chiefly that it exhibits 'the people' taught by paltry agitators to be violent, to be suspicious, to be jealous, to doubt their friends, and to bring discredit on their principles by a rash, theatrical and violent mode of asserting them. In substance the history is that of a vast crowd organised to follow despicable leaders, and led by them into folly, into peril, into failure. . . From the first, the men who put themselves forward as their representatives gave proofs of their radical political incapacity. In their egotism they could not combine for a common purpose. In their violence they terrified instead of conciliating the middle classes . . . they separated their party from all others in the realm by the frenzy and bitterness of their demonstrations.[6]

The tone here is clear enough. The politics of Chartism are judged by comparing them with the politics of established parties and found wanting. At a time when British political life was riddled with corruption, when politicians of all parties depended on patronage, the working class is castigated for 'theatrical' and 'frenzied' demonstrations. Anything which the middle classes found distasteful must be bad, since the aim of working-class politics should have been to conciliate this class.

The middle classes certainly believed themselves to be superior in every way to the classes above and below them in morality, knowledge and understanding. If one may generalise for a moment about so large a sector of society, it does seem to be the case that certain views were held with considerable confidence by almost every middle-class person. For one thing, they were agreed in believing very strongly in education. So strongly, indeed, that there is often the suggestion in their observations, as there is in those of their modern descendants, that anyone who is not educated is not anything. Literacy is the test of humanity, and information gained by means of the printed word is the most important, if not indeed the only kind of information that is worth having. Investigators were adept at finding out what the lower orders and their children did not know – the names of the prime minister, the twelve apostles, the queen of England, but they seldom waited to find out what they did know. The working people of early Victorian England may have had many among them who were ignorant, stupid and brutal. It should be noted, however, that the middle classes had many among *them* who were stupid, superstitious, religiose and complacent.

Take for a moment their attitude to education; it was the enlightened and reforming among the middle classes who advocated education as a cure for the evils of poverty and immorality which existed among the working people. Old-fashioned Tories doubted the propriety of any but the most basic religious education for the poor as tending to give them ideas above their stations.[7] But what sort of education did these middle-class reformers want for the lower orders? Two pamphleteers, writing in the early 1840s, eloquently advocated education as the solution for the country's ills. 'When it is considered that unless the efficacy ascribed to education is imaginary, unless the permanent improvement of the lower classes is impracticable, the misery we now see might have been averted, and without the sacrifice of any interest or the discomfiture of any class. . .'[8] Turn the page and the nature of the education to be provided is described: 'such education as would correct their prejudices, increase their self-respect, elevate their minds, and more especially impart the degree of moral and religious principle which would more effectually deter them from the habit of marrying without the means of rearing families in comfort'.[9] The authors of the pamphlet 'knew' that the cause of poverty in England in the 1840s was 'the excess of population over food'. This knowledge they derived from political economy, which was, they asserted, 'a science, not a theory or a system'. They attacked *The Times* for publishing 'dirge after dirge on the depressed condition of the labourer, without a word about imprudent marriages', and for considering the problems of the nation 'rather as a comet which has darted down upon society, and of which we know not the ways, than as a simple exemplification of a well-known and well-established theory'. What was worse, *The Times* was not only witholding this truth, but was inculcating error, by suggesting that the sorry state of the poor might be 'imputed to the neglect of the rich, to the avarice of the Landlords and to the stupidity of the farmers' rather than to the lack of self-control of the labourers.

Such publications were legion. Their spurious rationality and bogus scientific argument perpetuate an image of a scientifically-minded and enquiring class of truth-seekers, rather than of a group steeped in self-interest, religiosity and dogma before which the more earthy and limited culture of the working population had no reason to feel ashamed.

The cultural gulf was certainly great between the classes. The development of a middle ground later in the century, and the occasional success of a determined climber from the working class into the lower professions, has led many people to underestimate the profundity of this gulf. Outside the major cities the cultural and geographical differences between the classes were almost unbridgeable.

The typical areas of Chartist strength were outside the cities. They were, as has been shown, in the manufacturing districts, the provincial towns and above all in the outlying townships and villages around them. Here the regular meetings were held at which newspapers were read aloud and discussed, signature collection and fund-raising organised and operations like exclusive dealing and picketing arranged by members and supporters. The enormous demonstrations whose size, theatricality and frenzied oratory so angered and frightened middle-class observers were usually held on areas of common or waste land outside the towns, and men and women from all the surrounding townships marched with their banners and music to the meeting-place. Benjamin Wilson, of Halifax, described several such meetings in his own district, often held on Blackstone Edge, a high point on the Penine moors between Yorkshire and Lancashire. He remembered seeing the streets leading down into the town black with people for several miles after such a demonstration. The first of these rallies which he attended as a boy in his teens was on Peep Green, in the Spen Valley, on Whit Monday in 1839. He joined the Halifax procession and marched the nine miles or so to the meeting-place. On the way columns joined them from Bradford and Queenshead. At the meeting-place 'some thousands of people had already assembled, and for almost an hour we witnessed the continuous arrival of processions from different directions, with bands playing and banners flying'.[10] These huge numbers and the comparative isolation and independence of the districts from which the participants emanated were what worried middle-class observers most.

Disraeli caught this disquiet in his account of Wodegate, the manufacturing district, in *Sybil*.

At the beginning of the Revolutionary War, Wodegate was a sort of squatting district of the great mining region to which it was contiguous, a place where adventurers in the industry which was rapidly developing, settled themselves. . . It was a land without an owner; no one claimed any manorial right over it; they could build cottages without paying rent. It was a district recognised by no parish; so there were no ties and no meddlesome supervision. . . . There are no landlords, head-lessees, main-masters or butties in Wodegate. No church there has yet raised its spire; . . . even the conventicle scarcely dares show its humble front in some obscure corner. There is no municipality, no magistrate; there are no local acts, no vestries, no schools of any kind. The streets are never cleaned; every man lights his own house; nor does any one know anything except his own business. . .[11]

The inhabitants, Disraeli allowed, were world-famous for their skill as metal workers, but they were brutal, drunken, without any of the graces of civilised beings, and represented the truly destructive forces let loose by Chartism.

A much more sympathetic account of a similar community at almost exactly the same period was given by a local historian of the township of Failsworth, a small weaving community in Lancashire.

Here, on a rugged, elevated site . . . a sturdy people still speaking with rare force and humour the dialect of Lancashire, have, for a century or more lived a life thoroughly characteristic of the county in its occupations, customs and political and social energy. . . Time after time during the early part of the century . . . have the men and women of Failsworth marched into Manchester, sometimes with pikes and muskets in their hands, at others carrying banners with bold demands for political reforms.[12]

Like the inhabitants of Wodegate, the Failsworth people were beyond the reach of parson or magistrate. But far from living in animal ignorance, they set up their own school, where children were taught from Paine and Voltaire, until the church managed to bring it under control in the post-Chartist period. Like the inhabitants of Wodegate, they took part in many of the violent episodes of Chartism, moulding bullets and grinding pikes. They also shared with Wodegate and most of the manufacturing townships a liking for cruel sports like bear and badger-baiting, bull-running and cock and hen fighting.

The lack of control exercised by secular and ecclesiastical authority in such districts worried the middle class. The proposal by the Whig Government to set up constabulary forces in the rural districts was largely concerned, in the late 1830s, with the disciplining of these districts, which fell outside the boundaries of the boroughs. Working-class radicals believed that the new police forces would have as their main objects the enforcement of the new Poor Law, the reinforcement of the employers' interests in industrial disputes and the regulation and suppression of the sports and leisure activities of the working people. Among the evidence collected by the commissioners investigating the need for a rural constabulary force in 1836 was a submission from a correspondent in the worsted-manufacturing township of Clayton, just outside Bradford in the West Riding of Yorkshire. He welcomed the proposals for a police force. 'Of all the measures proposed for the Good of the Community which have engaged the attention of our present prudent administration, I apprehend few will be found more beneficial to this country in the promotion of good Order and the suppression of vice than the establishment of a Rural Police presently meditated by Government.' He went on to describe the district of Clayton, which consisted of four villages, Clayton, Clayton Heights, Old Dolphin and Queenshead, set about half a mile apart from each other in the hills between Halifax and Bradford, with a total population of 4,459.

> The mountaineers in most places are noted for generosity and simplicity but here they are infamous for knavery and cruelty, and the deplorable ignorance and rudeness of these savage villagers are not to be equalled in the Empire. There are fewer individuals in the township able to read and write than in any other place of equal size in England, and consequently the subjects which form topics of discourse and engage the minds of working men in other places are here never either discussed or understood, and whenever a number of the inhabitants are met together at an inn, obscene songs, the most disgusting conversation, brawling and fighting alone prevail. . . . In the Old Dolphin village containing 184 houses, there are upward of fifty illegitimate children, a Fact speaking little in favour of its inhabitants. In the township there are 14 beer shops – in these strongholds of the devil, shunned and detested by every honest man, every description of knavery is carried on and villainy concocted . . . card playing and gambling are carried on from morning to night without any attempt at secrecy . . . I have heard it said that since the establishment of Beer Shops wickedness has here been alarmingly augmented, a consequence of the practices at those places – I have heard a beer shop keeper in this neighbourhood declare that in his business 'it is the Gambling that brings in the custom and not the *Ale*'. . .

Policing to date had been carried on by one chief constable supported by a deputy for each village. The constable for Old Dolphin, where the writer lived, was an operative woolcomber earning 14*s*. a week: 'I have heard the deputy constable often declare that he durst not do his Duty, from fear of the Revenge that would be taken upon him at the expiration of the year of his appointment.'[13] The letter consists of five and a half foolscap pages of such description. Fierce and rough inhabitants whose practices included a brutal kind of fighting called 'poising', which closely resembled the 'purring' of the mining districts, met regularly in unsupervised beer-shops whose existence was a grievance to magistrates and to other respectable inhabitants. This mingled fear of unlicensed drinking and working-class subversion occurring in the alehouses was caught in the same year by a local historian in nearby Halifax, who concluded his account of the town with a description of a local beer-house, in which

> 'the incendiary and the unionist fraternise together; from hence under the influence and excitement of their too often adulterated beverage, they turn out at midnight . . . the one to fire the cornstack and the barn, the other to imbrue his hands in the blood of a fellow-workman, or peradventure the man to whom he was formerly indebted for his daily bread. . .'[14]

It happens, however, that we know a bit about other things that were happening in the beer-shops and loom sheds of at least one of the Clayton villages. Queenshead was the location of one of the earliest radical groups and one of the earliest temperance groups in the West Riding, both of which were in existence at the time the letter was written. In at the founding of both groups was John Bates, who described his early life in the area. He had been born in Queenshead in 1815 and lived there all his life. He recalled that 'The inhabitants were colliers, quarrymen and handloom weavers, who had to work very hard for a small wage, and were seldom able to taste any other articles of food than milk, porridge and potatoes.' Bates worked at the age of twelve as a driver in the colliery for 3*s*. a week, but later took up his widowed mother's trade of handloom weaving. During the Chartist period he became a powerloom weaver in a local factory. His ideas about politics and temperance were learnt from and discussed with his fellow-workmen –

> I acquired an interest in public affairs through meeting with a company of men on Saturday nights for the reading of a newspaper. We could only afford a newspaper in those days by putting our pence together. I was often asked to read aloud.[15]

A member of this group introduced Bates to the writings of William Cobbett, hence to radical politics and to the local radical association which was soon to become the Chartist Association.

Another member of the same association was John Snowden, a young woolcomber who joined in 1837 at the age of sixteen. Unlike Bates, who had been taught to read by his mother, Snowden could neither read nor write. He learnt the former skill in his early years as a radical, and in his old age liked to tell how, when he was arrested and imprisoned in 1842,

> the chaplain came round and asked them to read from the Bible in order to test their degree of education. Mr Snowden, with grim humour, selected the chapter in James 'Go now, ye rich men, weep and howl for your miseries that shall come upon you'. The chaplain, however, soon had enough of that doctrine, and closed the examination abruptly with 'That'll do, that'll do.'[16]

In spite of his late acquisition of the skills of literacy – he did not learn to write until he was over forty – Snowden became a leader among the West Riding Chartists. Christopher Shackleton, handloom weaver, considered the best speaker in the district and later to become secretary of the West Riding Chartists, Jonathan Bairstow, one of the most popular speakers in the Chartist movement in the 1840s and a member of the National Executive of the National Charter Association, and a number of other well-known figures came from the small village of Queenshead. It may also be remembered that Ben Wilson spoke of a column marching in from the village to the Peep Green meeting.

Clearly, then, there are at least two ways of looking at such a community. To the middle-class observer what predominates is the drunkenness, brutality and lack of formal moral education. Aspects of this view may have been shared by some of the working-class observers and inhabitants – working men and women formed the first temperance association, and were called infidels by the local churchmen for doing so. But temperance, and even more, radical politics, were their own form of 'self-improvement'. Singing and gambling would not have been regarded as serious sins by many of the Chartists – men like John Bedford Leno, Chartist printer, who earned his beer money as an apprentice by gambling and by singing in 'free and easy's' in his local public house. Indeed, the quality of the singing to be found in such surroundings was probably musically at least as high as that to be found in the drawing-rooms of their betters. Chartism grew in this atmosphere, and with it a conception of legality and forms of political action which were often at variance with middle-class conceptions. More than fifty years later John Bates recalled:

> Well, the Chartist riots proper took place in 1839 and 1848, when Frost, Williams and Jones were transported. A large number of plots were arranged in secret, and this movement developed a great deal in 1848, when the great

Revolution in France took place. I have attended several secret meetings at which we have planned revolution; but nothing came of them. . . I never did anything illegal except to attend meetings, and if I had to live over again I should not want to alter what I did.[17]

The important lesson from these two views of the same community is that the middle-class observer was condemning in a blanket way whole areas of differing experience. It is also a fact that changes in the aspirations of the people were coming from among the people themselves. This can be seen by taking the example of drinking and temperance. Although working-class radicals would not have agreed that all their problems were caused by excessive drinking, as middle-class commentators were wont to suggest, they were not unaware of the waste of time and energy which drinking could entail, and indeed many saw abstention from alcohol as a way of resisting exploitation. As Brian Harrison, the historian of the temperance movement, has shown, the middle-class temperance reformers did not welcome teetotal Chartists in their ranks, since intemperance was by no means the greatest of the complaints that were made against the working man. Attacks on drinking habits rarely came alone.

Indiscipline and drunkenness were alleged of almost every occupation in the manufacturing trades and districts. Such accusations were standard from the employers' side in times of wage disputes, but drinking habits were only a part of the customary practices which were under heavy attack in these years. The insistence on control over working hours and aspects of work, including the training of new entrants to trades, and the irregularity of the working week were usually linked together by critics and moralists. Drunkenness and indiscipline were twin evils. But just as a change was coming about in the attitude towards alcohol of many working-class families, so the four-day week was increasingly used not simply for drinking, but as the chance to develop interests and activities outside work. One old shoemaker writing later in the century recalled other ways in which Saint Monday was observed in the trade.

Four days out of six is the extent of endurance that any very ready workman can bear. It is because of this that men of Tom Horne's stamp are generally 'Fuddlers' – not necessarily in strong drinks, although this is the *rule* – or was when I worked on the seat some thirty years ago or more. . . . I know one man personally who would soak his stuff overnight, and turn out his dozen pair of French sewrounds during the following day by daylight. Four days were quite enough for him, however. He was what is known to the literary craftsmen as a 'book-fuddler' that is to say, when exhausted by close application to his work, instead of resorting to the shop's meeting-house to drink brawl and smoke . . . he would wander through the streets and lanes . . . of the City and West-End, where old books were found in super-abundance, and where he could revel in the luxury of the best writers. . . I have known many shopmates of this stamp.[18]

These and other indications suggest that the middle-class observers may not have seen all that was to be seen in the manufacturing districts. But later historians of Chartism often themselves picked up the tone and ideas of contemporary middle-class observers. Mark Hovell's description of the supporters of the anti-Poor-Law movement in the north is an example.

The movement was thus of extreme vehemence and violence. The rank and file were men already rendered desperate by continuous and increasing poverty, ignorant and unlettered men deprived or fearing to be deprived, of a resource on which they had long counted, men coarsened by evil surroundings and brutalised by hard and unremitting toil, relieved only by periods of unemployment in which their dulled minds brooded over their misfortunes and recalled their lost prosperity. . .

Hovell saw the agitation in the north as being

. . . without organisation. Its methods were far removed from the anti-corn-law league or the London Working Men's Association. It was not educative; it appealed not to reason but to passion and sentiment. Its leaders were not expert agitators, aiming at the conversion of public and Parliament, but mob orators, stirring up passions and spreading terror, hoping to frighten the government into a suspension or a repeal of the hated act.[19]

In a later passage he attributes the failure of early Chartism to the 'dog-like attachment' of the northern Chartists to local leaders and to O'Connor. The expression 'dog-like' is important. It echoes the imagery constantly used by middle-class observers, an imagery by which the common people are reduced to the status of animals, without souls, minds or culture.

Disraeli stands out among the novelists of the 1840s in the recognition he gives to the political autonomy and rationality of sections of the working-class radicals. But to the inhabitants of Wodegate he allows no rationality: 'It is not that the people are immoral, for immorality implies some forethought; or ignorant, for ignorance is relative; but they are animals, unconscious; their minds a blank; and their worst actions only the impulse of a gross and savage instinct.'[20] Lest this be set aside as in some way a Tory attitude of contempt, the same kind of imagery and assessment can be found in more 'liberal' writers, such as Elizabeth Gaskell and Charles Kingsley. Mrs Gaskell wrote:

> The actions of the uneducated seem to me typified in those of Frankenstein, that monster of many human qualities, ungifted with a soul, a knowledge of the difference between good and evil. . . . The people rise up to life; they irritate us, they terrify us, and we become their enemies. Then in the sorrowful moment of our triumphant power, their eyes gaze on us with mute reproach. Why have we made them what they are; a powerful monster, yet without the inner means for peace and happiness?[21]

Charles Kingsley described agricultural labourers in a Devonshire tavern, whose conversation was '. . . half articulate, nasal, guttural, made up almost entirely of vowels, like the speech of savages . . . coarse, half-formed growls, as of a company of seals. . .'[22]

These wretched creatures are even unfavourably compared with a Chartist crowd, and are so degenerate, their blood tainted by the 'filth and drunkenness' induced by war-time prosperity, that even an itinerant Chartist fails to stir them to action.[23]

In *Alton Locke*, it is Alton's address to a crowd of agricultural labourers – and it should be emphasised that Kingsley worked among such people in his rural incumbency – that provides the riot which puts him behind bars, for his impassioned political appeal only has the effect of setting the mindless multitude off on a rampage of looting and destruction.

Lady Charlotte Guest was in many ways a sympathetic observer, but in her diary the same kind of language appears. She wrote, recording a discussion with the curate at Dowlais: 'We talked about the poor and the feeling of the lower classes to the rich, and what he said quite confirmed my views of the unsound state of society and the necessity of educating or humanising the lower grade. . .'[24] A less sensitive observer wrote to a friend in the same year: 'When once the lower classes have felt their physical power, they are like dogs that have tasted sheep's blood.'[25] Caroline Norton joined in the discussion about Chartism on several occasions – again expressing the animal imagery in verse when she warned her fellow-aristocrats against ignoring the grievances of the factory workers:

> But if the weight which habit renders light
> Is made to gall the Serf who bends below –
> The dog that watched and fawned prepares to bite!
> Too rashly strained, the cord snaps from the bow.

Too tightly curbed, the steeds their riders throw –
And so (at first contented his fair state
Of customary servitude to know)
Too harshly ruled, the poor man learns to hate
And curse the oppressive law that bids him serve the great.[26]

Many more examples could be cited. Their significance is that even liberal and sympathetic observers saw the working people as having no culture of their own. The constant use of animal imagery is not accidental. Sometimes a writer was prepared to recognise in an outstanding individual some qualities of a pale reflection of a higher culture – Alton Locke, the self-taught poet, dreaming of higher things, Mary Barton, the busy little housewife whose house is described in terms of its resemblance to a 'real' household, Felix Holt, the self-sacrificing artisan radical. But with the partial exception of Disraeli, none was prepared to allow any political or other rationality to working-class characters. At best they are depicted as lost, confused and misguided. Those whose entanglements in class contradictions are too great even for the subtleties of Victorian plot devices die, like John Barton, Stephen Blackpool or Stephen Morley, expiating in the pathos or heroism of their last moments the mistaken decisions of their lives. But heroes invariably abandon radical politics, and basically for the same reason in all cases. The plots of all these novels concern the dangers of wakening the slumbering monster in society. Like the children's classic of a later generation, *The Wind in the Willows*, the characters in Victorian novels acted out their lives with the knowledge that the woods around them were full of threatening and dangerous creatures, creatures without individual names, who waited their chance to emerge under cover of darkness to loot, murder, rape, fire and destroy. They are the voiceless labourers in *Alton Locke*, the miners in *Felix Holt*, the denizens of Wodegate in *Sybil*, the strikers in *North and South*. They are also the Gordon rioters in *Barnaby Rudge* and the *tricoteuses* in *A Tale of Two Cities*, though distanced here in a historical setting. Invariably this evil mob – led by unscrupulous and self-seeking demagogues – turns against the moderate radicalism of the deluded meddler in politics. Their true leader is the unscrupulous demagogue, 'a fiend incarnate, whose heart Satan must possess entirely, for he has endowed his brain with talents which are but used for the purpose of desolation and destruction'.[27] The fear and incomprehension which was the typical middle-class response to the mass action of working people was caught by Tennyson in his poem 'Walking to the Mail':

I once was near him when his bailiff brought
A Chartist pike. You should have seen him wince
As from a venemous thing: he thought himself
A mark for all, and shuddered, lest a cry
Should break his sleep by night, and his nice eyes
Should see the raw mechanic's bloody thumbs
Sweat on his blazon'd chairs;[28]

What, then, does all this imply? That, basically, even the most sympathetic members of the middle class only empathised with a small selected part of the working class. For the mass they reserved an attitude of fear, suspicion and total lack of comprehension. Thus, if we are speaking of the possibility of combined political action between middle- and working-class politicians in these years, we are never talking about an all-out alliance between the mainstream parties of the two classes. Such middle-class men as did on occasion float the possibility of collaboration rejected, like the writer in the *Leader* with whom we started, the theatrical, the violent, the crowd action and anything which might frighten the middle classes. The riot scene, essential to every 'condition-of-England novel', presented in fiction this fear. The rising of the Welsh miners and iron workers in 1839 and the riots in the manufacturing districts in 1842 represented the reality.

The working classes, on the other hand, showed a strong inclination to follow leaders who preached a very simple doctrine of class hostility. A rhetoric of class conflict had been part of working-class radicalism for a generation before the publication of the Charter. By the late 1830s it can be found in the speeches and writings of all the popular radical leaders. Thus Feargus O'Connor in February 1838 was declaring that

> He knew that the working men were pressed down by the capitalists. He saw that instead of the capitalist being dependent on the labourer, as he ought to be, his sole attention was directed to the improvement of machinery, while the working classes were to be starved, or punished if they attempted to make a stand against so ruinous a system . . . he divided society into just two classes – the rich oppressors and the poor oppressed. The whole question resolved itself into the battle between labour and capital.[29]

This kind of analysis is to be found throughout the Chartist press. There were other arguments, including appeals to 'natural rights' and 'natural justice', but the language of class conflict was constant. The rich had somehow to be forced to recognise the rights of the poor.

Any discussion, therefore, of the relations between the Chartists and 'the Middle Class' must have in mind the strong sense of class identity on both sides. Other factors influenced the politics of the question. The middle classes had been an articulate presence in British political life since the seventeenth century. The working people had appeared only as a mob, or at the tail of middle-class movements – often, indeed, as an embarrassment to such movements. The working-class dissenters or the crowd supporting political demands had been used by the establishment to discredit the more respectable elements, and the taunt of rabble-rousing had been used against middle-class politicians as recently as 1832. Working-class radicals of the 1830s were well aware of the suspicion with which middle-class politicians regarded crowd action of any kind; middle-class politicians of whatever view did not want to sully their own movements with the taint of turbulence, or with the accusation of exciting those dark forces in society which all respectable opinion united to condemn.

It is also very important to remember that at no time did the classes meet on anything like equal terms. At the height of the political agitation one or two shopkeepers may have been driven out of business through organised boycotting by Chartists in very strong districts. But in the same years numberless Chartists and trade unionists were dismissed and blacklisted for behaving in a perfectly legal manner, quite apart from those who were prosecuted. Moreover, the control of the employers was used not only to limit the freedom of workmen and women to engage in political or trade-union action. It could be extended to cover almost every aspect of their lives. Chartism was concerned as much with the personal dignity and independence of working people as with the attainment of political rights – indeed, the two were inseparable. And many of the middle-class men who declaimed loudly against monopoly and patronage in the professional and commercial worlds were exercising patronage and encouraging dependence among their own employees. Any number of examples could be given. Abraham Fielden's brother was dismissed by the Fielden family for whom he worked as a gardener, for neglecting to touch his cap to a member of the family.[30] George Jacob Holyoake recalled that in Birmingham – a town in which some historians have posited a close social proximity between masters and men – the workers in the foundry at which he and his father worked were in a relationship of abject dependence with their masters.

> . . . the acting 'master' as he was called was mainly an unpleasant person. He was exacting and always spoke with harshness. I saw old men who were in such terror at his approach that they would strike their hands instead of the chisel they were using, and were afraid of dismissal or reduction of wages in

consequence of the incapacity which he witnessed, and which his presence caused. Piece-workers and day-workers were so continually subjected to reduced prices and wages that they never felt certain on Monday morning what they would receive on Saturday evening . . . there was continual resentment, sullenness and disgust, but no independence or self-dependence. If a man saved a little money, he carefully concealed that he had done so; if he could afford to dress cleanly and moderately well, he was afraid to do it, as his wages were sure to be reduced. . .[31]

Class domination was not confined to the work-place. All aspects of social life – dwelling-places, shops, drinking-places, recreational and instructional institutions, churches and chapel seating – were segregated on class lines. In Dundee in 1841 the magistrates issued a placard, warning potential interruptors of an Anti-Corn-Law meeting:

Whereas a meeting of merchants, manufacturers and shipowners in Dundee has been called under requisition to the Provost and by his authority . . . for the purpose of petitioning Parliament for the abolition of the Corn Laws. . . The Magistrates think it incumbent upon them to warn all classes of the community that the proposed meeting has been called in a regular and legal manner; that it is a meeting of certain classes, specified in the notice . . . and that no person not of the classes so called to meet, is entitled to force himself into the meeting . . . and that doing so would amount to an offence against the laws. . . .[32]

A 'public' meeting to discuss the Government's proposals for an education bill in Barnsley in 1839 expressly forbade the attendance of working men and women.[33]

It was unusual, and a sign of the tensions present in the Chartist period, for things to be spelt out in this way. A whole range of public activity was simply assumed to be the province of the higher orders, and the manner and language in which it was conducted effectively excluded even such working men as might technically be entitled to take part. When Ben Wilson decided to attend a vestry meeting in 1843, he found himself the only working man present.

. . . there being about twelve gentlemen present, comprised several of the largest ratepayers in the township. I felt uncomfortable, and wished I was nicely out. Mr Robert Wainhouse was chairman, and when he put a motion to the meeting he looked on to the table and said – 'Carried unanimously, I suppose'.[34]

Even when bereft of most of their other senses, citizens were held to retain the quintessential awareness of class. A. B. Granville reacted with horror in 1840 to the practice he saw in the Lincoln Asylum, of allowing private to mingle with pauper patients in the 'airing grounds'. 'The man of education, mad as he may be, may retain his feelings of delicacy and pride; he will be better dressed, and be shocked . . . at being associated with those whose coarse garments, coarse habits, rude manners, filthy tricks, and want of cleanliness mark them out as of an inferior class. . .' What is more, 'The sight of persons bereaved of their wits by hard inebriation from potent liquors, inducing the worst species of insanity, can ill accord with any anticipation of cure in the case of a gentleman or gentlewoman afflicted probably only with melancholy, or an aberration of a refined sort, as most of the mental disorders of that class of people are. . .'[35]

From both sides of the gulf separating the classes, men and women looked across with suspicion, mistrust and lack of comprehension. But on the middle-class side hostility to those below them was backed by increasing wealth, political status, control of a whole range of institutions, authority in essential areas – legal, educational and spiritual – and above all, of course, by the control they were able to exercise directly over their employees. Nevertheless, spokesmen from the middle class usually defined their class role as one of leadership and education, rather than one of control and oppression, let alone exploitation. The ideology expressed in the ideas of free trade and political economy was generally powerful enough to produce an absolute certainty amongst those who held it that its truth was self-evident and that all classes would eventually be persuaded to act in accordance with it.

The great majority of the spokesmen for the middle classes did not, in the Chartist period, consider that the active adhesion of members of the working class to their political organisations was something to be sought. On the contrary, they considered that the working classes must be educated and subdued. In so far as they acknowledged the existence of independent working-class institutions they perceived these as injurious or criminal, and regarded it as their duty to oppose them by every possible means. In 1860 Nassau Senior, Professor of Political Economy, argued against the idea that the British labouring classes should participate in the running of the schools at which their children were to be educated.

For fifty years they have been managing their own benefit societies. Almost all of them are founded on principles leading to inevitable insolvency. For fifty years they have been managing their own trade unions. There is not one which is not based on folly, tyranny and injustice which would disgrace the rudest savages.[36]

Any discussion, therefore, of the relationship between Chartism and the middle class must start from a number of propositions, the first of which is that the great majority of the articulate middle class wanted nothing to do with any kind of independent working-class activity. They regarded the working class as their inferiors in every way – in education, morality, achievement and aspiration, and considered that their own social function was to provide leadership and control for those below them. The suggestion which was often made and has been accepted implicitly by a number of historians, that, left to themselves, the middle classes would have reformed the political institutions of society in the interests of the greater participation in them by the lower orders in society, is backed by no evidence at all. On the contrary, an examination of the parliamentary division lists throughout the first sixty years of the nineteenth century shows that only a handful of committed radicals voted for an extension of the suffrage when they were given the chance to do so, and even among these very few considered the question to be one of urgency. So that when we speak of a 'middle-class alliance', or when such an alliance is advocated by Chartists, it refers only to a very limited section of the middle class. What is more, even those few middle-class politicians who did at any time toy with the idea of cooperation with leaders or members of the working class were always extremely particular about which members of the working class they were going to work with. At no time was an open alliance proposed between any middle-class political movement and the Chartist movement as such. Resistance to such an idea was so overwhelming on both sides, that it simply did not enter into the range of possibilities in the period. Those middle-class men who became Chartists were held to have deserted the interests of their class as surely as were those working men who became spokesmen for the Anti-Corn-Law League, or who wrote attacks on trade unionism.

The rhetoric which attributes the failure of Chartism to gain its political objectives to the alienation of influential middle-class opinion contains implicitly this view that, left to themselves or approached with deference and servility, the middle classes would have worked for the inclusion of the working people within the pale of the constitution. True, some of their critics suggested the same idea to the Chartists. Francis Close told the women Chartists of Cheltenham

> I would pledge myself, though only a private individual in the nation, that if the Chartists will lay aside the posture of rebellion, disarm themselves, and retire to the bosoms of their families; if they will cease to profane the Sabbath day by political meetings; if they become again peacable, kind and gentle to

their fellow-men and fellow-subjects, I for one would do all in my power to promote the removal of their grievances; and the nation would listen with attention to her loving and contented sons. . .[37]

When, however, the local Chartists did, for a number of reasons, cease to be publicly active in the late forties and fifties, the reverend gentleman made no move to fulfil his pledge. Instead he continued with his life's work of minstering to his wealthy parishioners, exerting his efforts to maintain the full control of the city's education in the hands of the established church, and battling bravely, and to an extent successfully, against the local theatre, the local racecourse, the local alehouses and the proposal to run railway trains on Sundays.

Those members of the middle class who were active in public life during the Chartist period had their hands very full with a number of measures by which they were consolidating their victory in the 1832 Reform Act. Municipal reform and the introduction of the rural police were two of the ways in which their authority was being imposed. Another, perhaps more important still, was the change in the composition of the magistracy. In some parts of the country at least the social make-up of this most important source of power and authority was changing during exactly the Chartist years. Even more than membership of the House of Commons, the constitution of the magistracy affected the nature of law and justice in England. Feargus O'Connor stressed the importance of this in 1842.

It must be clear to every sane man that the Reform Bill was forced from the Tory party by the new-born influence of the master manufacturers; that with their own party in power they have for ten years gone on establishing the details by which their principle of reform was to be made most beneficial to their order. The Poor-law amendment act, the Corporation reform bill, the Rural police bill, and above all the appointment of Whig magistrates, constituted those details. . .[38]

In a study of the Black Country magistracy, David Philips has shown that in that area the percentage of magistrates appointed from the landed aristocracy and gentry was, in 1835, 60·9; in the same year the percentage of coal and iron masters (employers in the dominant trades) was nil. By 1848 the percentage of landowners appointed dropped to 26·5, while that of coal and iron masters rose to 30·6. Adding to the coal and iron masters the percentage of other employers and 'men in trade' meant that by 1850 over 60 per cent of the Black Country bench was appointed from 'industry, trade or finance'.[39] No one would suggest that the members of the traditional landowning class from which the magistrates had formerly been recruited were biased in any way in favour of the working people. Nevertheless, the new entrants were men with a very specific interest in the administration of justice in their communities. Earl Talbot, Lord Lieutenant of Staffordshire in 1835 wrote to Lord John Russell that 'The rule has been in this county, not to place Gentlemen in the commission of the Peace who are in trade, or they might be called upon to adjudicate in cases where they have an interest.'[40] The interest of employers was often in the interpretation of recent industrial law – in the Black Country Philips cites the Master and Servant Act of 1823, the Truck Act of 1831, and the Mines Regulation Act of 1841. In the interpretation of these Acts, masters were often in judgement in cases in which they or their colleagues were participants. This was also a period in many industries in which industrial crime was being redefined in daily practice. Traditional 'perks' in the form of waste material, wood and coal for fuel, 'fents' – the ends of cloth left on the loom when a piece was completed – were being claimed by employers in the increasingly competitive atmosphere of the time. It is very probable, therefore, that even in such obvious acts of criminality as straightforward theft, there could be more than one interpretation of the situation. Certainly it appears that in the Black Country the new magistrates took a sterner view of industrial larceny, and sent a significantly higher proportion of cases to Quarter Sessions. Between 1835 and 1848 cases of industrial theft rose from 34 in the first year, or 9·4 per cent of total prosecutions, to 171 in 1848, or 20·6 per cent of total prosecutions. It did not need Feargus O'Connor to make the connections.

The years after 1832 saw the heightening of hostility between the middle and lower classes. In 1835 Daniel O'Connell entered into the Lichfield House compact with the Whig leaders and deliberately turned his back on many of his former allies. The Anti-Corn-Law League, established in the wake of the Chartist movement, was led exclusively by middle-class men, united to achieve a single issue, and achieved a following among liberals that the movement for the suffrage never approached. Both the Irish parliamentary policies and those of the League in its early days were policies of pressurising Whig administrations. Extra-parliamentary activity involving the working-class crowd was regarded with caution, and in fact the leaders of both these movements incurred working-class hostility in these years. O'Connell's attacks on trade unionism in 1837-8 disappointed his working-class admirers, whilst many of the League's leading men had been among the framers of the 1834 Poor Law. The Whig Cabinet was unanimous in opposing the commutation of the death sentences on the Welsh leaders in 1840, and the Government were extremely harsh in their arrests and prosecutions of local and national Chartist leaders during the winter of 1839–40. While liberals continued to hope for concessions from the Whigs, the Chartists found themselves increasingly facing prosecutions and attacks from the Government, and therefore more and more hostile towards the Government and towards those former middle-class radicals who now seemed to be courting Whig favour. The litmus test for the radicalism of the Chartists in these years was the two issues of trade-union rights and of hostility to the 1834 Poor Law. Universal suffrage was the basis of their programme, but a belief in it was not sufficient to define their radical position.

The Poor Law and the whole Malthusian philosophy were the chief reasons for the increasing alienation of Francis Place from the Chartists. Although he had been one of the instigators of the 1838 Chartist Petition, Place had also been a keen contributor to the making of the 1834 Poor Law Amendment Act, and had hoped for an appointment as a Poor Law Commissioner. The *Northern Liberator* described him as 'the very head and chief, the life and soul, of the Poor Law Amendment Bill'. This was no uninformed gibe, but part of an article by Augustus Hardin Beaumont, who knew Place well. As he wrote,

> On all other subjects but Malthusianism, Mr Place is a close, a candid, and a most even-tempered reasoner; but doubt the infallibility of his anti-population creed, and he is ready to treat you as the Homoousian Christians did their diphthongal controvertists the Homoiousians, in the fifth century. The only answers he will condescend to give are, 'You don't understand political economy; your words have no sense in them; they contain no distinct ideas'.[41]

Place had based his assistance to Lovett in the drawing up of the People's Charter in 1838 on an agreement that the WMA would allow no speeches from their platforms against the new Poor Law or in favour of socialism.[42] Although as the movement grew the agreement became an impossible one to keep, Place retained his beliefs, and was viewed with suspicion as a 'Malthusian' by many of the Chartists.

The winter of 1840–1 was one in which Chartists and liberals took stock. The Chartists had remained a united national movement since the beginning of 1838, and in those three years had attempted the tactics of mass meetings, drilling, firearm training and local confrontations with authority, as well as the collection of signatures, the bringing together of the Convention and the presentation of the national petition. The petition's rejection had been followed by an attempted rising, and by the imprisonment of hundreds of the most active men in the movement. The Chartists had retained their press, and had succeeded in setting up a national organisation in the late summer of 1840. But there was no doubt that the initial excitement and optimism had died down, and that the bitterness and difficulties of keeping the movement together in face of repression by the authorities had brought to the fore again some of the divisions which had been implicit in the movement since the days of the LWMA. The great majority of Chartists enrolled in the National Charter Association, but three new organisations were floated as alternatives. William Lovett and John Collins, while in gaol for their part in the Birmingham demonstrations, wrote a booklet, *Chartism, a New Organisation for the People*. In this they proposed a programme for building a national system of education, under democratic control, to be financed by a levy of a penny a week on all signatories of the Chartist petition. On this foundation was to be erected a structure of educational institutions at all levels from kindergarten to training college. The proposals had a lot in common with other Chartist projects like the Land Company and the various proposals for consumer and producer cooperatives. The Chartists, of all tendencies, were continually trying to establish their own institutions, to keep control of essential aspects of their lives, including education and worship, against the influence of the state or of profit-seeking speculators. In gaol Lovett had returned to his view that education was the only key to the liberation of the working people. Soon after he left gaol he wrote an open letter to his fellow working men, pointing out that the despotic rulers of Europe maintained their power only through the consent of the common people.

> Who but the people toil from birth till death, and thousands pine in misery, *to support those idle few in all their oppressions and debaucheries, and think it just to do so?* nay! bow down before the hireling priest who impiously declares *that God has ordained it!*
>
> Democrats of Europe – you who aspire to place liberty upon the throne of justice – to establish the laws on the basis of equality – and to awaken the dormant faculties of mind to appreciate the social and political happiness of our race – be assured that though the power of despotism can check the progress of knowledge it is the ignorance of our brethren which generates and fosters despots.[43]

Increasingly Lovett moved from the view that political rights would make education for all possible to the view with which he ended his life, that education must prepare people for political rights. From the time of leaving prison he spent more and more time on plans for the institutionalisation of formal education rather than for propaganda for political rights. With his usual short-sightedness on matters of organisation, he believed that a sufficient proportion of those who had signed the Chartist petitions could be persuaded to invest a penny a week to finance a nation-wide system of democratic schools for children and adults. When this means of financing his schemes did not work, he was increasingly driven to look for help from patrons in the middle and upper classes, although his principles were against such patronage.

The organisation through which Lovett's aims were to be achieved was the National Association for the Moral, Social and Political Improvement of the People. It had the support, moral and financial, of a number of MPs and middle-class educationalists and reformers. A few months after it had been founded, Henry Vincent came out of gaol and set out on a speaking tour of the West of England. At all his meetings he put forward the panacea of teetotalism as the solution to the ills of the working people, ending his speeches with the call for teetotal Chartist Associations in all districts. A third new organisation was the Birmingham Chartist Church, founded by Arthur O'Neil in 1841. All three tendencies were independent of each other, all three were supported to an extent by middle-class funds, but most important of all, all three held aloof from the National Charter Association. They were together the objects of the famous attack by Feargus O'Connor, in April 1841, on 'Knowledge Chartism, Christian Chartism and Temperance Chartism', which has been the basis for many assertions by contemporaries and historians, that O'Connor and the mainstream Chartists were opposed to education and temperance.

This interpretation of the matter is entirely mistaken. Education was at the heart of the Chartists' aims, and very many districts supported schools and Sunday schools. Many – perhaps most – Chartist leaders were either temperance supporters or teetotalers. Appeals to abstain from alcohol can be found coming at some time or another from nearly every leader, including some, like John West and Feargus himself, who became heavy drinkers later in their lives,[44] and clearly, from the evidence of their speeches and writings, most Chartists were Christians of one sort or another. Scotland had, indeed, had a thriving group of Chartist churches for some time, and temperance and teetotal associations flourished there as well as schools and Sunday schools. What was different in 1841 was that these particular three movements appeared to be putting forward their programmes as *alternatives* to the National Charter Association rather than as organisations under the general Chartist umbrella. The effect of the New Move, as the three

Associations were known, was to divide the loyalties of a few Chartists, but in the main, to separate off a small group of 'respectables', to return perhaps to the alignments of early 1838. Protests and support for O'Connor's attack poured in loyally from provincial Chartist centres. In Huddersfield, for example, a meeting called to discuss the question reaffirmed its confidence in O'Connor and unanimously viewed 'with feelings of indignation the base, cowardly and unjustifiable conduct of the unprincipled leaders of the "new move"'.[45] This did not prevent them from holding a teetotal Chartist tea party a few weeks later,[46] nor did the fact that they had their own Chartist chapel and school hold back their disapprobation of Lovett's action. Clearly it was the timing and the presumed motivation rather than the actual aims of the new move that so annoyed the Chartists. *The English Chartist Circular and Temperance Record* published by John Cleave and edited by James Harris was started early in 1841. It yielded nothing in its support for temperance, Christianity and education to the *National Association Gazette*, the organ of the 'new move', but it remained within the main stream of Chartism, supported the National Charter Association, and carried regular contributions from the leaders of the movement, including Feargus O'Connor.

An understanding of the attitude towards popular agitation of Lovett, Vincent and O'Neil is necessary for an understanding of the incursion into popular politics of Joseph Sturge in the winter of 1841–2, with his proposal for a Complete Suffrage Union which should heal the breach between middle-class radicals and a selected number of the working classes, and help to create a united front against the recently elected Tory Government.

The general election in the late summer of 1841 put the Whigs out of office for the first time since the Reform Act. The election has been described as the most corrupt of the century, and the return of the old corrupt practices, as well as the return of a Tory ministry, made some of the parliamentary radicals take stock. Disillusion with Whig politics, as well as the release from a strategy which had some hope of influencing the Government, gave more leeway for independent radical initiatives, and some of the spirit of 1832 was revived. Even the Whigs in opposition revived some of the rhetoric of reform. Released from his compact with the Whigs, Daniel O'Connell again raised the question of the repeal of the Union. In returning to the traditional measures of coercion in Ireland, Peel faced a formidable variety of opponents. 'I firmly believe,' he wrote to Sir James Graham, 'in the present state of things . . . there would be banded against the measure, that is against a measure of simple unqualified coercion, the Whig party, the Radical party, the Chartist party, the Anti-Corn-Law League party – all those parties, by whatever name they may be called, who are in favour of democracy, or of mischief and confusion.'[47]

Democracy, mischief and confusion; the three were inextricably bound up in the minds of politicians and members of the educated public. Any politician, then, who toyed even remotely with democracy felt particularly bound to separate it from mischief and confusion.

Joseph Sturge's proposals for a new campaign for parliamentary reform on a platform of complete suffrage originated at a meeting held during the Anti-Corn-Law League conference in Manchester in November 1841, organised by some of the League members who were dissatisfied with its narrow and self-interested programme.

The episode of the Chartists and the Complete Suffrage Union has sometimes been cited as an example of the inconsistency of Chartist leadership. In fact, it is a story of a basically consistent attitude on the part of the Chartists and of O'Connor, but the consistency can only be understood in the light of class attitudes on both sides. The Chartists' approach to the two major parties, indeed to any conventional politician outside their own movement, was always totally instrumental. They expected no disinterested good from either Whig or Tory, and tried to use the differences between them to extract advantages as the situation allowed. They expected both parties to act favourably towards them only if threatened or pressurised. When O'Connor, from prison, advised Chartists to vote Tory in 1841, it was not in the hope of establishing a Chartist-Tory alliance, but mainly with the idea of punishing the Whigs for their anti-working-class measures. If the Whigs had in the past been more radical on questions of limited parliamentary reform, some Tories had been much more hostile to the new Poor Law than their Whig counterparts. In any case, Chartist support for individual candidates in 1841 had not been along party lines. In Nottingham they had supported John Walter, a Tory with a record of vigorous opposition to the Poor Law. In 1842 they backed Sturge, who was running on a platform of the six points of the Charter. In neither case were they uncritical of the candidate for whom they pledged their small number of votes.

Sturge's move has often been described as a proposal for a 'middle-class alliance' with the Chartists. Of course, it was nothing of the kind. 'The' middle class, in and out of Parliament, had no time for Chartism, and Sturge was widely disavowed by his associates in the Anti-Corn-Law League as well as by his co-religionists for his intervention in the violent field of working-class politics.[48] Sturge was a philanthropist with a highly-developed moral sensibility. He regarded all violence as destructive, and found a basis for his philosophy of non-violent cooperation in the scriptures. Unlike most members of the Society of Friends, he had already, by 1842, taken some part in the radical politics of his native Birmingham. He had been a member of the Birmingham Political Union in 1832, and had chaired a public meeting opposing a centralised police force in 1839. From the chair at that meeting he had justified his participation.

> He knew there were some who considered that the few and wealthy should govern the poor and the many, but he could not find in his Bible, either in the doctrine or the example of Him whom all Christians professed to follow, a single passage to justify such an opinion or such a practice. It was the conviction of a Christian duty which brought him there that day, and which told him that he should resist by all means the government Police Bill. He felt that he would not be obeying the instructions of his divine Master 'to love his neighbour as himself', if he did not use any little influence which he might possess to prevent encroachments upon the liberties of his country, and it was also his duty to advocate the rights of the poorest individuals in the community to all the religious, civil and political privileges of the wealthiest in the land.[49]

He had already stood once for Parliament, in 1840, on a platform which included the separation of church and state, free trade, extension of the franchise, no property qualification for MPs, shorter parliaments, the ballot, the abolition of slavery throughout the world and the abolition of capital punishment. This political programme makes it quite clear that there was the possibility of a dialogue with the Chartists.

In the 'new move' and the tone of moderation to be heard from some of the released Chartist leaders, Sturge detected the possibility of detaching an influential group of Chartist leaders from the movement. He floated his proposal at the autumn meeting of the Anti-Corn-Law League at Manchester, in a meeting of a few kindred spirits, including Francis Place. He made further enquiries and found the response favourable. He wrote to Place: 'I have turned my attention seriously to getting that part of the religious philanthropic public who do not commonly mix in politics to take the subject up, and the result has been most encouraging.'[50] The plan was canvassed in 180 English boroughs and a group of supporters formed, mainly from among Anglican and dissenting clergy.

One of the first acts of the new organisation was to prepare a memorial to the Queen asking for an extension of the suffrage. This was to be presented by Sharmon Crawford, an Irish member with a record of support for such measures and a signatory of the People's Charter. It is perhaps a further indication of the lack of enthusiasm among members for any suffrage extension that the CSU memorial, in spite of its respectable backing, received only twenty more votes in the House of Commons than the Chartist petition. The terms of the memorial were inoffensive compared with those of the 1842 petition, which included in its preamble a demand for the repeal of the Act of Union with Ireland and of the 1834 Poor Law Amendment Act. Nevertheless, the CSU memorial obtained only 69 votes, compared with the 49 obtained by the Chartist petition.

The first conference called by Sturge, in February 1842, of supporters of his organisation together with a select band of Chartists and former Chartists, adopted the whole of the six points of the Charter. This having been agreed, further discussion was adjourned until a further conference. The Chartist press, particularly the *Northern Star* and the *English Chartist Circular*, carried on a debate and discussion as to the value of the cooperation that the Complete Suffrage Union was offering. Sturge himself was respected by many of the Chartists – O'Connor called him 'a most excellent person – a man – as the world goes – a century before his order in all the distinguishing qualities which mark progression. . . . In fact, I declare at the outset that I esteem Mr Sturge more than the whole party with which he is mixed up.'[51] The two issues over which there was disagreement seemed trivial. One was the replacement of the term 'universal suffrage' by 'complete suffrage', the other was the dropping of the name of the People's Charter, even though retaining the programme of the six points.

The issues were, however, explosive, and concealed deep divisions. Even the most respectable of ex-Chartists were not prepared to drop the name of the Charter. They sensed clearly that the name stood for a whole cluster of values and experience which could not be expressed only in a political programme, and that any movement which dropped the name would lose the following in the country. *The National Association Gazette*, organ of the 'new move', argued for the retention of the name, and of the expression 'universal suffrage'. Although welcoming the Sturge initiative, it rejected the reasons for the change of name, particularly the one that 'the advocates of the Charter had brought upon themselves considerable odium amongst the middle classes by violent and extravagant conduct'.

To us the constant harping upon this one string of violence has ever appeared an indication either of weakness or insincerity. . . We strongly deprecate this eternal allusion to the violent conduct of the working classes; and if those who are fond of making it would but enquire into the circumstances under which working men were incited to violence, and above all remember the iniquitous prosecutions of the Whig government by which venial excitement was turned into 'seditious libel' they will, we are sure, see the propriety of ceasing from the reiteration of a charge to which the working classes are no more liable than any other set of men who have engaged in resolute political agitation.

The *Gazette* went on to point out that anyone prejudiced against the Charter by name was not likely to view its aims with any lesser degree of prejudice. It listed the achievements of Chartism, and insisted:

The working classes WILL NOT by the application of any entreaties abandon the name of the Charter. . . . From this resolution there is no spell potent enough to move them. The Chartist leader who would counsel them to depart from it would for ever peril his political reputation, let his name be O'Connor, Lovett, Brewster, or any other name under heaven. . . . The Charter signifies equal rights for all men. Toryism means equal justice for landlords; Whiggism means equal justice for ten-pound householders; the Charter means equal justice for all men.[52]

The issue was not fought out immediately. But the acceptance of the six points by Sturge and the CSU was a good enough reason for the Chartists of Nottingham to switch their allegiance from Walter when Sturge presented himself as a candidate at the by-election there in the early summer of 1842. Nottingham was one of the strongest Chartist areas in the country, and one in which a wide franchise and a tradition of popular politics meant that a radical victory was not out of the question. Feargus O'Connor did in fact win it a few years later, the only Chartist candidate to be returned to the House.

Chartists from all parts of the Midlands poured into Nottingham to support Sturge. Ironically, the Tory candidate had the support of Joseph Rayner Stephens, who had abandoned the suffrage but remained a strong opponent of the Poor Law. In the fashion of contested elections in the nineteenth century, verbal warfare not infrequently escalated into physical battles. Thomas Cooper was present on an occasion which became famous. He described it in a letter home to his wife.

My Dear Love,

I have but a few moments. We had a grand affair in the market place last night. The Tory waggon with Stephens on it, was drawn up opposite ours. Our lads would not hear him. The Tory lambs, chiefly butchers, began to show fight – when O'Connor leapt like a lion from our waggon crying 'Now my side

Charge!' He fought like a dragon – flooring the fellows like ninepins – was thrown – forty men upon him – Sprang up again – seized a fellow by the leg who stood on the waggon tore him down (Stephens and the rest had cut) and then mounted the Tory waggon! What a shout then rent the air, amidst throbbing hearts! I shall never forget it! McDouall and others then crowded the waggon and it was dragged alongside ours – we stepped on to it and, successively, addressed the meeting . . . we remained in possession of the market place – O'Connor only lost his hat. We all marched singing round the streets at night – thousands upon thousands. . .[53]

The rough and tumble of electioneering tested Joseph Sturge's tactical alliance with the ultra-radicals, and no doubt hardened his attitude towards the association with Chartism. His Tory opponents made capital out of the incongruous association of Quakerism and Chartism, with a ballad.

Merrily danced the Quaker Sturge,
  And merrily sang his creatures;
We'll give the laws a Chartist purge
  And radicalise their features. . .

After taking Sturge through each of the six points, the ballad presented the Nottingham electors as Tories to a man, loyal to altar and throne.

Gloomily then danced the Quaker Sturge,
  More gloomily danced his *craturs*;
And O'Connor fled, as if in dread
  Of Vincent's agitators.[54]

Sturge was defeated at Nottingham, but the corruption involved in the election and the subsequent unseating of the successful candidate left the way open for further cooperation between radicals and Chartists. But the events of the summer of 1842, in which the manufacturing districts were swept by a wave of strikes, and some of the most violent and unruly episodes of the century occurred, only served to magnify the existing middle-class terror of the crowd. When the Complete Suffrage Union reconvened its conference in December, many of the Chartist delegates attending, including O'Connor himself, were on bail awaiting trial on charges of seditious conspiracy.

Four hundred delegates attended the conference, among them Thomas Cooper. He recorded in his autobiography the high hopes with which he saw the large number of respectable middle-class men present. In the aftermath of the defeat of the strikes, with so many Chartists under arrest, many on trumped-up charges, he thought that the size of the conference and the good representation of established professional men might convince the Government where other means had failed. His disappointment was therefore all the greater when he found that the middle-class members, without consulting even those 'safe' Chartists, their friends and allies in the 'new move', had arrived with a prepared and printed programme, determined that the conference should accept it *in toto*, or that they should withdraw. As is well-known, the opposition to this high-handed procedure was led jointly by Lovett and O'Connor, a combination rare in the history of Chartism. The Sturge party were defeated, and withdrew from the proposed alliance. The aim of the philanthropic liberals became clear as the conference progressed. Unless they could totally sever the 'respectable' Chartists from their existing leaders, there could be no question of cooperation. Lawrence Heyworth made it clear.

> 'We will espouse your principles, but we will not have your leaders' . . . and when the outcry against him grew stronger, he grew still more offensive. 'I say again' he shouted 'we'll not have you, you tyrants!' The good chairman now interposed and begged of him not to proceed in that style; or I think George White, and Beesley, and a few others who were heard swearing roughly, would have been disposed to try another and more conclusive way of arguing than mere speech. . .[55]

The account is Cooper's. Cooper makes it clear that the divisive issue was that of class attitudes. Loyalty to the name of the Charter and to the leaders of the Chartist movement meant loyalty to the experience of the past decade and to the men and women who had made up the agitation. In the tense atmosphere of 1842 only a minute number of the Chartists were prepared to accept the leadership of middle-class politicians. In that year the gulf between the classes was probably as great as at any time in the century. Although the public debate in the Chartist press about the overtures from the CSU was carried on in measured and diplomatic tones, private letters from participants in the political manoeuvres reveal some of the bitterness which in public erupted at meetings addressed by speakers like Vincent, Philp and O'Brien who remained for a time in the Sturgeite camp. In Birmingham, Sturge's home town, the Complete Suffrage Party, by encouraging and supporting the Chartist Church, and other radicals who were outside the National Charter Association, for a short time built up a sizeable branch of the CSU. In May 1842 'Commodore' E. P. Meade, Chartist lecturer in Birmingham, wrote to Thomas Cooper:

> Tommason from the vale of Leven is here – and lectured among the *Christian* Chartist humbugs, good souls! last night – and will lecture to the infidels poor

> devils! in the open air to-night. – O these pawky Scots will gang ony gait for a week mickle siller, *entre nous* – mind that, Johnnie Mason is na reicht weel affected towards Feargus, and, I believe, wad na mak a wry mou at a wee sip o' Sturge milk. The Sturgeites are advancing with rapid strides, their quarterly tickets are from 6d to £10 each, they have enrolled six hundred new members this week. . . By Heaven! Cooper, they will outgeneral us if we don't look out very sharp. . .[56]

Philp, Vincent and O'Brien were the only leading Chartists who appeared to have committed themselves to the CSU after the first conference. Vincent and O'Brien had not in any case joined the National Charter Association; Philp had not only joined, but was a member of the executive. His association with the Sturgeites led to his replacement in the elections in the early summer by Jonathan Bairstow.

Bronterre O'Brien's role in the whole affair is curious. Gammage's *History* was written very much under the influence of O'Brien, so that his account of events contains a great deal which is accessible nowhere else. This includes a lengthy defence of O'Brien's part in the CSU, and an account of some of his clashes with mainstream Chartists during that summer. The best explanation of his behaviour is probably that he was still at that time hoping to set up an alternative organisation to attract Chartist membership. There is a suggestion of this counter-organisation in a letter from George White to Thomas Cooper, undated, but written some time in the early summer of 1842.

> I have a regular war here with a factious crew of little minded fellows who are trying all in their power to raise an O'Brienite party in this town. They had gone so smoothly to work as to get themselves on the council, and eventually appointed themselves 'the Executive of Birmingham'. But I have floored the whole lot. They were discarded by an unanimous vote of the real lads, and are now forming themselves into the Washington Association. We have more trouble with pretended Chartists than either Whig or Tory – but we will floor the whole lot of the humbugs.[57]

O'Brien was at this time the editor and part-owner of the *British Statesman*, the funds to establish him in it having been raised by the Chartists through the agency of the *Northern Star*. He stuck firmly to the six points of the Charter in the paper, and his regular columns contained much of the old O'Brienite fire and brilliance. Nevertheless, like all his other ventures, it was short-lived. He sought the kind of following which O'Connor had gained, but it appeared once more that he would never gain popularity by attacking Feargus. In so far as his programme represented an alternative, in any but purely personal terms, to the leadership of O'Connor, it was on the question of the Complete Suffrage Union and cooperation with members of the middle class. It was a bad misjudgement to float that policy precisely at that time, however. Of the three leading Chartists who followed Sturge after the failure of the December conference, O'Brien was the least consistent. Vincent believed, and continued to act on the belief, that there were a number of essential questions on which middle- and working-class radicals could combine. He preached only on these questions, mainly on the need for the total rejection of alcoholic liquor and in favour of adult male suffrage, and he accepted the fees paid by middle-class organisations for doing so. He moved further and further from Chartism, accepting the role of a popular and charismatic lecturer to mainly middle-class audiences. He knew, and sometimes in his letters during 1842 commented a little ruefully on the subject, that he had become a middle-class attraction.

> On Monday night here I had a chapel full – chiefly middle men . . . and drove 'it' into them with a sledgehammer. . . I am a sort of . . . Punch among them, a knowing kind of fellow – some cheesemonger was heard to say 'I likes to hear his blessed voice'. . . But why boast? 'all that's bright must fade'; and even popularity based on cheesemen may perish. . .[58]

O'Brien, however, hoped always to retain both audiences, but succeeded with neither. He who had been the scourge of the middle classes in the early thirties was hardly likely to win their confidence overnight, while he clearly underestimated the degree of sheer, almost irrational, class hostility felt by the working people in the provinces. The result was that the *Statesman* died from lack of support early in 1843.

Robert Kemp Philp, the third of the Chartists who stayed with the Sturge party, worked for a time on the *British Statesman*, but after the paper's demise, he disappeared from radical politics.

The events of 1842 sharply underlined the rift which existed between the classes in Britain. Chartist autobiographers Cooper, Wilson and Brierley all saw this year as the most dramatic and eventful of their careers. William Lovett, astonishingly, records only the events connected with the CSU in 1842, and made no comment on the strikes and demonstrations in the country. In some ways the defeats of this year meant the end of open, participatory politics, and although the projected alliance between the ultra-liberals of the middle class and the respectable Chartists came to nothing in the highly-charged atmosphere of the century's worst depression, the CSU did in some ways herald the kind of popular liberalism that eventually replaced Chartism. Lovett perhaps foreshadowed the working-man Liberal in his attitude over the Sturge initiative. Although he insisted on the retention of the name of the Charter, and resented the fact that he and his associates of the 'new move' had not been consulted about the agenda of the second conference, he accepted completely the organisation of that conference, by which an equal number of delegates were to be chosen from among the electors and the non-electors. This system, he wrote,

> was not, as might be supposed, approved of by the O'Connorites, who took every opportunity of denouncing it as anti-democratic and unjust. The Complete Suffrage party, however, instead of defending it as a fair and just mode for choosing a deliberative assembly, where reason and argument were to prevail instead of the power of numbers . . . gave way on this very important point. . .[59]

Essentially, the question of numbers was central. As long as one middle-class man was held to be the equal of a thousand or more members of the working class, the middle class's own self-estimate was being accepted.

CHAPTER 11

The Strikes

THE foundation of the National Charter Association in the late summer of 1840 enabled the Chartists to regroup after the defeats of the winter. Many of the national and local leaders were still serving terms of imprisonment, others had emigrated in the aftermath of the failed insurrections and the ensuing arrests. Nevertheless, the Chartists up and down the country began a reorganisation which was soon to produce a second petition with more signatures than the first, and which continued to support a lively press and a considerable number of full-time lecturers in all the main manufacturing districts. If there was a falling-off of members, this was more evident among a certain type of leader than among the main body of supporters.

1840 did indeed see the dropping out of Chartism of some of the older 'Jacobin'-type radicals in some centres. Some, as Matthew Fletcher later recalled, were frightened away by the spectre of the 'raw head and bloody bones' that had become the image of Chartism after Newport. Others felt a relaxation of tension after the commutation of the death sentences on the Welsh leaders, and considered that the immediate threat to radical and dissenting opinion was no longer a life and death matter. Among others Chartism lost John Taylor, through illness as much as disagreement,[1] Dr Wade, Rev. Patrick Brewster, Baillie Hugh Craig, Matthew Fletcher and Rev. J. R. Stephens. Peter Bussey of Bradford, Thomas Ainge Devyr and Edward Ruecastle from the north-east were among those who emigrated to avoid arrest, while William Carrier, one of the ablest of the leaders of the West-Country Chartists emigrated soon after his release from prison. During 1842 the 'new move' and the advances of the Complete Suffrage Union removed one or two leaders, notably Henry Vincent and Robert Kemp Philp. But the main body of the movement remained unaffected, and support for the exiled Welsh leaders was added to the programme in every locality. The 'new move' seems to have had little effect outside the metropolis in dividing or weakening the movement.

The National Association of the United Kingdom for Promoting the Political and Social Improvement of the People was launched in 1841. Although it was in theory possible for individuals to be members of both the 'new move' and the NCA, the leaders of the National Association held aloof from the wider body. There were nearly eighty signatories of the original address of the National Association, of whom some later withdrew their names when friction developed with the Chartists. The signatories tended to be those already concerned with education and with organised temperance, and included, besides William Lovett and John Collins, Henry Hetherington, John Cleave, George Rogers and Henry Vincent from London, W. J. Linton from Essex, William Hollis from Cheltenham and John Goodwyn Barmby from Ipswich. Many of the signatories were men who had been associated with the movement at least since the publication of the Charter, and by no means all were opposed to the NCA. The list of subscribers to the fund to build a National Association Hall to further the educational aims of the 'new movers' however, was a different matter, and it is difficult not to imagine that some at least of those who subscribed were hoping to divert energies from the more radical activities of the Chartist movement. Lord Brougham donated £10, Sir Francis Burdett £5, George Grote and Sir John Easthope £10 each. J. Temple Leader donated £50 'per F. Place Esq.' and at least sixteen other Members of Parliament contributed. Like the early days of the LWMA, the Association seems to have represented an attempt to restore discipline to popular political action, and to promote educational rather than agitational activity.

The Chartists concentrated, in the winter of 1840–1 on building their organisation and supporting the families of imprisoned Chartists. In the course of 1841 most of the prisoners were released and joined in the consideration of the coming general election and the preparations for the second national petition.

The Chartists had little electoral power, but in some districts they had enough votes to make an electoral strategy important. For the most part, however, it was a question of the best way in which to use the occasion of the election to put their case, rather than to influence the outcome significantly. They used the hustings to quiz candidates, and in a few cases, following the plan put forward by Bronterre O'Brien, put up candidates, although without the serious intention of going as far as taking part in the poll, when the limitations on the numbers of electors would mean certain defeat. In Bradford in 1841 William Martin stood on the hustings, and was introduced by his nominator as a candidate who had been 'born within the precincts of Dublin University and [had] received the finishing touches to his education at three of the Whig Universities of England. The first was York Castle, the second Northallerton House of Correction, and the third at Lancaster Castle'.[2] At the last of these schools, Major Williams had found Martin to be 'A most dangerous, violent and unprincipled man, advocating physical force, destruction of property and anarchy in its worst form. He has been for years a political agitator in Ireland, Scotland and England, and says 'it is his intention to agitate for the Charter again when liberated". . .'[3] He had clearly lost no time, and received a massive show of hands vote at the Bradford hustings.[4]

In neighbouring Halifax the Chartists did not put up a candidate, but they pressed the Tory and Whig candidates hard. John Crossland, weaver and member of the weavers' central committee, asked Sir Charles Wood, Whig, why no action had been taken to relieve the plight of the weavers. Sir Charles replied that the only measure that could help them would be the repeal of the Corn Laws. The crowd at the hustings howled him down, and Benjamin Rushton declared that machinery was ousting weavers and combers, and that employers 'now do the work with a woman and a child, and take the labourer to a new scientific residence'. Here the Tory candidate rejected the language of political economy, and was himself a factory reformer and an opponent of the new Poor Law. He gained the support of the Chartists, but clearly as an anti-Whig gesture.[5]

The Tory victory created a new political atmosphere. The Chartists began a new programme, and O'Connor toured the country in the winter of 1841–2, encouraging the preparations for a new Convention to be held in the spring, and the collection of signatures to the petition.

It was a hard winter and trade was bad. In many districts the free traders, freed by the election result to oppose the administration wholeheartedly, sought to make common cause with Radicals and Chartists and to enlist their support for the aims of the Anti-Corn-Law campaign. In Worcester, for example, in February of 1842, a town meeting was requisitioned 'to inquire into the present distressed state of the country' by a combination of 'most of the Liberal members of the Town Council' and 'a large body of Radicals and Chartists'; 'at the appointed hour . . . every street, lane and alley in the city sent forth its crowds of distressed and dissatisfied poor, with artisans and mechanics till the large hall was crammed'. The local Anti-Corn-Law candidate wooed the audience with an attack on the new Tory administration:

> They pitted the farmers against the tradesman, the operative against his employer and man against man generally, in order to effect their grand purpose of plundering them all . . . Then they had talked of emigration as a means of remedying the national distress; . . . but he would say that the first emigration ship that set sail from this country might be filled with Dukes and Lords (immense laughter).

The move was, however, unsuccessful. A resolution against the Corn Laws was followed rapidly by a series of escalating resolutions, ending with the adoption by a great majority against the platform of the six points of the Charter. It was announced that the petition would lie for signing in the Market House next day. 'This farce having been enacted', reported the local paper, 'three groans for Bob Peel were proposed and given with much grace, followed by a similar compliment awarded to "Little Johnny Russell" and then the assembly dispersed.'[6]

At meetings all over England the arguments about the relative priority of the suffrage and the repeal of the Corn Laws were being rehearsed in the new political context. This was the period of which Gammage commented:

> There was – whatever may be thought of the policy – something heroic in the attitude assumed by working men on this question. It was a battle of the employer and the employed. Masters were astonished at what they deemed the audacity of their workmen, who made no scruple of standing beside them on the platform, and contesting with them face to face their most cherished doctrines. Terrible was the persecution they suffered for taking this liberty. Loss of employment usually followed, but it was in vain that their employers endeavoured to starve them into submission . . . [7]

It was in the argument over free trade and the Corn Laws that the Chartists came closest to articulating an alternative doctrine to that of the political economists. Most Chartists accepted an ideal of the removal of many restrictions on trade. They were certainly opposed to the taxation of essentials, particularly foodstuffs. But they knew that the existing protection did not benefit the farm labourer, and they believed that its removal would not benefit the urban worker, who would simply suffer a reduction in his wages if food were to become cheaper. In the manufacturing towns, employers and their spokesmen used the same rhetoric of 'freedom' as they used against the Corn Laws to attack trade unions and to oppose factory reform. The same philanthropic gentlemen who drew attention to the distress of the factory operatives unemployed through bad trade and high provision prices also supported the new Poor Law which deliberately lowered the standard of relief and imposed punitive conditions on those unemployed operatives who were forced to apply for it. The Chartists never accepted the doctrine of the primacy of economic laws. For them political control was needed to ensure that the results of economic expansion were not simply an increase in exploitation. An argument for some protection of certain industries, and of agriculture, was on occasion put forward by Chartists like John Campbell and Feargus O'Connor himself.[8] For the Chartists free trade was not an absolute, but an aspect of economic policy which must always be under political control. For many of the middle-class free traders, on the other hand, the question had the absolute quality of a religious belief.

However, much of the conflict between Chartists and the Anti-Corn Law League was not on the level of doctrine, but was an expression of the hostility which existed between employers and employees. The economic and political arguments gained their passions from the deep conflict between their exponents in their daily lives. Thus, when the Chartists of Midgley reported that a local manufacturer had reduced the wages of the worsted weavers in his employment, and had resisted all efforts made by the weavers' delegates to get some of the reduction restored, he was described as 'chief constable of the township, a great enemy of the Chartists, a liberal Whig, a Corn Law repealer and a great friend to the New Poor Law and Bastille system'.[9] In 1844 John West described Batley, home of the shoddy trade, as 'the great *depot* of "Devil's Dust" . . . a great nest of the Leaguers. The poor men are sadly coerced, and . . . dare not avow their principles.'[10]

The doctrines of *laissez-faire* political economy were seen as the ideology of the employers, and this fact alone, in the atmosphere of the 1830s and 1840s, would have been enough to damn them. The Chartists' alternative, which put political control at the head of their demands and which required that that control be used among other things to monitor the effects of changes in technology and in conditions of employment, was neither a reversion to an old paternalist view of the responsibilities of Government, nor a proposal for the complete replacement of existing property relations. It was a view of the role of Government which was rejected by the majority of political theorists of the nineteenth century. The view had some support in the House of Commons, notably from John Fielden and John Maxwell, who put up a lengthy fight for the supervision of the conditions of groups like the handloom weavers, and the payment of compensation for workers displaced by new technology, the compensation to be raised partly by a tax on the new machinery. Basically such demands were neither 'luddite' – in the sense in which that term has been used by many economic historians, that is to say senseless opposition to inevitable progress – nor necessarily socialist or even cooperative. They implied the injection into any notion of political economy of the conception of labour as the property of the working population, and as much in need of protection by the law as any other form of property. Any system which did not recognise this need was seen as tyrannical and exploitative. This conception was picked up by Disraeli, who put the argument into the mouth of Philip Warden, the handloom weaver: 'If a society that has been created by labour suddenly becomes independent of it, that society is bound to maintain the race whose only property is labour, out of the proceeds of that other property which has not ceased to be productive.' Warden recalled that all Europe had gone to war to avenge the expropriation of the estates of the French nobility, and that their own country had handsomely compensated them when they were restored. 'Yet we have lost our estates. Who raises a voice for us? . . . We sink among no sighs but our own. And if they give us sympathy – what then? Sympathy is the solace of the Poor; but for the Rich there is Compensation.'[11]

The weavers, however, were not an island of misery in a sea of prosperous trades. As recent writers have pointed out, the distress of 1842 was universal, but was probably most acute in the leading sector of the British economy, the cotton trade. The complaint which Disraeli articulated so clearly may be seen in the resolutions of the factory operatives as well as in the weavers' petitions. The Bolton spinners listed the injustices they complained of in a placard in 1842.

> . . . namely in the reduction of our wages, in unjust and unreasonable abatements, in forcing upon us unhealthy and disagreeable houses, in charging us unreasonable and exorbitant rents, and in meanly and avariciously employing apprentices to supersede the regular journeymen, and in various ways curtailing our wages by not paying up to the list that the masters almost unanimously agreed to, thus proving their unprincipled meanness and trickery . . .
>
> That this meeting is of opinion that a great deal of the distress in the manufacturing districts is owing to the improvements of machinery which have superseded manual labour, and created a redundant and burdensome population. And this meeting is further of opinion that the best means to be adopted would be to establish an efficient Ten Hours' Bill, with restrictions on all moving power; to immediately colonise the Crown Lands, which would thus employ the redundant population, and at the same time improve and augment the home trade . . .
>
> That it is the opinion of this meeting that the above evils arise from class legislation, and we are further of opinion that misery, ignorance, poverty and crime will continue to exist until the People's Charter becomes the law of the land . . .[12]

1842 was a year of strikes. The Chartist press carried reports throughout the early months of the year of action by masons, bobbin-weavers, nailers and other trades, with appeals for support and for funds. In supporting the appeal by the masons, the English Chartist Circular wrote:

We *Chartists* are constantly declaring that the cooperation of the *Trades* would go further towards securing the rights of *all* than the aid of any other class of men . . . Let us then endeavour to warm the hearts of these our fellows towards *us* by a generous demonstration of sympathy in *their* time of need.[13]

Outside London the sympathy had a less detached tone. In the Midlands a group of Chartists including the Birmingham leader John Mason were arrested for 'holding unlawful meetings' in districts in which the nailers were on strike in May and June. Duncombe protested in the House of Commons about the partial behaviour of the Black Country magistrates and the actions of the police in breaking up peaceful meetings. His protests gained only thirty-one supporting votes in favour of an investigation, and Mason and seven other Chartists were sent to prison.

In July the whole of the Black Country coalfield was brought to a standstill by a series of strikes against wage reductions. The local press noticed the prominence of Chartist speakers at meetings of striking colliers, and varied in its reports between pictures of thousands of colliers attending meetings addressed by Chartists, and claims that the colliers had no sympathy for the Chartists 'despite their zeal and keeping their political principles in the background'.[14] However, when a crowd of three to four hundred colliers threatened and frightened off fifteen blacklegs at the Parkfield colliery, their ringleaders included William Chatterton, a Chartist tailor from Bilston who was described as being 'in full work . . . and without any excuse for going to the disturbances'.[15] He was sentenced to a month's imprisonment with hard labour.

Whatever the view of Chartism held by the colliers, it soon became clear that Chatterton was only one of many local leaders who appeared at demonstrations and meetings throughout the district. In the third week in August, when Lancashire, the West Riding and the Scottish coalfield were all on strike, the *Wolverhampton Chronicle* reported:

One of the largest meetings held ever since the strike began took place on Thursday afternoon in a large field at Wednesbury. Men from Rowley, Lye, Brierley Hill etc. marched through Dudley, 10,000 of them with banners – 4/-d and a 9-hour day. There were said to be 20,000 people at the meeting. It was chaired by Danks, said to be a manufacturer and Chartist in Wednesbury. It was addressed by O'Neill, Linney, Pearson, Wilcox, Griffiths (Walsall) and

Cooper of Leicester. After the meeting 100 delegates met in the Chartist rooms in Wednesbury and persons were appointed to go to all the coalfields for a general organisation of colliers and the working class to stop all work.[16]

Arthur O'Neil's Christian Chartism, which was tolerated – even encouraged – within the radical city of Birmingham, was a danger in the coalfield, and he was soon to be arrested and imprisoned. Joseph Linney, who had already served a sentence for Chartist activity in 1839, was sentenced to two terms for his speeches during the strike, one of fifteen months, with a second of six months added to it. At the meeting on 3 August, he was reported as saying:

. . . he expected to meet hundreds, but he was pleased to meet thousands. He addressed the meeting as 'Fellow-countrymen, Brother Chartists and Oppressed Colliers'. He said the masters were calling out for protection. He bade them stick out. If they did, they would have their wages and all they wanted. Why? Because they knew they were a starving people and a starving people was a rebellious people. The masters say they can do without you. We'll show them if they can . . . Afterwards he said 'We'll divide the land and live upon it ourselves'.[17]

His second trial was for words spoken at an earlier meeting which were stronger, and definitely republican in tone. These he denied having spoken, and it is very probable that they had been coloured up by the very partial witnesses. Nevertheless, in the main the language was clear enough. O'Neil, Linney and the other Chartists supported the strike, urged the colliers to 'keep the peace and not return under 4/- a day', but at the same time stressed the political moral that labour and wages would never be fully protected until the workers had political power.

The most dramatic strikes of 1842 took place in the Midlands and the North. In London, however, this was also a time in which the Chartists and the trades worked closely together. Organisation was consolidated, with more than thirty localities in the metropolis and as many as twenty branches set up by particular trades.[18] Foremost among the Chartist trade groups here, as in the provinces, were the shoemakers. London master shoemakers had attempted a *rapprochement* with their journeymen in April 1842, to protest against the Tory Government's proposals to lower the tariff on imported footwear. The masters were somewhat embarrassed at finding themselves in opposition on a question of the principle of free trade, a principle which they asserted 'it was so desirable should be carried into full effect'. In their own trade, however, an exception had to be made. They therefore called their men to a meeting which, they insisted, should be concerned with trade matters only, and 'politics' were not to be raised. The suggestion was greeted with laughter by the men, and with cries of 'It's a political question!' The atmosphere got more heated, however, when William Benbow rose to address the meeting: 'not being appointed by the committee, they would not allow him, some asserting that he was not a shoemaker, until his hands convinced them to the contrary'.[19]

His attempt to speak caused so much furore that he agreed to withdraw for a time. It was not possible, however, to deny the floor to the young journeyman shoemaker John Skelton, who seconded the next resolution

> in a very eloquent address, in which he administered some very hard hits to the employers on their past treatment of their men; it was only when the shoe pinched them – when the misery was likely to approach their own door – that they once thought of the distress of the journeymen. . . . He called upon them to look to the working men and treat them as rational beings (Great cheering) The day was gone by when they were called a drunken set of men. He could tell them that the men could now calculate and look to their interest as well as Sir Robert Peel.

As soon as the resolutions were passed, the masters hastily left the meeting, leaving a hall full of would-be speakers, who adjourned to another large meeting-place at the Craven Head. Here the inhibition on politics no longer obtained, and Benbow was able to make his speech. He pointed out that he and his family had been shoemakers for a century past, and that William Cobbett had dedicated his grammar to 'William Benbow, shoemaker, of Manchester'. The shoemakers – in a 'shoemakers only' vote – agreed unanimously on a resolution:

> That this meeting fully agree with the resolutions passed at the Crown and Anchor, but are nevertheless of opinion that until the working classes of this country have the management of their affairs vested in their own hands, according to the principles laid down in the People's Charter, they will never be able successfully to struggle with those who oppress, injure, and deprive them of their employment.

The meeting ended with a show of hands from all those who would aid in procuring the return of Frost, Williams and Jones, which was unanimous.

London did not see a widespread strike movement on the scale of the provinces in the summer of 1842, but the procession which accompanied the second petition to the House of Commons in May was of enormous size, and there were considerable demonstrations in August when troops were despatched by rail to the industrial districts.[20]

Events in the early summer, including the presentation of the petition in May, have been overshadowed in the history of Chartism by events later in the summer. They were not as unconnected, however, as has sometimes been implied. The Convention was organised more efficiently than the 1839 one, with delegates limited to twenty-four from English constituencies and twenty-five from Scottish and Welsh. The petition itself, which was alleged by the Chartists to have well over three million signatures, was a more political document than its predecessor, for it contained in its preamble specific demands for the repeal of the Poor Law Amendment Act, and of the Union of Britain and Ireland. Even Duncombe, staunch ally as he was of the Chartists, was slightly embarrassed by the repeal demand, and explained it as meaning that the Chartists believed that universal suffrage would in fact mean the repeal of the Union – a statement with which he did not agree. The rejection of the petition – or rather, the rejection of Duncombe's proposal that the petitioners be heard at the bar of the House – by a derisory vote of 287 to 46 certainly exacerbated the class bitterness in the manufacturing districts. The Chartists who read reports of the proceedings in Parliament – and these were published in the *Star* as well as in other papers – soon realised that attacks upon them came not only from opponents of universal suffrage, but from the so-called supporters of their petition. Outstanding in the debate was the speech of John Arthur Roebuck, whose attack on O'Connor as 'a malignant and cowardly demagogue' gave the perfect lever for Graham in his reply for the Government. Many provincial radicals and Chartists had long ago abandoned petitioning as a possible solution to their problems. The reception of the 1842 petition must have disillusioned many more with constitutional procedures.[21]

The petition was rejected in May after the petition presented by the Complete Suffrage Union had been rejected in April by almost as great a majority. The 'respectables' re-grouped in London, under the leadership of the elderly Francis Place, for a further perspective of years of wire-pulling and peaceful persuasion. In the factory districts and the country generally, peaceful petitioning had once again been shown to be ineffective as a means of obtaining relief.

A month after the rejection of the petition a further cause for Chartist anger occurred with the death in prison of Samuel Holberry, leader of the Sheffield insurrection of 1840. Most of the Chartists who had been imprisoned in 1839 and 1840 had by now served their sentences. Holberry, however, had received the longest sentence, four years' imprisonment with hard labour. Even the prison inspectors, whose account of prisoners' conditions was always optimistic, had been critical in the 1841 report of the conditions under which Holberry was confined. But the move from Northallerton which they suggested was delayed too long, and he died on 21 June 1842. The news was received by a movement which was angry at the rejection of the Charter and desperate at the distress and industrial conflict in the main manufacturing districts. Jonathan Bairstow wrote to Cooper when he heard the news.

Poor, brave Holberry is dead. I received the astounding intelligence in a letter from York in the middle of a lecture last night – I was struck dunb – I staggered, my head reeled to and fro like a drunken man's – I felt mad – I spoke on for upwards of two hours – my God what an impression – the crowd meeting all seemed bursting – never such a feeling in the world did I see. Better than 40 members were enrolled at the close of the meeting . . . [22]

Memorial meetings were held in all the main districts. A public funeral in Sheffield was attended by an estimated 50,000. Harney made a graveside oration, and a hymn, 'Great God is this the patriot's doom!', was composed for the occasion by the Leicester stockinger-poet John Henry Bramwich.[23] It has been suggested that Holberry was a nonentity whose death provided a convenient martyr for the Chartists at that moment. This is far from being the case. He was not the only Chartist to die in prison, then or later. His fellow-prisoner John Clayton had died shortly before him and others were to suffer the same fate later in the forties. Holberry was well-known in his part of the country, a local leader of some standing. Major Williams had a number of conversations with him whilst he was in prison, and found him 'a man of considerable resolution and talent'. He was only twenty-seven at the time of his death and was undoubtedly killed by the conditions under which he was imprisoned.[24]

Accounts of the suffering of working people in the manufacturing districts of Britain during the spring and early summer of 1842 have some of the quality of reports of famines and other 'natural' disasters. Poor rates rocketed, and the new system groaned under the strain. In spite of the regulations, outdoor relief was given in many cases to unemployed workmen, but the workhouse test and tasks like stone-breaking for a minimal pittance continued, together with the removal of children to the workhouse, and sometimes of whole families. In June a proposal to suspend the operation of the new Poor Law was supported by only twenty-nine members of the House of Commons. 'We can tell the Tory Premier, and ex-Whig leader that this minority of 29, whom they call a faction, speak the sentiments of four-fifths of the people – all but those who feed and fatten upon the plunder of the industrious millions' thundered O'Brien in the *British Statesman*.[25]

The strike of colliers which began in Staffordshire in early June spread throughout the coalfield, and in July the shortage of coal for the potteries meant that many potters were also idle. In June the Anti-Corn-Law writer William Cooke Taylor made a tour of the northern manufacturing districts. He reported not only great distress but widespread support for Chartism. From Burnley he wrote:

> I found them all Chartists but with this difference, that the block-printers and handloom weavers united to their Chartism a hatred of machinery, which was far from being shared by the factory operatives. The latter also deprecated anything like an appeal to physical force, while the former strenuously urged an immediate appeal to arms.[26]

He commented on the rapidity with which political news reached Lancashire, and told of hearing parliamentary debates which had been reported in the morning paper discussed before he himself had yet seen that morning's edition. In Colne he reported that

> . . . Chartism, and particularly the phase of it which threatened an appeal to physical force, appears to be advancing with fearful rapidity in this part of the country. More than twenty said, 'We used to think that something better would turn up, but we have waited so long that hope itself is worn out; we must do something for ourselves, because those above us will do nothing for us.'

The *Northern Star* was being read throughout the districts of Lancashire that he visited, as it was in the heckling sheds of Dundee and the combing shops of the West Riding.

The outbreaks of strikes in June and July have been described by some historians as 'spontaneous'. G. D. H. Cole considered them to have been so: 'The strikes were spontaneous; the Chartists as a body had nothing to do with bringing them about, however active individual Chartists may have been among the factory workers.'[27] Theodore Rothstein suggested that 'the Chartists could not but be aware that the movement had been started without them'. But local studies have shown a close interrelation between the Chartist movement and the actions of the trades in all districts. Chartist participation varied from place to place. There seem to have been fewer known Chartists among the colliers' leaders, although in some cases the experience of the strike itself made them into Chartists. In Lancashire, however, there can be no doubt about Chartist involvement, while in the West Riding the turn-outs and the welcome for the strikers from across the Pennines were organised by the Chartists in all the main centres.

The strikes in Lancashire were spearheaded by the powerloom weavers, who with the cotton spinners had, since 1840 at least, been in the forefront of the battle over wages and prices. The cotton industry – the most highly-mechanised sector of British industry – was the most susceptible to fluctuations in trade and the most competitive of all British industries. The powerloom weavers' union had been defeated in a dramatic strike against wage cuts in Stockport in 1840, and conditions for the workforce had got worse since then. Employers pointed to a collapse of profits in the winter of 1841–2 as justification for further lay-offs and wage reductions. For the operatives the only hope of change seemed to lie in intervention at government level. Strikes had been tried in most of the main areas, and resulted only in defeat. The Anti-Corn-Law League claimed that the repeal of the Corn Laws would bring down home food prices and thereby relieve distress without the need for an increase in wages, and would also open up new possibilities of trade for British goods, thereby increasing general prosperity and enabling the working people to increase their earnings.

So convinced were the League members of the unanswerable character of their case, that they so far overcame their suspicion of trade societies as to sponsor, under the aegis of the Operative Anti-Corn-Law Association, a joint conference in Manchester of delegates from trade unions, workshops and other working-class organisations. In the heart of Cottonopolis, however, the delegates turned their backs on the League and its programme, and passed a resolution in favour of concentrating on the Charter 'as alone worth fighting for.'[28] Lancashire was at one with Worcester on this point, and the efforts of the League only seemed to increase the tenacity with which the trades clung to the need for a political dimension to their activities. Again and again trade union addresses and resolutions returned to the same point: ' . . . the baseness of our political system, and the consequent tyranny of capitalists, whom the laws allow to ride roughshod over prostrate labour . . . drives the labourers to associate for common protection, since the law affords them none'.[29] When the workers whom Cooke Taylor had seen advocating Chartism in June and July came out on strike early in August, they did so under the leadership of trade societies which had considered the wage question, the campaign against the Corn Laws and other social questions, like the operation of the Poor Law, during the depression, and had decided that political power was the only answer. It was the trade societies and not the Chartist delegates who, meeting in Manchester, declared that the strike must be for the

Charter. And it was not only the textile unions, but the engineers and smiths who gave this lead. The proposals for inter-trade cooperation were initiated after the first turn-out, by a meeting of the five engineering trades delegates, the millwrights, engineers, smiths, iron moulders and mechanics, who passed resolutions advocating the Charter and calling for a delegate meeting of all the trades in the district.[30] It was this meeting, called for 15 August, which achieved such significance in the subsequent account of the Plug riots. Of the 85 trades attending, 58 voted immediately for a strike for the Charter, 19 had no mandate but to support the majority decision and only 7 were instructed to vote for a strike for wages alone.[31]

Such discussions were not confined to Lancashire. In August 1842 the *Dundee Warder* published the result of a poll of the factories in the town on the question of a possible strike. They were asked whether they would strike for a wage increase, for the Charter, or in support of strikes in other factories or industries for either of these objects. Of the town's 51 textile mills, 46, employing 1,513 men, were represented at the delegate meeting which heard reports from delegates on the answers. Five factories, employing 124 men, were unrepresented, although in the case of most of these shops, another delegate answered for them. The enquiry was conducted while the Lancashire operatives were still on strike, with the activities in England clearly the model for the kind of industrial action being proposed.

In nine of the factories there was a clear majority against any kind of strike action. These were mostly small firms. In all the others support was expressed for strike action, but in almost every case in a form which specifically excluded a simple industrial action for wage increase. The majority of the firms were small – the largest employed 100 men – and it is clear that in many cases the wage question had already been raised, and the employers' answers to an extent accepted. At Baxter's, Maxwelltown, the 24 weavers were told by their master that he would give them a rise as soon as the other masters did. He told them to bring the key to him when they left the factory, and their looms should be returned to them when they came back. Here the decision was to strike immediately. Mr Ferguson told his men that he felt for their situation but could give them no rise. His 61 employees declared themselves 'ready to strike for the Charter, but not for wages'. They were prepared to 'use means to keep others out' once the strike was begun. This was the general line. The great majority of firms reported either that they would support a strike if it were general, or that they would support a strike if it were political. The 75 men at Blaikie's would 'not identify themselves with the movement for wages, but turn out for political privileges'. At Walker's Mill the 29 employees 'considered the whole distress occasioned by class legislation – would not strike for wages, but for the Charter'. At Johnson's Lower Factory where 70 were employed, it was considered that a national strike would be the best thing, and advised 'measures to be entered into immediately for carrying the same'. The 29 men at Walker's Mill 'considered the whole distress occasioned by class legislation' and had voted 'not to strike for wages but for the Charter'. The 70 employees at Steel and Hutton were ready to 'go full hog, but not for wages'.

Clearly the Dundee workmen, like the more desperate Lancashire operatives, did not consider that their problems – of wages or of political status – could be dealt with by deals with individual employers. The few representatives of other trades at the same meeting agreed with the textile workers: 29 mechanics at Baxters would strike 'not for wages but for the Charter'; 30 shoemakers would 'come out for the Charter'; 36 tailors would 'support other trades in obtaining a rise'; the 12 confectioners would go with the majority. The 200 unemployed present agreed that if a strike was national, they would not take the places of those who came out.[32]

Against such a background, it is clear that the strike movement of the summer of 1842 was not something which occurred 'spontaneously' which the Chartists then tried to exploit and turn into a political movement.

To begin with, the strikes in Lancashire and the turn-outs across the Pennines occurred in areas with a continously high level of radical and Chartist activity. As Richard Otley said at his trial, 'in the manufacturing districts there are, at least, four out of every five of the working classes, that either are actually Chartists or hold Chartist principles. This being the the case, it is quite impossible that there should be a turn-out for wages without having a great number of Chartists among the turn-outs.'[33] The strikes took place after a long series of wage reductions, many of which had been unsuccessfully resisted by local actions. The spring of 1842 had seen a renewed campaign of political action to draw the attention of the Government to the plight of the industrial districts. The response to both the Chartist petition and the middle-class petition for reform had been a dusty answer from those in authority. At their trial for conspiracy in 1843 the Chartist leaders laid great stress on the economic grievances which had actuated the strikers, but it must be recalled that they were facing a very serious charge, and were on occasions disingenuous. Richard Pilling, whose defence speech has been taken by many historians to be the statement of a simple working man concerned only with the immediate aims of improving his own and his family's material situation, in fact opened the famous speech on a 'political' note.

Gentlemen of the jury, it is stated by one of the witnesses that I was the father of this great movement – the father of this outbreak . . . But I say it is not *me* that is the father of this movement but that house. Our addresses have been laid before that house, and they have not redressed our grievances and from there and there alone, the cause comes.[34]

Pilling and his fellow-Chartists knew perfectly well that they had very little chance of getting the wage and price lists they were demanding by a simple, localised strike. They went, from the very beginning, for a confrontation with all the local employers, calling out trades and occupations which did not have specific wage grievances as well as those which were resisting wage cuts. Reports given at the trial or collected by the prosecution show a highly political atmosphere from the start.

A report of a meeting on 15 August at Stockport, attended by between five and six thousand people, was giving by a police witness who had taken fairly extensive notes. The speakers were nearly all well-known as Chartists. The chair was taken by John Wright, a 32-year-old cotton spinner, of Shaw within Crompton, known locally as Jack O'Betty's; he had been arrested for his part in the strikes, although he was not among those tried in the mass conspiracy trial. He had already served a term of imprisonment in 1840 for Chartist activities. First speaker was John Newton, who proposed:

that whoever introduced any subject not connected with that of wages should be put down; he told them they must get their wages, and if they could not, they must ask their masters why they could not give it them; and if they told them it was through the 'top shop' (the government), they must ask their masters to go with them as commanders and sergeants, and find them with bread and cheese on the road.

The chairman objected to the proposal for going to London, and James Allison, Chartist and powerloom weaver, brought the question back again to wages. When Richard Pilling came to the platform, he said:

Fellow-townsmen, for I may so call you, having lived amongst you for so long, and having been at so many meetings, by thousands, and having been in prison. I do not know whether it would be safe for me to own it or not; but I may avow that I have the honour to be the father of this movement, and the sole cause of your being ladies and gentlemen at the present time; for the masters of Ashton had thought proper to offer a reduction of 25 per cent upon their wages. I then caused the bellman to go round and call the meeting, swearing by the God of heaven, that, if the reduction took place, we would annihilate the system and cause the day of reckoning . . . at every meeting they came to a resolution to work no more till they got the same wages as they had in February 1840.[35]

The demand for the wage rates of 1840 for the cotton weavers and spinners, and the tactic of forcing out *all* workers – including railway navvies, timber yard workers and building workers, most of whom do not seem to have had particular wage grievances, show that the leaders of the strike were deliberately spreading it beyond the confines of their own industry, and were putting pressure on all the employers as citizens as well as industrialists. The wage cuts which they were opposing had been imposed over two and a half years, and had been unsuccessfully opposed by local strike action during that time. The demand for the restoration of the 1840 prices was a political as well as an industrial demand. An intercepted letter from Ashton said: 'Now's the time for Liberty. We want the wages paid 1840 if they won't give it us Revolution is the consequence we have stopt every trade – Tailors Cobblers Brushmakers Sweeps Tinkers Carters Masons Builders Colliers & c and every other trade . . . '[36] Significantly, it was the Chartists among the strike leaders who were often the most insistent on the aim of the 1840 wage demand. It was often the crowds and the non-Chartist speakers who linked the strike to the attainment of the Charter. William Bell, of Heywood, who does not appear either before 1842 or afterwards as an active or vocal Chartist, was arrested for seditious speech at an Oldham meeting on 19 August. He was a special constable, but told the meeting that 'it was not a question of wages now, it was for the Charter and if they could only obtain that, they would fix the price of labour and when and how it was to be paid'.[37]

A mass meeting of strikers in Ashton on 15 August heard the Chartist tailor, Albert Wolfenden, report to them on the meeting of trades' delegates. He reported that no final decision had been reached on the relative importance of wages and the Charter. The constable who reported the meeting said: 'I heard a question asked . . . whether the people would have the wages or the Charter and they held up hands for both.'[38]

The constable at Royton deposed that he met the local bellringer on 12 August, announcing a meeting. Warned that he might get himself into trouble, the bellman replied 'Well, Scott, we are ready for anything, we will not clam.' At the meeting of men and women which he assembled, the secretary of the local Chartists spoke and warned against committing any breach of the peace. It was arranged that the crowd should reassemble every morning and evening at five o'clock, and the whole body then set out for Rochdale to turn out any mills in that district that might still be working. Men with banners led them, and many of the marchers held loaves on sticks up over their heads. 'When they passed me they said "Come along with us and you shall have something to eat."' When they were joined by a contingent from Oldham and another from Shaw, the constable reckoned that about twelve thousand of them marched on towards Rochdale, the women leading the singing as they marched.

A day or two later at the regular meeting, Benjamin Dunkerley, a pensioner, addressed the crowd and told them 'they could not have a fair day's wage for a fair day's labour without the Charter'. After the Chartist secretary had again called on them to be peaceful and to remain out until they were assured of a fair reward for their labour, a speaker clambered up on to the cart which served as a platform and accused the other speakers of leading the people astray. He asked if the meeting was to discuss politics or a fair wage for a fair day's labour.

> He then moved for a shew of hands to take the sense of the meeting whether their object was to discuss politics or the wages question. The meeting carried the question in favour of politics and cried out 'damn him, put him out of the cart for a fool as he is.'[39]

At Staleybridge on 13 August, the constable deposed that a large meeting assembled.

> There were eight or ten thousand – a great number of strangers who came from Glossop way. They appeared to be many of them railway labourers; they had large sticks in their hands and came very turbulently into the town, and calling out for the Charter and waving their sticks and shouting – there was great shouting at that meeting – it excited a great deal of alarm in Staleybridge.[40]

All recent work on 1842 has enforced the view that the question of whether or not the strike should become more 'political' was not simply a matter of the Chartist leadership attempting to impose a political direction on an essentially industrial action. Apart from the clear evidence of support from both trades and crowds for the idea of a strike for the Charter, there was the additional dimension of the political machinations of the Anti-Corn-Law League. Feargus O'Connor and Frederick Engels both believed that the strikes in Lancashire had been deliberately provoked by supporters of the League as a means of pressurising the Tory Government. Many Chartists shared this view – Benjamin Rushton expressed it in his speech to the strikers in Halifax. The statement by James Acland, former radical and now an itinerant lecturer for the League, that 'the people would either have the Charter or a repeal of the Corn laws within three weeks, as the mill-owners had come to the determination of closing all their mills, and turning all their hands out' received wide circulation, although it seems to have been a piece of reported speech resting on O'Connor's recollection.[41] While the evidence does not support a concerted and Machiavellian policy deliberately pursued by the League *tout entier*, O'Connor's suggestion of divided counsels is borne out by some of the statements made by leading figures in private – such as C. P. Villers's contention that 'the *brickbat argument* is the only one that our nobles heed', and Cobden's assessment of the Complete Suffrage Union as 'something in our *rear* to frighten the aristocracy'. The employment by the League of men like James Acland and Timothy Falvey does imply at least a flirtation with the idea of using the tactics of crowd arousal. Certainly the episode of the clash with the Chartists in Manchester in March 1842 had shown that the League was not above hiring Irish muscle to provoke and sustain violent disturbances at their opponents' meetings, as well as to defend their own against interruption.

There is, however, no apparent evidence that the League did deliberately foment political strikes in 1842. This is not to say that some employers, who may have been League members or supporters, were not averse to the closure of mills at a time when order books were empty. Nor did they hesitate to use the situation once it had arisen. The accusation of exploiting the strikes for political ends after they had started could more properly be levelled against the League than against the Chartists. Many of the Chartists felt that their plight was being exploited, and there were magistrates who agreed with them. William Duffey, Manchester tailors' delegate to the 15 August trades conference, spoke of the provocative actions of the League, and of their inconsistency.

> The people . . . had taken a hint from Messers Brooks, Cobden, Robert Gardener and others; and they (the people) would not now be diverted from their purpose. Some members and lecturers of the Anti-Corn Law League . . . were now carrying staves as special constables; and, after having conjured up this agitation to the highest possible pitch, they were now endeavouring to intimidate the working men because they chose to think for themselves. . .[42]

From Derby a magistrate complained that an Anti-Corn-Law leaflet had been put into nearly every house in Derby 'without reference to the station or political feeling of the occupier.' The leaflet complained of was an address signed by P. A. Taylor, chairman of the League, which put down the current suffering and distress to the 'monopoly in food, upheld by a landowning legislature and a subservient ministry'. Many of the Tory magistrates and authorities suspected the League of deliberately stirring up the dark forces in society.[43]

Whether or not it represented deliberate provocation, a wage reduction of 25 per cent, such as that made at Ashton, was bound to result in action. The trades leaders had already unsuccessfully appealed to some employers to consider short-time working rather than wage-reductions. Whether or not the Chartist leaders in the industrial areas had called for strikes, it seems inevitable that they would have occurred. In the Manchester district as in the Potteries and the Staffordshire coalfield, the articulate leaders in the strike movement were the Chartists. Not all the Chartists wanted the question of the Charter kept to the fore. Some of them realised that a successful resistance to a wages reduction would have been a very significant demonstration of industrial power in the context of the summer of 1842, and would have been satisfied with that. It may be this view which prevailed among some unionists like those at Oldham who voted against the idea of a strike for the Charter. Certainly many of those who, like O'Connor, were chary of the idea of a strike for the Charter were so because they feared an unsuccessful strike would damage the Chartist movement, not because they considered the two questions unconnected.

The Chartists must have expected, as Cooper said, that the turn-outs were likely to lead to a general rising. In anticipation of this, and as a method of keeping up the spirit of the strikers and keeping the demands before the public, they organised meetings, processions, demonstrations. They stressed the need for discipline and organisation, and discouraged any move towards looting or the destruction of property beyond what was needed to stop the factories. As Christopher Doyle claimed at his trial,

> . . . in all the agitations that have taken place in this country for what is called Chartism, I think you will recollect that, generally speaking, if there be any party who more than another ought to be thanked for preserving the peace, it is the Chartist body . . . their constant motto has been 'peace, law and order'. Of course wages became mixed up with the Chartist question – a fair day's wage for a fair day's work; . . . I believe, Gentlemen, that the labour of the people of this country will never be protected until the working classes have a voice in making the laws they are called on to obey.[44]

But while keeping the peace, the leaders had to spread the strike. Not only were new trades and industries involved, but from Lancashire and Staffordshire determined efforts were made to move into other districts and to connect up the striking areas. Troops were present in both areas in large numbers, and clashes were inevitable. The meeting of trades delegates which had called for a continuance of the strike until the Charter was achieved was held on 12 August. A meeting of Chartist delegates had been summoned for 17 August in Manchester to preside over the installation of a memorial to Henry Hunt in James Scholefield's Every Street chapel. The delegates had already been elected, but as they set out for Manchester they realised that they would have other matters than the Hunt memorial to discuss. Thomas Cooper, travelling from Leicester, had spoken on his way at several places in Staffordshire. In his autobiography he describes the intense excitement of his two days of travelling and speaking – the enormous meetings, his avoidance of the police, his arrest and finally his arrival on foot at Crewe station, from which he set out in a state of intense excitement to join the other delegates in Manchester.

By this time Cooper had already become deeply involved. He had spoken to meetings throughout the district, culminating in the meeting at Hanley at which the resolution was unanimously passed 'that all labour cease until the People's Charter become the law of the land'. He directed the frustration and enthusiasm of the crowds to the business of stopping those works that were still operating. But his hearers did not stop at such peaceful demonstrations. Cooper himself later admitted that he had 'struck a spark which kindled all into combustion'. The combustion did not end in the district until police stations had been destroyed, prisoners released, poorhouses torn down, and the homes of unpopular magistrates and coal-owners sacked and burned. This was the crowd of the middle-class nightmare – the Potteries riots were indeed the basis for the riot scenes in *Sybil*. Apart from those who were wounded by bullets from troops who fired on the crowd at Burslem on 16 August, however, there were no killings or serious wounding by the crowds even here. The destruction was of property – the property of unpopular people was destroyed, not their lives.

Cooper arrived in Manchester, convinced that 'the spread of the strike would and must be followed by a general outbreak'. Meanwhile the movement had been spreading from Lancashire across the Pennines into Yorkshire. In each district new supporters were enrolled and mills and factories were stopped. Local magistrates and police sent reports to the Home Office, and took precautions by calling up pensioners and swearing in special constables. In most districts enough respectable inhabitants came forward to make up a force of some pretensions. There were places, however, like Barnoldswick, where the operation proved difficult. Here, where wages of both handloom weavers and the factory workers on short time were around three to four shillings a week, the local magistrate reported that the township 'consists of people almost wholly of the lowest class; the few more respectable inhabitants are very objectionable to the people and naturally unwilling to take any active part fearing as they do that common result, private mischief . . . '[45]

From Huddersfield the magistrates reported on the arrival of the strikers; the leaders were described as 'all strangers, evidently in humble life – sensible, shrewd, determined, peaceable . . . the burden of their speeches was to destroy no property, to hurt no human being, but determinedly to persist in ceasing from labour and to induce others to do the same until every man could obtain "a fair day's wage for a fair day's work"'. The same writer reported next day that 'the native operatives are quiet, but evidently wish success to what may be called an insurrection'.[46] At Dewsbury the strike was complete, and the local magistrate reported that on one day thirty-eight mills had been stopped by the mob, and at five o'clock the crowd in the town centre heard two speeches given from the market cross, one by a stranger, the other by a local shoemaker named Sheldrake. The speakers urged them to keep the peace, not to return to work until they had the Charter, and to reassemble next morning to receive instructions about that day's programme. The report concluded: 'the rioters have not yet proceeded to outrage, but we cannot help perceiving that this state of things cannot last much longer, the rioters seem almost famished for want of food.'[47] In the towns of Leeds and Cleckheaton, strong forces of troops and special constables, combined with far less supportive activity from the local population, prevented the crowds from entering.

Halifax was one of the strongest Chartist centres in the district, and was the location of one of the biggest clashes between Chartists and troops. The strikers crossed from Rochdale into Todmorden on 12 August. The next day they moved up to Hebden Bridge, closing all mills, drawing the plugs from the boilers and letting off the mill-dams on the way. While some of the strikers returned each night to their homes, the crowd was swelled each day by local workers. Although some observers claimed that most of the people who took part in the action were 'outsiders', all those arrested in Halifax were local men. F. H. Grundy, a civil engineer working on railway construction in the town at the time, said that 'few of the people, excepting enthusiasts among the enthusiastic marched many miles from home, because multitudes were seen returning to the various towns passed through . . . I had unusual opportunities of noticing them closely, and was surprised at the number whom I recognised as factory hands round about, and navvies . . . '[48] Benjamin Wilson also insisted that the people who attacked the soldiers were 'neither Lancashire people or people from a distance, but principally young men from the surrounding districts'.[49]

Contemporary accounts and reminiscences of the clashes provide a vivid series of pictures of the events of the next two or three days. At dawn on 15 August an excited crowd – hearing that the approach of the strikers was imminent – assembled on Skircoat Moor. Ben Rushton addressed them, condemning the masters who had reduced wages 'for the purpose of obtaining the repeal of the Corn Laws', urging the people to support the strike and to keep the peace. The magistrates intervened to disperse the meeting, so the crowd formed into a procession and marched towards Luddenden Foot to meet the Todmorden and Hebden Bridge turn-outs on their way to Halifax.[50] Some mills on the road were stopped; handloom weavers who joined the strike threw their shuttles into a common bag which was deposited in a public house. One participant remembered the day: 'It was a remarkably fine day, the sun shone in its full splendour. The broad white road with its green hedges . . . was filled with a long black straggling line of people, who cheerfully went along, evidently possessed of an idea that they were doing something towards a betterment.'[51] The contingents met, and 'Ben Rushton stepped aside into a field and led off with a speech. . . Before the speaking a big milk can was obtained and filled with treacle-beer.' Some went into nearby houses and were given food.

In the late morning the procession re-entered Halifax, about five thousand strong, singing Chartist hymns and the One Hundreth Psalm.[52] 'The women went first, four abreast, and were followed by a long procession of more or less pretensions. They then dispersed, under orders given by a man on horseback, who told them what mills to visit.'[53] Meanwhile, from the direction of Bradford, another procession of between four and five thousand marchers were approaching.

> The sight was just one of those which it is impossible to forget. They came pouring down the wide road in thousands, taking up the whole breadth – a gaunt, famished-looking, desperate multitude armed with huge bludgeons, flails, pitchforks and pikes, many without coats and hats, and hundreds upon hundreds with their clothes in rags and tatters. Many of the older men looked

footsore and weary, but the great bulk were men in the prime of life, full of wild excitement. As they marched they thundered out . . . a stirring melody. . . [54]

The soldiers were unable to prevent the two contingents from joining. The Riot Act was read, and the main body separated into smaller groups which went round closing any mills that still remained open. The military commander in his report spoke of the way in which any large crowd which was confronted would melt away, often dispersing across the fields, and reassemble in another part of town, sometimes joining with the parties which came into Halifax from at least three different directions along the main roads. During the first day a number of arrests were made. The prisoners were interrogated by the magistrates, and finally reduced to eighteen serious offenders who were kept in custody overnight before being transferred by rail to Wakefield for charging. The strikers retired to the moor above the town where many of them spent the night in the open air. Many women were among them, leading the singing of Chartist hymns and songs. One observer remembered them fifty years later: 'Perhaps the women were at this time the more valiant. Approaching to the very necks of the horses they declared they would rather die than starve, and if the soldiers were determined to charge, they might kill them . . . ' Some taunted the men with cowardice, and one, speaking of the prisoners who were in custody, declared: 'If I were a man, they sudn't long be there.'[55]

Next days things took a more serious tone. The arrested men were taken early to the nearest railway station, which was at Elland, where they were put on the train for Wakefield and gaol. The crowd missed the prisoners and their military escort, so no rescue was attempted. Instead they prepared an ambush for the returning soldiers. Grundy, whose office was on the Halifax–Elland road, found that road, on the morning of 16 August, 'Like a road to a fair or to the races . . . all busy, women as well as men – rushing along the various lanes over my head with arms and aprons full of stones . . . ' At this point high wooded banks overlook the road, and Grundy set out to warn the troops of their danger. On the pretext of a routine inspection of the bridge he was building, he set out from his office.

I have hardly gone a dozen yards from my door when heavy hands are on my shoulders, and I turn to see two of my *own* men.

'Thou munnot go to t'brigg to-day, sir.'

'Why, what nonsense is this?'

'We be main sorry sir, varry, but thou mun come back again. Thou'rt to go whoam into t'house, and we two are to watch thee, like. Thou'lt nobbut be murdered, and then cannot do ony guid. There are a matter of fower thousand folk looking on; so coome sir. Thou'rt not to be fettled, but thou'rt to be kept inside o' t'house.'

At length the soldiers and the omnibus in which the prisoners had been taken returned.

They slow into a walk as they breast Salterhebble Hill. Then a loud voice shouts 'Now, lads, give it 'em!' From every wall rises a crowd of infuriated men, and down comes a shower of stones, bricks, boulders, like a close fall of hail . . . 'Gallop! Gallop!' comes the order, as their leader spurs his horse up the steep hill. But the men, jammed together, cannot gallop. They come down pell-mell, horses and riders. Those who can get through ride off at speed after their officer . . . Then the command came 'Cease throwing'. Eight horsemen, bleeding and helpless crawled about the road, seeking shelter . . . Down come the hosts now, and tearing the belts and accoutrements from the prostrate hussars, the saddles and bridles from the horses, they give three cheers and depart.[56]

A report was sent to Leeds, with an urgent call for more troops.

A most terrible affair has occurred at Salterhebble, and at the time I write it is feared there will be many lives lost before the day is over. I scarcely know how to inform you in a few lines the dreadful state of things in Halifax and the neighbourhood.[57]

The soldiers were not slow in taking their revenge. They sallied forth from their billet in full strength, rode down the crowds, and 'followed the flying people for miles . . . Many a tale of wounded men lying out in barns and under hedges was told . . .' A report sent to the Home Office lists eight wounded, four dangerously. At least two of these died, and one soldier. Thirty-six men were sent for trial, and several received severe sentences, including one of life transportation, for their parts in the rioting.

The mills went back slowly, and by 12 September the clerk to the Halifax magistrates was able to report 'business carried on as usual with the most perfect order and security'.[58]

1842 was the year in which more energy was hurled against the authorities than in any other of the nineteenth century. More people were arrested and sentenced for offences concerned with speaking, agitating, rioting and demonstrating than in any other year, and more people were out on the streets during August 1842 than at any other time. It was the nearest thing to a general strike that the century saw. Whole districts stopped work. Thomas Cooper recalled the effect on the Chartist leaders looking from the railway carriage that was taking them to the 1842 convention in Manchester.

> So soon as the city of Long Chimneys came in sight, and every chimney was beheld smokeless. Campbell's face changed, and with an oath he said, 'Not a single mill at work! something must come of this, and something serious too!'[59]

Many historians, as has already been noted, dismissed the events of that summer as a 'spontaneous' response to bad trade conditions which had very little to do with Chartism. The Chartist leadership nationally was divided in its response to the outbreaks. Lovett's National Association poured forth a stream of platitudes as if nothing had happened to the working population about which it professed to care. Perhaps no other reason for the utter failure of the organisation needs to be sought than this enormous insensitivity to the concerns of the great body of the working class. Perhaps it is merely an index of the isolation and self-absorption of the old Lovett who was writing in 1876 that he failed to recall those months of tumult. Ben Brierly, by contrast, recalled the strike of 1842 as the 'culmination' of the Chartism he remembered. For him it was a time of meetings, newspaper-reading, and pike-sharpening, in anticipation of the expected 'smash-up'.

> I entered into the movement with all the zest of youth, and rushed into danger heedless of consequences. I was present at 'plug-drawings' everywhere, disguised by appearing in my shirt sleeves, my paper cap, and the leather apron I wore at my velvet loom . . . [60]

Thomas Cooper's life was changed dramatically by the events of July and August 1842. He told in his autobiography of the narrowness of his escape from the same fate as William Ellis. Indeed, had he not had the word of a magistrate as alibi he would have joined Ellis on the convict ship, since the same perjured witness whose evidence condemned the young potter claimed to have seen Cooper arm-in-arm with him at the scene of the fire. As it was, the sentence of imprisonment he received checked his career as a political agitator and led him back to his earlier literary ambitions. His account of 1842 is of very great interest. Protesting, as all old Chartists did, his adherence to a belief in law and order, he recalled that the magistrate questioned one of the hostile witnesses about his attitude.

> 'He procalimed "Peace, Law and Order" and shouted it aloud' said one of the meanest of the witnesses, with a laugh.
>
> 'But *how* did he say it?' asked Mr. Mainwaring; 'did he say it as if he meant it?'
>
> 'Oh, no!' cried Dirty Neck, as the fellow was called in the Potteries; 'it was only *innuendo*.'[61]

Cooper recalled his anger at this answer, and yet it perhaps represents an important matter. In a way, it was precisely the legality and orderliness of the Plug rioters and strikers that was most threatening. Witnesses in many areas reported the banners with 'Peace Law and Order' on one side, and slogans such as 'Political Equality' on the other. Leaders urged their followers to keep the peace, and led them into the mills to draw the plugs. Strikers linked arms and 'swept' reluctant workers out of the mill-yards and along the road with the marching strikers. Cooper recalled that he spoke at the Manchester conference in favour of supporting the strike and his reason.

I told the Conference I should vote for the resolution because it meant fighting, and I saw it must come to that. The spread of the strike would and must be followed by a general outbreak. The authorities of the land would try to quell it; but we must resist them. There was nothing now but a physical force struggle to be looked for. We must get the people out to fight; and they must be irresistible, if they were united.[62]

It is not so surprising that a hostile observer should detect an innuendo in Cooper's cry of 'Peace Law and Order'. The eager crowds who heard him were looking for signals other than the simple words of his address. He had, as he recalled in his account, made a passionate speech attacking the Government, taking as his text the sixth commandment, 'Thou shalt do no murder'. In his speech he had shown, with a mounting series of examples, that the authorities had violated the commandment in all their actions – from the slaughter of conquered peoples and the imposition of colonial rule to the establishment of the new Poor Law and the starvation of the weavers, nailers and stockingers of the country in which he was speaking.

I fear I spent so much time in describing the wrong, and raising the spirit of vengeance in those who heard me, that the little time I spent in conclusion, and in showing that those who heard me were not to violate the precept 'Thou shalt do no murder' . . . but that they were to . . . forgive their enemies, produced little effect in the way of lowering the flame . . . [63]

Recalling his part in the events – a part which was being played throughout the manufacturing districts by the leaders of the movement – Cooper commented

Now thirty years have gone over my head, I see how rash and uncalculating my conduct was . . . I had caught the spirit of the oppressed and discontented thousands, and, by virtue of my nature and constitution, struck the spark which kindled all into combustion.[64]

The walls of the towns and villages broke out in placards, most of them having a short life before being torn down or pasted over. Magistrates banned meetings by placards, respectable householders like those in Blackburn protested against the strikes and disorder, and begged leave 'to tender our services to the magistracy with a fixed determination to employ all our power and influence in the maintenance of Loyalty to our Sovereign, obedience to the Law and full protection of the rights and liberties of the peaceful and industrious'.[65] By contrast, the placards put up by the Chartists resounded with poetic exhortation:

To the Colliers of
England and Wales.
Strike! Colliers! Strike for the Charter!

In your hands is reposed such a power as the tyrant few, who oppress and grind the faces of the poor, cannot withstand. Without *coal* the lordly aristocrat cannot cook his luxurious meal. Without coal the *Steam Engine* whose iron arm has beggared so many of your poor fellow-countrymen, willing to work – murdered thousands of *innocent children* in our Cotton Mills yearly – reduced thousands of tender mothers to a worse state than brute beasts, and hung their pale limbs with filthy rags – without coal this giant monster, the Steam Engine, cannot work. Your labour, my honest friends, supplies it with strength, for without Coal it is powerless. Stop getting Coal, for Coal supports the money-mongering Capitalists.[66]

CHAPTER 12

The Charter and the Land

SOME of the early Chartists reached the high point of their radical careers in 1839. For many of those who came into the movement then as very young people, 1842 was the year in which they were called on to act on their principles, and to take immediate risks including standing against armed troops. Many Chartist leaders found themselves in 1842 facing both directions – the troops and police were ahead, but at the same time there was the need to restrain their followers from acts of violence and desperation. On the whole, considering the enormous numbers involved, the level of violence was low. More people were, however, arrested in 1842 than at any other period in the Chartist movement, and more were transported. We know less about the Chartist prisoners of this period as individuals, but, as with the earlier arrests, the support of the prisoners and their families occupied a great deal of the time and resources of the Chartist localities after 1842.

The years after 1842 saw fewer confrontations with authority than the first four years. 1848 was a dramatic year in Europe, when middle-class radicalism and liberalism flared up in many European cities. The urban artisans were involved in many cases, notably of course in Paris, and the Chartists in Britain followed the events of that year with enthusiasm. 1848 saw the last of the great national Chartist efforts, the last petition presented to Parliament, and the end of the mass platform. After that year, and in fact the tendencies can be seen earlier, Chartism divided into a number of different movements. These have provided many speculations for historians, and the publications of the late forties and early fifties produced some of the most interesting political discussions of the period. As a mass movement, however, Chartism declined rapidly after 1848. The limits of popular action seem to have been reached, and the later organisations which replaced the National Charter Association were less ambitious and less far-ranging in their aims.

During the late forties, some of the most interesting aspects of the Chartist movement developed. It was in these years that local associations set up schools, cooperative societies, reading-rooms and mutual improvement groups. The Chartist Land Company operated from 1845 to 1850, and seemed to offer the chance of self-help and self-activity for which so many people in the industrial areas longed. The thousands of members of the Land Plan, the large number of branches and the wide spread of its membership suggest a support for the ideas and the leadership of the Chartists even in years in which great demonstrations and widespread petitioning did not occur.

Chartism had always combined political demands with attempts to bring about practical improvement in the lives of its members and supporters. In the first decade following the Reform Act of 1832, the working people pressed for the widening of the terms of the Act, and for their own inclusion in the political system. By the end of 1842, however, every tactic had been attempted with no success. Hundreds had been arrested, hundreds, probably thousands, more had emigrated, either in despair or actually to avoid arrest. The years that followed saw the development of social and educational organisations, and in 1848 a final attempt to bring together British Chartism and the Irish repeal movement and to make contact with European revolutionary events.

The conspiracy trial of April 1843, in which O'Connor and the other Chartist leaders were in effect acquitted, was something of a victory for the movement. There had been, however, many arrests, imprisonments and transportations among the lesser leaders. Added to the names of the Welsh leaders for whom pardon and return were sought and demanded after 1842, was that of William Sherrat Ellis, a young potter sentenced on perjured evidence for the crime of arson after the riots of that year. 'His *real* crime,' wrote Thomas Cooper, 'was – daring to promulgate the great truth that *the Many ought not to be slaves to the Few!*' Ellis, like many of the younger Chartists, was a teetotaler, a great reader and a former Sunday school teacher. If he was a danger to the authorities it was not as a 'firebrand', but as a serious and devoted organiser and educator.[1] Cooper maintained that his real crime was to have been voted into the chair at a recent county meeting, at which the Chartists attended in force. The meeting had been called to congratulate the Queen on the birth of the Prince of Wales, and under Ellis's chairmanship, an alternative wording to the resolution, pointing out the poverty and suffering in the county at the same time as offering the congratulations, had been adopted. From the time of the meeting, the authorities had been determined that Ellis should be punished and the sentence of twenty-one years' transportation, passed after he had been found guilty on the flimsiest of evidence by a jury of middle-class citizens, was in reality a punishment for that episode. Cooper and Ellis spent an hour together in prison after their respective sentences, and talked about Chartism and the future.

He spoke of the coming age of universal brotherhood, of the world-spread establishment of the great community. I soon perceived his attachments to the doctrines of socialism; and we communed together until we forgot the dungeon, in our visions of that glorious fraternityof happy beings which Earth, now groaning beneath her weight of misery, shall one day exultantly bear . . .[2]

Socialism – in the form of cooperation and community-building – was one of the questions that occupied the Chartists of the forties. The foundation, in 1844, of the Rochdale Cooperative Society, with the formula of dividend paid on purchases that was to become the key to a century of successful cooperative trading, was the work of a group of Chartist flannel weavers.[3] Throughout Lancashire and Yorkshire and many other manufacturing districts cooperative trading societies were set up, among whose founders were invariably a large number of Chartists. Most of these earliest societies included education among their aims, and had part of their funds set aside for this purpose. Many also included programmes of home colonisation, and carried forward into the second half of the century some of the aims of the Land Plan, but in a more limited form. Just as the political impulse of Chartism became constricted into the narrow confines of popular liberalism in the second half of the century, so the social impulses which the Chartists took into the cooperative movement became subservient to the practicalities of retail trading. Although the importance of cooperative trading in working-class communities should not be understated, it was still, by the end of the century, very far from the communitarian vision of William Ellis and his associates.

1845 saw two important events in the Chartist movement, the launching of the Land Plan, and the adhesion of a new leader, Ernest Jones, who was to carry the movement into the fifties.

When O'Connor published the report of the Lancaster conspiracy trial in 1843, he published at the same time *The State of Ireland*, a pamphlet written in 1798 by his uncle, Arthur O'Connor.

The re-publication at that time had two aims. One, emphasised in Feargus's introduction and dedication 'to the working classes of England and Ireland', was to highlight the political problems of Ireland, and to stress the continued relevance of the United Irishmen's programme, which included the main points of the Charter and reform of land tenure. The second aim was to bring before the Chartists the question of land ownership and cultivation. In the same year of 1843, O'Connor began the publication in parts of a pocket-sized work, *The Management of Small Farms*, which was then issued as a book at 1*s*. a copy and went into several editions in the following years. These two publications marked the beginning of the Chartist Land Scheme.

The Management of Small Farms makes interesting reading today. Like its author, the Land Plan has had a generally bad press until recently. Many of the arguments which make up the introductory sections of the book, however, have a very contemporary ring. Modern concern with ecology and the problems of labour and the distribution of wealth in a highly-mechanised economy is foreseen in many of Feargus's arguments, which are not based on the idea of a return to the land for all or even for most of the working people, but are concerned with the problem of choice. His attack on large-scale mechanised production is based on the monopoly which it gives to a small number of employers over the lives and wages of whole populations, and the proposals for small farming projects, like those put forward by the cooperative and redemption societies, are for alternatives which could offer a way of escape or at least a form of competition which would keep up urban wages. This concern was not new. As well as Arthur O'Connor, its proponents included William Cobbett, whose influence on many radicals was that of a small proprietor as well as a political reformer. Many of the working people who emigrated in the Chartist period sought a more rewarding way of life on the land, and it should be remembered that many of them found it. Land ownership, control and cultivation were involved in the politics of all political groups in the nineteenth century, and proposals for allotments, smallholdings, cooperatives communities and emigration societies existed in nearly every part of the political spectrum. The Chartist version, launched first at the National Convention in April 1845, and formalised in December of that year at a special convention called in Manchester for the purpose, was participatory and democratic in structure, although not socialist in its form or its organisation.

The later Chartists, including most of the autobiographers, were dismissive of the Land Plan. Its history did not in the end bring much credit on the Chartist movement or on O'Connor, although, as so often, his critics underestimated the deliberate opposition mounted against him by the authorities. Among the rank and file members, however, memories of the plan were more generous. Benjamin Wilson wrote:

Feargus O'Connor tried to grapple with the land question. He formed a company on the small farm system and purchased several large estates and a great many thousands became members, including several of my friends, and although trade was bad, they cheerfully made great sacrifices to raise the money. Feargus had a great many difficulties to contend against, for he had nearly all the press in the country against him, whilst a great many got on the land who had no knowledge of it, and what with the opposition outside and the dissatisfaction within, the company was thrown into Chancery. Two or three from Halifax went on the land, but the scheme was before its time; yet I believe the day is not far distant when it will be successfully carried out.[4]

A full history of the scheme and its problems remains to be written. The material is available, and some valuable preliminary studies have been made. In particular, a recent essay by Eileen Yeo shows that, so far from the legal problems of the Land Company having arisen from the amateurishness of its founders, a deliberate policy was pursued by Parliament and the courts of excluding the possibility of a popularly-owned and controlled organisation of smallholders.[5] Even limited liability, essential to the protection of small businesses and cooperative ventures, was not available as a protection for the Chartists.

As a practical venture, the Land Plan failed. The comfortable small houses which were built under O'Connor's direction remain, many of them, to this day as monuments to the integrity of Chartist planning in an age increasingly devoted to shoddy. On some of the estates the smallholdings flourished – mainly in districts in which market gardening was possible, rather than spade husbandry of traditional farming crops. One of the original allottees told a reporter in 1888 that the chief failure had been that many of the allottees were industrial workers who had no knowledge of agriculture.[6] As a means of holding together the Chartist movement in the second half of the decade, however, the Land Plan must certainly be seen as an important part of the Chartist movement. So far from constituting a diversion from the main course of Chartism, as some have claimed, it seems much more likely that the Plan served to hold together a movement which otherwise might have split sooner into a variety of tendencies. As a glance at the organisations of Chartism shows, the districts which retained Chartist organisations in 1848 were the same as those which had branches of the Land Company. Nearly every Chartist leader in the main localities was associated with the Land Company. In the membership lists, names like Benjamin Rushton of Halifax, John Vallance of Barnsley, Thomas Sidaway of Gloucester and hundreds of others appear as shareholders. In the localities men like Samuel Cook of Dudley and Joseph Linney of Bilston were officers and organisers of local branches, while at the level of national leadership, office-holders and directors included many of the leading figures of the period. Philip McGrath, Christopher Doyle and Thomas Martin Wheeler were all officers as was, in spite of his later denials, Ernest Jones. George Candelet, a delegate to the trades conference in Manchester in August 1842, and one of the defendants in the conspiracy trial, wrote a pamphlet in support of the Plan,[7] and most of the radical journals which were not actually socialist in their outlook wrote about the Plan with sympathy.

As John Saville has shown in what is probably the most important discussion of the Land Plan,[8] historians of Chartism have made the mistake of looking at the Plan out of the context in which it was launched. Just as the politics of Chartism have often been mis-read through failure to take account of the context of national politics, so the removal of the land policy of O'Connor to the twentieth century has missed some important points about it. It has already been noted that home colonisation, community-building and emigration to land-based communities in America were part of the programmes of the many Owenite and other socialist groups in the thirties and forties. There was also a strong current of dissenting Christian land-based communitarian activity in Britain in those years.[9] But policies of the development of smallholdings and allotments were not confined to the utopian part of the working-class movement. Among philanthropists and political economists there was also serious discussion both of the idea of large gardens and allotments for rural labourers to compensate for the loss by enclosure of common rights and common grazing, and of other machinery for making land more available to the less wealthy sections of the population. Private property in land, particularly the concentration of land ownership in the hands of a small number of families, through whom, by the custom of primogeniture, it became an increasingly static and powerful monopoly, was seen by liberals as a block to the development of genuinely liberal democracy in Britain. Although the traditional political economists tended to agree that large farms were preferable to small, on grounds of economic theory – productivity per man being clearly a more important measure of success than productivity per acre by their standards – there were economists who had their doubts, as well as politicians and philanthropists who deplored the depopulation of the countryside and the unplanned growth of cities. Commentators as different in outlook as John Stuart Mill and the *Halifax Guardian* looked with some favour on the Chartist Land Plan. Mill, after describing the plan and its organisation, declared: 'Should its issue ultimately be unfavourable, the cause of failure will be in the details of management, not in the Principle.'[10] The *Halifax Guardian*, a Tory paper with some sympathy for the factory reform and anti-Poor-Law movements, noted in 1848:

The invention of the £10 franchise has not reduced, nor checked, the increase of the pauper list, and Free Trade has not *yet* increased the wages of the factory operatives. Even the Chartists are beginning to recognise the non-connection of political changes with general social benefit, and are more wisely looking to 'the land' for their sole chance of regeneration.[11]

Such opinions do not, of course, necessarily justify the scheme, or answer the critics within and around the movement who saw it as a deviation from 'true Chartism'. Such critics were, however, in a very small minority at the time. Some of the fiercest criticism came from the pen of Alexander Somerville, himself a long way from the Chartists. He believed that the Land scheme and its passionate supporters in the factory districts were not genuinely concerned with setting up smallholdings, but were a cover for the Chartists' 'true' aim of land nationalisation and the confiscation of property.[12] However, it has not always been remembered that Somerville was not a disinterested observer. Like many of the Irish 'lambs' in 1841, Somerville was instigated to attack the Chartists by the officials of the Anti-Corn-Law League, and he expected payment for his services. When he was not paid, he exposed his relations with the League in a pamphlet, in which he pointed out that he had not only, by his writing, provided ammunition for most of the subsequent attacks on the Land Scheme, but had also involved himself in unpopularity – indeed in physical danger – by his writing. 'So vehemently had O'Connor excited the Manchester mobs against me in 1847, that after assaults in the streets, thrown in the mud at night, my life threatened and my steps dogged night and day by emissaries of O'Connor, I left Manchester and resided in London.'[13] In spite of his sufferings on their behalf, his patrons had refused to pay him, and he complained bitterly to Bright in 1852: 'You and the men of the League and the proprietor of the *Manchester Examiner* induced me to waste months of time and incur heavy expenses in the controversy against O'Connor. You and they have left me to bear all the expenses and all the odium. I call that injury.'[14]

Somerville's writing, in the *Examiner* and in other papers, together with the criticisms of the Land Plan from O'Brien at the time and from other ex-Chartists later, have perhaps given historians a view of the scheme as very much more eccentric than it actually was. Perhaps the comment of a contemporary Chartist, towards the end of the lifetime of the plan, is nearer the mark.

Travel in England, north or south (but more in the north than the south) and in every parish you will hear of local land societies, sometimes originating with trades unions, and other times with land associations. Trace all these societies to their fountain-head, and you will find in them the impress of the mind of Mr. O'Connor . . . [15]

The Chartists had tried petitioning, they had tried the weapons of the strike, the mass demonstration, even an attempted rising. As the decade proceeded they were turning to self-help of various kinds, trying against the odds of lack of means, alternating overwork and unemployment and the increasing presence of police and military in their communities, to set up their own institutions. The Land Plan provided an organising focus in all the localities. The estates as they were bought and put into operation seemed to provide islands of practical Chartism in the country. So far from diverting attention from the political movement, it was almost certainly the existence of the Land Company that kept the movement together, provided an additional reason for the regular reading of the *Star*, and offered a focus of activity beyond the discredited process of petitioning.

CHAPTER 13

1848

AFTER 1845, a great deal of Feargus's ferocious energy was absorbed by the land scheme. He was personally involved in organising, raising money, setting up the colonies and supervising the settlement of allottees. In the *Star* he coupled the continued demand for the suffrage with the defence of the Land Plan and with accounts of small cultivator systems in other parts of Europe. In 1847 he founded and edited, in association with Ernest Jones, the *Labourer*, a monthly journal devoted to the Land Plan. In Parliament he pressed on with attempts to secure the legality of the scheme, and to bring about amendments of the law to achieve this. Nearly every leading Chartist was at some time involved in the scheme. In September 1846, Ernest Jones was given a paid position in the company, as secretary to one section, and probably held the post until he was appointed to the editorial staff of the *Northern Star* at the end of 1846.[1]

Jones has been treated more seriously by historians than many of the other Chartist leaders for a number of reasons.[2] He was one of the few leading Chartists who made the transition from Chartism to Liberalism, becoming as he did a leading figure in the Reform League in the sixties, and a parliamentary candidate in the first election after the 1867 Bill. He was a close associate of Marx and of Engels, both of whom wrote for his journals. He left more personalia than most Chartists, since he came from a higher social class. He was a poet, some of whose verse retained its popularity in radical circles into the early years of the modern labour movement. Perhaps, above all, he appealed as a 'modern' political leader who was easier for Chartism's early historians to understand than many of his predecessors.

Ernest Jones was born in 1819 into a family whose roots were in the military and landowning classes of the *ancien regime*. His father, a retired army officer who had fought in the Peninsular War, was attached to the court of Ernest Augustus, Duke of Cumberland. When Queen Victoria ascended the throne, Ernest Augustus assumed the crown of Hanover, from which the Salic law of male inheritance precluded Victoria. The Duke was the Chartist leader's godfather – an ironic connection between the most conservative member of the British royal family and a leader of popular radicalism. Jones was born in Berlin and educated for the first twenty years of his life in Germany. He was bilingual in German and English, as well as being fluent in French and Italian and well versed in the classical languages. In his own recollections he often mentioned an incident in his childhood when, at the age of eleven, he ran away from home and was found wandering in the Black Forest, on his way 'to help the Poles' in their rising against the Russians in 1830. In England he read for the bar, married the daughter of a conservative landowning family, published a few verses in fashionable journals, enjoyed a lively social life among rather Bohemian literary and theatrical London circles, and generally followed the life of a minor and not very wealthy member of the British upper classes until 1845. In that year a series of family disasters and unwise property speculations found him bankrupt.

Jones's conversion to Chartism in the middle forties may have been the result of a combination of Byronic romanticism, failed literary ambition, and the collapse of the upper-class life-style to which he aspired. It was, however, none the less genuine for that, and he was to spend the rest of his life as an active radical, never free of financial and family cares, never fully accepted into middle-class radical circles, nor fully at home among the working men who made up his following. Although a skilful orator, he lacked the charisma of an O'Connor or a Hunt, and never achieved the status of the gentleman demagogue – a figure which had, indeed, had its day in British working-class history by the time he appeared on the scene. He was, nevertheless, a national leader of some stature, and was remembered by the last generation of Chartists who had not known the founders of the movement.

Jones approached O'Connor in 1845, and Feargus agreed to support the publication of his *Chartist Songs and Fugitive Pieces*. The collection appeared in 1846, and was an immediate success with the Chartists. In the time before its publication, Jones had spoken at his first mass demonstration, at Blackstone Edge, between Yorkshire and Lancashire. A crowd of between twenty-five and thirty thousand people at a great outdoor camp meeting heard him speak, and one observer later remembered: ' . . . it was one of the most telling and effective speeches I ever heard, replete with the various figures and graces of oratory . . . Mr. Jones was on all hands hailed as a great accession to the movement, and before the meeting separated his arms and hands must have ached from having them so cordially grasped and shaken.'[3] The same writer considered that, with the exception of Feargus O'Connor, 'no public man at all approached Mr. Jones in popularity'. He commented above all on Jones's 'enthusiasm'. Clearly the quality of personal energy and commitment which made O'Connor an outstanding leader was also to an extent present in Jones.

1846, when Jones first became a Chartlist, was a year in which the Chartists could still command great rallies on the scale of the camp meeting at Blackstone Edge. By the end of that year the movement was again considering its policy for parliamentary elections, and the elections which took place in the summer of 1847 saw some of the most successful campaigns ever fought by the Chartists. Feargus O'Connor was elected for Nottingham, running in joint candidature with John Walter junior, a Tory. In Halifax Ernest Jones ran as a Chartist, in conjunction with the radical Edward Miall, editor of the *Nonconformist*, and a former member of the Complete Suffrage Union. They ran a lively campaign, filling the town with exciting meetings of thousands of non-electors, and carrying all before them at the hustings. Although Jones, who was a congenital optimist, hoped to win the seat, he was predictably at the bottom of the poll, although his very respectable vote of 279, in an electorate of not much more than 1,000, was a high peak in Chartist electoral support in the town.[4] Political alignments in 1847 were confused. The Tory Government, which had passed the repeal of the Corn Laws under the guidance of Peel, had fallen on an issue of Irish coercion. Political loyalties were unstable – protectionist Tories were disgruntled by the repeal of the Corn Laws, many nonconformists and Anglicans were disaffected by the Government's recent 'soft' attitude to Irish education, shown in particular by the grant to the Catholic training college at Maynooth. The Ten Hours Bill had passed both Houses of Parliament by a combination of supporters which had not followed party lines. In the atmosphere of 1847, electors were better-disposed towards Chartist candidates than at any other election. Jones's vote, and Philip McGrath's 220 at Derby as well as O'Connor's victory – with 1,340 votes – at Nottingham, represent the high point of middle-class support for Chartism.

The election campaigns and O'Connor's victory re-enthused the Chartist movement. Preparations were made for a third national petition – to be presented this time by their own leader in the House of Commons. The winter of 1847 was a bad one. Benjamin Wilson recalled:

> In this year flour was very dear, reaching the price of 5s per stone, whilst trade was also very bad. This was the time to make politicians, as the easiest way to get to an Englishman's brain is through his stomach. It was said by its enemies that Chartism was dead and buried and would never rise again, but they were doomed to disappointment. . . . Amongst combers, handloom weavers and others, politics was the chief topic. *The Northern Star* was their principal paper,

and it was a common practice, particularly in villages, to meet at friends' houses to read the paper and talk over political matters . . . [5]

The last petition, and the political re-awakening that was to characterise 1848, were therefore started well before events in Continental Europe provided a new inspiration.

By 1848, Chartism had become the accepted political standpoint of the working people of Britain. The fading of support in the fifties was a fading of the belief in politics as an agent of change and improvement, rather than a decline in the belief in the suffrage and in Chartism generally. Henry Mayhew's account of the costermongers in London is well-known.

The politics of these people are detailed in a very few words – they are nearly all Chartists. 'You might say, sir,' remarked one of my informants, 'that they *all* were Chartists, but as its rather better you should be under than over the mark, say *nearly* all . . . ' I am assured that in every district where the costermongers are congregated, one or two of the body, more intelligent than the others, have great influence over them; and these leading men are all Chartists, and being industrious and not unprosperous persons, their pecuniary and intellectual superiority cause them to be regarded as oracles . . . [6]

If the Chartism of many of the costermongers consisted of a determined hatred of the police rather than an adhesion to the six points, the fact was that Chartism was the word which summed up for them their political attitudes. John Plummer, recalling his own politics in 1848, before he became converted to the views of the political economists, recalled the influence of Gerald Massey, the Chartist poet, whose work was then appearing in Harney's *Red Republican* and other radical journals. Although by the time his account was published he himself had given up radicalism and had become the protégé of Lord Brougham, he still considered, as late as 1860, that then, as well as in 1848, the opinions of Massey were 'most in accordance with the general tone of opinion entertained by the majority of working men of the present day'.[7]

The 1847 election revived Chartist enthusiasm in the main provincial centres. Huge meetings addressed by Chartist candidates were reported in the *Northern Star* as the election grew closer, and Harney and O'Connor began to predict a Chartist bench in the House. The potato famine in Ireland had brought that country's ills back into the headlines, and with the death of O'Connell in 1847, a major barrier to the recognition of the common interests of the popular movements in the two countries was removed. Cooperation between Irish and British workmen had existed in many provincial centres, in spite of the efforts of O'Connell and of the Catholic Church to prevent it. In the winter of 1847 this increased considerably, to the alarm of the Home Office, where such collaboration was regarded as much more serious than the agitation of the British Chartists alone. Other voices were heard. Refugees from various German states, from the Austro-Hungarian Empire and from France, had, since 1845, been organised in London in the Society of Fraternal Democrats. Reports of meetings and social events in which Chartists took part with the refugees appeared in the *Star* – at times to the annoyance of O'Connor, who considered that Ireland, France and America were sufficient of a world coverage for the newspaper, and that the small (and it has to be admitted) rather quarrelsome socialist and other refugee groups from Central Europe had little to say that would interest the main *Star* readership. Harney, however, the editor, and Jones who since 1846 was working as literary editor of the paper, were passionately interested in all that concerned popular and revolutionary movements throughout the world. Harney had made the acquaintance of Frederick Engels in 1844, beginning a friendship that was to last his lifetime, and Jones soon became intimate with the family of Karl Marx, whom he first met in 1847. Engels knew James Leach, leader of the Manchester Chartists, and other of the Manchester men. Both Marx and Engels watched the Chartists with close attention, wrote for their journals, discussed their ideas and activities in private correspondence, and almost certainly drew some of their descriptions of working-class behaviour and ideas from their observation of the movement. By the winter of 1847-8, Chartism was an internationally-known movement, and in Britain it was a movement which reached out towards Europe and towards the areas of European emigration in which former Chartists had settled.

Collection of signatures to the third petition was well under way by the end of February, when Europe was aroused by the revolution in France. The declaration of the French republic was seized on with enthusiasm by the Chartists. 'France has the Republic, England shall have the Charter' became a national slogan.

The French revolution of 1848 was very different, in Chartist eyes, from the risings of 1830. Peter McDouall referred sarcastically to the 1830 events in France as 'the late revolution which merely deposed a Bourbon and substituted a baboon',[8] but, like everyone else in the movement, he saw the 1848 republic as the beginning of a new age in Europe. It was at this time that many new younger men came into the Chartist movement, and, as Benjamin Wilson reported from Halifax, 'it had become a common practice to march through the streets in military order'.[9]

The Halifax Chartists, like those in most districts, called a meeting to greet the new republic. They had held a crowded meeting only a week or two earlier, at which Ernest Jones, who now styled himself the 'true representative' of Halifax, spoke for two and a half hours on the state of the country and the virtues of the Land Plan.[10] For their meeting on France, however, they had no national speakers. All the resolutions at the crowded meeting in the Oddfellows Hall were introduced by local men. The chairman was Jonathan Gaukroger, an elector who had been one of Jones's proposers at the hustings a few months earlier. He urged the principles of moral force on the audience, but was booed for doing so by what the local paper described as 'the younger element' among them. Isaac Clisset, bill-poster, proposed the first resolution, that

> This meeting rejoices with the republicans of France that they have completely overcome their enemies and established the power of the people of that nation; having set an example worthy of imitation by all nations crushed beneath the tyrannical sway of kingcraft, but more especially to those nations governed by a tyrannical oligarchy.

James Boden, a woolcomber who worked as assistant to James Haigh, 'the Chartist butcher', spoke to the next resolution. He was seconded by George Webber, weaver, and supported by John Snowden, woolcomber and one of the town's leading radicals. The meeting passed with enthusiasm, the resolution that

> It is the opinion of this meeting that the sufferings and privations which the working classes of this country are at present enduring is a consequence of class legislation, and that no permanent relief can be obtained until the people's charter becomes the law of the land; and should this measure of justice be much longer withheld, nothing can prevent the people from aspiring after and ultimately obtaining, a similar change in the constitution to that which the French people have so recently obtained . . . [11]

Similar meetings were held in these weeks throughout Britain. Henry Solly recalled that his own enthusiasm and that of the more radical members of his congregation led him to call a meeting of welcome to the new regime in his church – to the horror of some of his more wealthy supporters.[12]

Plans for the new petition were rushed ahead. On 11 March the *Northern Star* announced that a convention was to be called in London to supervise the presentation of the petition and to consider further action. Delegates were to be elected at open-air meetings as in the earliest days. If the meetings were not on the scale of those of 1838, and clearly they were not, they were nevertheless bigger and more enthusiastic than any that had been held for several years. In Halifax a meeting, estimated by the *Star* at ten thousand and by the local paper at between three and four thousand, enthusiastically elected Ernest Jones as the town's delegate. Forming into columns as they left the meeting, the Chartists marched past the barracks, where they were cheered by the soldiers as they passed. Within a few days of this incident, the soldiers were transferred to Dublin. On the day of their departure, local Chartists, to the number of around five thousand, turned out and accompanied them to the railway station, accompanied by a brass band and tricolour flag, 'with the evident hope', as the local journal put it, 'of cultivating a mutinous spirit in their ranks'.[13]

Once again, the preparations for the presentation of the petition were accompanied by consideration of what to do in the event of its rejection. In the Chartist strongholds, guns were bought and pikes were sharpened again. Drilling was reported in Lancashire and the West Riding, and this time there is no doubt that serious insurrectionary plans were being made in the nation's capital. As before, the evidence for all this is shadowy – the trials revealed only the tip of the iceberg. Most of the Chartists who remembered the events subsequently were cautious in their accounts, and often presented themselves as having been restraining influences. Ben Wilson, who never himself fell foul of the law, recalled that

> Bill Cockroft, one of the leaders of the physical force party in Halifax, wished me to join the movement. I consented and purchased a gun, although I knew it was a serious thing for a Chartist to have a gun or a pike in his possession. I saw Cockroft, who gave me instructions how to proceed until wanted, which did not occur as the scheme was abandoned . . .[14]

He recalled another friend who had been moulding bullets in his cellar in that year, and spoke of others who had narrow escapes, and many who were actually arrested. In London, Robert Crowe considered that the Chartist Movement

> . . . did not develop its full power until about 1846, but that soon, our agitation, both in England and Ireland, rose to fever heat. The Young Irelanders were in fierce conflict with the adherents of O'Connell, repudiating his 'peace at any price' doctrine. On all sides, especially in the north of England, men were arming; bold and defiant utterances were heard on every hand. . . .[15]

For the younger generation of Chartists, of whom Wilson and Crowe were examples,[16] 1848 represented the high point of their Chartist experience. Since most of the men who survived to tell the nascent labour movement in the 1890s about their Chartist experiences were of this generation, 1848 assumed a greater importance than it may have merited in the overall history of Chartism, the more so as it was the year of European revolutions. A reminiscent interview with Harney by Edward Aveling in 1897 called him 'A straggler of 1848', even though he had been associated with the movement from its inception.

The European revolutions of 1848, however, were a response to political and social conditions totally unlike those in Britain. The British middle class had achieved a propaganda victory of considerable proportions by the repeal, in 1846, of the Corn Laws – the symbol of landed supremacy. If anything they were more alienated from the militant working-class movement after this, since they had no need of crowd turbulence to use as a threat in the background of their repeal campaign. In fact, after the repeal of the Corn Laws, the working-class movement was marginally more sympathetic to the group of traditionalist and ultra-radical MPs who had managed to secure the Ten Hours Act in 1847, than to the mainstream of Whig-Liberal politicians. The question of repeal of the Union with Ireland, central to Chartist demands and programme, had almost no middle-class support outside Ireland.

Ireland itself was probably more like the subject countries of Continental Europe in feeling in 1848 than England was. The conflicts between the leaders of the English and Irish movements may in some part illustrate this difference. Since O'Connell had disavowed the Chartists and trade unionists in 1838, he and his close followers had done their best to keep the movements apart. Ireland and her relations with Great Britain remained central to the programmes and concerns of the Chartists in spite of this, however, and there were a great number of Irishmen among the local and national leaders of the movement. In 1842 the repeal of the Union was included in the preamble to the Chartist petition, along with the repeal of the 1834 Poor Law. In 1847 the first subject on which Feargus spoke as an MP was Ireland, and in December 1847 he moved for a select committee to inquire into the effects of the Union upon Ireland.[17] The death of O'Connell, followig the appalling horrors of two years of famine, changed the nature of Irish nationalist politics. O'Connell's insistance on non-violent methods, his loyalty to the British crown, and his strong belief in the doctrines of political economy were all called into question.

Young Ireland, originally mainly a literary group, turned

increasingly towards politics, and began to invoke traditions other than the O'Connellite. In 1846 the group seceded from O'Connell's Loyal National Repeal Association, and in 1847 formed the Irish Confederation. Like O'Connell, however, they initially repudiated any association with the English Chartists or with their Irish counterparts, the Irish Universal Suffrage Association.[18] When W. H. Dyott, a printer and secretary of the IUSA applied to join the Confederation, he protested against a speech made by one of the leaders of Young Ireland, Thomas Maegher, who had publicly boasted that he was 'no democrat'. The secretary returned Dyott's subscription.[19] Young Ireland's journal, the *Nation*, had already made clear on many occasions that it was 'not a Jacobin journal', and that its editors rejected any association with the Chartists, not only because of the latter's rhetoric of physical force, but also because the editors considered that 'some of their five points are to us an abomination'.[20] Their quarrel was not initially with the Chartists alone, but with the whole republican tradition of the United Irishmen, leaders of the 1798 rising. In England many of the Irish Chartists, including Feargus himself, came from that tradition which was ultra-democratic, mainly republican, and insurrectionary. One indication that the attempt to keep the two traditions apart had not been completely successful, even before 1848, is the fact that repealers in London were organised into the Emmet brigade from as early as 1843. Robert Emmet was the last leader of the United Irishmen, whose unsuccessful attempt at a rising had led to his public execution and decapitation in Dublin in 1804. For the Chartists Emmet was a great hero, his name was toasted at radical dinners, and his defence speech was circulated as a pamphlet and performed as drama or as a recitation in many different parts of the country.[21] The O'Connellite Repeal movement, however, disapproved of the revival of such memories: 'although we revere and respect his memory, we view with horror the principle that brought him to an untimely end',[22] and urged its members not to attend meetings or performances of his trial.

But by the end of 1847 things were changing. The years of O'Connell's leadership had not prevented Ireland from becoming the most depressed country in Europe. Ruled by fiat and coercion, her population decimated by a famine that had been worsened in its effects by the arbitrary nature of the land tenure system and by the free trade dogmas of the British Government and administrators, Ireland offered neither livelihood nor hope to her population. When John Mitchel broke in desperation from the Young Ireland group to form his own journal and his own policy, it was to the traditions of 1798 that he appealed. His journal was entitled *The United Irishman*, and even before the French revolution he was making overtures of friendship to the Chartists. In a leading article at the end of February 1848, he urged his readers not to dismiss Chartism. 'Every Chartist is a *Repealer* to begin with; and all English labourers and artizans are Chartists.'[23] Irish Chartists like Patrick O'Higgins and W. H. Dyott wrote in his columns, and regular reports of English Chartist activities as they concerned Ireland were published there.

But in the event the Irish rising of the summer of 1848 was even less effectual than those in other parts of Europe. Some of the latter at least achieved temporary gains for liberalism and nationalism. At Balingarry all that was enacted was a farce. Irish politics had not prepared the nation for insurrection, and the peasantry were broken and debilitated by the years of famine. The combination of middle-class nationalism and peasant and artisan discontent that had produced explosions throughout Europe produced in Ireland only a failed rising and a despairing flow of emigrants.

Within Britain itself, where there was little if any middle-class support for the working-class movement, the Chartist attempt to force democracy upon the constitution was met with a solid and confident system of authority backed by all sections of the middle and upper classes.

The revolutions in Europe did, however, introduce an element of unease on the part of the authorities which had been absent from the earlier crises. The Chartists proposed to call a mass meeting in London on 10 April, from which a procession would walk to the Houses of Parliament to present the petition. The 1842 petition had been accompanied by such a procession, and the petition had been handed in with neither violence nor disorder. In 1848, however, arming, drilling and republican oratory induced a more guarded attitude from the authorities. The open association of the Confederate movement with the Chartists in England added to the unease. Collection of signatures to the petition was hurried on. Again, it seems likely that the most committed amongst the Chartists had lost patience with petitioning, for there is little mention of it at the meetings in support of the French. The lack of numbers, and the alleged high incidence of forgeries discovered after the petition had been delivered, have been used to ridicule the Chartist efforts of 1848. The lowest estimate of genuine signatures, however, was round 1½ million, and it must be remembered that the number of signatures was never a clear index of Chartist enthusiasm or activity.

The disaffection in Europe was reflected in the Chartist journals as the year turned. Ernest Jones published a fifty-verse poem in the *Labourer*, called the 'March of Freedom', attacking monarchies and empires throughout the world.

Lopsided thrones are creaking
For 'Loyalty' is dead;
And commonsense is speaking
Of honesty instead

And coming freedom whispers
'Mid the rushing of her wings
Of loyalty to nature,
Not loyalty to kings . . .

Bohemia's mountains echo
Tones of Ziskra's drum
And the nobles see in thought
The modern Hussites come.

E'en Russia's frozen north
Is dawning on our ken
And sends Bakounine forth
To tell us it has *men* . . .

Still onward Freedom wandered
Till she touched on British soil
Elysium of money
And *Tartarus* of toil . . .

'Why weeps your sorrowing sister,
Still bleeding, unredressed,
'Neath *Russell*, England's *Nicholas*,
The Poland of the West.

Cry 'Liberty to Erin!'
It is a debt you owe;
Had *ye* not armed his hand
He ne'er had struck a blow . . .

Then Hurrah for the Charter,
On Shannon, Thames and Tweed!
Now, scythemen to the harvest!
Reap, ye who sowed the seed![24]

The Fraternal Democrats had, for several years, been issuing appeals to the democracy of Europe. 1848 was the year in which these declarations and appeals seemed to be bearing fruit. On the night of 24

February, Thomas Frost, a young Chartist printer from Croydon, was attending a meeting of the Fraternal Democrats in central London. On the platform were representatives of the participating nations, France, Germany, Hungary, Italy, Poland, whose national flags were draped around the hall. Harney was speaking for Britain, and Carl Schapper, painter and adventurer, for Germany.

> Suddenly the news of the events in Paris was brought in. The effect was electrical. Frenchmen, Germans, Poles, Magyars sprang to their feet, embraced, shouted and gesticulated in the wildest enthusiasm. Snatches of oratory were delivered in excited tones, and flags were caught from the walls, to be waved exultingly, amidst cries of *Hoch! Eljeu! Vive la Republique!*. Then the doors were opened, and the whole assemblage descended to the street and, with linked arms and colours flying, marched to the meeting-place of the Westminster Chartists in Dean Street, Soho. There another enthusiastic fraternization took place, and great was the clinking of glasses that night in and around Soho and Leicester Square . . . [25]

The Bradford Chartists welcomed the French revolution with a camp meeting on Peep Green, at which the local paper reported them as singing:

> Britannia's sons, though slaves you be!
> God, your creator, made you free;
> And life to all, and being, gave
> But never, never, made a slave.
>
> All men are equal in his sight –
> The bound, the free, the black, the white;
> He made them all – them freedom gave
> He made the man – man made the slave.

George White, Irish woolcomber from Bradford, made the main speech, and other speakers included Samuel Kydd, shoemaker member of the national executive, Benjamin Rushton, Ovenden, fancy weaver, and John Smith, Irish shoemaker from Bradford.[26]

In Manchester the influx of the O'Connellite Irish to the popular movement was probably most significant statistically, for it was here that the greatest number of recent immigrants were to be found and the divisions had been most entrenched. O'Connor himself went to Manchester and then to a mass meeting at Oldham Edge to celebrate the new alliance. Here, at a meeting chaired by powerloom weaver Richard Pilling, O'Connor called upon each man in the crowd of thirteen thousand to 'swear with him to high heaven, uncovered, never to abandon the cause until freedom had been obtained'.[27]

The close connection between Irish and English politics has been too often neglected in the study of Chartism. 1848 was to show many examples of this connection. O'Connell's Loyal National Repeal Organisation in the early forties had been based on the same organisational principles as his earlier Catholic Association, and on the political strategy of that organisation. It relied on 'moral force' only, and on the massive display of numbers, organised through and supported by the church, as well as by its own paid staff. It organised a series of enormous public meetings, culminating in one at Clontarf in October 1843, to which perhaps a million people were expected to turn up. The Government called O'Connell's bluff and banned the meeting. To avoid bloodshed, or at best uncontrolled violence, O'Connell called it off. Moral force was defeated at Clontarf. The Chartist strategy for April 1848 may be seen in part as an intended re-enactment of Clontarf, but without the failure of nerve.

The decision to call a monster Chartist meeting to send off the third petition was taken at the Chartist Convention which met in London on 4 April. The Convention was to organise the meeting, supervise the presentation of the petition on the same day, and in the event of the petition's rejection, the Convention was to transform itself into a National Assembly which should take over the government of the country. The Chartist tactics, in short, were to be a combination of Irish repeal politics, Chartist political and social programmes and French revolutionary tactics.

Was 10 April a failure for the Chartists, and could things have gone differently on that day? Certainly there were neither the numbers nor the determined action which the Convention had hoped for. Ernest Jones was later to blame the Chartists for their failure to support the Convention, and the meeting, and for not 'withholding from the gin-palace the money that would have given strength to their Democratic senate'.[28] He also blamed lack of unity among delegates for the overall failure of the Chartist movement. But all these must be seen as symptoms rather than as causes of Chartist weakness, if weakness there was, in 1848.

The Chartists throughout Britain were certainly alert and active. Many of the younger men who had entered the movement in the last two or three years had been waiting for the kind of signals which were now coming from Europe. But the strength of Chartism had lain in the participation of whole communities and of whole trades. It had also lain in an unquestioning belief in the efficacy of political change to bring about social improvement. In the late forties many of these ideas were no longer so potent. Many trades had begun to organise for more limited but achievable aims. Cooperative societies and friendly societies, land company branches and redemption societies[29] were offering forms of social self-help in which men and women had invested time and money. Much of the achievement in these areas would be threatened by violent confrontations with authority. And, locally and nationally, the Government was preparing for confrontation. Special constables – something of a joke in 1842 – were now supported by efficient police forces in many districts. Electric telegraph communication traversed the country – and the Government took over control of the whole system in anticipation of national response to the Convention's lead in April. Troops could now be moved rapidly by rail, and the Government had already demonstrated, in Glasgow, that it was prepared to use troops, to fire on crowds, and to kill rioters.

Before 10 April, blood had been shed in Europe and in Britain. The French republic had not been achieved without bloodshed in the streets of Paris. In London the authorities prepared for violent confrontation. Special constables were sworn in in large numbers,[30] the Queen was sent for safety to the Isle of Wight, the military command of London was given to the Duke of Wellington, who deployed a prodigious force of military throughout the capital.[31] London had already, earlier in the year, experienced street rioting against the income tax and against the local administration of the Poor Law. In Glasgow violent anti-Poor-Law riots had occurred in which troops had fired on the crowd and six men had been killed. These were protests by starving people against the lack of provision by the Poor Law authorities, and involved looting of shops, especially food shops. No Chartist leaders were among those transported for their part in the clashes, and it may well have been, as the Glasgow delegate, James Adams, later declared at the Convention, that the Chartists had tried to restrain the rioters. Nevertheless, Chartist slogans were shouted, and cries of *Vive la Republique* were heard. Such actions have fired off revolutionary risings, and the authorities were more nervous as the day of the London demonstration arrived. Disraeli wrote on 8 March: 'all are swamped and merged in the mighty theme of how Europe, or perhaps England, is to be governed. 6 shot at Glasgow; here cockney riots of little boys.'[32] Later in the month, he wrote to his sister: 'Affairs are very bad, but in my opinion will be much worse. All one can hope for now is to put one's house in order during the temporary lull – if there be one.'[33] Government prohibitions, street violence in Europe and in Britain, divided councils at the national Convention, all combined to produce an ambivalent attitude among the Chartists themselves. Some accepted that the day of the presentation of the petition was to be peaceful, if defiant, in tone. Others, like Frederick Lessner and John Beford Leno, were convinced that violence was inevitable, and that arms should be carried.[34] Leno and his friends stayed away from the meeting when it became clear that the leaders had forbidden the carrying of arms. In those days, he later recalled, 'I believed more in fighting that I do now. In truth, I was for rebellion and civil war, and despaired of ever obtaining justice, or what I then conceived it to be, save by revolution.'[35] It is impossible to know how many took up the same attitude, or how far it contributed to the comparatively low numbers. It may well be the case that one part of the potential crowd stayed at home through fear of violence, while another did not attend because of its formal prohibition.

As the day of the meeting approached, respectable opinion became increasingly apprehensive. Thackeray wrote an article in the *Morning Chronicle* of 14 March, endeavouring to bring home to its readers the urgency of the situation. He wrote in his diary, however:

> Wrote an article on the Kennington Meeting for the M.C. . . . I tried in vain to convince the fine folks at Mrs. Fox's that revolution was upon us: that we were wicked in our scorn of the people. They all thought there was poverty and discomfort to be sure, but that they were pretty good in themselves; that powder and liveries were very decent and proper tho' certainly absurd.[36]

Thomas Cooper, although he still kept the title of 'the Chartist' on the title pages of his books, was by now a minor member of London's literary intelligentsia, and, perhaps significantly, spent the evening before 10 April at a literary soirée at the home of Garth Wilkinson. He wrote later: 'In the year 1848 . . . the Chartists were wilder than they were in 1842 or than the members of the First Convention were in 1838. Experience had rendered me a little wiser than to suffer myself to be mixed up in any plot, however plausible: so I kept out of them all . . . '[37] It may be, however, that the invitation which so pleased Cooper, to attend the evening at the Wilkinson household on the night before the Chartist demonstration, was connected with his Chartist past. In his correspondence Garth Wilkinson showed the same ambivalent attitude towards the Chartists and the proposed meeting that is to be found in many of the more radical members of the middle class. A few days earlier he had written to his wife:

> London is in a state of panic from the contemplated meeting of the Chartists, 200,000 strong on Monday; for myself, nothing that happened would in the least degree surprise me: I expect a Revolution within two years: there may be

one within three days. The *Times* is alarmed beyond measure. I have it from good authority that the Chartists are determined to have their wishes granted . . . [38]

In his report of his dinner party, he refers to Cooper as 'the Chartist poet'.

Richard Whiting, a small boy at boarding school in London at the time, recalled the excitement of the day. The children were kept indoors, discussing the expected revolution, while their fathers paraded as special constables, and the headmaster went into the centre of London to observe the day's events and to prepare for any necessary action.[39] Citizens and friends who enrolled as special constables never ceased to talk about the events. They ranged from a bevy of London coal-whippers to the exiled Louis Napoleon, soon to be the surprising beneficiary of the events of 1848 in France. They included Richard, the son of Count Metternich, and, in Richard Whiting's words, 'everybody who had a character or a position to lose . . . ' Nassau Senior's daughter recalled that 'Every man I knew was a special constable' and that the ladies of her neighbourhood predicted bloodshed. One whose son was a special constable declared, 'If only I had another son I should not mind.'[40]

Many of the special constables, like Whiting's father, had been more or less pressurised into signing on. Others had signed on in romantic enthusiasm to defend their country and its government from revolution. One former special recalled years later that he had kept his baton for many years after 1848, but that he had 'often wondered what on earth I should have done with it, had we come to blows. I used to picture myself encountering a tall Irishman with a long spear, ready to run me through, and I did not relish the picture . . . '[41]

Whatever the motivations of the specials, another group of middle-class men took an active part in trying to defuse the potentially violent sitution in April 1848 by peaceful means. Charles Kingsley and the group with which he was associated, who later became known as the Christian Socialists, began their political activity on 10 April, and followed it up in the next few days with posters, placards and speeches urging peaceful behaviour and promising support for the redress of grievances to those who accepted their advice. The fact that Kingsley – a character with great histrionic talent – on one accasion leapt on to a Chartist platform, declaring 'I am a Church of England clergyman – and a Chartist' has left some people, including some historians, with the idea that he was sympathetic to Chartism. In fact, Kingsley, a humane and determined man, but certainly no democrat, was one of Chartism's most effective opponents. His wife, writing many years later, was at some pains to make clear her husband's real attitude, and that of his journal *Politics for the People*, stressing the latter's 'loyal, conservatist tone . . . and the gravity, if not severity, with which it attacked physical force Chartism, monster meetings, and the demand for universal suffrage by men who had neither education nor moral self-government to qualify them for a vote'.[42] To have sympathy for people living in poverty, and to be prepared to engage in a dialogue with some Chartists represents perhaps a significant change in certain middle-class attitudes, of which Kingsley was one of the pioneers. But as for his attitude towards the strategy of the Chartists on 10 April 1848, it is only necessary to read Kingsley's contemptuous account in his Chartist novel, *Alton Locke*, to realise his intense and absolute hostility.

The authorities and the respectable inhabitants of London were alarmed by Chartism itself, but perhaps much more than had been the case up until then, by the two additional factors of the French example and the open association between the Irish Confederates and the Chartists. The language of leading confederates, like Dr Reynolds of Liverpool, was very much more belligerent and insurrectionist than the usual run of Chartist oratory, and probably contributed to the speedy passing, early in April, of the so-called 'gagging bill', which made seditious speech a felony and considerably increased the penalties.[43] There were, in any case, statutes already in existence which had not been invoked on earlier occasions – for example, it was in fact illegal for a petition to be presented by more than twenty people to the House of Commons, and it was, of course, illegal to hold a meeting within one mile of Westminster Hall.[44] These restrictions had been ignored by the authorities on the occasion of the 1842 petition, and on other occasions since, but in 1848 they were invoked. The earlier demonstrations and minor riots in the London streets had already shown that the Metropolitan Police were prepared to forbid actions under these statutes. When the meeting at Kennington Common was declared illegal by the Home Office, and it became clear that the authorities were prepared to enforce their prohibitions, the Chartist Convention had to decide on the tactics it would pursue, and on the extent to which it would defy the police and the Government.

The story of 10 April 1848 has been told so many times – by participants, observers and historians, that an attempt to reverse the accepted picture of events may seem perverse. Fortunately a study has been made of the events of the day which for the first time puts them into the context of London politics and of national politics, and which also examines the way in which the story has been distorted subsequently.[45] There is space here only to describe briefly what happened, and to look at some of the implications.

Faced with the tense situation, the hostility and armed preparations of the authorities, and with changing attitudes among their followers, the Chartist leaders, meeting in the Convention, responded in several different ways. Bronterre O'Brien, back again in the Chartist ranks, was for complete acceptance of the demands of the authorities, for winning support and admiration and hence possible future cooperation from middle-class allies by cautious and reasonable behaviour. He sneered at Ernest Jones, whose talk of the support available from armed Chartists in the north of England he found totally unconvincing. But he was in a very small minority. Jones was full of enthusiasm for his northern 'constituents', and argued for organisation and planning in the movement. His perspective was still very much that of Continental Europe, and he saw the Convention as the provisional government of Britain. O'Connor, as usual, steered between extremes. His whole tactic was based on the mass showing of numbers – in the petition, the meeting and the procession. He was, however, always aware of the danger of clashes with authority which could escalate into bloodshed. He had always declared that the aim of the Kennington Common meeting was the peaceful demonstration of numbers. Had there been any other intention, it is hardly likely that the meeting would have been held south of the river (Kennington Common being where the Oval cricket ground is today). Until the very morning of the demonstration McGrath, chairman of the Convention, was trying to persuade the police commissioner to allow the procession, but when it became clear that the prohibition was to be enforced, the Chartists decided to proceed with the meeting, defying that prohibition, but to abandon the procession, and to allow a small group of their leaders to take the petition to the Commons in a cab.

On the night before 10 April, London was tense and excited. Duncombe wrote to O'Connor, urging caution,[46] and Thomas Allsop urged on Feargus a policy of defiance with the minimum of violence.

> Nothing rashly. The government must be met with calm and firm defiance. Violence may be overcome with violence, but a resolute determination not to submit cannot be overcome. . . . Aim not to destroy the government, but to render a class government impossible.[47]

The morning of the 10th saw London crammed with military, and police – many of the latter armed. Chartists leaving the northern parts of the city passed these evidences of official preparedness on their way to their meeting. The bridges in particular were well guarded; a little to the south of Blackfriars Bridge Gammage noted a group of fifty police armed with cutlasses, in addition to the pensioners (ex-soldiers) on the steamboat pier north of the river and some hundreds of police on the south bank. Arrived at the common, O'Connor was sent for to a tavern where Richard Mayne, commissioner of police, impressed on him the intention of the authorities to enforce their prohibition of the procession. He agreed, however, that they would not attempt to disperse the meeting if good order was maintained. O'Connor then addressed the gathering – numbered at perhaps 20,000 – and for those beyond the reach of even his stentorian tones, other leaders spoke in different parts of the common from other platforms – including Philip McGrath, Ernest Jones, G. W. M. Reynolds, John West and George Julian Harney. Although there was ample evidence of the Irish presence, including banners with *Ireland for the Irish*,[48] the Irish speakers were Chartists rather than Confederates.

When the meeting broke up, the Chartists dribbled slowly back to the city, well behind the cabs, which, the first three carrying the petition[49] and the fourth O'Connor and the NCA executive, had been allowed across the bridge immediately. The crowds were allowed through only in small groups, and although a few doughty spirits contested the police control to the extent of the odd scuffle, in general the police and troops demonstrated a complete control of the bridges by which alone the Chartists could reach the centre of government.

> When they came back at night, angry, hungry, footsore, they found the bridges barred and the sullen canon between them and the palaces, public offices, banks, and, what was still more of a hardship . . . their miserable homes. They were filtered over in detachments at last and kept on the run till they reached their hovels dead beat . . . [50]

So Richard Whiting recalled, attributing the whole arrangement to the military strategy of the Duke of Wellington. But Wellington was certainly opposing an army that was not there. There is little doubt that the majority of those attending the meeting had no intention of fighting. If battle was contemplated, it was to have been after the rejection of the petition.

The petition was duly presented – in its large physical bulk – to the House of Commons. Before O'Connor was required to speak to it, however, it was referred to a committee for examination, and in a remarkably short time the committee reported that, far from having the claimed five and a half million and more signatures, it contained barely two million, of which many were palpable forgeries, and others bogus or obscene. (*Punch* printed a cartoon showing the response of Colonel Sibthorpe, the most ultra-Tory Member of the House, to the information that he appeared as a signatory.) O'Connor declared that he would not, in view of this, move the acceptance of the petition by the House, and the Convention was again faced with planning the next stage of operations.

As in 1839, the delegates to the Convention decided to go back to their constituents. Although many textbooks and commentators have dated the end of Chartism as 10 April 1848, this was not at the time seen as a final end to the movement, nor does it appear to be a decisive date. The spring and summer of 1848 saw a great deal of activity, many arrests and trials, and several attempts at rising – or at least riots which took on a more serious complexion than anything that had occurred since 1842. The end of the year, with the leaders of the movement in prison, the Land Company in legal difficulties, the *Star* beginning to lose support and direction and the 'year of revolutions' in Europe having ended in a rearrangement of traditional authority rather than in any significant shift of power towards the populations as a whole, is perhaps a better date. Even this misses many important elements of Chartism and many local organisations which did survive for a decade or more. April 1848, however, was far from being any kind of a halt to London Chartism. In the city the number of meetings increased, marches by day and by night continued into the summer. In the entry for 3 June in his journal, Greville wrote:

> The Government are now getting seriously uneasy about the Chartist manifestations in various parts of the country, especially in London, and at the repeated assemblings and marchings of great bodies of men. Le Marchant told me that two months ago he received accounts he thought very alarming of the wide-spreading disaffection of the people . . . and that many of those who on the 10th of April went out as special constables declare they would not do so again if another manifestation required it . . . [51]

In the provinces, after the initial sense of disappointment at the failure of the petition and the indecision of the Convention, activity continued to increase throughout the summer. In May John Mitchel was tried in Dublin, and sentenced to transportation. Demonstrations of protest erupted throughout the active centres of Chartism – nightly marches took place in Nottingham, Manchester and Ashton, and troops were stationed in Manchester to prevent the gathering there of marchers from all the surrounding districts on the night of 31 May.

So far from Chartist feeling declining in the immediate aftermath of 10 April, there seems to have been an increase in violence in the response of many of the younger Chartists, who were now talking of revolution or of military action to rescue Mitchel and other imprisoned leaders. This violent talk, and in some places, action, led to a polarisation within the movement, and to the withdrawal from activity of more moderate elements. The Mayor of Nottingham reported that some of the language of speakers at the demonstrations there had been 'disavowed by those who have hitherto been the Chartist leaders in this town'. The arrests of leaders with a following in the major centres of dissaffection began soon after Mitchel's sentence.

Relief – perhaps something of an over-reaction to the frenzied preparations for conflict on 10 April – led many observers to declare that Chartism was at an end. Richard Cobden was among these, and was taken to task by the Tory *Halifax Guardian*.

> Mr. Cobden declares the Chartists to be 'a small insignificant and powerless party'. There are a few people in Lancashire and Yorkshire who can tell him a different story. And if Mr. Cobden will accept a single engagement to report for the *Halifax Guardian* the next Chartist demonstration he will either alter his story or prove himself vastly inferior in candour and intelligence to the ordinary newspaper reporter. . . . We are no Chartists . . . We have no wish to over-rate the number or import of the Chartist body. But men who muster in tens of thousands to demonstrate their attachment to a political principle are neither 'small' nor 'insignificant'.[52]

Halifax, Leeds and Bradford were areas of great activity in the early summer, when pitched battles between police and Chartists resulted in arrests and rescues in rapid succession. Bradford's delegate to the National Assembly, which on 1 May took the place of the Convention, was David Lightowler, a man who had been associated with the insurrectionary end of Chartism since 1839.[53] His selection as delegate was therefore of some significance. By the end of May the situation in Bradford, where a large number of the Chartists had always been Irish, and where the Irish were said now to number half the Chartists,[54] was so turbulent that Peter McDouall was sent by the Chartist executive to take charge. He found the Chartists drilling in uniform, and setting up a National Guard. When contingents came to a meeting from other West Riding towns, the Halifax men marched 'in sections, each headed by an officer, wearing white blouses and black belts, the Chartist rosettes and green caps with red bands, which had a very imposing effect when the military bearing and steady march of the men was considered. On they came with music playing, banners flying, and the glittering pikes flashing in the sun.'[55] For a time the West Riding Chartists disputed the control of Bradford with the police. A local blacksmith, Isaac Jefferson, was at the centre of much of the organisation and of some of the more dramatic events. One of the chief local manufacturers of pikes, he was described as 'a burley middle-sized man, with a profundity of whisker and moustachio, without neck cloth, attired in a velveteen shooting jacket and wearing a cap of knight templar form'.[56] The police made several unsuccessful attempts to arrest Jefferson – who was known locally as Wat Tyler – but his great strength and the support of the Chartists in his district defeated them for a long while. On one occasion their handcuffs were too small for his wrists – on another he was immediately rescued. There is no doubt that some of the members of the association and many of the Irish believed that some kind of rising would occur in the summer of 1848. At the trial of the local Chartists in the winter of 1848, evidence was produced of plans for an organised rising of some kind in August, and Benjamin Wilson's discreet evidence much later supports the suggestion. When Ernest Jones was arrested, in June, George Webber declared:

> Ernest Jones was the real representative of Halifax, and no sooner did the intelligence reach Halifax on Wednesday night that Jones had been imprisoned, than a meeting – a torchlight meeting – took place on their highest mountains, and it was resolved that if a similar sentence should be passed on Jones as had been done on Mitchel, though they should stand alone, they would erect barricades and bid defiance to the bloodthirsty Government of England . . . if necessary proclaim the republic of Yorkshire and Lancashire.[57]

Ernest Jones had been arrested in Manchester on 6 June, for a speech which he had made in London, at Bishop Bonner's Fields, on 4 June. In the wake of Mitchel's sentence, London was alive with rumours of fighting in Dublin. On that Sunday evening, Jones had referred to the possibility of an Irish revolt, urged his hearers to stay clear of all partial outbreaks and rioting, reported outbreaks in Manchester and Bradford, and urged on the Chartists the immediate setting up of organisations which could handle their demands in a controlled way. Within the meaning of the new Act, many phrases certainly sounded seditious.

> Rest assured that I shall not preach a miserable, namby pamby doctrine of non-resistance and passive obedience. But at the same time I shall preach a doctrine

of manly firmness and not hot-headed impetuosity. If you mean to do anything, see well first if you have the power to do it; and then, having made up your mind, do not let even death itself prevent you from carrying it into effect. . . . Only preparation – only organisation is wanted, and the Green Flag shall float over Downing Street and St. Stephens. Only energy is wanted – only determination – and what will be the result? Why, that John Mitchel and John Frost will be brought back, and Sir George Grey, and Lord John Russell will be sent to change places with them.[58]

The audience at Bishop Bonner's fields, and at the many meetings held in London and the provinces, was not, perhaps, the traditional Chartist audience. The presence of police and military turned all the meetings into potential clashes, and the kind of family and community attendance which had characterised the huge demonstrations of 1838 and 1839 was no longer possible.

The summer of 1848 was a violent one in parts of the provinces, and those leaders who had a following in London, Lancashire or the West Riding were arrested and imprisoned by the autumn. The number of Chartists arrested and punished was considerably less than in 1839-40 or than in 1842. Nevertheless men like Ernest Jones, Peter McDouall, George White, James Leach and John West and nearly three hundred others were sent for trial, and most of them spent at least a year in prison. While they were there the final collapse of the Land Company took place.

O'Connor was caught up in the vain attempts to preserve his Land Plan, and these coincided with the onset of the malady which drove him mad and then killed him.[59] The *Northern Star* changed hands, being owned for a short time in 1852 by Harney, but neither it nor any of the journals which Ernest Jones began after he left prison in 1851 ever paid their way. Chartism as a mass movement was over, and although it took a decade to die, it persisted only as a marginal force in British social history in those years.

CHAPTER 14

Conclusion

THE question of why Chartism declined, and of why its decline was so relatively rapid and complete, has never been satisfactorily answered. For some writers the answer was self-evident. If Chartism was basically a gut reaction to hunger and to the disorganisation caused in traditional industries by the early experience of industrialisation, then clearly the better economic climate which accompanied and followed the Great Exhibition of 1851, the increasing stability of Britain's major industries in that period and the organisations which these conditions allowed to develop among the new industrial workforce are enough to account for its decline and death. With the death of 'hunger Chartism' the rational side of the movement moved into the organisation of consumer cooperatives, new model trade unions, reading-rooms, mechanics' institutes, local government, friendly societies and all the various organisations which the skilled workers developed in the third quarter of the nineteenth century. Some versions of this explanation imply that the process was to some extent a betrayal by the skilled and regularly employed (the 'aristocracy of labour') of the aspirations of their less fortunate fellows. This idea is a familiar one, and may include the idea of a conscious move by the employing class to divide the skilled workers from the rest. Another explanatory framework is offered by the view that the Chartist period represented a conflict between a consciously hegemonic middle class and the traditional culture of the British working class. The end of this conflict was signalled by the end of Chartism, and by the incorporation of the articulate members of the working class into the traditions and values of the middle class.[1]

Each of these explanations has some force, but none really explains the matter satisfactorily. It is certainly true that in many major industries the third quarter of the century was one of greater stability. But it was not for that reason one of class collaboration. Indeed it would be strange if the long history of conflict within industry were to have ended suddenly with a brief spell of prosperity. Some of the bitterest industrial conflict in history occurred in major sectors of British industry in the 1850s. The Preston cotton strike, the engineering lock-out, strikes in the building, brickmaking, and other industries produced violence, hunger and conflict. And the prosperity was in any case not as striking or as long-lasting as some historians have suggested. The fifties were for many very hard years. W. E. Adams, a printer, recorded in his diary his experiences of seeking work in the early part of 1855.

It was the winter of the Crimean War – the severest as regards weather, the dreariest as regards depression, the direst as regards distress, that we had had for years. I find in my old diary a note on the state of the country – 'Everywhere the cry is want of work. In Macclesfield especially, steady men, industrious men, have great difficulty in obtaining bread. . . The weavers "play" nearly as often as they work, some of them oftener. . . One young man in Newcastle-under-Lyme, now compelled to seek bread by "busking" . . . a thrower by trade, [he] said he had been offered 6s. 6d a week at a factory in that town.'[2]

On his journey through England Adams was unable to find work at his own trade and everywhere met distress among the major trades of the country. And yet this was a year in which political activity was minimal, and which saw no kind of mass Chartist action, with the exception of the turn-out of 20,000 people in London at the funeral of Feargus O'Connor. Life for the unskilled, the outworkers and the casually employed was very little, if any, better in the early fifties than in the forties, as the investigations of Mayhew and of the *Morning Chronicle* demonstrated.

Popular experience did not register a total change of perspective in the early fifties which would be enough to account for the decline of Chartism as a focus for hope of improvement. Industrial conflict among the skilled workers and continuing grinding poverty among the unskilled, with seasonal and trade recessions occurring as before if not, perhaps, with the extreme hardships of the 1839–42 period, present a picture which was like enough to the Chartist years, but which produced no mass demand for political reform. The appeals of political reformers, middle-class or former Chartist leaders, elicited no mass response at all. To explain the position by the suggestion of a betrayal of the mass of the working class by a privileged aristocracy of labour who should have been the natural leaders, but who achieved their own stability and therefore lost interest in the mass of their fellows, is not a sufficient or convincing explanation. The leaders of the Chartists were by no means recruited only from the skilled and better-off trades. Had the less skilled workers wanted to continue the struggle for political rights, leaders would not have been lacking. Men like John West, Macclesfield silk handloom weaver, and George White, woolcomber, died in poverty twenty years after the end of Chartism without having deserted the cause. They had not spent the years after its end living in luxury, but had worked at their trades amongst the same people whom they had led during the Chartist years. Indeed, in the 1860s when agitation for parliamentary reform revived under the leadership of the Reform League, very many of the old Chartist leaders in the localities, men like George Webber, Halifax weaver, John Skelton, Matthew John, Moses Simpson of Hanley, and others up and down the country, emerged to take the lead in local reform initiatives. These men had never abandoned the idea of political reform, but it had assumed for them a different place in their priorities for action.

The suggestion that the militancy of Chartism had been conquered by the attitude and values of the middle class in England, and that the decline of the movement is to be attributed to this may in some ways be nearer to the truth of what happened. It is however a great over-simplification of a complex process. It would clearly be wrong simply to suggest that a working class which could spend a quarter of a century in building up its trade unions, friendly societies and cooperative stores in the teeth of the determined hostility of employers, shopkeepers and the bourgeois press, had been conquered by bourgeois ideology. Nevertheless, the reasons for the end of Chartism are to be sought in the field of ideas as well as in the field of direct economic experience.

Many of the ideas and beliefs which were to become potent in the later years of the nineteenth century may be grouped within a generally 'middle-class' definition. The interests of the commercial class seemed clearly to be served by the philosophy of free trade and non-interference by government in commerce and industry. Elevated into a philosophy, the creed of *laissez-faire* was taken into all aspects of life. The market had its own benevolent laws, population growth was regulated by factors in human nature and human behaviour which were almost entirely outside the control of any government, every individual in society had within himself the potential for his own realisation if he was left alone to work for himself with the minimum of government control of his activity or taxation of his income. The Chartists had countered this philosophy with their own alternative, but there were, even at the height of the Chartist movement, areas of overlap. Like the commercial classes, the working class resented the power of patronage and the enormous control of areas of social life which was exercised by landowners and their ecclesiastical allies. For reasons which were in many ways different, members of both middle and working classes resented the attempts to control opinion, whether by restrictions on speech and publication or by the clerical control of education. Within both classes, though not identically organised or motivated, there were movements against the irrationality, corruption and low standards of personal morality which the rulers of traditional society had countenanced for too long. Cooperation between the classes on these questions, however, had not taken place during the Chartist years, because the Chartists could not believe that any group of people who were not prepared to concede the principle of universal suffrage could be sincere about a moral critique of the existing political system. What was more, they did not believe that even the limited reforms of Corn Law repeal and factory reform could be gained except from a Parliament elected by universal suffrage. When the Chartists clashed with the Anti-Corn-Law Leaguers, they did so partly because they distrusted the self-interested arguments of the employers, but partly also because they saw the single-issue campaign for repeal as a diversion from the much more important campaign for the suffrage. Nevertheless, working-class radicalism contained its own non-political ideas – those of socialism stemming from Robert Owen, and reinforced to some extent in the late forties by the newer Continental socialist ideas. As the propaganda of free trade became more powerful throughout the forties, and the increasingly economic analysis of power and influence, the certainties about political solutions became less certain. To an extent the Chartist Land Plan, and certainly the early and increasingly successful consumer cooperatives, the friendly societies and the nationally-organised trade unions which were being established as the forties drew to a close, seemed to show that some successes could be achieved without the suffrage.

To the Leaguers' declaration that repeal of the Corn Laws would mean lower food prices, better trade and greater freedom, the Chartists replied that repeal would make little difference without political power, and that it could not in any case be passed through the existing House of Commons. When, in 1846, the Corn Laws were repealed, and when, apparently, trade improved in many sectors of industry (1848 and 1849 were said to be the two best years in the worsted industry for many years) the prophecies of the Chartist leaders took a beating. When, in 1847, an unreformed House of Commons also passed the Ten Hours Act, introduced by the radical John Fielden, the possibilities of pressurising the existing structures seemed to be demonstrated. The Chartists and many members of the working class developed doubts about the absolute priority of political reform. When Ernest Jones came out of prison in 1850, it was against his own party that he was arguing when he made his famous speech: 'Some tell you that teetotalism will get you the Charter: the Charter don't lie at the bottom of a glass of water. Some tell you social cooperation will do it; cooperation is at the mercy of those who hold political power . . . '[3] Already by 1850 the fundamental importance of the Charter had been undermined. The prophecies of the Chartist leaders had foundered, those of the Anti-Corn-Law League had assumed credibility. The Corn Laws had been repealed – before universal suffrage. Industry had picked up – and had done so apparently as the result of repeal. The Ten Hours Act had been passed by a Whig administration. More regularity of employment meant the possibility of self-help organisations, from trade unions and co-ops to friendly societies, and the revival of prosperity had to some extent softened the operation of the new Poor Law after the defeat of the 'bashaws' and the transference of the supervision of poor relief to direct government control in 1847. This was probably the fundamental break with political solutions. As the decades proceeded, people increasingly looked to parliamentary action simply to protect autonomous organisations. Workers wanted freedom for trade unions to operate rather than government intervention in wage bargaining. They wanted protection for the funds of their own organisations of self-help, rather than government aid. If they continued to hate the workhouse, as they did, they tried to protect themselves from entering it by savings and the mutuality of co-ops, trade unions and insurance groups. A number of Chartist leaders went into branches of working-class insurance in the twenty years after 1850, and these years saw a great increase in societies for that purpose. Obviously all these organisations tended to be mostly made up of regularly employed and better-paid workmen, making very little impact on the lives of the very poor. But they contributed to the general turning away from political solutions to problems. Even amongst the unskilled workers in the later years of the century trade unionism preceded the formulation of a new programme of political reform and government intervention. The working class had arrived at a non-political ideology by a rather different route from that of the middle class. Nevertheless the process had brought elements of the two classes together. The leaders of the working class still wanted the suffrage, the essential badge of citizenship. Leaders of all the major trade unions were to be seen on the platform of the Reform League in the early sixties. But they used the vote when they got it, to vote for the 'non-political' Liberal Party, accepted the leadership of John Bright and W. E. Gladstone, and accepted at the hands of the Liberals a system of state-organised education for their children, having been apparently converted to a belief in the neutrality of political institutions. The working people lost faith in political solutions before they – or some of them – became converted to Liberalism. The change in tone of the politicians' addresses to the people and the libertarian rhetoric of Gladstonian Liberalism completed the conversion in the sixties and seventies.

However 'unhistorical' the question may be, nearly everyone who studies Chartism ends up by suggesting reasons for its failure, or by suggestions of areas in which Chartists achieved successes. If we accept that movements for change rarely achieve the specific change they are seeking, nevertheless, is it possible to see changes in British society which may be directly attributed to this powerful and widespread movement?

As far as the achievement of the six points went, the Chartists failed completely. Their aim of one man one vote was not achieved until after the Second World War, and their vision of a Parliament regularly and frequently responsible to the whole people was never achieved. Working men were admitted cautiously and piecemeal into the electoral system between 1867 and 1919, but as more and more players were allowed on to the field, the rules of the game were being constantly changed. The power of the non-parliamentary elements of government, the civil service, the judiciary, and the various advisory organisations, grew in the same period, and these were accessible only to those who had been educated within a system from which working people were totally excluded. The first working men to enter Parliament did so through the cordon sanitaire of Liberalism. They were 'safe' men who had already demonstrated their reliability by cooperation with the Liberals in local politics or in industrial negotiations. George White or Abram Hanson would never have made the grade. The few wild men who slipped through the mesh before the First World War had little impact on the basic structure of political power and dominion.

The Chartists' aim of a free, universal system of education, controlled by the communities in which the children lived, also died with Chartism. The post-Chartist years were characterised by a series of Factory Acts with educational provisions, paralleled by the growth of a network of 'provided' schools, provided by rival religious bodies and supported by government grants which culminated in the 1870 Act, after which school attendance was gradually made compulsory. Some small degree of community participation was permitted in the areas where school boards were set up, but the life of the school board as an institution was short, and it did not live to flourish in the era of universal suffrage. Schools in the second half of the nineteenth century served mainly to instil ideas of Christian dogma – religious instruction remains the only subject whose teaching in English schools is compulsory – to establish basic literacy and counting – arithmetic was taught but not mathematics – and to teach politeness, punctuality, cleanliness and other social virtues. The type of child for whom one writer urged the need for education was ' . . . the very boy to become a Chartist victim; jealous of his schoolfellows and tenacious of his rights; never capping to his teachers or moving off the pavement to his betters; covetous of ease and pleasure, but inclined to the most degrading idleness . . . [and with] treachery towards rightful authority . . . '[4] The presence of such children in the 1840s was a powerful spur to the school and Sunday school movements of the following decades. Modern writers disagree as to the extent of the re-defining of social and cultural attitudes of the working people achieved by the educational system in the second half of the nineteenth century. It seems clear, however, that though the volume of provided schools expanded, the control which working people exercised over their children's education lessened considerably. The Chartist aim of an education system in the hands of the local people moved further away in the post-Chartist period, and eventually disappeared from sight.

In other areas of social provision, Chartist aims were not achieved during the hundred years which followed. Some of the worst and most ideologically-inspired aspects of the 1834 Poor Law were modified in practice, some as the result of popular protest, some because the cost to the ratepayers of the full implementation of the new system would have been prohibitive, but the workhouse test and the remnants of the Settlement Acts persisted into the depression years between the two world wars. The demand that relief should be given to those unable to work through no fault of their own, as a matter of right and in conditions of personal dignity and respect, was scarcely on the agenda for the hundred years after the defeat of Chartism. There is in fact a strong case for saying that for all their poverty and long hours of work, the men and women of the early industrial districts which produced Chartism had more say in many important aspects of their lives than their more prosperous descendants.

Perhaps the most important gain in the Chartist period was in the sphere of independent working-class organisations with limited aims. The legal recognition of trade unions, the *de facto* recognition of apprenticeship regulation by the unions, of wage bargaining and the negotiation of other aspects of working conditions by at least some trades, were gained in these years in the face of a determined resistance by most employers and a strong ideological opposition from the powerful dogma of political economy. To an extent cooperative societies and friendly societies also represented victories. If a humane and dignified system of poor relief did not emerge in local or national government, the skilled workers and others in regular employment were able to make their own provision through these organisations. By dropping, or rather by ceasing to believe in, the efficacy of political change as the lever of social change and the establisher of social justice, the working people lost the unity of the Chartist period, the strong sense of the interrelatedness of the demands of all sections of the propertyless and unrepresented. They accepted a re-definition of the nature of power and of politics, accepting the division between 'political' and 'industrial' activity which Chartism had never recognised. Within this new division they made certain advances in the 'industrial' sector which ensured some share for the workers in the great industrial expansion of Victorian Britain.

Chartism could be seen as the political dimension of the way of life of the producers in early industrial Britain. The vote was the badge of citizenship but also the lever by which the property of the labourer, his labour, could be given the same protection in law, and receive the same respect in the community, as the property of the landowner or the entrepreneur. A Chartist alternative programme for nineteenth-century Britain could have meant less rapid centralisation, much more local autonomy in all fields, a slower rate of industrialisation and economic growth generally, probably no new imperialism, and a check on the size of economic units. Clearly a lower standard of life for many, a greater participation in government by all, and therefore probably slower, less efficient government. It would probably have meant state control if not state ownership of land and of major transport – roads and railways certainly. In so far as it achieved anything, it was in these directions that Chartist success should be looked for. The development of trade unions, co-ops and friendly societies probably did slow up industrialisation in some ways. The new Poor Law remained a solitary landmark of centralisation for decades – the police, for instance, were introduced more slowly and more definitely under local control, and the Poor Law reverted to greater answerability and a less centralised structure after 1849. Whether the increasing concern with urban sanitary reform of the post-Chartist decades had much to do with Chartism is doubtful – probably asian cholera was the more effective goad.

In the field of education, the Chartist vision was lost. George Mart, Chartist potter who gave evidence to the Commission on the Employment of Children and Young Persons in 1841, told the commissioners that he had educated his children, although a poor man, at his own expense, since he did not like 'the system of education pursued in the national schools, where they instil the principle of paying deference to superiors, when we are all the same flesh and blood . . . '[5] Subsequent generations of working-class parents seem to have accepted the system with little question.

Police forces developed in all districts, trained in crowd control and instructed to discourage all forms of crowd action, political or recreational, which could represent a possible disturbance of order. Many forms of action and entertainment, however, such as fairs, community celebrations, political and trade processions and traditional sports, were put down as much by the encouragement in educational institutions and the press of a more rational, modernising outlook as by direct attack. Regular working hours helped encourage hobbies and individual pastimes in place of communal celebration of rare shared leisure, and this inevitably affected all forms of joint activity. The Sunday school scholars' Whitsun walk and the primary schools' dancing round a be-ribboned maypole reduced older forms of community action to children's games. A more sober and rational but a more fragmented working population developed. The rough and the respectable had to an extent worked together in the Chartist movement. In later years they became separated, even hostile. Self-righteousness and self-indulgence polarised the bad side of each, while school, press and pulpit emphasised the value of self-help and individual achievement, at the expense of family and community values.

But perhaps the ethos of Chartism could anyway not have survived into the great urban centres of the later nineteenth century. It needed the small communities, the slack religious and moral supervision, the unpoliced public street and meeting-place. The control which such communities could exercise over shopkeepers, constables, schoolteachers, local preachers and even Poor Law guardians was greater than anything that could take place in the cities or in the rural villages. As society in Britain became increasingly polarised between a de-populated countryside and large urban centres, the unifying influence of a common living area and shared institutions lessened. Such working-class organisations as survived combined a degree of local autonomy with membership of national networks, substituting shared values of social identity between skilled and regularly-employed workers throughout the country for the community of neighbourhood. Many groups who had at times played an important part in Chartism –

women, immigrant, unskilled and semi-skilled workers, individual home-based artisans like cobblers, tailors, blacksmiths, small printers, as well as radical lay preachers and other local orators, ceased to be part of the labour movement. Organisation moved from the home, the inn and the street to the large workshop and the trades club. It is not necessary to posit a lower level of commitment or of class consciousness among the organised workers of the later nineteenth century. Their movements were different. They accepted the scale of modern industry, and the arguments for a continual expansion of scale in industry and government, indeed they embodied the values of centralisation and economies of scale in their own organisations. They had no desire to hold back the clock, to retain control over many of the areas which had seemed essential to the Chartists – education, policing, community leisure activities. Only in the workshop did they maintain the battle for control to any real extent, and even here they accepted, like all their generation, the inevitability of technical 'improvements', the uncontrollability of economic laws.

APPENDIX

Location and Timing of Chartist Activity

FIGURES in column 2 are of the population given in the *Parliamentary Gazetteer* for 1841, or in a few cases of very small places not given there, are from Capper's *Topographical Dictionary of the United Kingdom* for 1813. Clearly such figures are fairly notional, since the names given by Chartists to their localities rarely coincided with parliamentary boundaries. They do, however, give some indication of the size of the areas in which activity took place. Figures in brackets are of signatures to the first Chartist petition as listed in the *Northern Star* in June 1839, and after this figure on occasion is the number of female signatures (marked *f*), which were in some cases given separately. Other lists of signatures from districts vary slightly from the figures given here, but the proportion is usually about the same as between major districts. The figures do not add up to the full number of signatures, as some were entered for districts rather than for towns or villages. A star in any of the columns indicates some recorded activity of the type or on the date indicated. The figures in column 4 are for NCA membership cards taken out in one year between 1842, in all cases taken from the *Northern Star*. The following key is to the names of the organisations shown in column 3. By the end of 1840 nearly all localities had become NCA groups.

(C)	Church occupation in summer 1839	PA	Political Association
CA	Chartist Association	PU	Political Union
Ch	Chartist church or chapel	RA	Radical Association
DA	Democratic Association	RCA	Radical Chartist Association
DCA	Democratic Chartist Association	RRA	Radical Reform Association
F	Female Radical Association	Ref A	Reform Association
GNU	Great Northern Union	TT	Teetotal Chartist Association
IUSA	Irish Universal Suffrage Association	USA	Universal Suffrage Association
NPU	Northern Political Union	WMA	Working Men's Association
NU	Northern Union	Y	Young Chartists' Association

Appendix: Location and Timing of Chartist Activity

Place	*Population 1841*	*1839*	*NCA*	*1842*	*1844*	*1848*	*Land Branch*	*Company Members*
Aberdare	6,471		440	*				
Aberdeen	63,000 (8,116)	F WMA				*	*	
Abergavenny	4,230					*	*	
Abersychan		F WMA						
Accrington	6,908	RA	*	*		*	*	*
Ackerworth	(14,800)	*						
Addington	237							*
Airdrie		*					*	
Alexandria		*					*	
Alfreton	7577							*
Alloa	8,000 (896)	Ch WMA				*		*
Alnwick	6,626	NPU			*	*	*	
Alva	1,600 (400)	F WMA					*	*
Alyth			*	*				
Ambler Thorn		RA	*	*				
Anderston		*Ch						
Annan		*						
Arbroath		*TT		*		*		*
Argoed		*						
Ashburton	3,841 (480)	WMA						*
Ashby-de-la-Zouche	5,652	(C) F PU Y					*	*
Ashton-under-Lyne	46,304 (5,000, 1,312*f*)		350	*	*	*	*	*
Astley		RA	*	*			*	
Atherston	3,743							*
Auchenewin		*						
Auchterarder		*						
Auchtermuchty		*						
Austerland (Oldham)		*						*
Aycliffe	1,372	DA						
Ayr		WMA					*	
figures for Ayrshire	(20,738)							
Bacup			*	*F				*
Badbury (Swindon)	2,459							*
Balfron		*						
Banbury	12,333 (2,198)	WMA TT	*	*		*	*	*
Bangor	7,232	*						
Bannockburn	(3,000)	*						
Barnard Castle	4,452							*

Appendix: Location and Timing of Chartist Activity

Place	*Population 1841*	*1839*	*NCA*	*1842*	*1844*	*1848*	*Land Branch*	*Company Members*
Barnley	(4,800)	*						
Barnoldswick	2,844	RA	*	*		*	*	*
	(6,000)							
Barnsley	10,330	Ch F NU	480	*	*	*	*	*
	(3,645)	RA						
Barnstable	7,902	WMA	*	*	*	*	*	*
	(440)							
Barrhead		*F				*		*
Basley						*		
Bath	53,000	(C) Ch F	420	*		*	*	*
	(8,000)	WMA						
Bathgate	(4,000)	*						
Batley	14,278	NU	*	*		*		
Baxenden			*	*				
Bedford	4,187	WMA						*
Beith			*	*				*
Belfast	70,000		IUSA					*
Bellshill		*						
Belper	9,885	WMA	290 F	*				*
	(1,211)							
Benton Lane End		NPU						
Benwell and	1,433	NPU						
Elswicke	1,789							
Beverley	8,730					*		
Bilston	20,181	F	1,000	*	*	*	*	*
Bingley	11,850		170	*		*	*	*
Birkenhead	8,000		*	*			*	*
Birkenshaw			*	*				
BIRMINGHAM	183,000	(C) Ch F	1,200	*	*	*	*	*
	(86,180)	PU Y						
Aston	45,718		*	*				
Birstall	29,723	RA		*		*		*
Bishop Wearmouth		*	450	*				
Bishops Itchington								*
Black Hill							*	
Blackburn	37,000	x (C)	280	*		*	*	*
	(4,631)							
Blackwood (Newport)	526	F WMA		*	*			
Blagdon	1,178		*					
Blairgourie		RA					*	
Blandford	407	WMA						*
	(554)							
Bleana (Mon)		*					*	*
Blisworth	882	WMA						*

Appendix: Location and Timing of Chartist Activity

Place	*Population 1841*	*1839*	*NCA*	*1842*	*1844*	*1848*	*Land Company Branch*	*Members*
Bocking	3,437	WMA						
Bolton	51,000	(C) F	700	★	★		★	★
	(16,600)	WMA		(18,500)				
Bonhill	298	X						
Bonsdale	(355)	X						
Borrowsford	(3,496)	X						
Boston	12,942	RA	★	★			★	
	(3,074)							
Boulogne (France)							★	★
Bourton-on-the-Water	943							★
Box	2,274	WMA						
Bradford (Wilts)	12,012	F Ch	★	★		★	★	★
	(2,368)	WMA						
BRADFORD (Yorks)	67,000	(C) Ch F	1,500-	★	★	★	★	★
(Parish pop. 105,257)	(10,049)	NU WMA	1,900					
Allerton		★						
Baildon	3,280	X						
Bowling Lane	8,918	F	★	★			★	
Clayton	4,347	NU						
Clayton Heights		RA						
Clayton West	1,440	★						
Daisy Hill			★					
George Street			★					
Great Horton	17,615	DCA F	★	★	★	★		
Heaton	1,573	NU						
Idle	6,212	RA						
Lidget Green		F NU						
Manchester Rd		★ F						
Manningham	5,622	TT WMA			★			
Nelson Court		★ F						
Nelson Street		★ F						
Oakenshaw		NU						
Wapping		★ F	★					
White Abbey			★	★	★			
Bradley	(400)	★						
Baintree	3,670	WMA			★	★	★	
	(1,372)							
Bramley	970		★					
Brampton		★ F						
Brandon (Suffolk)	2,002							★
Brechin		★						
Brecon	5,354						★	
Brentford	2,174	PU						

Appendix: Location and Timing of Chartist Activity

Place	*Population 1841*	*1839*	*NCA*	*1842*	*1844*	*1848*	*Land Branch*	*Company Members*
Brereton	667						★	
Bridge of Weir		★						
Bridgend		★						
Bridgeton		★ Ch F						
Bridgewater	10,449					★	★	★
Bridlington	6,070							★
Bridport	4,787						★	
Brierley Hill	491		★	★		★		
Brighouse	5,421					★		
Brightlingsea	2,055	★	★					★
Brighton	47,000 (12,757)	F PA RA WMA	420	★		★	★	★
Brinksway								★
Bristol	124,000 (8,160)	(C) F TT WMA Y	920	★			★	★
Broadtown			★					
Bromham	1,558	WMA	★					
Bromsgrove	9,671 (2,200)	WMA	★	★		★		
Brymbo	1,217	★						
Buckfastleigh	2,576 (240)	WMA						
Buckley	190	★					★	
Buckwell End								★
Burnley	10,699	WMA	570	★	★	★	★	★
Burnsley	(373)	★						
Burton-on-Trent	8,136		★	★				
Burwash	2,093	Radical Newspaper Club						
Bury	62,301 (18,800)	F RA	★	★	★	★	★	★
Bury St Edmunds	12,538						★	
Busage (Glos)		★						
Busby	148					★	★	
Butterleigh	155							★
Byers Green	489						★	
Caerleon	1,174 (380)	WMA			★			
Caermarthen	(1,013)	WMA						
Caernarvon		★						
Callander		★						
Calverly	21,039			★				
Cambourne	10,061	★			★			
Cambridge	24,000		★	★			★	★

Appendix: Location and Timing of Chartist Activity

Place	Population 1841	1839	NCA	1842	1844	1848	Land Branch	Company Members
Campsall	2,149 (176)	★						
Campsie		★ Ch	USA	★			★	
Canterbury	15,435 (228)	RA	★	★				
Cardiff	10,000						★	★
Carlisle	22,000 (7,566, 1,792*f*)	F RA	120	★	★	★	★	★
Carlsdyke								★
Cassop	1,076						★	
Castle Donnington	(288)	★						
Castle Eden	588					★	★	
Cawthorne		NU						
Cefn Mawr						★		
Ceres		RA				★		
Chalford			★	★				
Chard	5,788	RA	★	★		★		
Chatham	21,431		★	★				
Chatteris	4,813		★	★				
Cheddington	439						★	★
Chelmsford	6,789 (930)	WMA	★	★		★		
Cheltenham	31,411 (1,720)	(C) F WMA	270	★	★	★	★	★
Chepstow	3,366						★	★
Chester	24,000	★ (C)	★	★			★	
Chesterfield	11,231 (654)	WMA	★	★			★	★
Chichester	8,512 (643)	★						
Chickenley		RA WMA	★	★				
Chilton and Naseby	(160)	★						
Chippenham	5,438	WMA						
Chirwell						★		
Chorley	13,139 (2,900)	★ (C)	★	★		★	★	
Chorlton-on-Medlock	28,336		★	★				★
Chowbent		RA	★	★				
Cirencester	6,014	(C) WMA					★	
Clackmannan	5,000 (400)	WMA						
Clayton West	1,440	NU					★	
Cleator	763					★		

Appendix: Location and Timing of Chartist Activity

Place	*Population 1841*	*1839*	*NCA*	*1842*	*1844*	*1848*	*Land Branch*	*Company Members*
Cleckheaton			⋆	⋆		⋆		
Clitheroe	6,765	⋆	400	⋆		⋆	⋆	⋆
Coalbrookdale			⋆	⋆				
Coatbridge						⋆		
Cockermouth	4,940	RA	⋆	⋆				
Cockerton	482		⋆	⋆				
Coggleshall	3,408	WMA	⋆					
Colchester	18,000 (2,092)	WMA	⋆	⋆		⋆		⋆
Colne	8,615	RA	220	⋆	⋆	⋆	⋆	
Combe Down		WMA						
Compstall Bridge			⋆	⋆				
Comrie		⋆						
Congleton	9,222		⋆	⋆	⋆		⋆	⋆
Corbridge							⋆	
Coundon	990						⋆	
Coventry	31,000 (3,860)	PU	250	⋆	⋆	⋆	⋆	⋆
Cradley	2,686			⋆				
Craig				⋆				
Craig Vale				⋆				
Crayford	2,408						⋆	
Cretoun	(192)	⋆						
Cricklade	2,128		⋆			⋆		
Crieff						⋆	⋆	⋆
Croespenmaen		⋆						
Crook	257		⋆					
Croydon	16,712	⋆	⋆	⋆	⋆	⋆	⋆	
Crumlin		⋆						
Cullompton	3,909 (516)	⋆				⋆	⋆	
Cummersdale					⋆			
Cumnock		WMA				⋆		
Cupar	(7,366)	⋆Ch						
Cupar Angus		⋆					⋆	
Cyfartha		⋆						
Dalby (Ayrshire)								⋆
Dalkeith		RRA						
Dalry								⋆
Dalston (Carlisle)	2,874	RA	⋆	⋆		⋆		
Darlaston	8,244					⋆		⋆
Darlington	11,877	(C) F WMA	⋆	⋆		⋆	⋆	⋆
Dartford	5,619							⋆
Darvel		⋆Ch						

Appendix: Location and Timing of Chartist Activity

Place	*Population 1841*	*1839*	*NCA*	*1842*	*1844*	*1848*	*Land Branch*	*Company Members*
Darwen	12,348		*	*				
Daventry	4,565 (972)	WMA	*	*F		*	*	*
Davyhulme			*	*				
Dawley	8,641		*	*				*
Great Dawley								*
Dawley Green								*
Dawlish								*
Delph			*	*				
Denny							*	*
Derby	33,000 (8,000)	RA WMA	370	*	*	*	*	*
Dereham	4,278							*
Desborough	1,388 (132)	*	*	*	*			*
Devizes	4,631							*
Devonport	43,532	WMA					*	
Dewsbury	23,806	(C) NU RA	580	*	*	*	*	*
Doghouse		*F						
Dolgellau	3,695	*						
Dollar		*						
Doncaster	11,245	WMA	*	*		*		
Dorking	5,638 (786)	WMA						*
Doun		*						
Dowlais		(C) WMA					*	*
Downe	444	WMA						
Doyle			*	*				
Driffield	3,477						*	
Droylsdon	(2,968)	*	*	*			*	*
Dublin			IUSA	*	*	*		*
(county)	373,000							
Dudley	31,000	PU WMA	*	*	*	*	*	
Dukestown		*						
Dukinfield	22,394 (3,454)	*	*	*	*			
Dumbarton		*						
Dumfries	(2,180)	WMA			*	*		
Dundee	63,000	F PU WMA Y Ch	*	*		*	*	
Dunfermline	20,000 (6,050)	F WMA				*		
Dunning		*						

Durham – see under Northumberland and Durham district

Appendix: Location and Timing of Chartist Activity

Place	*Population 1841*	*1839*	*NCA*	*1842*	*1844*	*1848*	*Land Branch*	*Company Members*
Dursley	2,931	*						
Dutwell								*
Eaglesham		* Ch						
Earle Shilton	*1,287*	*						*
Earlston								
	(200)	*						
East Leak(e)			*					
East Retford	2,680							*
East Woodside		* F						
Eastbourne	3,015	*						
Ebbw Vale		WMA		*			*	
Ebley		WMA						
Ecclefechan		*						
Eccles	33,792	WMA	200	*				*
Edgeworth	1,697	*						
Edgley								*
Edinburgh	166,000 (16,686)	USA	*	*	*	*	*	*
Edington	1,136	WMA						
Elderslie								*
Elgin		*						
Elland	6,479	FRA	*	*		*	*	*
Elm (Cambs.)	951							*
Ely	6,824							*
Epping	2,424	WMA						
Etruria								*
Exeter	31,000 (2,560)	WMA				*	*	*
Failsworth	3,879	RA	*	*		*	*	*
Falkirk		USA					*	*
Falmouth	7,695		*	*				
Farnley Tyas	844							*
Feckenham	2,800				*			
Foleshill	7,063						*	
Forest Hertford								*
Forfar	8,817 (900)	FRA						
Friston	91	WMA						
Frome	19,213 (1,653)	WMA	*	*				*
Furze Hill								*
Gainsborough	7,842 (874)	*		*		*	*	
Galston								*
Gasstown							*	

Place	*Population 1841*	*1839*	*NCA*	*1842*	*1844*	*1848*	*Land Branch*	*Company Members*
George Mills							*	
Giggleswick	3,467							*
Gillingham	6,059							*
Girvan								*
Glasgow	275,000 (80,000)	Ch (2) F USA	*	*	*	*	*	*
Glossop	22,898 (4,506)	*	*	*	*			*
Gloucester	14,152 (844)	WMA	300	*		*	*	*
Golkham							*	*
Gomersal	8,030	WMA RA						*
Goole	2,850							*
Gorbals		* Ch F						
Gosport		WMA						*
Govan		*						
Grampton		* F						
Grantham	8,691							*
Great Harwood	2,273		*	*				*
Great Malvern	2,911							*
Greenleigh								*
Greenock	36,000	* Ch				*		
Greenstead	601	WMA						
Grindleton	902		*	*				
Guernsey	26,666							*
Hadleigh	3,679	WMA						
Hag Gate		RA						
Hale								*
HALIFAX (*Parish pop. 130, 743*)	28,000 (13,036)	(C) F RA	460	*	*	* F	*	*
Luddenden		RA	*	*				*
Midgley	2,667	RA	*	*				
Mixenden		RA	*	*				
Mixenden Stones		RA	*	*		*	*	*
Mytholmroyde		RA	*	*				*
New Pellon		RA						*
Norland	1,670		*	*				
Northowram			*	*				
Ovenden	11,799	RA	*	*			*	*
Ripponden		RA	*	*				*
Southowram			*	*				
Stainland	3,759	RA	*	*				

(and see Elland, Queenshead (Queensbury) which are sometimes listed with Halifax)

Halstead	5,710 (515)	WMA					*	*

Place	*Population 1841*	*1839*	*NCA*	*1842*	*1844*	*1848*	*Land Branch*	*Company Members*
Hamilton		* Ch F				*	*	
Hanging Heaton		NU						
Hanley	8,609	F PU WMA	1,100	*				*
Hardwick								*
Harleston	539	CA	*	*				
Harlow	2,315	WMA						
Harpool								*
Hartlepool	5,236							*
Harwich	3,829							*
Haslingdon	8,063	*					*	
Hastings	11,607							*
Haswell	3,981	DCA F					*	
Hatfield Broadoak	1,968	WMA						
Hathern	1,252	PU		*				
Hawick	(1,368)	F TT WMA					*	*
Hazel Grove		RA	*	*				*
Heanor	6,282	WMA						
Hebden Bridge		Ch RA	300	*	*	*		*
Heckmondwyke	3,537	DA RA	*	*		*		*
Hedge End							*	
Helston	3,584							*
Henley	3,622						*	
Heptonstall	4,791		*	*				
Hereford	10,921	DA WMA						
Heywood	14,856	RA	*	*	*	*		*
High Wickham								*
Hightown								*
Hilperton	973	WMA					*	
Hilton							*	
Hinckley	7,291	*		*		*		
Hindley	5,459	F WMA			*			*
Hinton St Mary	361							*
Holbrook	774	F	*	*				
Hollingwood		*	*	*	*			
Hollingworth	2,012		*	*				
Holt (Wilts)	1,044 (180)	WMA						
Holytown								*
Hooking Norton	1,032							*
Hooley Hill			*	*				
Horbury	2,683		*					
Horncastle	4,521							*
Horton				*				

Place	*Population 1841*	*1839*	*NCA*	*1842*	*1844*	*1848*	*Land Branch*	*Company Members*
Howden	4,860		*	*		*		
Howick	112							*
HUDDERSFIELD	25,000 (19,432)	NU WMA	630	*	*	*		*
Almondbury	35,859	GNU WMA	*	*				
Berry Brow			*					
Dalton	3,906		*					
Farnley Bank	1,530	NU	*					
Holme	713		*					
Holmfirth			*	*			*	*
Honley	5,383	NU	*	*				
Kirkheaton	1,647		*	*				*
Lepton	3,875		*					
Linfit			*					
Linthwaite	3,301		*					
Lockwood	4,303		*		*			
Marsden	2,403		*					
New Mill			*					
Newsholme	55		*					
Paddock		*						
Rastrick	3,482		*					
Shelley	1,772		*					
Stocksmoor			*					
Thurstonland	1,872	Ch	*					
Yew Green			*	*				
Hulin	(180)	*						
Hull	67,000 (3,091)	(C) F TT WMA	550	*			*	*
Hulme	26,982	F NPU RA						
Hyde	10,151	(C) F WMA	*	*		*	*	*
Hyson Green		*				*		
Inverleven		*						
Ipswich	25,000 (7,020, 292*f*)	F WMA	140	*		*	*	*
Irvine		WMA	*					
Isham	397	*	*	*				
Ivestone	448							*
Ivinghoe	1,843							*
Ivingwide							*	
Jedburgh	(694)	*						
Johnstone	289	* Ch						
Juniper Green		*						
Keevil		WMA						

Appendix: Location and Timing of Chartist Activity

Place	*Population 1841*	*1839*	*NCA*	*1842*	*1844*	*1848*	*Land Branch*	*Company Members*
Keighley	13,413	F RA	200	*			*	
Kelso	(670)	*						
Kendal	18,027 (2,117)	WMA	*	*				
Kenilworth	3,149		*		*			
Kettering	4,867 (1,632)	F RA TT	100	*			*	*
Kettle							*	
Kexby	269						*	
Kidderminster	20,753 (1,832)	F WMA	*	*	*	*	*	*
Kilbrachan		Ch						
Kilburnie		PU	*	*				
Kilmarnock	(12,095)	Ch F WMA	*		*	*	*	*
Kilsyth		*						
Kingsholme	139							*
Kingston Deverill	420			*				
Kingston-on- Thames	9,760 (500)	WMA	*	*				
Kinross							*	
Kip		*						
Kirkaldy	15,820 (2,362)		*				*	
Kirkintilloch		*						
Kirrieumuir	(1,679)	F PU						
Knaresborough	9,947 (500)	*			*		*	*
Lamberhead Green								*
Lanark	(8,647)	* Ch						
Lancaster	24,707 (916)	RA	*	*				*
Laneshaw Bridge		NU						
Langley			*					*
Largs	(168)	*						
Lasswade			*	*				*
Market Lavington			*	*		*	*	*
West Lavington	1,554		*	*			*	*
Leadgate						*		
Leamington	12,864 (1,000)	WMA	*	*	*	*	*	*
Ledbury	4,591 (163)	WMA						
LEEDS	152,000 (4,800)	F NU RA TT	1,325	*	*	*	*	*
Beeston	2,175		*					

Appendix: Location and Timing of Chartist Activity

Place	*Population 1841*	*1839*	*NCA*	*1842*	*1844*	*1848*	*Land Branch*	*Company Members*
Daw Green		FNU	★					
East Bierly		★	★					
East End		DA						
Gomersall	8,030	RA						★
Holbeck	13,346		★	★				
Hunslet	15,852		★	★				
Kirkstall		F						
Stanningley				★			★	
West End		RA						
Lees		WMA	★	★		★		
Leicester	53,000 (13,126)	F PU TT	3,100	★	★	★	★	★
Leigh	22,229 (15,071)	(C) F RA WMA	★	★			★	★
Leith		Ch USA WMA				★		
Lennox Town		★						★
Lepton	3,875	★ F						★
Leslie		★						
Letham		★						
Levenshulme								★
Lewes	9,199 (2,966)	RA						
Lincoln	16,172 (460)	★				★		
Linfield	(3,640)	★						
Links of Kirkaldy								★
Linlithgow		★ Ch						
Litchfield							★	
Little Chiveral								★
Littleborough	77						★	★
Littleton Pannel	507						★	★
Littletown (Yorks)				★	★	★		
Liverpool	286,000 (20,689)	WMA	800	★	★	★		★
Liversedge	5,988	RA	★	★				
Llanelly	11,155	WMA					★	
Llanidloes	4,261	PU WMA	★	★			★	
Llanhilleth	662 (1,748)	★						
Llantwit Verdre							★	
Lochee							★	
Lochwinnoch		★						
London	1,873,676 (60,786)	(C) DA RA WMA	★	★	★	★	★	★

Appendix: Location and Timing of Chartist Activity

Place	*Population 1841*	*1839*	*NCA*	*1842*	*1844*	*1848*	*Land Branch*	*Company Members*
Bermondsey	34,947	CA DA TT	*	*	*		*	*
Bethnal Green	74,088	CA RA WMA	*	*	*	*F		
Blackheath	20,198						*	
Bloomsbury		CA	*	*		*		
Bow and Stratford			*	*				
Brixton								*
Brompton	9,515	F	*	*	*			
Camberwell	39,868		*	*	*	*	*	*
Chelsea	40,179	WMA	*	*	*		*	
Chiswick	5,811	DA						
City	•	CA Ch F Y	*	*	*	*	*	*
Clapham and Wandsworth	19,720 (170)	WMA	*					*
Clerkenwell	56,756	CA	*	*	*		*	
Craven Head (Drury Lane)			*	*				
Cripplegate						*	*	
Crown and Anchor Waterloo Town			*	*	*			
Dalston								*
Deptford		DA	*	*	*			
Dockhead			*	*				
East London (Globe Fields)		DA F TT USA	*	*	*			*
Edgware Road							*	
Finsbury			*	*	*	*	*	
Greenwich	29,755 (382)	*	*	*	*		*	
Grosvenor Square		CA						
Hammersmith	13,453 (336)	CA DA	*	*	*	*	*	
Holborn		CA						
Hoxton			*			*		
Hoxton New Town						*		
Islington	55,690	DA WMA			*	*		
Kensington	26,834	CA DA WMA	*	*	*		*	
Kentish Town						*		
Kings Cross						*		
Kingsland Rd		CA						
Knightsbridge		CA			*			
Lambeth	115,888	CA DA PU TT WMA Y	*	*	*	*	*	

Place	*Population 1841*	*1839*	*NCA*	*1842*	*1844*	*1848*	*Land Branch*	*Company Members*
Lewisham	12,276				★			
Limehouse	21,121						★	
Marylebone		Ch DA	★	★	★	★	★	★
Mile End Road (and Carlton)		F	★	★	★			
Moorfields								★
New Kent Road							★	★
Newington	734		★	★				
Norton Folgate	1,674						★	
Old Bailey			★					
Old Kent Road		DA						
Paddington	25,173							★
Pentonville		CA				★		
Pimlico		WMA						
Putney	4,684	WMA						
Queenhithe		CA						
Ratcliffe-cross	11,874				★			
Regents Park		RA RCA						
Rotherhithe	13,917	RA			★			
Saffron Hill					★			
Shadwell	10,060	USA						
Shoreditch	83,432	CA DA	★	★		★	★	★
Smithfield		CA						
Somerstown			★	★	★	★	★	
Southwark	98,648	DA RA	★	★	★			★
Spitalfields	20,436						★	
Stepney	63,723		★	★			★	★
St Andrews		CA			★			
St Giles	54,292	★						
St Lukes	49,829	CA	★	★				★
St Martins Lane					★			
St Pancras	129,763	CA DA WMA	★	★	★			
Stoke Newington	4,490		★	★				
Tower Hamlets	1,107	DA F	★	★	★	★	★	
Turnagain Lane					★			
Walworth	23,299	CA	★	★				★
Wandsworth	7,614 (200)	F WMA	★	★				
Westminster	222,053	DA WMA	★	★	★	★	★	★
Woolwich	25,785					★	★	
Whitechapel			★	★	★			
Long Buckby	2,145 (284)	WMA	★	★ F	★			
Long Govan					★			

Place	*Population 1841*	*1839*	*NCA*	*1842*	*1844*	*1848*	*Land Branch*	*Company Members*
Long Preston			★	★				
Longton	1,718		480	★		★	★	★
Loughborough	10,170	(C) PU TT	800	★	★	★	★	★
	(6,180)	WMA						
Lower Houses		★						
Lower Lowell								★
Lower Moor			★	★				
Lowton	2,150	WMA						
Ludworth	1,476							★
Lustleigh	311							★
Luthermuir		★ TT						
Lye Waste		★	★	★				
Lyme	2,756	★						
Lynn	16,039	★	★			★	★	★
	(550)							
Lytchett Matravers								★
Macclesfield	24,137	F PU	★		★	★		★
	(4,140)	WMA						
Maesycwmmer		★						
Maidstone	18,086					★	★	★
Maldon	3,967		★	★		★		★
Malmesbury	2,367		★			★		
Malton	5,317	★	★	★			★	
Malvern Wells	819							★
MANCHESTER	242,983	(C) F PU	2,800	★	★	★	★	★
	(7,930)	TT Y		99,680				
Brown St		TT Y	★	★				
Miles Platting			★	★				
Redfern St			★	★				
Stand St			★	★				
Manchline		RA						
Mannington	20							★
Manningtree	1,255		★	★				
Market Rasen								★
Market Weighton			★					
Markinch		★				★		★
Marple	3,462		★	★				
Marsden	2,403	F NU RA		★				
Marsham (Bucks.)								★
Marston Green	(700)	★						
Mauchline		WMA	★					
May (Dorset)							★	
Maybole		★						
Meldrum	(720)	★						
Melingriffith							★	

Appendix: Location and Timing of Chartist Activity

Place	*Population 1841*	*1839*	*NCA*	*1842*	*1844*	*1848*	*Land Branch*	*Company Members*
Melkesham	6,236	*	*	*				
Mells	1,261						*	*
Menai	8,364	*						
Mere (Wilts)	3,139		*	*				
Mereclough		*						
Merthyr Tydfil	34,977 (14,710)	(C) WMA	1,100	*	*	*	*	*
Middlesbrough	6,000						*	*
Middleton	15,488	F PU RA WMA	*	*			*	*
Middlewich	4,755 (800)	*						
Millbank					*			*
Millbottom			*	*				
Millbridge				*				
Milnfield								*
Milnrow			*	*				
Milton (Stirling)		WMA						
Milverton	2,154							*
Mirfield	6,919		*	*		*		
Mitcham	4,532	WMA						*
Mold	10,653	*		*			*	
Moniferth	(340)	*						
Monkton Deverill	207		*	*			*	
Monmouth (*county pop. 134, 355*)	5,446 (6,670, 1,000*f*)	*F					*	
Montgomery	1,208						*	
Montrose	16,000 (2,000)	*F	*					
Morley	4,087	RA						
Mosley								*
Mossley			*	*	*			*
Mottram	21,215		*	*	*	*	*	*
Mount Skipton in Wadsworth		NU						
Mountsorrel	1,536	*F	*	*				
Musselburgh		*						
Nantwich	5,921		*	*				
Nantyglo		*						
Narberth (Pembs)	2,620	*						
Neath	4,970						*	
New Cumnock		*						
Newark-on-Trent	10,220						*	*
Newbridge							*	

Place	*Population 1841*	*1839*	*NCA*	*1842*	*1844*	*1848*	*Land Branch*	*Company Members*
Newburgh	111	* Ch						
Newbury	6,379	*						
	(876)							
New Mills	(320)	RA	*	*		*		
(Derbyshire)								
New Scone		WMA						
NEWCASTLE-UPON-TYNE	70,000	(C) F NPU	1,000	*	*	*	*	*
	(11,000)	RA						
Barlow		WMA						
Barlow Fell		NPU						
Bensham		NPU						
Cramlington	2,634	NPU						
Earsdon	9,429	NPU						
Felling		NPU						
		WMA						
Greenside		NPU						
		WMA						
Hepburn		NU						
Hexham	4,742	NPU						*
Holywell	1,164	WMA						
Ouseburn		NPU						
		WMA						
St Peters Quay		NPU						
Salt Meadows		NPU						
Seghill		F NPU						
Sheriff Hill		NPU						
		WMA						
Spital Tongus		NPU						
Stanhope	7,063	NPU						
Swallwell	1,030	NPU						
Usworth	1,030	NPU						
Walker		NPU						
Washington	2,396	NPU						
Wigton		Ch NPU						
Newent	3,099						*	*
Newfield	345					*	*	*
Newmilnes		Ch WMA	*					
Newport (IOW)	3,858	*	*	*				
	(574)							
Newport (Mon.)	13,766	F WMA	400	*		*	*	*
	(1,700)							
Newport (Salop)	2,497						*	*
Newton (Ayr)							*	
Newton (Cambs)	114							*
Newton Abbot						*	*	*

Appendix: Location and Timing of Chartist Activity

Place	*Population 1841*	*1839*	*NCA*	*1842*	*1844*	*1848*	*Land Company Branch*	*Members*
Newton Heath			*	*				
Newton Mearns								*
Newton St Loe		*						
Newtown	9,000 (3,476)	PU						
Normanton	1,323		*	*		*		
North Bradley	2,427	WMA	*	*				
Northallerton	5,273	*						
Northampton	21,000 (38,000)	F TT WMA	600	*		*	*	*
Northumberland and Durham								
Bishop Auckland	3,776	DCA PU	190	*				*
West Auckland	2,310		*	*			*	
Bedlington	3,155	F PU	*					
Blaydon		NPU						
Blyth	123	PU						*
Broomside		DCA						
Carville		NPU						
Chester-le-Street	16,359	DA					*	
Collier Row		DCA						
Coxhoe	3,904	F WMA				*		
Durham	14,151 (7,591)	*	*	*	*	*		*
Easington Lane		DCA					*	
Elswick	1,789	NPU						
Fatfield		CA NPU						
Gateshead	20,000	PU						*
Gosforth Row	3,020	NPU						
Haswell	3,981	CA						
Hazelrigg		NPU						
Helton		CA						
South Helton		CA						
Horworth		CA						
Houghton	16,833 (2,764)	CA						
Kelloe	11,223	DCA F						
Lumley	1,796	CA						
Moorsley	821	CA						
New Durham		CA F						
North Shields		NPU				*		*
Pittington	4,577	DCA						
Quarrington Hill		DCA F						
East Rainton	1,414	CA						
Middle Rainton		CA						

Appendix: Location and Timing of Chartist Activity

Place	*Population 1841*	*1839*	*NCA*	*1842*	*1844*	*1848*	*Land Branch*	*Company Members*
West Rainton	1,054	CA						
Sacristan Colliery		NPU						
Shildon	2,631	PA						
Shin(e)y Row		DCA NPU						
Snippers Gate		DCA						
South Shields	23,000	DCA F PU			*	*	*	*
Stockton-on-Tees	10,071	DCA F					*	*
Sunderland	17,022 (460)	Ch DA	750	*		*	*	
Thornley	2,730	CA F					*	
Northwich	1,365						*	
Norwich	62,344 (6,646)	(C) Ch DA F	300	*	*	*	*	*
Nottingham	53,091 (14,496)	(C) Ch F WMA	1,650 F	*	*	*	*	*
Arnold	4,509	DA	*	*		*		*
New Basford			*	*				
Old Basford			*	*				
Beeston	2,807	WMA						
Bulwell	3,157		*				*	
Calverton	1,339		*	*				
Carrington	229				*		*	*
Caythrop Lambley								*
Hucknall Torkard	2,680		*	*				
Hucknall-under-Huthwaite	887		*	*				
Lambley	983		*	*				
Mansfield	9,788 (1,100/3)	(C) WMA				*	*	*
New Lenton			*	*				*
Radford	10,817		*	*	*			
Sutton-in-Ashfield	6,563 (1,100/3)	F WMA	300	*		*	*	*
Wodehouse	(1,100/3)	*						
Nuneaton	7,105 (2,120)	*					*	
Nuttall	669	PU						*
Ochiltree and Sorn			*	*				
Old Shildon						*	*	*
Oldbury	142					*		
Oldham	42,595 (13,566)	PU	900	* F 15,000	*	*	*	*
Ongar	15,805	WMA						
Openshaw	2,280		*	*				
Ossett	6,078	RA						*

Appendix: Location and Timing of Chartist Activity

Place	*Population 1841*	*1839*	*NCA*	*1842*	*1844*	*1848*	*Land Branch*	*Company Members*
Oswaldthwistle	6,655		*	*			*	*
Otley	11,143					*	*	*
Oundle	3,037		*	*				
Over (Darwen)	2,863	*						
Overton			*	*				
Oxford	23,834 (383)	*	*	*		*	*	*
Padiham	3,789	RA				*	*	
Paisley	48,000 (13,546)	* Ch F				*		
Parkhead								*
Partick		* F	*					
Penicuik		* Ch						
Pennington	388							*
Pennydarren		*						
Penrith	6,429	RA					*	*
Penshurst	1,470							*
Penyane			*	*				
Penzance	8,578	WMA					*	
Perevale								*
Pershore	2,446						*	*
Perth	(26,954)	*F					*	
Peterborough	6,107			*			*	*
Pilkington		*	*	*		*	*	*
Pitson Moor		F						
Plymouth	36,527 (2,250)	WMA	*	*		*	*	*
Pocklington	2,552		*					
Pontillanfraith		*						
Pontypool	2,865 (6,000)	(C) WMA						
Pontypridd		*						
Portsea	43,704 (1,308)	WMA					*	*
Portsmouth	9,354	*		*				*
Portwood (Cheshire)								*
Potovers			*	*				
Potteries		PU	*	*	*	*	*	
Powick	1,704							*
Prescot	35,902		*	*				
Preston	53,482 (18,533)	(C) F RA	330	* 24,000	*	*	*	*
Prestwich		PU RA	*	*				
Prestwick	50	*						
Printley (Glos)								*

Appendix: Location and Timing of Chartist Activity

Place	*Population 1841*	*1839*	*NCA*	*1842*	*1844*	*1848*	*Land Branch*	*Company Members*
Pudsey	10,002	WMA		*				
Queenshead (Queensbury)		NU RA	*	*		*		
Radcliffe	5,099		*	*				
Radcliffe Bridge		WMA						
Radstock	1,447	WMA						
Raglan							*	
Ramsbottom		RA WMA						
Ratcliffe	11,874		*	*				
Rattray		WMA						
Raunds	1,653		*					
Rawreth	387 (123)	WMA						
Reading	19,000 (2,212)	*					*	*
Redditch		* Y	*	*	*		*	
Redmarley						*	*	*
Redruth	9,305		*					
Rhayader	(600)	*						
Rhymney		*						
Rickmandsworth	5,026							*
Ripley	1,235							*
Risca	1,072	*						
Rochdale	84,718 (9,050)	(C) F RA	470	*	*	*	*	*
Rochester	11,743						*	*
Romford	5,317 (237)	WMA	*		*	*	*	*
Romsey	5,347							*
Rossendale						*	*	*
Rotherham	13,439	WMA	150	*		*	*	*
Rothwell	7,462 (210)	*						
Rowell			*	*				
Royston	2,002	*						*
Royton	5,730		*	*	*			
Ruddington	1,835		*	*	*			
Rugely							*	
Rutherglen								*
Sabden	(440)	RA	*	*				
Saddlescombe	(472)	*						
Saddleworth	16,829	*						*
St Andrews						*		
St Helens	17,849					*	*	
St Ninians		Ch WMA						

Place	*Population 1841*	*1839*	*NCA*	*1842*	*1844*	*1848*	*Land Branch*	*Company Members*
St Rollox		* Ch						
Salcoats		*						
Salford	53,000	FUSAY	500	*	*	*	*	*
Salisbury	10,086 (400)	*	100	*			*	
Sandbank								*
Sanquhar		*						
Sawley	1,933		*	*				
Saxmundham	1,097 (6,936)	*						
Scarborough	10,060	*						
Seal	1,618 (101)	*						
Selby	5,376	FRA	*					*
Selkirk	(275)	*						
Selston	1,982		*	*	*			
Settle	2,041		*	*				
Shaftesbury	3,170 (528)	WMA	*	*				
Shaw			*	*				
Shebbear	1,160							*
Sheepshead	3,872	PU						
Sheerness			*	*			*	
Sheffield	111,090 (16,829)*	(C) F WMA	2,000	*	*	*	*	*
Shelf	3,050	*						
Shelton	12,115		*	*			*	
Shettleston		* Ch						
Shipley	2,413		*	*				
Shotley Bridge						*		
Shotts		*						
Shrewsbury	21,517 (850)	*					*	*
Sible Hedingham			*	*				
Silby (Leics)								*
Silk Willoughby	225							*
Silsden	2,346		*	*				
Sinclairtoun		FRA						
Sittingbourne	2,352							*
Skegby	775		*	*				
Skipton	6,870	RA		*				
Slaithwaite	2,925	*						
Sleaford	3,382					*	*	
Smallthorne					*			
Smethwick	5,020						*	

Appendix: Location and Timing of Chartist Activity

Place	*Population 1841*	*1839*	*NCA*	*1842*	*1844*	*1848*	*Land Branch*	*Company Members*
Sniggs End							*	*
South Hetton			*					
South Molton	(1,320)	*						*
Southampton	27,744 (500)	WMA	*		*	*	*	*
Southwick		WMA						
Sowerby Bridge	8,163	RA	170	*		*	*	*
Spalding	7,778						*	
Stafford	9,245		*	*				
Stainton						*		
Staleybridge (*pop. included in Ashton-under-Lyne*)	(4,863)	F RA	200	* 10,000	*	*	*	*
Stanley (Glos.)	2,200	WMA						
Starmlow								*
Staunton	172	*					*	
Staveley	3,315							*
Stenhousemuir								*
Stewarton		WMA						
Stirling	12,000 (7,250)	F WMA					*	*
Stockport	84,282 (10,781)	(C) F TT WMA Y	800 (14,000)	* Y	*	*	*	*
Stoke-on-Trent	48,093		*	*				
Stonehouse	9,712	WMA						*
Stony Stratford	1,757						*	*
Stourbridge	7,481 (4,040)	WMA				*		
Stow-on-the-Wold	2,140	*					*	
Stowmarket	3,043	WMA						
Stratford (Essex)	201							*
Stratford-on-Avon	3,321 (420)	*			*			
Strathaven		* F	*					
Stratton St Margaret	1,565		*			*		
Stricking	(110)	*						
Strood	2,881							*
Stroud	8,680	(C) WMA	*	*	*	*		
Stroudwater	(3,728)	*	*	*				*
Strutton-by-Stow								*
Sudbury	5,085					*		*
Sunderland	17,022	* F						
Sutherland	(2,160)	*						

Place	*Population 1841*	*1839*	*NCA*	*1842*	*1844*	*1848*	*Land Branch*	*Company Members*
Sutton Courteney	1,378						★	
Sutton (Keighly)							★	
Swaffham	3,358							★
Swainley	(461)	★						
Swansea	19,115 (3,363)	WMA						
Swindon	2,459					★	★	
Tavistock	6,272 (1,366)	WMA	★	★	★			★
Teignmouth	2,883					★	★	★
Tetbury	2,982 (163)	★						
Tewkesbury	5,862 (1,056)	F WMA	★				★	★
Thetford	3,934							★
Thorn								★
Thornhill	7,201				★			
Thornton (Bucks.)	101							★
Thornton (Leics.)	1,375		★			★		
Thrislington	24						★	
Thurmaston	1,229						★	★
Tillicoutry	4,000 (800)	F WMA				★	★	★
Timsbury	1,666	★						
Tipton	18,891		★	★		★		
Tiverton	10,040 (951)	WMA				★	★	★
Todmorden	7,311 (7,328)	★F	500	★F	★	★	★	★
Tollcross			★					
Tonbridge	12,530 (461)	Ref A						
Tonge	2,423 (168)	PA						
Torquay	4,085		★			★	★	
Totnes	3,849 (1,250)	★						★
Tottington	340	F RA						
Tradeston			★					
Tredegar		★		★				★
Trowbridge	11,050 (5,160)	Ch DA F WMA	500	★	★	★	★	★
Truro	3,043	WMA			★	★		★
Tulloch		WMA						
Tunbridge Wells	8,302			★			★	

Appendix: Location and Timing of Chartist Activity

Place	*Population 1841*	*1839*	*NCA*	*1842*	*1844*	*1848*	*Land Branch*	*Company Members*
Tunnicliffe		WMA						
Tunstall								★
Turriff		★						
Tyldesley		FWMA						★
Uddingston		★						
Uley (Glos)		★						
Ulverstone	8,778 (630)	★	★	★				
Uncoat			★	★				
Upper Hanley		F						
Upper Stanton	300							★
Upton-on-Severn	2,696	★					★	★
Uxbridge	3,219					★		
Vale of Leven		★Ch				★		
Ventnor				★	★	★		
Wakefield	29,992 (2,962)	FWMA				★	★	
Walpole Lynn								★
Walsall	20,800	PU	★	★	★		★	★
Walsoken								★
Waltham Abbey	4,177	WMA						
Walthamstow	4,873 (300)	★						
Walton-le-Dale	6,659							★
Wanborough	992					★		
Warminster	6,211 (1,200)	★	★	★				
Warrington	21,000 (1,500)	★	★	★		★		
Warwick	9,775				★	★	★	★
Wednesbury	11,625 (1,600, 400*f*)	★F					★	
Wellingborough	5,061 (1,011)	WMA	★	★				★
West Bromwich	26,121 (3,300)	★						
West Houghton		★						★
Westbury (Somerset)	647	WMA						
Westbury (Wilts)	7,588 (1,024)	WMA	★					
West Kilbride	(1,960)	★						
West Linton	567	★						
Westleigh		WMA						★
West Wanbury								★

Appendix: Location and Timing of Chartist Activity

Place	Population 1841	1839	NCA	1842	1844	1848	Land Branch	Company Members
Weston	(62)	*						
Whilton	401		*	*				
Whitburn	1,061	*						
Whittington								*
Wigan	51,988	RA	150	*	*	*	*	*
				(10,000)				
Wigston	2,189					*		
Wigton	6,432	(C) F RA	*	*				
	(400)	WMA						
Willenhall								*
Wilmington	845	*						
	(329)							
Wilmslow	4,973		*	*			*	
Winchcombe	2,613	WMA					*	*
Winchester	10,732	WMA						*
	(200)							
Windy Nook		NPU				*	*	
Wingate Grange							*	
Winlaton	5,326	F NPU	*	*	*		*	*
		WMA						
Winsley	2,646	WMA						
Wishaw	206					*	*	
Witham	3,158		*	*			*	*
Witney	5,707					*		
Wivenhoe	1,599		*	*				
Wolverhampton	70,370	PU	300	*			*	
	(1,960)							
Worsley	8,337							*
Woodhouse	1,309		*	*				
Worcester	25,793	WMA	*	*			*	*
	(1,500)							
Worksop	6,197						*	
Worsborough Common	3,800 (3,326)	NU						
Wotton-under-Edge	(1,344)	F WMA			*	*	*	*
Wreckenton		NPU						
Wroughton	1,963					*		
Wyesham			*					*
Yarmouth	24,086	WMA				*	*	
	(411)							
Yeovil	7,043		*	*		*	*	*
York	38,321	F NU	150	*	*	*	*	*

Bibliographical note

THE manuscript and printed sources on which this book is based are listed in the *Bibliography of the Chartist Movement* which I compiled in 1978 with Professor J.F.C. Harrison. Specific references are given in the notes to the chapters of this book, but I have not attempted to reproduce the bibliography. Where new work has been done since 1978 I have tried to mention it in footnotes, but inevitably there will be some recent work which is not cited. The main manuscript sources which have been used are the papers in the Public Record Office, of which the following series are most often cited. The Home Office papers, particularly the series HO 40 and HO 45, *Correspondence and Papers, Disturbances*, and HO 20 *Prisons* have been extensively consulted, the Treasury Solicitor's papers, particularly the series TS 11 relating to State Trials, provide a great deal of material, including documents impounded from arrested Chartists. The series PL 26 and 27 which are cited in 1842 are the records of state trials held in the area covered by the Palatinate of Lancaster. Board of Trade and Chancery records (BT and C) contain material relating to the Chartist Land Company. The *Bibliography* contains information about other series which include Chartist material. The other manuscript sources which have been used include the Allsop papers in the British Library of Political and Economic Science, and the Minikin-Vincent papers in the library of the Labour Party. Other sources are mentioned in the notes to chapters.

Notes

Introduction

1. For a listing of published and unpublished work on Chartism until 1976, see J. F. C. Harrison and Dorothy Thompson, *Bibliography of the Chartist Movement* (Hassocks, 1978). Books and theses on local aspects of Chartism completed since 1976 include Carol Sue Bebb, 'The Chartist Movement in Dundee' (unpub. B. Phil, St Andrews, 1977); Owen Ashton, 'Chartism and Radicalism in Cheltenham and Gloucester' (unpub. Ph.D., Birmingham, 1980); John Ryan, 'Religion and Radical Politics in Birmingham 1820–1850' (unpub. M. Phil, Birmingham, 1979); Robert Fyson, 'Chartism in North Staffordshire' (unpub. Ph.D., Lancaster, 1983); Robert Sykes, 'Popular Politics and Trade Unionism in South-east Lancashire' (unpub. Ph.D., Manchester, 1982); and David Goodway, 'Chartism in London' (Ph.D., London, 1979), published as *London Chartism 1838-1848* (1982).
2. The most important recent study is J. A. Epstein, 'Feargus O'Connor and the English Working Class Radical Movement 1832-41' (Ph.D., Birmingham, 1977) and the same author's book, *The Lion of Freedom* (1981).
3. John Belchem, 'Radicalism as a "platform" agitation' (Ph.D., Sussex, 1974). See also the same author's 'Feargus O'Connor and the collapse of the mass platform' in J. A. Epstein and Dorothy Thompson (eds), *The Chartist Experience, Studies in Working-Class Radicalism and Culture, 1830-1860* (1982). Professor John Saville of Hull University and Dr David Large of the University of Bristol are also working on the year 1848 in Britain.
4. Mark Hovell, *The Chartist Movement* (1925 edn), p.164.
5. Asa Briggs, 'Feargus O'Connor and J. Bronterre O'Brien', in J. W. Boyle (ed.), *Leaders and Workers* (Cork, n.d. (1968?)), p.27.
6. For an account of Maxwell and Fielden's efforts on behalf of the handloom weavers, and Fielden's attempts to repeal the 1834 Poor Law Amendment Act, see Paul R. Richards, 'The State and the Working Class 1833–1841: M.P.s and the making of Social Policy' (unpub. Ph.D. thesis, Birmingham, 1975).

1. The Politics of the Reformed Parliament

1. Benjamin Wilson, *The Struggles of an Old Chartist: What he Knows and the Part he has Taken in Various Movements* (Halifax, 1887), p.3.
2. H.O. 20/10.
3. *London Mercury*, 11 March 1837.
4. William Cobbett, *Legacy to Labourers* (1834).
5. *Poor Man's Guardian*, 26 May 1832.
6. Angus Macintyre, *The Liberator* (1965), p.46.
7. Ellenborough, *Diary*, 15 February 1833, cited in Macintyre, op. cit., p.48.
8. *3 and 4 William IV cap 4* (1833) Suppression of Disturbances Bill.
9. *Nottingham Review*, 22 February 1833.
10. For a fuller account of O'Connell's relationship with the Chartists, see James Epstein, *The Lion of Freedom*, pp. 39-53. For O'Connor's accusations against O'Connell, see *A Series of Letters from Feargus O'Connor Esq. Barrister-at-Law, to Daniel O'Connell . . . containing a Review of Mr O'Connell's Conduct during the Agitation of the Question of Catholic Emancipation etc.* (1836).
11. *Report of the Proceedings of the Great Public Meeting etc.* (Birmingham, 1833).
12. R. G. Kirby and A. E. Musson, *The Voice of the People*, p.452.
13. For a slightly fuller discussion of this question, see my 'The Irish and English radicalism before the Famine' in Epstein and Thompson (eds), *The Chartist Experience* (1982).

14. For accounts of these activities see G. D. H. Cole, *Attempts at a General Union* (1953); Kirby and Musson, *The Voice of the People*; Iorwerth Prothero, *Artisans and Politics in Early Nineteenth Century London* (1979), pp.301-7; and E. P. Thompson, *The Making of the English Working Class* (1964), *passim*.
15. Cited in Joyce Marlow, *The Tolpuddle Martyrs* (1971), p.94.
16. For a recent account of the case, see W. H. Fraser, 'The Glasgow Cotton Spinners 1837', in John Butt and J. T. Ward (eds), *Scottish Themes* (Edinburgh, 1976).
17. Letter Pitkethly to Broyan, H.O. 40/47 f530.
18. *The Cotton Spinners' Farewell* (Newcastle, 1838). Discovered by Roy Palmer and reprinted in full (with suggested tune) in his *Ballad History of England* (1979), p.115.
19. *Northern Star*, 14 May 1838.
20. *Northern Star*, 31 March 1838.
21. *London Dispatch*, 10 Dec. 1837.
22. A. Alison, *Some Accounts of my Life and Writings. An Autobiography*, edited by Lady Alison (Edinburgh, 1883).
23. Letter in *London Dispatch*, cited in Alfred (Samuel Kydd), *History of the Factory Movement*, Vol. 11, p.844.
24. *Ibid*, p.109. This was the occasion of his famous speech in which he said that if the magistrates refused to act on complaints against abuse of the Act 'bring with you your children, and tell them to ask their grandmothers for a few of their old knitting needles, which I will instruct them how to apply to the spindles which will teach these law-defying magistrates to have respect for . . . the factory law'.
25. Angus Macintyre, *The Liberator*, pp.139-46.
26. The debate in the House of Commons was reprinted in full in Charles Wing, *Evils of the Factory System Demonstrated by Parliamentary Evidence* (1837, repr. 1967), pp.383-430. For Feargus O'Connor's comments on the debate and O'Connell's part in it, see *A Series of Letters to Daniel O'Connor Esq M.P.* (1836), pp.83-98.
27. An attempt by the metropolitan police commissioner to use the police to clear the streets of radical meetings. A prohibited though entirely peaceful meeting was dispersed, and a policeman stabbed in the scuffling. A London jury returned a verdict of 'justifiable homicide'. See Gavin Thurston, *The Clerkenwell Riot* (1967), and for the context see T. M. Parssinen, 'Association, convention and anti-parliament in British radical politics, 1771-1848', *English Historical Review*, Vol. LXXXVIII (July 1973), No. CCCXLVIII.
28. H.O. 73 – *Answers to questions sent out by Constabulary Commissioners, for the returns to the questionnaire. First Report of the Commissioners Appointed to Inquire as to the best means of Establishing an Efficient Constabulary Force in the counties of England and Wales* (1839), for the report. For attitudes to the police during the Chartist years, see R. D. Storch, 'The Plague of Blue Locusts', *International Review of Social History*, Vol. XX (1975), Part 1.
29. *Poor Man's Guardian*, 3 January 1835.
30. *Penny Political Magazine*, 17 September 1836, cited in Wiener, *War of the Unstamped*, p.223.
31. Hansard, Third series, XXXVI col. 1014. For a full account of Fielden's opposition to the Bill in the House of Commons, and his attempt in 1838 to get it repealed, see Paul Richards, 'The State and the Working Class 1833-1841: M.P.'s and the making of Social Policy' (unpub. Ph.D., Birmingham, 1975).
32. Kydd, *History of the Factory Movement*, Vol. II, p.76.
33. *Bronterre's National Reformer*, 11 March 1837.
34. *Bronterre's National Reformer*, 7 Jan. 1837.
35. *Halifax Guardian*, 8 Oct. 1836.
36. *Northern Star*, 5 May 1838.
37. *Halifax Courier*, 22 June 1895.
38. *Northern Star* 27 Jan. 1838.
Halifax Guardian, 23 Jan. 1838 (this account reprinted in full in *The Early Chartists*).
39. Joseph Rayner Stephens, *A Sermon Preached at Primrose Hill, London, on Sunday May 12th 1839* (1839).
40. *Northern Star*, 2 February 1839.
41. *The Charter*, 10 March 1839.
42. R. G. Gammage, *The History of the Chartist Movement* (1894 edn), p.61.
43. *Twopenny Dispatch*, 10 September 1836.
44. *Northern Star*, 23 June 1838.

Notes

2. The Chartist Press

1. Two very full accounts of the unstamped are to be found in P. Hollis *The Pauper Press* (1970) and Joel Wiener *The War of the Unstamped* (1969 Ithaca). Much of the information in the following paragraph is taken from these works.
2. H.O. 20/10. For Benbow see I. J. Prothero, 'William Benbow and the concept of the "General Strike"', *Past and Present*, No. 63 (May 1971), and entry in *Dictionary of Labour Movement Biography*, John Saville and Joyce Bellamy (eds), Vol. 3.
3. George Laval Chesterton, *Revelations of Prison Life* (2 vols, 1856), Vol. 1, pp. 195, 204.
4. J. A. Epstein, 'Feargus O'Connor and the Northern Star', *International Review of Social History*, Vol. XXI, Part 1 (1976). A fuller discussion of some of the points in this section will be found in this article, and in my 'La Presse de la Classe Ouvrière Anglaise, 1836-1848' in Jacques Godechot (ed.), *La Presse Ouvrière 1819-1850* (Paris, 1966).
5. D. J. Rowe, 'The London Working Men's Association and the People's Charter', *Past and Present*, No. 36 (April 1967).
6. J. A. Epstein, *The Lion of Freedom*, Chapter 1, for the pre-Chartist radical career of O'Connor.
7. Letter William Cobbett to Joshua Hobson (Tolsen Memorial Museum, Huddersfield).
8. J. Wiener, *War of the Unstamped*, p.109. And see the press reports of the great Guildhall meeting called in March 1836 by the middle-class Association for the Abolition of the Stamp Duty on Newspapers.
9. Cited in J. Wiener, *op. cit.*, p.271.
10. *New Weekly True Sun*, 19 March 1836.
11. *London Dispatch*, 17 December 1836.
12. *Bronterre's National Reformer*, Vol. 1, No. 1 (7 Jan. 1837).
13. *Ibid*, Vol. 1, No. 11 (18 March 1837).
14. *Halifax Courier*, 6 September 1884.
15. Angela V. John, 'The Chartist Endurance: Industrial South Wales, 1840–1868', *Morgannwg*, Vol. XV (1971).
16. For example, his 'Address to the Women of England' in Vol. 1, No. 13. The Ellis biography is in Vol. II, beginning at No. 143.
17. A valuable series of letters to Cooper is in T.S. 11/600, 601, 602.
18. *Notes to the People*, Introduction to Vol. 1, 1851.
19. The *Northern Tribune*, 19 May 1855. The paper was absorbed by the *Reasoner* in 1855.
20. For a full account see J. A. Epstein, 'Feargus O'Connor and the Northern Star', *International Review of Social History*, Vol. XXI, Part 1 (1976).
21. G. J. Holyoake, *Life of Joseph Rayner Stephens* (1881), p.86.
22. *Northern Star*, 23 June 1838.
23. George Robinson to Thomas Cooper, T. S. 11/601 X/L05 744 .
24. *Newcastle Weekly Chronicle*, 7 November 1896, letter from Thomas Hayes, Lower Crumpsall, Manchester.
25. Autobiography of Thomas Wood, engineer, of Bingley, reprinted in John Burnett (ed.), *Useful Toil* (1974), p.308.
26. Ben Brierley, *Home Memories and Recollections of Life* (1886), p.23.
27. Brophy to Cooper, 20 November 1841. T.S. 11/600.
28. Samuel Fielden, 'Autobiography' reprinted in Philip S. Foner (ed.), *The Autobiographies of the Haymarket Martyrs* (New York, 1969).
29. *Northern Star*, 23 February 1839.
30. William Robertson, *The Social and Political History of Rochdale* (Rochdale n.d. [?1889]), p.15.
31. W. J. O'Neill Daunt, *Eighty-five Years of Irish History 1800-1885* (1886), Vol. 1, p.268.
32. In the second half of 1839 the circulation of the *Star* averaged over 30,000; in 1840, 18,500; in 1841, 13,000; 1842, 12,500. After this sales fell more steeply, to 7,500 in 1844, 6,000 in 1846. The figures rose again to around 11,000 in 1847 and 12,000 in 1848. O'Connor claimed to have sold 21,000 copies of the issue of 15 April 1848. For 1849 the figures averaged 7,000 weekly, and for 1850, 5,000. For more detailed figures and for comparisons with other provincial weeklies, see Donald Read, *Press and People 1790-1850. Opinion in three English Cities* (1961), appendix.
33. Frank Peel, *Spen Valley Past and Present* (Heckmondwyke, 1893), p.319. Samuel

Shaw, of Hyde, remembered his mother reading the *Star* aloud to his father and friends in the kitchen. Thomas Middleton, *History of Hyde* (Hyde, 1934) p.122, and there are many more such accounts.

34. F. G. and R. M. Black (eds), *The Harney Papers* (Assen, 1969), p.62.
35. *Northern Star*, 3 March 1839. Two weeks later, O'Connor was complaining that Harney 'looked upon the *Northern Star* as his property' and 'endeavoured to make it the organ of socialism and to merge the question of Chartism and the question of socialism'. For an interesting discussion of the divisive effects of republican and other ultra-radical ideas on the mass movement, see John Belchem, 'Republicanism, Popular Constitutionalism and the Radical Platform in early nineteenth century England', *Social History*, Vol. 6, No. 1.
36. British Museum, Add. MSS. 27,820, f 25.
37. *Northern Star*, 21 Sept. 1839.
38. Thomas Ainge Devyr, *The Odd Book of the Nineteenth Century* (New York, 1882), Chapters XI, XII, XIII.
39. Benjamin Wilson, *Struggles*, p.19.

3. 'We, Your Petitioners'

1. *Bronterre's National Reformer*, 4 Feb. 1837.
2. *Northern Star*, 16 June 1838.
3. *London Dispatch*, 24 Feb. 1839.
4. *Northern Star*, 14 March 1840.
5. W. Lovett, *Life and Struggles*, p.95, n. 1 refers to this episode as though he had only heard of it much later. In fact, there was considerable discussion in the radical press at the time, and cuttings relating to the warnings against O'Connell given by other radical MPs are in the cuttings books of the Lovett collection in Birmingham public library.
6. Graham Wallas, *Life of Francis Place* (1918 edn.), p.371.
7. Matthew Fletcher, *Letters to the Inhabitants of Bury* (Bury, 1852), Letter IV, pp.4-5.
8. e.g. *Fleet Papers*, 20 March 1841.
9. *The Times*, 21 May 1839.
10. *Bradford Daily Telegraph*, 7 March 1895.
11. T. M. Parssinen, 'Association, Convention and Anti-Parliament in British Radical Politics, 1771-1848', *English Historical Review*, No. 88 (July 1973). I. J. Prothero, 'William Benbow and the Concept of the General Strike', *Past and Present*, No. 38 (Dec. 1967).
12. D. McForan, 'Birmingham Radicalism 1815-1820' (unpub. M.A. thesis, Birmingham University, 1982).
13. Add. MSS. 27,821 Appendix D f 161.
14. Fletcher, *Letters*, Letter IV, p.7.
15. J. A. Epstein thesis, p.262.
16. Add. MSS. 34,245 A.
17. T. M. Kemnitz, 'The Chartist Convention of 1839', in *Albion*, Vol. 10, No. 2 (summer 1978). Parssinen, loc. cit.; Epstein, thesis and *Lion of Freedom*, pp.138-194.
18. Probably James Taylor of Rochdale.
19. Fletcher, *Letters*, Letter IV, p.8.
20. Vincent to Minikin, Oct. 1838.
21. *Newcastle Weekly Chronicle*, 5 Jan. 1890.
22. Lovett, *Life and Struggles*, p.172.
23. *Northern Star*, 4 May 1839.
24. Lovett, *Life and Struggles*, p.180.
25. The other proposals were: withdrawal of savings from banks and savings banks, conversion of all paper money into gold, arming, putting up Chartist candidates at the hustings, exclusive dealing, the resolve not to be diverted from the charter by any other agitation, and a promise to obey 'all the just and constitutional requests of the majority of the Convention'. These proposals were to be put to simultaneous meetings throughout the kingdom.
26. *Northern Star*, 15 June 1839.
27. Rev. Francis Close, *The Female Chartists' Visit to the Parish Church . . .* (1839), pp.26-7.
28. *Justice of the Peace*, Aug. 1839.
29. *Hansard*, Vol. XLIX, 3rd series, col. 1200.
30. *Northern Star*, 10 Aug. 1839.
31. W. Napier, *Life and Opinions of General Sir Charles James Napier* (1857), Vol. II, p.59.
32. Ibid, p.42.
33. Ibid, p.42.
34. Ibid, p.89.
35. Lord Broughton (James Cam Hobhouse), *Recollections of a Long Life* (1909), Vol. 5, pp. 220, 222.
36. Holyoake, *Life of Stephens*, p.165.
37. Holyoake, 'G. D. H. Cole', *Chartist Portraits* (1941); T. M. Kemnitz and Fleurange Jaques, 'J. R. Stephens and the Chartist Movement', *International Review of Social History*, Vol. XIX, Part 2 (1974).

4. The Newport Rising

1. *Trial of Feargus O'Connor and Fifty-eight Others* (1843), p.x.
2. Lord Broughton, [J. C. Hobhouse], *Recollections of a Long Life* (ed. Lady Dorchester) (1909), Vol. V, p.240.
3. David Williams, 'Chartism in Wales', in Asa Briggs (ed.), *Chartist Studies*, pp.233-4. See also the exchange of letters between Lord John Russell and John Frost in the *Annual Register*, 1839.
4. For the fullest discussion of the events of November 1839, see David Williams, *John Frost* (1939), A. R. Schoyen, *The Chartist Challenge* (1958) and A. J. Peacock, *Chartism in Bradford* (York, 1969). John Baxter of Sheffield University is working on an extended study of the insurrectionary aspects of the Chartist movement, while David Jones of Swansea University will shortly begin a total reassessment of all the evidence, Welsh and English, concerning the events at Newport.
5. Broughton, *Recollections*, Vol. V, p.240.
6. Broughton, *Recollections*, Vol. V, p.242.
7. *Chartist Studies*, pp.240-1.
8. *Newcastle Weekly Chronicle*, 5 Jan. 1890.
9. *Manifesto of the General Convention*, printed in full in Lovett, *Life and Struggles*, p.172.
10. Peacock, *Bradford Chartism*, for the best recent account.
11. Napier, Vol. II, p.126.
12. Three letters, Taylor to Lovett, in Lovett Collection, Birmingham Central Reference Library.
13. Alexander Wilson, 'John Taylor Esq, M.D., of Backhouse, Ayrshire,' *Ayrshire Archeological and Natural History Society Collections*, 2nd series, Vol. 1 (1947-9).
14. Burland, MS Annuals, pp.197-8.
15. T. A. Devyr, *The Odd Book of the Nineteenth Century* (New York, 1882), pp.194-5.
16. *Last Farewell to England of Frost Williams and Jones*, Broadside ballad (Shrewsbury, 1840). Printed in full in Roy Palmer, *A Ballad History of England* (1979), pp.118-19.
17. Thomas Cooper, *Purgatory of Suicides* (1845), Book 5, St. XII. This passage was omitted from Cooper's *Collected Works* published later in the century.
18. *Midland Counties Illuminator*, 1 May 1841. There were a large number of street ballads about the Newport rising, many, like that printed in John Ashton's *Modern Street Ballads* (1888), very far from hostile. One verse of 'A New Hunting Song' went

John Frost in Wales a-hunting went, and well knew how to ride,
He had a fine-bred Chartist horse but got on the wrong side.
If he had held the reins quite firm in his own hand,
They'd ne'er have hunted him into Van Dieman's Land.

5. Leaders and Followers

1. *A New Song to be Sung* . . . etc. (Birmingham, n.d. [1840]). Reprinted in full in Roy Palmer (ed.), *A Ballad History of England* (1978).
2. e.g. *Northern Star*, 9 July 1842, 'we insert no nominations for council without trades and residences'.
3. For an analysis of the 476 trades represented among Chartist prisoners held in England and Wales, according to information supplied to Parliament by the Home Secretary, see Christopher Godfrey, 'The Chartist Prisoners 1839-41', *International Review of Social History*, Vol. XXIII (1979), Part 2. The list itself is published in the Parliamentary Papers and the *English Chartist Circular*; see n. 39, p. 382 below.
4. These are reports based on interviews with 73 Chartist prisoners in the winter of 1840-1, and are in the series H.O. 20/10. They consist of answers to questions on a pro forma interview sheet, with additional notes in some cases on conversations. For a fuller discussion of them, see James Epstein and Christopher Godfrey, 'H.O 20/10: Interviews of Chartist Prisoners, 1840-41', *Bulletin of the Society for the Study of Labour History*, No. 34 (1977).
5. MS Membership Book of the Great Horton Chartist Association, 1840-1866, in Bradford Central Library.
6. B.T. 41/475, 5 and 6.
7. *Yorkshire Gazette*, 27 Oct. 1855, which also gives information about the numbers who claimed from different Yorkshire towns.
8. Select Committee on the National Land Company: *Parliamentary Papers* (Reports

from Committees), Session 1847-48, Vol. XIX.

9. Alice Mary Hadfield, *The Chartist Land Company* (Newton Abbot, 1970) pp.60-4.
10. Thomas Frost, *Forty Years Recollections* (1880) p.96.
11. For the London membership assessments, David Goodway, *London Chartism*, pp.16 and 17. It can be argued that he makes too many calculations based on what are clearly very inadequate numbers of known Chartists, but provided that the somewhat notional quality of the numbers is recognised, the tables are interesting. David Jones's list is in *Chartism and the Chartists*, pp.134-5. The thesis by Christopher Godfrey, *Chartist Lives: the Anatomy of a Working-Class Movement* (unpub. Ph.D., Harvard, 1978) contains some valuable short biographies and analyses based on them, as well as some tables based on NCA committee membership. It is, however, inevitably biased as a statistical study by the availability of biographical material, and by the factors discussed here which governed the publication of committee names.
12. Biographies continue to appear in *Dictionary of Labour Movement Biography*, edited by Joyce Bellamy and John Saville, and work is in progress on others.
13. Napier, Vol. II, p.83.
14. H.O. 20/10.
15. For an expansion of this point, see my review article, 'Radicals and their Historians' in *Literature and History*, No. 5 (Spring 1977), pp.104-9.
16. Hansard, *Parliamentary Debates*, 23 May 1848 (cols 1309 – 10).
17. J. A. Epstein, *The Lion of Freedom* (1982), pp.90 ff.
18. *The Harney Papers*, pp.241-2.
19. There are one or two letters from O'Connor to Harney in *The Harney Papers*, and a number of letters to Thomas Allsopp in the collection in the London School of Economics. The memoirs of O'Neil Daunt are full of personal anecdotes and recollections. Daunt was a boyhood friend, although a political opponent in later life. He spoke of O'Connor's charm, humour and gifts of mimicry and repartee, and of his manners which 'in private [were] courteous and refined, in public . . . were hearty, rattling and impulsive . . . '
20. Napier, *op. cit.*, pp.48-9.
21. W. J. O'Neil Daunt, *85 Years of Irish History*, p.244.
22. Thomas Frost, 'The Life and Times of John Vallance', *Barnsley Times*, May 1882.
23. Adam Rushton, *My Life as Farmer's Boy, Factory Lad, Teacher and Preacher* (Manchester, 1909), p.64.
24. Samuel Fielden, 'Autobiography', reprinted in P. S. Foner (ed.) *The Autobiographies of the Haymarket Martyrs* (New York, 1969).
25. Charles Wilkins, *History of Merthyr Tydfil* (Merthyr Tydfil, 1867), p.92.
26. F. P. [Sir J. Frederick Pollock] to George Maule, 7 October 1842 (unnumbered letter in TS 11/600). Letters to Sir James Graham, the Home Secretary, on the same lines from Pollock are in the Graham papers, Bundle 54A, dated 9 and 12 October 1842 (microfilm in Cambridge University Library).
27. Napier, Vol. II, pp. 83, 88-9.
28. Stan Shipley, *Club Life and Socialism in mid-Victorian London* (Oxford, 1971), records a few of these men. They seem to be the model taken by Mark Rutherford for the character of Marshall the cabinet-maker in *Clara Hopgood* (1896). He is a serious, rather humourless rationalist, who spent 'many of his evenings away from home at political meetings'. The novel is set in the 1840s, although written half a century later.
29. W. J. Linton, *Memories* (1895), p.42.
30. E. Belfort Bax, obituary notices of Fr. Engels, *Justice*, 24 August 1895.
31. Letter from Thomas McConnell, *Bronterre's National Reformer*, 28 January 1837.
32. H.O. 20/10.
33. *John Watkins to the People* (1844), p.12.
34. O'Brien to Allsop, Letter no. 21, n.d. [Sept. 1847?].
35. O'Brien to Allsop, Letter no. 2, 17 June 1840.
36. O'Brien to Allsop, Letter no. 22, n.d. [Sept. 1847?].
37. White to Cooper, 27 July 1842, T.S. 11/601.
38. *Midland Counties Illuminator*, 17 April 1841.

6. The Manufacturing Communities

1. *London Democrat*, 18 May 1839.
2. See L. W. Smith, 'The Kidderminster Carpet Industry, 1800-1850' (unpub. Ph.D. thesis, Birmingham University, 1982).
3. *National Reformer*, 8 May 1847.
4. For example, the very interesting series of letters in the local paper by Joseph Lawson, re-published as *Progress in Pudsey* (Stanningley, 1887) and the series 'Halifax 60 years ago, and the Progress it has made' in the *Halifax Courier* in February 1893 onwards.
5. William Brown, *Reminiscences of Flax Spinning* (Dundee, 1861), pp.19-20.
6. James Myles, *Rambles in Forfarshire* (Dundee, 1850), cited in Carol Sue Bebb, 'Chartism in Dundee'.
7. *Dundee Advertiser*, 23 May 1834, cited in Carol Sue Bebb, 'The Chartist Movement in Dundee' (unpub. B. Phil thesis, St Andrews, 1977).
8. William Lovett, *Life and Struggles*, p.25.
9. Joseph Gutteridge, *Sunlight and Shadows* in Valerie E. Chancellor (ed.), *Master and Artisan in Victorian England* (1969), p.98.
10. 'An Old Potter' [Charles Shaw], *When I was a Child* (1903), p.50.
11. See D. A. Reid, 'The Decline of St. Monday', *Past and Present*, No. 71 (Spring 1976) for a fuller discussion of this question.
12. See E. P. Thompson, *The Making of the English Working Class*, Ch. 9, for an account of the pre-Chartist experience of the weavers and their petitions.
13. Paul Richards, 'The State and early industrial capitalism: the case of the Handloom weavers', *Past and Present*, No. 83 (May 1979).
14. *Reports of the Handloom Weavers' Commissioners*, 1840, Part III, p.590.
15. Benjamin Disraeli, *Sybil* (Penguin edn), p.150.
16. *The Reverend Humphrey Price to his Native Townsmen, the Kidderminster Carpet Weavers* (1836).
17. 'Memorabilia of the late John Hartley . . . Hebden Bridge Chartist, Radical, Socialist and Co-operator', cuttings from *Todmorden and District News*, summer 1903 (in Halifax Public Library).
18. J. F. C. Harrison, *Learning and Living, 1790-1960* (1961), p.237.
19. Testified by the lists of founders and directors in the many half-century booklets and volumes issued around the turn of the century, and in the more recently-issued centenary volumes, particularly from Lancashire and the West Riding.
20. 'An Old Potter' [Charles Shaw], *When I was a Child*, (1903) pp.67-9.
21. Tr. and ed. Barrie M. Ratcliffe and W. H. Chaloner, *A French Sociologist Looks at Britain, Gustave d'Eichthal and British Society in 1828* (Manchester 1977), p.47.
22. J. Lawson, *Progress in Pudsey*, p.9.
23. Manifesto 'To the Working Men of Barnsley', June 1838, reprinted in *Barnsley Chronicle*, 29 June 1889.
24. 'Address of the Female Political Union of Newcastle upon Tyne to their Fellow Countrywomen', *Northern Star*, 2 Feb. 1839 (reprinted in *The Early Chartists*).
25. See below, pp.182-5.
26. Harrison and Hollis, *Robert Lowery*, pp.164-5.
27. Benjamin Wilson, *Struggles*, p.16.
28. *Northern Star*, 2 Jan. 1841.
29. Ibid.
30. *Colchester Gazette*, 1 August, 1935, reprinted in Arthur Brown, *English History from Essex Sources'* (1952), p.175.
31. W. E. Adams, *Memoirs of a Social Atom*, Vol. I, pp.92-9.
32. Clive Barker, 'The Chartists, Theatre Reform and Research', *Theatre Quarterly*, Vol. I, No. 4 (December 1971). Trevor H. Lloyd, 'Dr. Wade and the Working Class', *Midland History*, Vol. II, No. 2 (Autumn 1973).
33. W. E. Adams, *Memoirs of a Social Atom*, Vol. I, p.142. A collection of Willey's ballads is in the Madden Ballad Collection, Vol. 23, in Cambridge University Library.

7. The Women

1. *London Dispatch*, 24 Feb. 1839.
2. *Northern Star*, 10 March 1839. Total number of Birmingham signatures to the first petition was 86,180.
3. *Northern Star*, 11 May 1839.
4. The fullest accounts of Chartist women's activities are C. E. Martin, 'Female

Chartism, a study in Politics', unpub. M. A. dissertation, University of Wales (Swansea), 1973; my 'Women and Nineteenth Century Radical Politics' in (eds.) Juliet Mitchell and Ann Oakley, *The Rights and Wrongs of Women* (1976); Malcolm Thomis and Jennifer Grimmett, *Women in Protest* (1982), esp. Ch. 6; and David Jones, 'Women and Chartism' in *History*, vol. 68, no. 222 (February 1983).

5. J. A. Epstein, 'Some Aspects of Working-class Politics, Organisation and Culture: Nottingham Chartism in the 1840's' in J. A. Epstein and Dorothy Thompson (eds), *The Chartist Experience* (1982) for this and other aspects of the women's participation in Nottingham.
6. Benjamin Wilson, *The Struggles of an Old Chartist* (Halifax, 1887), p.15.
7. *Notes to the People*, Vol. II, p.709 (Merlin reprint, 1967). The letter, written in 1852, was signed by Abadiah Higginbothan, corresponding secretary of the Sheffield Women's Rights Association. There is no indication as to whether this group is in direct continuity with the Female Chartist Association of 1839.
8. *English Chartist Circular*, Vol. 2, No. 91.
9. *English Chartist Circular*, Vol. 2, No. 33.
10. William Lovett, *Life and Struggles*, p.141n.
11. *The People's Charter* (3rd edn), 1838, p.9.
12. Reginald John Richardson, *The Rights of Woman* (1840), reprinted in *The Early Chartists*, p.124.
13. *Ibid*, p.126.
14. *English Chartist Circular*, Vol. I, No. 13 (April 1841).
15. *Scottish Chartist Circular*, 9 Dec. 1839.
16. *Northern Star*, 2 Feb. 1839.
17. H.O. 45/55.
18. *Bradford Observer*, 4 Oct. 1838.
19. For a discussion of Owenism and feminist ideas see Barbara Taylor, *Eve and the New Jerusalem* (1983).
20. *Halifax Courier*, 25 August 1892.
21. *Annals of Barnsley* p.117.
22. B.T. 41/474.
23. *Trial of Feargus O'Connor and Fifty-eight Others* (1843), p.397.
24. *National Reformer*, new series, 22 March 1847.
25. Thomas Cooper, *Life*, p.6.
26. John Bedford Leno, *The Aftermath* (1892), p.30.
27. Cited in L. W. Smith, 'The Kidderminster Carpet Industry 1800-1850' (unpub. Ph.D. thesis, Birmingham University, 1982).
28. Frank Peel, *Old Cleckheaton, with reminiscences of some of its worthies* (1884), p.126.
29. *The Labourer*, Vol. IV, 1848, p.252. Compare this passage with the article on 'Servants' in the *English Chartist Circular*, Vol. I, No. 8, in which the whole idea of domestic service is condemned outright.
30. *National Reformer*, new series, 27 March 1847.
31. The proportion of women in full-time work fell between 1841 and 1851 and then remained fairly constant until 1871 (the actual numbers increased, as population was rising). During these thirty years the proportion of fully employed women working in the textile trades declined, while that of those in domestic service increased steadily. (Summarised from Mitchell and Deane, *Abstract of British Historical Statistics*, p.55.)
32. *Reynolds's Weekly Newspaper*, 8 Sept. 1850.
33. Thomas Frost, 'The Life and Times of John Vallance', *Barnsley Times*, 1882 (cuttings in Barnsley Public Library).
34. J. B. Leno, *Aftermath*, p.4.
35. *Ashton Reporter*, 30 Jan. 1869, and see my 'Women and Radical Politics'.
36. Vincent–Minikin correspondence, *passim*; and see reports of many of these meetings in *Northern Star*, 1838-9.
37. *Annual Register*, 1839.
38. *Western Vindicator* 28 Sept. 1839.
39. *Northern Star*, 17 March 1838, records a donation to the National Rent from the Ancient United Order of Druidesses, meeting at the Waggon and Horses Inn, Ossett Streetside, Elland.
40. *Boot and Shoemaker*, 8 Feb. 1879. Among the active Elland women was Mary Grasby, wife of James, who went on to become a nationally known figure and a member of the NCA executive in the later forties.
41. *Northern Star*, 24 Feb. 1838.
42. Georg Weerth, *Collected Works* (Berlin, 1956), Vol. 11, p.39.
43. Ibid, p.192.
44. *Northern Star*, 9 March 1839. My attention was drawn to this reference by Jonathan Smith of York University.

45. *English Chartist Circular*, Vol. 1, No. 33 (Aug. 1841).
46. *Northern Star*, 4 Aug. 1839.
47. *Halifax Guardian*, 16 Dec. 1848.
48. *Northern Star*, 9 May 1845.
49. See for a fuller account of Nottingham women, J. A. Epstein, 'Some Aspects of working-class Politics . . . ' (*op. cit.*)
50. *Northern Star*, 8 Dec. 1838.
51. William Roworth, *Observations on the Administration of the New Poor Law in Nottingham* (Nottingham, 1840).
52. *Nottingham Review*, Nov., Dec. 1838, *passim.*
53. *Northern Star*, 6 May 1843.
54. *Nottingham Mercury*, 16 May 1839, cited in Epstein, *loc. cit.*
55. *Northern Star*, 8 Dec. 1838. Account also based on *Northern Liberator*, 8 Dec. 1838.
56. *Northern Star*, 2 Feb. 1839 (reprinted in full in *The Early Chartists*).
57. *Northern Star*, 19 Jan. 1839.
58. *Northern Liberator*, 26 Jan. 1839.
59. *Northern Liberator*, 13 Dec. 1839.
60. *Northern Liberator*, 8 June 1839.
61. *Northern Star*, 16 April 1838.
62. Vincent–Minikin corr. Letter, 7 Aug, 1838. Vincent spoke of 50,000 women, 'all neatly and cleanly attired'.
63. Report from Wilson, 17 Dec. 1839, H.O. 40/50.
64. *Birmingham Journal*, 27 Aug. 1842.
65. Ibid. For a fuller account of this episode, see John Ryan, 'Religion and Radical Politics in Birmingham 1830-1850' (unpub. M.Litt. thesis, University of Birmingham, 1979).
66. *Northern Star*, 27 April 1839.
67. *The Charter*, 27 Oct. 1839.
68. *A Return from each gaol and House of Correction etc.* (1840). Edward Hamer, *The Chartist Outbreak in Llanidloes* (Llanidloes, 1867), *passim.*
69. *A Return from each gaol and House of Correction etc.* (1840).
70. H.O. 20/10.
71. H.O. 20/10 – inverview with Samuel Holberry.
72. Burland, *Annals of Barnsley*, p.113.
73. Benjamin Disraeli, *Sybil* (Penguin edn, 1980), p.424.
74. Ibid. pp.451-2.
75. *Northern Star*, 18 Feb. 1843.
76. Letter Jane Jones to Ernest Jones, n.d. [1851] (Seligman Coll.).
77. *Advocate and Operative Reporter*, 20 Nov. 1832, cited in R. G. Kirby and A. E. Musson, *The Voice of the People* (Manchester, 1975), p.6.
78. Letter, George White to Mark Norman, 18 Oct. 1849, in F. G. and R. M. Black (eds), *The Harney Papers* (Assen, 1969), p.88.
79. Letter Vincent–Minikin, 2 Oct. 1838.
80. *Cheltenham Free Press*, 28 Nov. 1840.
81. *Cheltenham Free Press*, 14 Oct. 1843.
82. *Northern Star*, 2 Jan. 1841. The *Star* had a regular column of 'Young patriots', from which all the following examples are also culled.
83. *Northern Star*, 27 Feb. 1841.
84. *Northern Star*, 13 March 1841.
85. Cited in R. Fyson, *Chartism in Northern Staffordshire* (Stafford, 1981), p.23.
86. *The Times*, 25 and 28 Oct. 1842.
English Chartist Circular, Vol 2, no. 90. September 1842.
87. *Essex Standard*, 21 Dec. 1838, re-printed in A. J. Brown, *English History from Essex Sources* (1952).
88. *Sheffield Telegraph*, 6 April 1839.
89. Rev. Francis Close, *A Sermon Addressed to the Female Chartists of Cheltenham*, 1839, p.17. The Cheltenham Female Radical Association had 300 members in June 1839, according to the *Western Vindicator*, 29 June 1839.
90. H.O. 40/42, ff 175-7. Letter, Longridge to Howick, 10 June 1839, and see *Northern Liberator*, 8 June 1839.
91. *Western Vindicator*, 28 Sept. 1839.
92. e.g. *Northern Star*, 17 Dec. 1840 – 'Mrs. Anna Pepper delivered a lecture to the female Chartists in Bradford on the political duties of women'.
93. *Northern Star*, 7 May 1842.
94. Ibid, 14 Jan. 1843.
95. Ibid, 2 July 1842.
96. Ibid, 8 July 1843.
97. *Annual Register*, 5 Dec. 1842, cited in Caroline Martin, 'Female Chartism'. Lloyd's *Illustrated London Newspaper* on 27 Nov. 1842 carried a report which could have been tongue in cheek that 'a marriage is on the *tapis* between Mr Thomas Slingsby Duncombe, M.P. and the celebrated *patriotess* Miss Mary Ann Walker'.

98. *Northern Star*, 17 Feb. 1838.
99. Ibid, 20 May 1843.
100. Ibid, 13 Feb. 1847.
101. H.O. 45/2410 (3).
102. For a discussion of the limits on the public participation of women in middle-class reform movements, see Alex Tyrrel, '"Woman's Mission" and Pressure Group Politics in Britain, 1825-60' in *Bulletin of the John Rylands University Library of Manchester*, Vol. 63, No. 1 (Autumn 1980).
103. For example, Emma Martin chaired a meeting of the 'female inhabitants of London' at Millbank in support of Frost, Williams and Jones in January 1840 (*Northern Star*, 1 Feb. 1840) and Mrs Chapelsmith seems to have sided with the Chartists when they clashed with the League in Bradford in September 1841 (*Northern Star*, 18 Sept. 1841).
104. MS Letter Elizabeth Pease to Wendell and Ann Phillips, 29 March 1842, MS A. 1.2. Vol. 12(2) Anti-Slavery letters to Garrison no. 94 in Friends Library, Euston Road.
105. MS letter Elizabeth Pease to Wendell and Ann Phillips, Ibid, Vol. 12 (2), No. 79.
106. MS letter Elizabeth Pease to Wendell and Ann Phillips, 29 March 1842, Ibid, No. 94.
107. MS letter William Shaen to his sister, 6 July 1841 (Symington Papers, Box 19, Leeds Public Library). Shaen was a solicitor by profession, and a Unitarian. He was a member, with Linton, Cooper and others, of the Peopies' International League in 1849.

8. Traders and Professional Men

1. The limitations on the sale of such goods, and a case in which a joiner was prosecuted for selling a workbox which he had made outside his own parish, were taken as the theme of a novel, *Gideon Giles the Roper*, published in 1841 by the novelist friend of Thomas Cooper, Thomas Miller.
2. *Poor Man's Guardian*, 7 Sept. 1833.
3. See biography of Cleave in DLMB, vol. IV.
4. C. Godfrey, thesis, pp.505-6.
5. Obit. *Huddersfield Weekly News*, 13 May 1876; Cecil Driver, *Tory Radical*; J. F. C. Harrison 'Chartism in Leeds' in Briggs (ed.), *Chartist Studies*; and C. Godfrey, thesis, p.508.
6. D. E. F. Sykes, *Huddersfield and its Vicinity* (Huddersfield, 1898), p.302.
7. Thomas Dunning, in D. Vincent (ed.), *Testaments of Radicalism*, p.135.
8. Wilkinson, *Barnsley Obituaries* (scrap book in Barnsley Central Library), p.57 (obit. of Thos. Lingard, Nov. 1878).
9. H.O. 20/10.
10. C. J. Hunt, *The Book Trade in Northumberland and Durham to 1860* (Newcastle, 1975); obit., notice in *Newcastle Weekly Chronicle*, 31 March 1883; Ernest Jones papers, Seligman Collection, Columbia.
11. *English Chartist Circular*, 1841-3, *passim*.
12. Obit. of Binns, *Northern Star*, 5 Feb. 1848.
13. G. Godfrey, thesis, p.561.
14. T.S. 11/601.
15. T.S. 11/601.
16. *The Life of Thomas Cooper, written by himself*, Chs 13–25 and *passim*.
17. *Midland Counties Illuminator*, 20 Feb. 1841, and see David Williams, *John Frost*, p.257.
18. H.O. 20/10.
19. John Latimer, *Local Records or Historical Register of Remarkable Events which have occurred in Northumberland and Durham, Newcastle-upon-Tyne and Berwick-upon-Tweed. 1832-1857* (Newcastle, 1857), p.245.
20. *Northern Liberator*, 7 Sept. 1839.
21. Obit., *Northern Star*, 1838.
22. *Northern Star*, 10 Aug. 1839.
23. George Barnsby, *The Working Class Movement in the Black Country* (Wolverhampton, 1977). For the detailed information about Linney, I have been very much helped by the series of biographies of Black Country Chartists compiled by John Rowley and Eric Taylor, which will eventually appear in the DLMB.
24. Information from John Rowley, as yet unpublished.
25. David Williams, *John Frost*, for a fuller picture of the fascinating character Zephenia Williams.
26. Angela V. John, 'The Chartist Endurance: Industrial South Wales, 1840–1868', *Morgannwg*, Vol. XV, 1971.
27. *Northern Star*, 27 May 1843.
28. Report dated 10 Aug. 1839 to the Home Office of a meeting held by the Bradford Chartists, and the resolutions passed at it.

(Harewood Papers, Leeds City Library.) Vevers moved a resolution protesting against the brutality of the authorities in Birmingham, and was confirmed by the meeting as one of the three reserve delegates to the Convention, the other two being Benjamin Rushton and Samuel Healy.

29. *The Charter*, 5 May 1839.
30. Letter (n.d.,? November 1839) to Halifax magistrates from Thomas Aked and James Rawson, in possession of the Halifax Antiquarian Society, held in the archives of the Calderdale Library. It is reproduced on the cover of *The Early Chartists*.
31. *Lines on Busy Peter's Escape from Bradford, by Reuben Holder*, Broadside, n.p. n.d. (?Bradford, 1839). The first two lines are quoted in Frank Peel, *Spen Valley Past and Present* (Heckmondwyke, 1893), p.315.
32. Thomas Frost, *Forty Years Recollections*, p.112.
33. *Commonwealthsman and Chartist Advocate*, 2 April 1842.
34. A. J. Peacock, *Bradford Chartism 1838–1840*, and C. Godfrey, thesis, for fuller biographies of Bussey.
35. Obit. in *Northern Star*, 15 Jan. 1848; Land Company details, B.T. 41.
36. R. Challinor and B. Ripley, *The Miners' Association: A Trade Union in the Age of the Chartists* (1968), p.17 and *passim*.
37. H.O. 20/10.
38. *Newcastle Weekly Chronicle*, 19 July 1879.
39. For Pitkethly's visit to the United States and his relations with the radical Dr Smyles (cousin of the better-known Samuel Smiles), see Michael Brook, 'Lawrence Pitkethly, Dr. Smyles and Canadian Revolutionaries in the United States, 1842', *Ontario History*, Vol. LVII (1965), No. 2, and *A Letter addressed to Mr. Pitkethly, of Huddersfield Yorkshire, by Dr. John Smyles* (1842).
40. Entry in DLMB, vol. V, by John Rowley and Eric Taylor, and the Samuel Cook collection at Dudley Public Library, which is well worth a visit.
41. Biographical details and publications of both men are listed in C. Godfrey, thesis, and see T. A. Devyr, *Odd Book*.
42. Haslam appears to have lived to a considerable age – if he is the Charles Janica Haslam whose death in Newcastle is recorded in the *Yorkshire Evening Press* of 20 February 1902, at the age of 91. He is described as having been a Chartist, active in Manchester.
43. Devyr, *Odd Book*, p.177.
44. Alex Wilson, *The Chartist Movement in Scotland* (Manchester, 1970); Christopher Godfrey, thesis.
45. *Allsop Collection*, British Library of Political Science, University of London (London School of Economics).
46. DNB, Vol. 1. Holyoake also has something to say about Allsop in *Sixty Years of an Agitator's Life* and *Life of Stephens*.
47. *The Operative*, 2 Feb. 1838.
48. Brief references to Allsop in three of Harney's letters to Engels suggest that he was a mutual friend. *Harney Papers*, letters 295, 296, 337.
49. See below, p.324. For full text of letter Allsop to O'Connor, see DNB entry.
50. *Trial of Feargus O'Connor and 58 Others* (1843), p.383. Other Chartist grocers included John Goding of Cheltenham, who was also a poet and later a historian of the town, Thomas Bird, of Bury, Reuben Allcorn and Joseph Bray of Huddersfield, James Diggles of Bradford, and John Newman of Bristol.
51. R. B. Pugh, 'Chartism in Somerset and Wiltshire', in Briggs (ed.), *Chartist Studies* (1958), p.184.
52. Devyr, *Odd Book*, pp.208-11.
53. W. R. Ward, *Religion and Society in England, 1790-1850* (1972), *passim*; *Trial of Feargus O'Connor and 58 others*.
54. T. H. Lloyd, 'Dr. Wade and the Working Class', *Midland History*, Vol. II, No. 2 (Autumn 1973).
55. Thomas Cooper, *Life*, pp.254-5.
56. For this handbill and for information about Price see L. A. Smith, 'The Kidderminster Carpet Industry, 1800-1850' (unpub. Ph.D. thesis, Birmingham University, 1982).
57. *Northern Star*, 26 Nov. 1842.
58. H.O. 20/10.
59. Angela V. John, loc. cit.
60. *Annals of Barnsley*, pp.186-8; T.S. 11/600, letter Brophy to Cooper, 21 Dec. 1841.
61. 'Sermon at Hebden Bridge, August 18 1849' in G. J. Holyoake *Life of Joseph*

Rayner Stephens (London, 1881), pp.131-2.

62. F. W. Hackwood, *Handsworth Old and New* (1908), p.81, for a brief biography of O'Neil, who is in general very well documented. For an account of the whole episode, John Ryan, 'Religion and Radical Politics in Birmingham 1820-1850' (unpub. M. Litt. thesis, Birmingham, 1979).

9. Labourers and the Trades

1. C. Godfrey, thesis; *Times* obit. 11 Aug. 1882.
2. Letter Loveless to Lovett, 13 April 1833, BM AdMS 37949 ff 409.
3. *Essex Standard*, 20 Dec. 1839 (report quoted from *Morning Post*).
4. Letters, William Loveless, Pymore, nr. Bridport to George Loveless, in Essex and then in Canada, 1842-1847. In the possession of Miss M. E. Loveless, of Regina, Canada. Copies are in Regina Office of the Archives of Saskatchewan.
5. *Northern Star*, 9 Jan. 1841.
6. See Appendix for list of places with Land Company branches and Land Company members. It is probable that many of the members in small country towns were also farm workers.
7. *Cambridge Chronicle*, 28 March 1846, cited in A. J. Peacock, 'Village Radicalism in East Anglia' in J. P. D. Dunbabin (ed.), *Rural Discontent in Nineteenth Century Britain* (1974), which contains many valuable insights for the study of rural society in the Chartist period.
8. R. B. Pugh, 'Chartism in Somerset and Wiltshire' in Briggs (ed.), *Chartist Studies* (1958), which contains other examples of rural Chartism in those counties.
9. Walter Long to Home Secretary, 9 March 1839, H.O. 40/48, cited in Pugh, loc. cit.
10. H. Fearn, 'Chartism in Suffolk' in Briggs (ed.), *Chartist Studies*, p.161.
11. In addition to the chapter by A. J. Peacock already mentioned, see D. J. V. Jones, 'Thomas Campbell Foster and the rural labourer: incendiarism in East Anglia in the 1840's', *Social History*, Vol. 1, No. 1 (Jan. 1976), and David Williams, *The Rebecca Riots* (Cardiff, 1965).
12. Charles Kingsley, *Yeast* and *Alton Locke*, Benjamin Disraeli, *Sybil*, and Alexander Somerville ('One who has whistled at the Plough'), 'Notes from the farming districts', originally published in the *Anti-Bread Tax Circular*, 1842-1847 and reprinted in Vol. 1 of *Somerville's Works* (Manchester, 1852).
13. *Northern Star*, 30 June 1838.
14. Extracts from Thom's paper, *The Lion*, published in the *Northern Star*, 9 June 1838.
15. *Northern Star*, 9 June 1838. For a full account of the events, see P. G. Rogers, *The Battle in Bossenden Wood* (1961); E. P. Thompson, *The Making of the English Working Class*, pp.800-801; J. F. C. Harrison, *The Second Coming* (1978); and Nigel Parratt 'The Battle in Bossenden Wood and the Press' (unpub. B. A. dissertation, Birmingham University, 1974).
16. *Trial of Feargus O'Connor and Fifty-Eight Others* (1843), pp.281-2.
17. Adam Rushton, *My Life as Farmer's Boy, Factory Lad, Teacher and Preacher* (Manchester, 1909), p.66.
18. *London Dispatch*, 2 June 1839.
19. Published Cheltenham, 1848. For Willey, see Owen Ashton, 'Radicalism and Chartism in Gloucestershire, 1832-1848' (unpub. Ph.D. thesis, Birmingham University, 1980).
20. J. McGacken to G. Cornwall Lewis Esq. M.P., H.O. 45/OS 2410 AE Misc 1848.
21. *The Labourer*, Vol. 1 (1847), pp.198-9.
22. Henry Solly, *These Eighty Years*, Vol. I, pp.389-95.
23. According to the 1851 census, in England and Wales 1,904,687 were engaged in agriculture, 828,892 in the combined textile industries, 398,756 in building and 243,935 in boot and shoemaking. Dudley Baxter, in 1867, including 157,000 boot and shoe workers among his estimated top 20 per cent of the labouring population, but put them in his lowest skilled category, as earning on average between 21 and 23 shillings a week. This would seem to be a fair idea of their position in the Chartist years, and would suggest that about 86,000 of them were not of skilled status, and earned very much less than the skilled rate. Bezer said that his cousin, the snob who taught him, could earn £1 a week with the help of wife and children but that he, a single man, could never make more than

half that, in spite of very long hours of work. For a valuable account of the organisation of this and other trades in the metropolis during the Chartist period, see David Goodway, *London Chartism 1838-1848*, Part 4, pp.153-217.

24. John James Bezer, 'The Autobiography of one of the Chartist Rebels' in David Vincent (ed.), *Testaments of Radicalism* (1977), p.176.
25. *Boot and Shoemaker*, 22 Feb. 1879.
26. Barrie M. Ratcliffe and W. H. Chaloner (eds), *A French Sociologist Looks at Britain* (1977), p.92.
27. *Boot and Shoemaker*, 28 June 1879.
28. *Aberdeen People's Journal*, 19 and 26 Feb. 1887.
29. *Boot and Shoemaker*, 8 Feb. 1879, from which all quotations referring to Hanson in the next three pages are taken unless otherwise indicated.
30. *The Operative*, 31 March 1839.
31. *People's Charter*, 3rd edn, August 1838.
32. For a description of the play and of its production under Cobbett's direction, see George Spater, *William Cobbett: the Poor Man's Friend* (1982), Vol. 2, p.602 n. 4.
33. Benjamin Wilson, *Struggles*, p.3.
34. *Halifax Guardian*, 25 May 1839.
35. Obit. from *Barnsley Chronicle*, in Wilkinson, *Barnsley Obituaries*, p.57.
36. Thomas Frost, *Forty Years Recollections*, p.33 and *passim.*
37. *Boot and Shoemaker*, 3 Aug. 1878.
38. David Goodway, *London Chartism 1838-1848*, p.16.
39. *Return from each Gaol and House of Correction in the United Kingdom from January 1, 1839 to June 1840, stating (1) The name of every person confined for charges for printing and publishing Seditious or Blasphemous Libel, or for attending any Seditious Meetings, or for any offence of a Political Nature; the nature of the Charge; the term of the sentence suffered, (2) The Treatment before and after conviction . . . (4) Comparative treatment of Persons Confined for Misdemeanor before and after Conviction and Sentence* (Parliamentary Papers: Accounts and Papers 1840 xxxviii). A list is also published in the *English Chartist Circular*, 1 Jan. 1840.

    H.O. 20/10 Confidential Reports made by the Inspectors of Prisons upon the cases of all Political Offenders in custody on 1 Jan. 1841.
40. Arthur Brown, 'The Chartist Movement in Essex', *Chartism In East Anglia* (1951), p.5.
41. T. M. Kemnitz, 'Chartism in Brighton' (unpub. Ph.D. thesis, University of Sussex, 1969).
42. *Beehive*, 14 March 1868.
43. 'Thomas Phillips, a Yorkshire Shoemaker in Philadelphia' in *Pennsylvania Magazine of History and Biography* (April 1955). See also Clifton K. Yearly, *Britons in American Labour: A History of the influence of United Kingdom immigrants on American Labour, 1820-1914* (Baltimore, 1957).
44. John Plummer, *Songs of Labour . . . and other Poems* (1860), p.xxvii and *passim.*
45. Frank Peel, *Old Cleckheaton* (1884), p.115.
46. Graham Wallas, *Life of Place*, p.36.
47. Charles Kingsley, *Alton Locke*, p.77.
48. Robert Crowe, *Reminiscences of an Octogenarian* (New York, n.d. – 1902?), p.5.
49. For an account of the problems of the London tailors and the background to the 1834 strike, T. M. Parssinen and I. J. Prothero, 'The London Tailors' Strike of 1834 and the collapse of the Grand National Consolidated Trades Union.' *International Review of Social History*, Vol. XXII (1977), Part I, pp.65-107.
50. First published as a tract 1849, included as foreword in second and subsequent editions of *Alton Locke.*
51. *Reynolds's Political Instructor*, 13 April 1850. Cuffey's Convict Records describe him as 4′ 11″ tall, with 'shin bones and spine deformed'.
52. Ibid, and see the similar comments by Thomas Frost, *Forty Years' Recollections*, p.150.
53. Letter W. P. Dowling to *Galway Vindicator*, reprinted in *People's Paper*, 22 May 1852. For biography and bibliography, see entry by Iorwerth Prothero in DLMB, Vol. IV.
54. This and other information in the following paragraphs is, unless otherwise noted, from Brian Harrison and Patricia Hollis (eds), *Robert Lowery, Radical and Chartist* (1979). This edition of Lowery's memoirs is preceded by a biographical introduction,

and also includes some of the subject's speeches.
55. *Northern Liberator*, 25 June 1839, speech reprinted in full in Harrison and Hollis, *op. cit*.
56. *Northern Liberator*, 7 Jan. 1839.
57. *Northern Star*, 18 July 1840.
58. *Northern Star*, 14 Dec. 1839.
59. *Northern Liberator*, 25 Jan. 1840.
60. Obituary notice in *National Reformer*, 20 and 27 July 1861, and see the useful summary in C. Godfrey, thesis.
61. C. Godfrey, thesis.
62. Arthur Brown, 'The Chartist Movement in Essex', in *Chartism in East Anglia*.
63. C. Godfrey, thesis; Yearley, *Britons in American Labour*.
64. *Northern Star, passim*; *People's Paper*, 2 July 1853; and information from Jonathan Smith, York.
65. *Northern Star, passim*, Godfrey, thesis, etc. At least six other localities had tailors among their officers.
66. *Northern Star*, 6 May 1843.
67. H. Fearn, 'Chartist Activity in Suffolk', in *Chartism in East Anglia: Three Essays* (Cambridge, n.d. [1951]).
68. *Trial of Feargus O'Connor and Fifty-eight Others* (1843), p.275. There were 9 tailors among Chartists under arrest in 1840 (PP op. cit, 1840) and 3 among the 66 arrested Sheffield Chartists in August 1839.
69. Robert Crowe, *Reminiscences* . . . p.5.
70. Ibid, p.7 (the following paragraph is summarised from Crowe, *Reminiscences*).
71. *Reynold's Political Instructor*, 16 March 1850.
72. *Reynold's Political Instructor*, 2 Feb. 1850.
73. David Goodway found 98 Chartist tailors in London, and assessed the element of participation at 2.40 – below many other trades. But this could perhaps be connected with the comparative anonymity of tailors, who are always referred to as being very radical as a trade. Land Company lists give a fairly predictable picture, with tailors relatively more numerous away from the manufacturing districts. Thus Leeds had 14 out of 198, whereas Barnsley, with 9 out of 457, and Bradford, with 23 out of 792, had proportionately far fewer. Manchester had 26 tailors out of 1,516 members, while the rest of Lancashire had 34 out of 4,193.
74. H.O. 40/43.
75. Joseph Lawson, *Progress in Pudsey*, p.132.
76. H.O. 20/10.
77. An Old Potter [Charles Shaw], *When I was a Child*, p.175.
78. *Northern Star*, 22 and 29 July 1848.
79. For Booley, Arthur Brown, 'Chartism in Essex', Hugh Fearn, 'Chartism in Suffolk' in Briggs (ed.), *Chartist Studies*, and B. J. McKinlay, 'The Geelong People's Association and Robert Booley' in *Labour History* (Australia), No. 15 (November 1968).
80. H.O. 20/10.
81. *Hampshire Times*, 8 April 1839; *Southampton Free Press*, 4 April 1839.
82. *The Chartist Experience*, pp.152f.
83. Biography in *Northern Star*, 20 Nov. 1847.
84. H.O. 20/10.
85. DLMB, vol. V, entry by John Rowley.
86. W. J. Linton, *Memories* (1895), and F. B. Smith, *Radical Artisan* (Manchester, 1973).
87. William Lovett, *Life and Struggles*, pp.84-5 and *passim*.
88. The case is the subject of a full-length treatment in Richard Moran, *Knowing Right from Wrong* (New York, 1981).
89. Facsimile in Moran, op. cit., p.117.
90. A. J. Peacock, 'Chartism in York', *York History*, No. 3 (n.d. ?1975).
91. John Rule, 'Richard Spurr of Truro, small town Radical', *Cornish Studies* 4/5 (1976-7), pp.50-5.
92. Thomas Frost, *Forty Years Recollections*, pp.119-20.
93. Thomas Frost, *Forty Years Recollections*, pp.119-20.
94. *Democratic Review*, Feb. 1850 (Merlin reprint), pp. 341, 410.
95. *English Chartist Circular*, Vol. 1, No. 23.
96. E.g. *Condition of the Working Class*, p.134, where he states that the 'class' of factory operatives 'is the most intelligent and energetic of all the English workers . . . It stands as a whole, and the cotton-workers pre-eminently stand, at the head of the labour movement . . . '
97. *Northern Star*, 2 March 1839 (speech reprinted in *The Early Chartists*, pp.181-4).
98. 'The Autobiography of Samuel Fielden', Philip S. Foner (ed.).
99. See the interesting series of letters from Vincent to his brother-in-law John Minikin

in the Labour Party Library, Transport House, London, which fully cover Vincent's travels as a LWMA missionary.

100. For the cotton-spinners' strikes in 1830-1, see Kirby and Musson, *Voice of the People*, pp.133-48, and Nicholas Cotton, 'Popular Movements in Ashton-under-Lyne and Staleybridge before 1832' (unpub. M. Litt. thesis, Birmingham University, 1977).

101/102. H.O. 20/10.
And see R. J. Sykes in *The Chartist Experience* for the involvement of cotton operatives generally.

103. *Report of Select Committee on the Sale of Liquor on Sunday*, PP 1867-8 XIV (402) p.385.

104. *Northern Star*, 4 May 1839.

105. *Ashton-under-Lyne News*, 2 Oct. 1869.

106. *Northern Star*, 10 Aug. 1839.

107. H.O. 20/10. Doyle gave his religion as Catholic.

108. Ann Swift, *George Cooper: Stockport's Last Town Crier* (Stockport, 1974), p.30.

109. *Trial of Feargus O'Connor and 58 Others*, pp.60-1.

110. *York Courant*, 17 Aug. 1843.

111. *Northern Star*, 3 Aug. 1846.

112. *Bolton Chronicle and South Lancs Advertiser*, 25 March 1848.

113. *Northern Star*, 16 Dec. 1848.

114. H.O. 45/269.

115. There is a biographical entry by Naomi Reid in Vol. IV of the DLMB.

116. H.O. 20/10.

117. *Northern Star*, 20 Oct. 1838.

118. Benjamin Wilson, *Struggles*, p.13.

119. Benjamin Brierley, *Home Memories* (1886) p.24.

120. *Manchester and Salford Advertiser*, 1 June 1833, and C. Godfrey, thesis.

121. Material mainly found in Burland, MS Annals, *passim*, and Wilkinson, *Barnsley Obituaries*, p.154 (*Barnsley Chronicle*, 1 and 8 Dec. 1877). Entry in DLMB, vol. IV.

122. Wilkinson, *Barnsley Obituaries*, pp. 148, 153.

123. Article in *Beehive* about James Crabtree, reprinted and included in Wilkinson, *Barnsley Obituaries*, p.151.

124. *Barnsley Times*, 15 April-29 July 1882.

125. Alex Wilson, *The Chartist Movement in Scotland* (1970), *passim*.

126. Thomas Cooper, *Life of himself* (1877), p.347.

127. E. and R. M. Black (eds), *The Harney Papers*, p.80.

128. Cited in D. J. Rowe, 'The Chartist Convention and the Regions', *Economic History Review*, 2nd Series, Vol. XXII (1969), No. 1.

129. *Northern Star*, 2 March 1839. For Pilling's defence, see *Trial of Feargus O'Connor and Fifty-eight others* (1843). The two speeches and the two men are discussed and compared in Edouard Dolleans, *Le Chartism* (Paris, 1912-13).

130. Gammage, *History*, p.65.

131. E. J. King, *Richard Marsden and the Preston Chartists* (1982).

132. See, for example, the vivid and lively account of the high days of the weavers in Willie Thom, *Rhymes and Recollections of a Handloom Weaver* (1844), p.3.

133. Felix Hebden, *Memorabilia of the late John Hartley* (cuttings from the *Todmorden and district News*, 1903).

134. 'A Leaf from the Annals of a Shoemaker's Garret', *The Labourer*, June 1847.

135. *People's Paper*, 30 June 1853.

136. *Halifax Courier*, 19 Aug. 1892.

137. Frank Peel, *Spen Valley Past and Present*, pp.318-19.

138. Above, pp.217-18.

139. There are a number of letters White to Cooper in TS 11/601, and some of his letters from prison in *The Harney Papers*. He wrote frequently in the *Star* and other Chartist journals.

140. There is a beginning of a biography of White in the unpublished MA thesis by Ken Geering, 'George White, a nineteenth century workers' leader'. (University of Sussex, 1973). He deserves a fuller study, as a central figure in mainstream Chartism and a very interesting character in his own right.

141. *Halifax Courier*, 6 Sept. 1884, obit. of John Snowden.

142. For purposes of counting, I have included colliers, coal-miners, pitmen and pit labourers in the heading 'coal-miner'. Some of the Welsh prisoners who gave their occupation as 'miner' would almost certainly have been iron-miners.

143. *Northern Star*, 7 July 1838, cited in Peter Cadogan, *Early Radical Newcastle* (Consett, 1975), p.116.

144. W. E. Adams, *Memoirs of a Social Atom*, Vol. 1, p.292.
145. The autobiographies which contain their Chartist memoirs have already been referred to several times. In addition both Adams and Frost wrote reminiscences in the newspapers they edited, and encouraged others to do the same. Thomas Frost's less well-known *Reminiscences of a Country Journalist* (1886) is in many ways the more interesting of his two books to social historians.
146. David Goodway who gives this figure for London Chartist printers adds the reservation that it may over-represent the active members of the trade, since a large number of the names only appear in a single early LWMA list.
147. W. E. Adams, *Memoirs of a Social Atom*, Vol. 1, Ch. XXIX.
148. H.O. 20/10.
149. L. D. Smith, thesis; and R. Fyson, forthcoming thesis (Ph.D., Lancaster) on 'Chartism in North Staffordshire'.

10. The Chartists and the Middle Class

1. Mark Hovell, *The Chartist Movement* (1918), p.164 for a classic statement of this view.
2. R. N. Soffer, 'Attitudes and Allegiances in the Unskilled North, 1830-1850', *International Review of Social History*, Vol. X, Part 1 (1965).
3. D. J. Rowe, 'The London Working Men's Association and the "People's Charter"', *Past and Present*, No. 36 (April 1967).
4. *Northern Star*, 4 March 1848.
5. J. B. Smith to Thomas Cooper, 14 March 1842, T.S. 11/601.
6. *The Leader*, 26 May 1855.
7. For a sympathetic account of some early factory schools, and the concern they caused the Tory philanthropist Lord Ashley, see Rhodes Boyson, *The Ashworth Cotton Enterprise* (1970), pp.127-32.
8. *An Appeal to the editors of the Times newspapers in behalf of the Working Classes* . . . by two lay members of the Church (1845), p.10.
9. *Ibid*, p.8.
10. Benjamin Wilson, *Struggles of an Old Chartist; What he knows and the part he has played in various Movements* (Halifax, 1887), p.3.
11. Benjamin Disraeli, *Sybil* p.202.
12. Percival Percival, *Failsworth Folk and Failsworth Memories* (Manchester, 1901), p.19.
13. Rickinson Pickhills to Constabulary Commissioners, 29 Nov. 1836, H.O. 73/3 f310.
14. J. Crabtree, *A Concise History of the Parish and Vicarage of Halifax* (Halifax, 1836), p.18.
15. *John Bates of Queensbury, the Veteran Reformer* (Queensbury, 1895), p.1 and *passim.*
16. *Halifax Courier*, 6 Sept. 1884.
17. *Bradford Daily Telegraph*, 7 March 1895.
18. Shopmate, 'Old Tom Horne', *Boot and Shoemaker*, 22 February 1879, p.95.
19. *Mark Hovell*, op. cit., p.86.
20. Benjamin Disraeli, *op. cit.*, p.204.
21. Elizabeth Gaskell, *Mary Barton* (1848), p.199.
22. Charles Kingsley, *Yeast* (London, 1890 edn), p.60.
23. Ibid, p.61.
24. Lord Bessborough (ed.), *The Diary of Lady Charlotte Guest*, Vol. 1, p.211.
25. Letter, Aubrey de Vere to Mrs Henry Taylor, 2 April 1848, *Correspondence of Henry Taylor* (n.d.), p.183.
26. Anon (Caroline Norton), *A Voice from the Factories* (1848).
27. G. P. R. James, *The Jacquerie*, cited in Nicholas Rance, *The Historical Novel and Popular Politics* (London, 1975), p.138.
28. Tennyson, *Poems and Plays* (Oxford, 1967), p.76.
29. *Bolton Free Press*, 24 Feb. 1838.
30. Samuel Fielden, loc. cit.
31. George Jacob Holyoake, *Sixty Years of an Agitator's Life* (1906 edn), p.17.
32. Anon, *Memoranda of the Chartist Agitation in Dundee* (Dundee, 1889), p.17.
33. James Burland, MS Annals of Barnsley, pp.122-5. The Chartists presented a letter protesting against their exclusion to the chairman, Earl Fitzwilliam, as he left the hall.
34. Benjamin Wilson, *Struggles*, p.7.
35. A. B. Granville, *Spas of England, Vol 2, the South and Midlands* (1841), pp.97-8.
36. Nassau Senior, *Resolutions and Heads of the People* (1860).

37. Rev. Francis Close A.M., *A Sermon Addressed to the Female Chartists of Cheltenham* (1839), pp.28-9.
38. Feargus O'Connor (ed.), *The Trial of Feargus O'Connor and Fifty-eight Others* (1843), p.vi.
39. David Philips, 'The Black Country Magistracy 1835-60; a changing local elite and the exercise of its power', *Midland History* (Spring 1967), pp.161-91. For an account of the blatant intervention in the local politics of Huddersfield by the appointment of magistrates (and hence *ex officio* poor law guardians) sympathetic to the Whig Government, see John W. Knott, 'The Devil's Law' (unpub. Ph.D. thesis, Canberra, 1981), Chapter VII.
40. Talbot to Russell, 9 September 1835 (Outletter Book of Lord Talbot, 1822-1842, Staffordshire Record Office), cited in Philips, loc. cit., p.168.
41. *Northern Liberator*, 30 Dec. 1837.
42. Graham Wallas, *Life of Francis Place* (1898), p.330.
43. *English Chartist Circular*, Vol. 1, No. 3 (Feb. 1841).
44. *Northern Star*, 30 April 1842 and *passim*.
45. *Northern Star*, 1 May 1842.
46. *Northern Star*, 31 July 1842.
47. Peel Papers, BM Add. MSS. 40498 fs 79-84, Peel to Graham, 12 June 1843, cited in Norman Gash, *Sir Robert Peel* (1972), p.407.
48. *Free Trader*, No. 3 (Feb. 1842) for a denunciation of Sturge, Miall and the C.S.U.
49. *Birmingham Journal*, 15 Nov. 1838, cited in John Ryan, 'Religion and Radical Politics in Birmingham 1830-1850' (unpub. M. Litt. thesis, Birmingham University 1979), p.56. See this thesis for a detailed account of Sturge and the C.S.U. in Birmingham.
50. Sturge to Place, n.d. [February 1842?] (Birmingham Reference Library).
51. *English Chartist Circular*, Vol. 2, No. 58 (1842).
52. *National Association Gazette*, 19 Feb. 1842.
53. Thomas Cooper to Mrs Susan Cooper, n.d. [August 1842?], TS/11/601.
54. Broadside, 'A New Song, In glorification of the Six Points of the Charter' from Walter papers (microfilm in Berkshire Record Office, *D/Ecb*).
55. Thomas Cooper, *The Life of Thomas Cooper* (1971 reprint), pp.224-5.
56. E. P. ('Commodore') Meade to Thomas Cooper, May 1842, TS 11/601.
57. George White to Thomas Cooper, n.d. [1842?], TS 11/600.
58. Henry Vincent to John Minikin, 13 July 1842.
59. William Lovett, *Life and Struggles*, p.234.

11. The Strikes

1. Alexander Wilson, 'John Taylor, Esq, M.D., of Backhouse, Ayrshire (1805-42)', *Ayrshire Archeological and Natural History Society Collections*, 2nd series, Vol. 1 (1947-9).
2. *Bradford Observer*, 25 November 1905.
3. H.O. 20/10.
4. *Northern Star*, 27 June 1841.
5. *Halifax Guardian*, 26 June 1841.
6. *Berrows Journal*, 24 Feb. 1842.
7. Gammage, *History*, pp.216-17.
8. John Campbell's pamphlet, *An Examination of the Corn and Provision Laws, from their first enactment to the Present Period* (M/c 1841) was widely used and quoted by Chartists.
9. *Northern Star*, 23 May 1840.
10. Ibid, 10 Feb. 1844.
11. Disraeli, *Sybil*, p.118.
12. *Bolton Free Press*, 20 Aug. 1842.
13. *English Chartist Circular*, vol. 2, no. 62 (March 1842).
14. *Wolverhampton Chronicle*, cited in George J. Barnsby, *The Working Class Movement in the Black Country 1750-1867* (Wolverhampton, 1977), p.105.
15. *Wolverhampton Chronicle*, cited in ibid, pp.105-6.
16. *Wolverhampton Chronicle*, 17 August 1842.
17. *Northern Star*, 13 August, 1842.
18. David Goodway, op. cit., and Iorwerth J. Prothero, 'London Working Class Movements, 1825-1848' (unpub. Ph.D. thesis, Cambridge University, 1967).
19. *Northern Star*, 12 April 1842, from which the whole of the following account is taken.
20. See description in David Goodway, *London Chartism*, pp.51-2.
21. Hansard, Third Series, vol. LXIII, cols. 13-91; see especially the speech of Thomas Babington Macaulay.

22. Letter, Bairstow–Cooper, 22 June 1842, TS 11/601.
23. Gammage, *History*, pp.214-15. John Henry Bramwich was a stockinger who had served for sixteen years as a regular soldier, before returning to the trade in Leicester. He was a member of Thomas Cooper's 'Shakesperean Chartists' and contributed to the Chartist hymn book compiled by Cooper. He died of TB in 1846.
24. H.O. 20/10, and see the entry by John Baxter in DLMB, vol. IV.
25. *British Statesman*, 25 June 1842.
26. *Morning Chronicle*, 18 June 1842.
27. G. D. H. Cole, *A Short History of the British Working Class Movement*.
28. *Northern Star*, 5 March 1842.
29. *Manchester and Salford Advertiser*, 17 April 1841 – address of Manchester hatters.
30. *Northern Star*, 13 Aug. 1842.
31. *Northern Star*, 20 Aug. 1842.

    For a full account of these events and a discussion of the relationship between Chartism and the trades, see R. Sykes, 'Popular Politics and Trade Unionism in South East Lancashire' (unpub. Ph.D. thesis, University of Manchester, 1982).
32. Dundee Warder 16 August 1842 – cited in full in Carol Sue Bebb, 'Chartism in Dundee'.
33. *Trial of Feargus O'Connor and Fifty-eight others*, p.246.
34. Ibid, p.248.
35. Ibid, p.54.
36. H.O. 45/264ff 70.
37. PL 27 11 PT ERD/418.
38. Ibid.
39. Ibid.
40. Ibid.
41. *Trial of Feargus O'Connor*, p.404.
42. *Trial of Feargus O'Connor*, p.168.
43. H.O. 45/264ff 35.
44. *Trial of Feargus O'Connor*, p.270.
45. H.O. 45/264ff 10.
46. H.O. 45/264ff 30.
47. H.O. 45/264ff 92.
48. F. H. Grundy, *Pictures of the Past* (1879), p.100.
49. Benjamin Wilson, *Struggles*, p.6.
50. *Halifax Guardian*, 20 Aug. 1842.
51. *Memorabilia of the late John Hartley*.
52. *Illustrated London News*, 22 Aug. 1842.
53. F. H. Grundy, *Pictures of the Past*, p.69.
54. Frank Peel, *Rising of the Luddites, Chartists and Plug-drawers* (1880, reprinted 1967), pp.338-9.
55. *Halifax Courier*, 19 Aug. 1892.
56. F. H. Grundy, *Pictures of the Past*, pp.98ff.
57. H.O. 45/264ff 76, 77, 78, 79. The file includes a vivid account sent to Leeds by a press reporter who was an eye-witness.
58. H.O. 45/264ff 220.
59. Thomas Cooper, *Life*, p.206.
60. Benjamin Brierley, *Home Memories and Recollections of Life* (1886), p.24.
61. Thomas Cooper, *Life*, p.213.
62. Ibid, p.208.
63. Ibid, p.189.
64. Ibid, p.197.
65. H.O. 45/269.
66. Placard, printed by G. Shoreham, Hanley; Copy in H.O. 45/269.

12. The Charter and the Land

1. *English Chartist Circular*, Vol. 2, No. 145 (1843). In his rather disappointing account of the experiences of the Chartists in the convict settlements, George Rudé seems to be unaware of Ellis's standing and importance in the Midlands. (*Protest and Punishment*, Oxford, 1978, pp.134 and 216.)
2. *English Chartist Circular*, Vol. 2, No. 147. This brief life, together with a selection of Ellis's letters, continues in seven issues of the journal.
3. G. D. H. Cole, *A Century of Cooperation* (1944).
4. Benjamin Wilson, *Struggles of an Old Chartist*, p.14.
5. Eileen Yeo, 'Some problems of Chartist Democracy' in Epstein and Thompson (eds), *The Chartist Experience* (1982). For studies of the Land Plan, see Joy McAskill, 'The Chartist Land Plan' in Briggs (ed.), *Chartist Studies*, and Alice Mary Hadfield, *The Chartist Land Company*, Newton Abbot, 1970. Peter Searby, 'Great Dodford and the later History of the Chartist Land Scheme' in *Agricultural History Review*, Vol. XVI, Part 1 (1968), and W. H. G. Armytage, 'The Chartist Land Colonies, 1846-1848' in *Agricultural History*, Vol. 32 (1958). Most of the general histories have some account of the Land Plan.

6. *Jacksons Oxfordshire Journal*, 11 Feb. 1888.
7. *A Letter addressed to Oddfellows, Foresters, Druids etc., calling their attention to the National Land and Labour Bank etc.* by George Candelet, Hyde (1848).
8. Introduction to R. G. Gammage, *History of the Chartist Movement* (Cass reprint edition, London, 1969), pp.48-62.
9. J. F. C. Harrison, *The Second Coming*, for the best account of millenarian movements in these years.
10. J. S. Mill, *Principles of Political Economy* (2nd edn, 1849), Bk 11, Ch. X, section 7. Cited in Saville, op. cit., p.53.
11. *Halifax Guardian*, 12 Feb. 1848.
12. Alexander Somerville, *The O'Connor Land Scheme Examined*, 1847.
13. Alexander Somerville, *Cobdenic Policy, the Internal Enemy of England*, 1854.
14. Ibid.
15. Letter to the Editor from 'an unlocated member', *Reynolds's Political Instructor*, Vol. 1, No. 18 (2 March 1850).

13. 1848

1. Ernest Jones MS diary (Manchester Central Reference Library) entry for 30 Sept. 1846. Later in life Jones denied that he had ever knowingly held a position in the Land Company. By this time he was a convinced Free Trade advocate. His strong point was never, however, veracity about his own past.
2. Jones was among the first Chartist leaders to be given a scholarly biography by a modern Labour historian. He was one of the few actual Chartists included in G. D. H. Cole's pioneering *Chartist Portraits* (1941) and a selection of his writing with a lengthy biographical preface was published by John Saville in 1952. There are also a great many biographical pamphlets published during the 1868 election and after his death the following year. The following brief account of his life is made up from these sources, and also from an examination of family and personal papers in the Seligman collection in the Special Collections Library at Columbia University, New York, in the possession of the late Thorold Jones Esq., in Chethams Library and the Central Library Manchester, and other smaller collections in the Bishopsgate Institute, the International Institute of Social History, Amsterdam, and a series of letter from Jones to K. Marx and Frederick Engels, kindly supplied to me on microfilm by the Marx–Engels Institute, Moscow.
3. Anon., 'Jottings on Ernest Jones and his times', *Preston Guardian*, 20 Feb. 1869.
4. Other candidates' votes were: Ernest Miall, 'anti-state Church candidate', 348; Sir Charles Wood, Whig, 506; Henry Edwards, Tory, 509. Very few known Chartists appear in the poll book among Jones's voters, and he had only 3 'plumpers'.
5. Benjamin Wilson, *Struggles*, p.10.
6. Henry Mayhew, *London Labour and the London Poor* (1861), Vol. I, p.20 (although the volumes were published in 1861, many of the interviews were done at least ten years earlier).
7. John Plummer, *Songs of Labour*, p.xxii.
8. *Northern Star*, 22 Aug. 1840.
9. Benjamin Wilson, *Struggles*, p.10.
10. *Halifax Guardian*, 12 Feb. 1848.
11. *Halifax Guardian*, 18 March 1848.
12. Henry Solly, *These Eighty Years*, Vol. II, p.40.
13. *Halifax Guardian*, 6 April 1848.
14. Benjamin Wilson, *Struggles*, p.13.
15. Robert Crowe, *Reminiscences of an Octogenarian* (New York, 1902), p.8.
16. Wilson and Crowe were both born in 1824, and so would have been very young in 1838. Crowe, indeed, had not left Ireland at that date. Many of the leading Chartists in 1848 were about this age, and represented a new influx since 1842.
17. Hansard, *Parliamentary Debates*, third series, XCV (1847), 796-7.
18. For a brief account of Chartism in Ireland, see my 'Ireland and the Irish in English radicalism before the famine' in J. A. Epstein and Dorothy Thompson (eds), *The Chartist Experience* (1982).
19. W. H. Dyott, *Reasons for seceding from the 'seceders' by an ex-member of the Irish Confederation* (Dublin, 1847), p.9.
20. *The Nation*, 15 Aug. 1847. Cited in C. Gavan Duffy, *Four Years of Irish History* (1883), p.450.
21. See my 'Ireland and the Irish in English radicalism' in *The Chartist Experience*.

22. *Freemans Journal*, cited in J. H. Treble, 'O'Connor, O'Connell and the Attitudes of Irish Immigrants towards Chartism in the North of England 1838-1848' in J. Butt and I. F. Clarke (eds), *The Victorians and Social Protest* (Newton Abbot, 1973), p.225, n.93.
23. *United Irishman*, 26 Feb. 1848.
24. *The Labourer*, Vol. III (1848), pp.100-108.
25. Thomas Frost, *Forty Years Recollections*, pp.128-9.
26. *Bradford Observer*, 16 March 1848.
27. *Bolton Chronicle and South Lancs Advertiser*, 25 March 1848. *Northern Star*, 25 March 1848.
28. *Northern Star*, 10 Aug. 1850.
29. See, e.g., J. F. C. Harrison, *Social Reform in Victorian Leeds* (Thoresby Society Monograph, Leeds, 1954) for an account of a successful society which started in 1847.
30. Numbers cited vary from around 60,000 to a quarter of a million. I have not attempted to count or to assess the various estimates. Clearly the numbers were considerable.
31. See the copy of his memorandum of 5 April 1848, in P. R. O., W.O. 30/81, X/1 9895, in which he appears to be deploying several regiments of troops, enforcing the closure of all parks, and putting all major arteries of communication under military surveillance. Since the troops were not in fact employed, I have not made any attempt to compare the actual deployments with the memo, but all reports insist on a very considerable military presence on 10 April.
32. Cited in R. T. Ward, *Chartism* (1973), p.200. See this whole section for an interesting series of snippets from concerned members of the Government and their friends in April 1848.
33. *Lord Beaconsfield's Correspondence with his sister, 1832-1852* (pocket edition, 1928), p.273.
34. Frederick Lessner, *Sixty Years in the Social-Democratic Movement Before 1848 and After* (1907), p.16.
35. J. B. Leno, *Aftermath*, p.28.
36. Gordon M. Ray (ed.), *The Letters and Private Papers of W. M. Thackeray* (1946) Diary 10-15 March, No. 457, Vol. II, p.364.
37. Thomas Cooper, *Life* (Leicester, 1971, edn), p.311.
38. J. J. Garth Wilkinson Correspondence, letter J. J. G. W. to his wife, 7 April 1848. Swedenborgian Society Archives, MS K 124.
39. Richard Whiting, *My Harvest* (1915), p.11.
40. M. C. M. Simpson, *Many Memories of Many People* (1898), pp.117-18.
41. E. Marston, in *Notes and Queries*, 17 Feb. 1906, where other such reminiscences may be read.
42. H. Kingsley, *Charles Kingsley's Letters and Memories of His Life edited by his wife* (6th edn, 1877), p.162.
43. After the passing of this Act, John Mitchel re-named his journal *The Irish Felon*.
44. 13 Chas 11, cap 5.
    57 Geo 111, cap 55.
45. John Belchem, 'Feargus O'Connor and the collapse of the Mass Platform', in Epstein and Thompson (eds), *The Chartist Experience* (1982), and see also his thesis 'Radicalism as a "Platform" agitation in the periods 1816-1821 and 1848-1851' (unpub. Ph.D. thesis, University of Sussex, 1974).
46. *The Life and Correspondence of Thomas Slingsby Duncombe* (London, 1868), Vol. I, p.375.
47. Letter printed in full in the entry for Allsop by G. J. Holyoake in the *Dictionary of National Biography*.
48. Account in *United Irishman*, 15 April. Most accounts record the presence of this slogan.
49. Gammage, *History*, p.316.
50. Richard Whiting, *My Harvest*, p.11.
51. Philip Morrell (ed.), *Leaves from the Greville Diary* (1929), pp.579-80.
52. *Halifax Guardian*, 27 May 1848.
53. Frank Peel, *Spen Valley Past and Present*, p.314, and *Northern Star, passim*. I am grateful to A. J. Peacock for allowing me to read an unpublished MS on Bradford Chartism which continues the story after the period covered in his Borthwick paper, and which pieces together the events of 1848 there.
54. H.O. 45/2410 (4) AB.
55. *Northern Star*, 27 May 1848.
56. *Bradford Observer*, 4 May 1848.
57. *Halifax Guardian*, 17 June 1848.
58. *Northern Star*, 10 June 1848, reprinted in John Saville (ed.), *Ernest Jones*, p.102.
59. I have described Feargus's symptoms to various medical people, and they seem to correspond to those of GPI, the last stage of

syphilis, which killed many well-known figures in the nineteenth century. If this is indeed what killed him, it should be noted that it is a disease which destroys the mind at a specific stage in its development, and is not one which would produce symptoms of madness at an earlier stage. In fact there is no indication that Feargus was of anything but fully sound mind until the onset of his final madness in 1850.

14. Conclusion

1. For this view see Francis Hearn, *Domination, Legitimation and Resistance* (1978).
2. W. E. Adams, *Memoirs of a Social Atom*, Vol. 1, pp.292-3. See also Henry Broadhurst's account of the winter of 1858-9, when he spent four months tramping without finding a single day's work. John Burnett (ed.), *Useful Toil*, p.317. Both these men were young, skilled and mobile.
3. *Northern Star*, 26 Oct. 1850.
4. R. F. Morse, *A Course of Lectures to Sunday School Teachers by a clergyman of Birmingham* (Birmingham, 1854), p.79.
5. *Royal Commission on the Employment of Children and Young Persons*, 1841, reproduced in R. Fyson (ed.), *Chartism in North Staffordshire* (Stafford, 1981).

INDEX

Index

Index

Index

Index

Index

ABOUT THE AUTHOR

Dorothy Thompson is a lecturer in modern history at the University of Birmingham in England, and has also taught at Rutgers, the University of Pittsburgh, Brown University, and Dartmouth College. She has written and edited several volumes on English labor history. Together with her husband, historian E. P. Thompson, she is extremely active in the European disarmament movement. She lives in England.